THE END OF
ORGANIZED CAPITALISM

THE END OF ORGANIZED CAPITALISM

Scott Lash and John Urry

Polity Press

First published 1987 by Polity Press in association with Blackwell Publishers
Reprinted 1988, 1991, 1993

Editorial office:
Polity Press
65 Bridge Street,
Cambridge CB2 1UR, UK

Marketing and production:
Blackwell Publishers
108 Cowley Road,
Oxford OX4 1JF, UK

British Library Cataloguing in Publication Data

Lash, Scott
    The end of organized capitalism.
    1. Capitalism
    I. Title   II. Urry, John
    330.12'2   HB501

    ISBN 0-7456-0068-9
    ISBN 0-7456-0069-7

Typeset in 10½ on 12pt Times by
System 4 Associates, Gerrards Cross, Buckinghamshire
Printed in Great Britain by
T.J. Press (Padstow) Ltd, Padstow, Cornwall.

Contents

Acknowledgements

The authors and publisher are grateful to the following publishers for permission to reproduce extracts from:

R. Aminzade, *Class, Politics, and Early Industrial Capitalism* (State University of New York Press, New York, 1981)

Department of Trade and Industry, *Historical Record of Census of Production 1907–1970* (Business Statistics Office, DTI, London, 1978)

S. Fothergill and G. Gudgin, *Unequal Growth* (Gower Publishing Group, Aldershot, 1982)

L. Hirschhorn, *Beyond Mechanization* (MIT Press, Cambridge, Mass., 1984)

W. Korpi, *The Working Class in Welfare Capitalism* (Routledge and Kegan Paul, London, 1978)

W. Korpi, *The Democratic Class Struggle* (Routledge and Kegan Paul, London, 1983)

B. R. Mitchell, *European Historical Statistics 1750–1970* (Macmillan, London and Basingstoke, 1975)

D. Perry and A. Watkins (eds), *The Rise of the Sunbelt Cities* (Sage, Beverly Hills, 1977)

D. Petzina, W. Abelhauser and A. Faust, *Sozialgeschichtes Arbeitsbuch III* (C. H. Beck, Munich, 1978)

M. Piore and C. Sabel, *The Second Industrial Divide* (Basic Books, New York, 1984)

J. Ross, *Thatcher and her Friends* (Pluto Press, London, 1983)

B. Sarlvik and I. Crewe, *Decade of Dealignment* (Cambridge University Press, Cambridge, 1983)

P. Taylor and N. Thrift (eds), *The Geography of Multinationals* (Croom Helm, London, 1982)

F. Tipton, *Regional Variations in the Economic Development of Germany During the Nineteenth Century* (Wesleyan University Press, Connecticut, 1976)

Preface

We are immensely grateful to social scientists in various countries who have helped us in the writing of this book. Its historical and comparative nature has made us particularly dependent upon the assistance and encouragement of many scholars in many places. In different ways all of the following have provided advice, help, criticism or encouragement: Nick Abercrombie, Bengt Abrahamsson, Paul Bagguley, Philip Cooke, Simon Duncan, Mike Featherstone, Mats Franzen, Anthony Giddens, Derek Gregory, Ulf Himmel-strand, David Keeble, Jim Kemeny, Anders Kjellberg, Olivier Kourchid, Jane Mark Lawson, Brian Longhurst, Claus Offe, Mike Savage, Dan Shapiro, Wolfgang Streeck, Göran Therborn, Rolf Torstendahl, Sylvia Walby, Alan Warde, Sam Whimster, Annie Witz.

We are also pleased to acknowledge the grants from the University of Lancaster Research Fund, The Swedish Institute, the Nuffield Foundation and the Institute of Sociology, Lund, to this project.

We are most grateful to Maeve Connolly, Kay Roberts, and Chris Quinn for their excellent typing of the manuscript.

Lancaster
March 1987

1

Introduction

In a sparkling passage in the otherwise maligned *Manifesto of the Communist Party*, Marx and Engels wrote of the

> Constant revolutionising of production, uninterrupted disturbance of all social conditions, everlasting uncertainty and agitation distinguish the bourgeois epoch from all earlier ones. All fixed, fast-frozen relations . . . all swept away, all new-formed ones become antiquated before they can ossify. All that is solid melts into air, all that is holy is profaned . . .[1]

Bourgeois or capitalist society, then, is one of intense change, particularly in relation to where people live and how their lives are organized over time. According to Marx and Engels, as production is revolutionized in order to bring about massive savings of labour-time, people's relationships to each other across space are transformed since

1 Capitalism has 'pitilessly torn asunder the motley feudal ties that bound man to his "natural superiors".'
2 The need for a constantly expanding market 'chases the bourgeoisie over the whole surface of the globe and destroys local and regional markets'.
3 The 'immensely facilitated means of communication draws all . . . nations into civilisation' (for 'civilisation' we can read 'modernity').
4 Enormous cities are created and this has 'rescued a considerable part of the population from the idiocy of rural life'.
5 Political centralization is generated as independent, loosely connected provinces 'become lumped together into one nation'.
6 Masses of labourers 'organised like soldiers' are 'crowded into the factory', the proletariat 'becomes concentrated in greater masses'.
7 The development of trade unions is 'helped on by the improved means of communication that are created by modern industry and that place the workers of different localities in contact with one another'.[2]

Marx and Engels in the *Manifesto* are very much the analysts of 'modernity' and indeed see the bourgeoisie as a profoundly revolutionary class, setting in motion an extraordinary train of events, creating more formidable and sophisticated forces of production than all the previous centuries had managed.[3] People's lives are thus controlled by a revolutionary bourgeois class – by a class with vested interest in change, crisis and chaos. The citizen in this modern era must learn not to long nostalgically for the 'fixed, fast-frozen relationships' of the real or fantasized past, but to delight in mobility, to thrive on renewal, to look forward to future developments in their conditions of life. As a world of change, it is a world which swings wildly out of control, menacing and destructive. The bourgeoisie thus moves within a profoundly tragic orbit. It has unleashed tremendous powers, but these powers are destructive as well as constructive, producing as well as resolving conflicts. Within this uncontrollable maelstrom the temporal and spatial structuring of people's lives are continuously transformed.

What Marx and Engels do in the *Manifesto* is thus to presage a massively influential set of social developments which have characterized western societies roughly from the end of the nineteenth century onwards. What we want to suggest, however, is that this era of 'organized capitalism' that they in part outline has, in certain societies, come to an end, and that there is a set of tremendously significant transformations which have recently been literally 'disorganizing' contemporary capitalist societies – transformations of time and space, of economy and culture – which disrupt and dislocate the patterns that Marx and Engels so brilliantly foresaw.

In this claim that organized capitalism is – if sporadically and unevenly – coming to an end, in our claim that we are moving into an era of '*disorganized* capitalism', we are contravening the conventions, not just of 'orthodoxy', but of a good deal of solid and reasoned social science opinion. We risk offence, not especially to fundamentalists among Marxists and Weberians, but to purveyors of some of the more creative and better thought-out work which draws on these two traditions. In this context both Marxists and Weberians will generally contend that we are living in increasingly *organized* societies. Marxists will speak of 'monopoly capitalism', characterized by the increasing concentration of constant and variable capital complemented by the unidirectional tendency towards centralization of money capital. They will speak of 'finance capitalism', most notably marked by the interpenetration of money capital and productive capital. They may speak of 'state-monopoly capitalism' or 'late capitalism', in which a low-growth and low-profitability phase of capitalist development is counteracted through a combination of state economic subsidies and growth in size of the public sector. Weberians will similarly claim that contemporary society is imbued with increased levels of organization. They will point to the seemingly teleological growth of state bureaucracy in both capitalist and state socialist countries. They will point to an ineluctable rationalization in our whole gamut of institutions – of the school, the police, the civil service, the factory, trade unions and so on. They will view this process of further organization as the obverse side of secularization, in which the dissolution of internal constraints is progressively replaced by normalizing, individuating and ordering external constraints. We risk offence then to some of the best Marxist and Weberian opinion in this book's contention that contemporary capitalism is undergoing a process of disorganization.

We must begin here by clarifying our terms. The notion of 'organized capitalism' has a considerable pedigree dating back to Hilferding and was particularly developed by Jürgen Kocka and several other contemporary social historians.[4] For these writers organized capitalism begins in most countries in the final decades of the nineteenth century as a consequence of the downward phase of the Kondratieff long wave which began in the mid-1870s. In Kocka's summary formulation, organized capitalism consists of the following inter-related features:[5]

1 The concentration and centralization of industrial, banking and commercial capital – as markets became progressively regulated; in comparison with the preceding epoch of 'liberal capitalism', special growth in producers' goods industries; the increased interconnection of banks and industry; and the proliferation of cartels.

2 The growth of the (famous) separation of ownership from control, with the bureaucratization of control and the elaboration of complex managerial hierarchies.

3 The growth of new sectors of managerial/scientific/technological intelligentsia and of a bureaucratically employed middle class.

4 The growth of collective organizations in the labour market, particularly of regionally and then nationally organized trade unions and of employers' associations, nationally organized professions etc.

5 The increasing inter-articulation between the state and the large monopolies; and between collective organizations and the state as the latter increasingly intervenes in social conflicts; development of class-specific welfare-state legislation.

6 The expansion of empires and the control of markets and production overseas.

7 Changes in politics and the state, including: the increasing number and size of state bureaucracies, the incorporation of various social categories into the national political arena; the increased representation of diverse interests in and through the state; and the transformation of administration from merely 'keeping order' to the attainment of various goals and national objectives.

8 Various ideological changes concerning the role of technical rationality and the glorification of science.

We would add to Kocka's enumeration the following further features:

9   The concentration of industrial capitalist relations within relatively few industrial sectors and within a small number of centrally significant nation-states.

10 The development of extractive/manufacturing industry as the dominant sector with a relatively large number of workers employed.

11 The concentration of different industries within different regions, so that there are clearly identifiable regional economies based on a handful of centrally significant extractive/manufacturing industries.

12 The growth of numbers employed in most plants as the economies of scale dictate growth and expansion within each unit of production.

13 The growth and increased importance of very large industrial cities which dominate particular regions through the provision of centralized services (expecially commercial and financial).

14 A cultural–ideological configuration which can be termed 'modernism', one aspect of which is Kocka's point (8) above; the other aspect is counterposed to such rationality and scientism and embraces, *inter alia*, aesthetic modernism and nationalism.

Clearly not all of these developments occurred either simultaneously or in the same way in all western countries. In order to examine the varying developments in Germany, Sweden, Britain, France and the USA, it is necessary to distinguish between organization 'at the top' and organization 'at the bottom'. Organization at the top here includes, for example, the concentration of industry, increasing inter-articulation of banks, industry and the state, and cartel formation; organization 'at the bottom' includes, for example, the development of national trade union bodies, working-class political parties, and the welfare state. In this connection we shall argue that German capitalism was organized early on at both the top and the bottom (1873–95); American capitalism was organized fairly early on at the top but very late on and only briefly at the bottom; Swedish capitalism was only fully organized in the inter-war period at both the top and the bottom; French capitalism was only *fully* organized at top and bottom during and after the Second World War; and Britain was organized only late at the top but rather early at the bottom.

The following are three of the factors which we shall maintain determine the timing that, and the extent to which, the capitalism in each of these countries becomes organized. First, is the point in history at which it begins to industrialize. The earlier a country enters into its 'take-off', the less organized *mutatis mutandis* its capitalism will be. This is because countries which are later industrializers need to begin at higher levels of concentration and centralization of capital to compete with those which have already been industrializing for some time. Secondly, there is the extent to which pre-capitalist organizations survive into the capitalist period. Britain and Germany became more highly organized capitalist societies than France and the United States: this is because the former two nations did not experience a 'bourgeois revolution' and as a result, guilds, corporate local government, and merchant, professional aristocratic, university and church bodies remained relatively intact. Sweden interestingly occupies a mid-way position, in as much as the high level of state centralization during Swedish feudalism did not allow for the same flourishing development of corporate groups. And the third factor is size of country. For the industry of small countries to compete internationally, resources were channelled into relatively few firms and sectors. Co-ordination between the state and industry was then greatly facilitated, if not necessitated. At the same time there would tend to be higher union densities, more 'organization' of labour, where there were relatively few firms and sectors.

Following the same 14 points, we will now set out what is meant by 'disorganized capitalism':

1   The growth of a 'world market' combined with the increasing scale of industrial, banking and commercial enterprises' means that national markets have become less regulated by nationally based corporations. From the point of view of national markets there has then been an effective de-concentration of capital. This tendency has been complemented by the nearly universal decline of cartels. Such deconcentration has been aided by the general decline of tariffs and the encouragement by states, particularly the USA, to increase the scale of external activity of large corporations. In many countries there is a growing separation of banks from industry.

2   The continued expansion of the number of white-collar workers and particularly of a distinctive service class (of managers, professionals, educators, scientists etc.), which is an effect of organized capitalism, becomes an increasingly significant element which then disorganizes modern capitalism. This results both from the development of an educationally based stratification system which fosters individual achievement and mobility and the growth of new 'social movements' (students', anti-nuclear, ecological and women's movements etc.) which increasingly draw energy and personnel away from class politics.

3   Decline in the absolute and relative size of the core working class, that is of manual workers in manufacturing industry, as economies are de-industrialized.

4   Decline in the importance and effectiveness of national-level collective bargaining procedures in industrial relations and the growth of company and plant-level bargaining. (This accompanies an important shift from Taylorist to 'flexible' forms of work organization.)

5   Increasing independence of large monopolies from direct control and regulation by individual nation-states; the breakdown of most neo-corporatist

forms of state regulation of wage bargaining, planning etc., and increasing contradiction between the state and capital (cf. fiscal crises etc.); development of universalistic welfare state legislation and subsequent challenges from left and right to the centralized welfare state.

6   The spread of capitalism into most Third World countries which has involved increased competition in many of the basic extractive/manufacturing industries (such as steel, coal, oil, heavy industry, automobiles) and the export of the jobs of part of the First World proletariat. This in turn has shifted the industrial/occupational structure of First World economies towards 'service' industry and occupations.

7   The decline of the salience and class character of political parties. There is a very significant decline in the class vote and the more general increase in 'catch-all' parties which reflect the decline in the degree to which national parties simply represent class interests.

8   An increase in cultural fragmentation and pluralism, resulting both from the commodification of leisure and the development of new political/cultural forms since the 1960s. The decodification of some existing cultural forms. The related reductions in time–space distanciation (cf. the 'global village') likewise undermine the construction of unproblematic national subjects.

9   The considerable expansion in the number of nation-states implicated in capitalist production and the large expansion in the number of sectors organized on the basis of capitalist relations of production.

10   Decline in the absolute and relative numbers employed in extractive/manufacturing industry and in the significance of those sectors for the organization of modern capitalist societies. Increased importance of service industry for the structuring of social relations (smaller plants, a more flexible labour process, increased feminization, a higher 'mental' component etc.).

11   The overlapping effect of new forms of the spatial division of labour has weakened the degree to which industries are concentrated within different regions. To a marked extent there are no longer 'regional economies' in which social and political relations are formed or shaped by a handful of significant central extractive/manufacturiang industries.

12   Decline in average plant size because of shifts in industrial structure, substantial labour-saving capital investment, the hiving off of various sub-contracted activities, the export of labour-intensive activities to 'world-market factories' in the Third World, and to 'rural' sites in the First World etc.

13   Industrial cities begin to decline in size and in their domination of regions. This is reflected in the industrial and population collapse of so-called 'inner cities', the increase in population of smaller towns and more generally of semi-rural areas, the movement away from older industrial areas etc. Cities also become less centrally implicated in the circuits

of capital and become progressively reduced to the status of alternative pools of labour-power.

14 The appearance and mass distribution of a cultural–ideological configuration of 'postmodernism'; this affects high culture, popular culture and the symbols and discourse of everyday life.

A major part of this book is devoted to substantiating the above 'disorganization thesis'. To do so we will adduce large quantities of evidence from the recent experiences of five societies: Britain and France, the first to industrialize; the USA, the most capitalistic; Germany, the most 'organized'; and Sweden, the most corporatist and 'socialistic' of the leading capitalist nations. This leads on to the book's second central thesis, the 'comparative thesis': that the greater the extent to which a nation's capitalism has ever been organized the more slowly and hesitantly its capitalism, *ceteris paribus*, will disorganize. Thus we shall contend that crucial aspects of such disorganization are to be found in Britain and the USA from the 1960s, France from the late 1960s/early 1970s, Germany from the 1970s, and Sweden from the late 1970s/early 1980s.

The aim of this book is not just to amass large amounts of evidence in support of these two theses. Our objectives are also narrative. In the following we shall partly, by way of buttressing our 'disorganized capitalism' thesis, attempt to characterize how each society first became organized and subsequently disorganized. This narrative is partly structured through looking at organization and disorganization in the economy, in civil society and in the state. Here the ideal-typical national model – and variance from this will be detailed in the text – is the following: towards the end of the nineteenth century organization – via the concentration of capital – in the economy occurs, followed rapidly by the organization of classes and their interest organization in civil society; organization of the state follows much later, typically between the two world wars. Economic change, most notably in the effects on occupational structure connected with the accumulation of capital, is subsequently the precondition of *disorganization* of civil society. The latter, most visible in multiplication and fragmentation of interest groups – inside and outside of the labour movement – is itself the precondition of disorganization in the state, in the ideal-typical model, instantiated in, for example, the decline of neo-corporatism, the development of the catch-all party, and class dealignment.

We should also stress that what is meant here by 'disorganized capitalism' is radically different from what other writers have spoken of in terms of 'post-industrial' or 'information' society. Unlike the post-industrial commentators we think that capitalist social relations continue to exist. For us a certain level of capital accumulation is a necessary condition of capitalism's disorganized era in which the capitalist class continues to be dominant. When we argue for the increased centrality of the professional–managerial or 'service' class, we shall not contend that such salience poses an obstacle to the accumulation of capital. Indeed it has been on balance, we shall argue, functional for such accumulation. Moreover, we are far from sympathetic with the 'farewell to the proletariat' line of argument associated with writers of the 1980s with much closer historical links with the left such as André Gorz, or even the less forcefully stated marginalization of the working-class theses associated with Eric Hobsbawm and Claus Offe.[6] Indeed working-class struggles may increase – and arguably have increased – in disorganized capitalism. Consider for example, France, Britain and Italy from the late 1960s, or the industrial struggles of France, Britain and Germany of the early and middle 1980s. Our point is that these struggles in disorganized capitalism are more likely to be sectional; and more likely to be carried out with either community-centred (as in Lorraine metallurgy and British coal) or radical–democratic ideological resources than with characteristically class-struggle *mentalités*. Though this book does not pretend to be programmatically political, it does hold out an implicit argument for qualitative social change through some sort of alliance between working-class and 'new' social movements. This would have to be based on the development of a transformed oppositional political culture, whose complexion would not need to be reformist. Thus we should like to differentiate the (at least) implicit politics articulated here from the fundamentalist and often reductionist class politics of some contemporary Marxists.[7] Though we reject the broader framework of 'post-industrial' interpretations, we think that they have highlighted some important truths in regard to important aspects of contemporary societies. What we have attempted to do in this volume is to account for these in a framework which is far more sympathetic to the broad currents of neo-Marxism. We would incidentally stress that what we mean by 'disorganization' is not just a shift into a sort of high-entropy random disorder; disorganization is instead a fairly systematic process of disaggregation and restructuration which we have begun to outline in our 14 points above.

Chapters 2 and 3 are devoted to an explication of the development and profile of organized capitalism in Germany, Sweden, Britain, France and the USA. In this context we will speak of two 'moments' of organized capitalism: the first starting with the expansive phase of the Kondratieff cycle, beginning in the 1890s, during which capitalism begins to organize at the top; the second, involving organization at the bottom, which in most societies commenced during the inter-war period. Germany is closest to approximating the ideal type outlined above of organized capitalism, achieving high levels of organization very early on both at the top and the bottom. Germany's industrial–sectoral profile, for instance, displays the greatest preponderance of production of capital goods. We shall argue, contrary to common wisdom, that German banks were a conservative influence on industrial investment. None the less, the framework of financial institutions in Germany which was accessible to industry and the willingness of industrialists to borrow was greater than elsewhere.

Readers familiar with Perry Anderson's *Lineages of the Absolutist State* – which portrays a Sweden of the 'early modern period' as marked by autocracy, bureaucracy and military might – may have made the inference that Swedish capitalism would be as organized and rationalized, if not more so, than that of Germany.[8] We would rather describe Swedish development in a different way, as more of a hybrid between the German and English experiences. First, an unusually profoundly experienced eighteenth-century Enlightenment infused important elements of liberalism into nineteenth- and twentieth-century Swedish politics. Second, the fact that Sweden in the early years of organized capitalism competed in sectors in which there were lacunae on international markets meant that levels of capital concentration were rather low. Third, very little state intervention into the economy occurred until the inter-war period. If the key agents of organization in Sweden's early years of organized capitalism were (as we shall argue) merchant and then finance capital, then the crucial counterpart from midway into the inter-war period was social democracy. State intervention in the economy came increasingly to be the rule. Capital began to concentrate effectively, as Sweden's now more conventional organized capitalist industrial sectoral profile brought enterprises face to face with the largest international competitors. Perhaps most crucially Swedish capitalism began to organize rapidly at the bottom. The important years, however, of Swedish industrial growth, especially in relative terms, we shall underline were not the post-war years (and especially not the 1960s and 1970s when only British growth was slower), but were the very early years, the decades before and around the First World War.

In Britain, we shall argue, neither the idiosyncratic and much noticed role of financial institutions nor the more general phenomenon of slow organized capitalist growth can be understood apart from the broader, what we want to call the *Makler*, or 'middleman', nature of the British economy. Central to the British *Makler* economy have been the absolute size and international scope of the financial sector, the early export of capital goods, the early shift into production of services, and especially a sectoral profile in which concentration was focused not in the characteristically organized capitalist sectors but in consumer industries such as food and drink. It was the absence of horizontal and vertical integration, of diversification and modern managerial structures in the key organized capitalist sectors which we shall maintain was the decisive feature of Britain's *Makler* economy.

France was a growth laggard for most of organized capitalism, we shall argue, not because France was economically backward, but because it was rather economically 'forward', by being more British than Britain. France suffered from an extreme version of the British syndrome – too many small workshops, too much skilled labour, too localized markets, too little rapport between banks and industry – which posed enourmous obstacles to the organization of French capitalism. These phenomena, along with a very gentle process of urbanization and industrialization, also meant less harmful levels of dislocation in French economy and society. Though the 'triumph of the engineers' in their takeover of French management helped create respectable levels of growth in the first three decades of the twentieth century, it was the shift towards corporatism, and later Vichy's 'state corporatism', which in the low-growth 1930s and 1940s laid the groundwork for the rapid expansion of the rational planning decades of the 1950s and 1960s.

Finally, considerable attention is devoted to the USA, partly because more individuals have experienced what we take to be the beginning of capitalist disorganization in America than in all four of our other countries combined. Many social scientists are fond of making general statements about contemporary capitalism drawing on data relating to large numbers of small countries. For all of the value of such comparative analysis, over 40 per cent of the population living in advanced capitalist countries in the West in fact live in the United States. The size of the American population living under *non*-corporatist, low-welfare state disorganized capitalist relations is more than *three times* larger than the combined population of Austria, Switzerland, Denmark, New Zealand, Holland, Belgium, Finland, Norway and Australia; that is more than three times the size of those small countries most often cited as proofs of high levels of corporatization and organization of contemporary capitalism. In any event, chapter 3 notes that the early and thorough organization of American capitalism at the top was unmatched by such organization at the bottom, and that the American polity in organized capitalism's first moment (from the 1890s) was characterized by the state apparently acting as the instrument of the economically dominant class. Subsequently the 'progressivism' of the New Deal helped American capitalism to organize at the bottom and lent relative autonomy to the state. 'Progressivism', an ideology and a movement associated with the rising service class and related middle classes from the beginning of the twentieth century, is key to the understanding of American capitalist organization and disorganization. Our claim is that in the twentieth century some variety of 'progressivism' has always been the main source of opposition to unregulated capitalist accumulation in the USA. And that 'American exceptionalism' is due, not as much to an ethnically divided and weak working class, as to the very early presence, size and access to organization of the American new middle classes, and especially the 'service class'.

In chapters 4 and 5 the focus is on shifts in the spatial structuring of economy and society in the development of organized capitalism and especially in the transition from organized to disorganized capitalism. If the process of organization meant the spatial concentration of the means of production, distribution and social reproduction, disorganization has meant a spatial scattering or deconcentration of this gamut of social relations. This spatial scattering has been translated in terms of a decline of not just the city, but of the 'region' and the nation-state. It includes a process of, first, the spatial deconcentration of the various production processes within today's large firm. Second, of the disurbanization of the means of production, not just to the suburbs and Third World subsidiaries but to the countryside in the First World. Third, the disurbanization of executive functions and of commercial capital. Fourth, the spatial scattering of the means of collective consumption, which has meant the residential deconcentration of labour power, of the working class itself. Finally, the growth of the highly capitalized establishment – in industry, commerce, the services – and the corresponding decline in number of employees per workplace has resulted in the spatial deconcentration of labour on the shopfloor. One overriding consequence of all these spatial changes has been (and this for us is perhaps the key explanatory factor, though not ultimately the crucial determinant, of disorganized capitalism) the decline of working-class capacities. 'Class capacities' are a matter not just of the numerical size of a social class but the organizational and cultural resources at its disposal.[9] Not only has the size of the working class and especially its 'core' declined in disorganized capitalism, but spatial scattering has meant the disruption of communicational and organizational networks, resulting in an important diminution of class resources.

If the class capacities of the proletariat have been diminished in disorganized capitalism, the size and resources of the professional–managerial strata, or 'service class', have enormously increased. This is the subject matter of chapter 6. The rise of the service class, first and most dramatically in the USA, has been not just a function of the accumulation of capital (though it has been this too), but has been a matter of engineers, managers, planners, social workers and so on creating space for their own class formation through the expansion of universities and professional associations (organizational resources) and through the development of arguments justifying their position in terms of superior education and expertise (cultural resources). The service class has in this process, partly as cause, partly as effect, been a considerable factor in the growth of higher education in disorganized capitalism. Our claim here is that the service class which is an effect or outgrowth of *organized* capitalism, is subsequently, largely through its self-formation, an important and driving factor in capitalism's disorganization process. Our comparative argument in large part rests on the time of appearance and size of the service class – hence much of our discussion is devoted to the American case – and in large part on the differing balance in the various countries of private-sector versus public-sector fractions of the class.

Chapter 7 is devoted to bringing the discussion of chapters 2 and 3 up to date and into the era of disorganized capitalism. Here we will consider the decentralization of finance capital and especially the effects of the substantial privatization of international money which has undermined the capacity of states to pursue national economic policies. We will also consider changes in the organization of industry, the decline in mass production and the growth of more specialized markets and of specialty producers. We will also con-sider the varying patterns of class dealignment in voting patterns and of the growth of 'catch-all', non-class-based parties in the various countries. This latter discussion will be in the context of the decline and transformation of working-class capacities, the growth of the service class and of a split between its private- and public-sector fractions, and the range, extent and effects of 'new' social movements. We shall also consider the recent evolution of the welfare state, at its challenge from the right and the left, and at the ways that its growth has itself partly disorganized contemporary societies.

In chapter 8, concerned with changes in working-class organizational and cultural resources, it is argued that neo-corporatism is in decline. Often it is maintained that Sweden's industrial relations are the most highly corporatist of any country. With specially close analysis, based on original source materials, of recent developments in the Swedish case, we argue that here, too, the corporatist consensus has undergone fragmentation. We then in less detail turn to the breakup of Concerted Action in Germany, of corporatist type initiatives in France, especially after 1981, and the problems of getting neo-corporatist institutional arrangements off the ground in Britain, before some very brief discussion as to why there has been so little corporatism in the USA. Our more general case here rests on the situating of neo-corporatism in the framework of organization and disorganization and shifts in class capacities. Our view is that organized capitalism is in the main structured along capital–labour lines. Such structuration can take a class-versus-class form as in France and Germany, or a 'class-with-class' form as in Sweden and Britain. Given the institutional framework of Swedish trade unions and the employers' associations and the early assumption of power by Social Democracy, this class-with-class, or class-compromise structuring of Swedish organized capitalism took place from the late 1930s by means of working-class *organizational* resources and neo-corporatism. In Britain, the class compromise from the 1920s until the mid-1960s, from the first to second shop stewards' movements, came about not so much through corporatism, or organizational resources, but took a more *cultural* form. What we mean is that the codes of working-class communication during this period, while reinforcing collective identity, did not result in any substantial salience of fundamentally oppositional meanings. And that such codes were loaded strongly with significations of tradition and deference. It was the breakdown of such cultural coding beginning from the mid-1950s which was importantly responsible for the decentralized assertiveness of the British shopfloor from the mid-1960s.[10] The failed attempts to install neo-corporatist institutions from this time were a matter of trying to substitute an organizational solution where cultural modes of incorporation had broken down. But the instrumental collectivism and 'democratic anarchy' of the second shop stewards' movement should not be seen as an increase in class capacities *per se*. The instrumental collectivism was largely a matter of class fragmentation and the language of anarchic democracy of the shopfloor was not necessarily the Marxist-inflected language of *class* struggle.

German organized capitalism, by contrast, was fundamentally structured on a class-versus-class basis until Hitler's 'unmaking' of the German working class. Then, with the Third Reich, the Second World War and the Cold War, the East German and Soviet presence so disrupted working-class communicative patterns, so seriously reduced class cultural resources that, given an institutional and organizational framework already present on the ground, the way was paved for some 30 years of corporatist bias, culminating in the decade of Concerted Action ending in 1977. Working-class marginalization, in the polity and more specifically in social democracy itself, largely accounts, we think, for subsequent decentralizing tendencies. In France the marginalization of the working class – which in spite of low union density figures, has possessed substantial capacities[11] – has come about in the absence, for a number of largely organizational reasons, of a neo-corporatist intermezzo. In the USA, as we have suggested above, partly because the service class possessed such extraordinary resources so early on to pose opposition to capital, the working class never had the type of organized capitalist structuring presence that it had in Europe.

We should emphasize here that we are not pushing a thesis of the imminent demise of the proletariat. We think that the industrial struggles of the late 1960s and middle 1980s are evidence of the continued existence of considerable working-class capacities. The struggles of the late 1960s were, however, importantly infused with the (non-class-specific) radical–democratic discourse which also informed the contemporary social movements; and those of the mid-1980s often part of a bid to pre-empt the attempt of large capital to bid adieu to the proletariat.

The first part of chapter 9 deals with the problem of culture in the shift from organized to disorganized capitalism. The central issue here was first systematically formulated by Daniel Bell in *The Cultural Contradictions of Capitalism*, though a number of writers on the left, and notably much of the work of the Birmigham Centre for Contemporary Cultural Studies, have also addressed it.[12] The issue is the implications of the mass distribution of modernist/postmodernist cultural forms for relations of domination in contemporary capitalism. 'Modernism' we take to be a cultural–ideological configuration which breaks with what Frederic Jameson has called the 'realist' configuration of liberal capitalism.[13] That is, modernism breaks with a paradigm of representation in art and in theoretical discourse, and breaks with any sort of absolute or categorical conceptions in moral discourse. Hence the turn-of-the-century flourishing of non-representational painting and lyrical poetry coincided with the advent of sociologistic epistemologies and ethics in Durkheim and Weber. But modernism is not limited to high culture, and its assumptions pervade everyday discourse, for example in the assumptions of even popular Marxism and nationalism, that knowledge and morals are interest-linked.

We shall not exaggerate the differences between modernism and post-modernism. In terms of the implications for social relations in disorganized capitalism the most important fact is the *mass* distribution of postmodernist cultural forms through television, advertising, film, fashion and so on. It is this which is most important for relations of domination. The main differences are as follows:

1 Postmodernism is about the transgression of boundaries – between what is inside and what is outside of a cultural 'text', between reality and representation, between the cultural and the social, and between high culture and popular culture.
2 Whereas modernism and postmodernism (though much more ambiguously) can be said to break with an aesthetics of representation, the more Apollonian modernism stands in an affinity with the conscious mind that the Dionysian postmodernism with the Freudian id.
3 If communications in liberal capitalism are largely through conversation, and in organized capitalism (modernism) through the printed word, disorganized capitalism's (postmodern) communications are through images, sounds and impulses. That is, to draw on some concepts of J. F. Lyotard, modernism's *discours* is replaced by postmodernism's and disorganized capitalism's *figure*.[14]

We should, though, emphasize here that not all cultural forms in disorganized capitalism are 'postmodernist', but only that such forms take on added weight and have an elective affinity with disorganized capitalism. We also claim that there are important postmodernist characteristics of not only high and popular culture but of the discourse, styles and symbols of everyday life. We do not claim that postmodernist culture is necessarily 'liberating' or a culture of resistance, but that it can (as could modernism) provide cultural resources for either dominant or subordinate collective actors. Postmodernism on one side, with its glorification of commercial vulgarity, its promotion of 'authoritarian populism', reinforces relations of domination; on the other side, with its opposition to hierarchy, it is a cultural resource for resistance to such domination. Postmodernism, on one side, opposes a liberating 'desire' to a traditional and patriarchal superego; on the other side, the new putatively free id is – in many instances and to a large degree – itself recolonized by patriarchy in the interests of new forms of gender domination.[15] Finally, there are also all sorts of postmodernist cultural objects that have very little to do with domination at all; i.e. all cultural objects are not necessarily 'cultural resources'.

Two final remarks about culture in disorganized capitalism. First, domination through cultural forms takes on significance in disorganized capitalism which is comparable in importance to domination in the sphere of production itself.[16] Second, there is something importantly 'classless' about postmodernism. With its core assumption of the breakdown of boundaries, postmodernism finds an audience when the boundaries which structure our identities break down; that is, during personal experiences of 'liminality' during which identity is unstable. Bernice Martin argues that the 'birth of adolescence' in the 1950s among British working-class teenagers was accompanied by such a destabilization of identity and created conditions of reception for rock music and youth culture.[17] This partial revaluation of values in conjunction with the dissipation of constraints is associated and contemporaneous with the gradual demise of the so-called 'traditional' working class, arguably contributed to the anti-hierarchical attitudes which underlay the radical shopfloor democracy from the middle 1960s. At the same time, Martin notes, for the 'middle classes' in Britain in the 1960s, with the extension of education the category of 'youth' first makes its appearance, again with the beginnings of an even more extended period of liminality, of unfixed identity. Martin goes on to argue that the nature of work in the vastly proliferating 'expressive professions' (i.e. service class members in part of the public sector, the communications media, etc.) can mean that liminality extends right through adulthood. Middle-class youth, then, and the expressive professions in the service class are a potential audience for postmodernist culture, and potential sources of resistance to domination in disorganized capitalism. This partly, we think, explains their overwhelming presence in the so-called 'new social movements'. The point here is that much of such popular culture (which possesses important postmodernist attributes), whoever consumes it, is largely 'classless' in content and form, and the radical anti-hierarchical values and practices, the 'anti-authoritarian populism', it *can* engender are equally not particularly marked by class characteristics.

The reason why this book concludes with an analysis of culture is first because of the disorganizing effects of contemporary culture, and secondly because of the greater importance that relatively 'classless' cultural forms assume in the context of social life today. If social action always involves an intermingling of presence and absence, modern culture permits an extraordinarily heightened 'presence-availability', of social situations, events, myths and images which cohere around and 'construct' diverse 'subjects'. With the sea change in modern society, in which large organizations, workplaces and cities are of diminishing significance for each individual, the processes of forming, fixing and reproducing 'subjects' is increasingly 'cultural', formed in diverse ways out of a myriad of myths and images, of consumer products, of available 'life-styles' not at all based on where one lives or whom one knows, that is, on those who are immediately present.[18] Central to our analysis then is an investigation of the changing temporal and spatial contours of liberal, organized and disorganized capitalism. Table 1.1 summarizes the main features of such changes, at the level of the wider societal processes, giving the organizational forms and the various cultural changes which occur in each of the three phases.[19]

Table 1.1   Temporal and spatial changes in liberal, organized and disorganized capitalism

Phase of capitalist development	Predominant temporal/spatial organizational/ structures	Spatial changes within each territory	Predominant means of transmitting knowledge and executing surveillance
Liberal	Large-scale collapsing empires that had been built up around dynastic rulers or world religions; emergence of weak nation-states.	Growth of tiny pockets of industry. Importance of substantial commercial cities as well as the expansion of new urban centres in rural areas.	Handwriting and word of mouth.
Organized	Nation-states within the ten or so major western economies increasingly dominate large parts of the rest of the world through colonization.	Development of distinct regional economies organized around growing urban centres. Major inequalities between new industrial and non-industrial regions and nations.	Printing developed through 'print-capitalism'.
Disorganized	Development of world economy, an international division of labour, and the widespread growth of capitalism in most countries.	Decline of distinct regional/national economies and of *industrial* cities. Growth of industry in smaller cities and rural areas, and the development of service industry. Separation of finance and industry.	Electronically transmitted information dramatically reduces the time–space distances between people and increases the powers of surveillance.

2

The development of organized capitalism (1)

Chapters 2 and 3 are devoted to a lengthy analysis of the development of organized capitalism. They are intended to give the reader not only an idea what is meant by 'organized capitalism', but also to present him or her with an account of its differential development in five major countries (Germany, Sweden, Britain, France, and the USA). This is important, in part because it lays the groundwork for our subsequent cross-national analyses of capitalism's disorganizing process; it is important also because little of this sort of analysis exists in the available literature. The (few) comparative economic history textbooks often tend to ignore the role of the state, banks, social classes and the development of the welfare state, all of which are central to the account of the growth of organized capitalism presented here. There is even less available sociological analysis of such a comparative nature.

We begin with an account of Germany which, though it draws on new material, is not especially contentious in nature. Because Germany has come closest to approaching the organized capitalist ideal type, our objective here is largely to establish a touchstone for subsequent comparative analysis. Some may wish to turn directly to the analyses of Sweden, Britain, France and the USA which are more fully interpretive and at points we think, novel.

GERMANY: THE 'IDEAL TYPE'?

Why, briefly, has Germany been the organized capitalist society *par excellence*? First, German industry was highly bureaucratized very early on, both at management level and on the shopfloor. Second, the German state was interventionist and at the same time relatively autonomous. Third, German industry became highly concentrated in terms of fixed capital per enterprise, number of employees per enterprise, and vertical (forward and backward) integration and diversification. A large part of the increase in capitalization of German firms was due to simple horizontal integration, that is, to straight-forward takeovers and mergers. Fourth, German industry became highly cartelized. It is important to distinguish the impact of cartelization from that of the formation of employers' associations. Cartelization became highly important in the 1890s and is the German equivalent of the British holding company. It rightly belongs to the first step of organization, that is, organization at the top. Employers' associations assumed much greater importance just after the First World War, at about the time that organization at the bottom gave to German politics a very definite 'corporate bias'. Fifth, the joint-stock company assumed an unusual importance quite early on in Germany. Sixth, the interarticulation of banks with industry was more pervasive in Germany than elsewhere. And finally, Germany was the birthplace of the welfare state and of the mass political party.

   Let us address some of these points, first considering German organization at the top – capital concentration in heavy and the new industries, cartels, banks, the role of the state – and then looking at organization at the bottom – the welfare state and the issue of corporate bias in German politics. While we do not claim to challenge in what follows the thesis that Germany has been indeed the country which has most closely approximated the organized capitalist ideal type, we do want to show that the received wisdom on a number of these matters is overly simplistic.

Organization at the top

Proportionately, Germany at the turn of the century had the most developed heavy industrial sector of any western country. No other country at that time had such a high proportion of coal producers or iron and steel manufacturers among its top 100 industrial companies. In the United States, for example, which had a thriving and well-articulated development of heavy industry, a much larger proportion of the top companies was comprised of petroleum and food-processing companies. In France there was a marked lack of coal. British coal was very unconcentrated, and 20 of the British top 50 firms were in the area of food-processing, mostly breweries. Sweden had inordinately rich iron ore deposits, but a good deal of this was exported, and it was not until much later that a thriving Swedish steel industry was developed.[1]

   German economic development in the Kondratieff A-phase from 1850 to 1873 was closely tied to the growth of the railway system. The cyclical boom which began in 1869 was brought about through a burst of railroad expansion and underlay the *Grunderjahre* or founding years of the Reich, the period from 1870 to 1874 during which a large number of joint-stock companies were floated. The crisis which began in 1873 should not be overexaggerated: it was more a matter of falling prices and its length than of a sharp absolute fall in production. However, only in 1880 did German production again reach the level of 1872. The downturn of 1873–80, though, was accompanied by a large shakeout of labour and a significant improvement in productivity. Thereafter, as the British and French economies continued to stagnate, Germany entered into a period of steady growth which involved an increase in net domestic product of on average 2.5 per cent per annum over the 1880s. This growth, unlike that of the 1850s and 1860s, was not primarily fuelled by demand from the expanding German railways, but by exports and increased levels of consumer spending. The end of this decade of steady growth was accompanied by another flurry of the founding of joint-stock companies.

It is difficult to overestimate the preponderance of German heavy industry in Europe. From 1910 to 1913 Germany produced over two-thirds of European steel output, and during these same years mined over one-half of the coal and lignite extracted on the European continent.[2] The country which most closely approached Germany's industrial profile in this period was the United States.[3] Of the top 50 firms in industry and extraction in Germany in 1907 and in the USA in 1917 there were 13 coal or oil companies, while in Britain in 1905 the equivalent figure was only one. In 1907 26 of the top 50 firms in Germany and 20 in the USA were metal or machine-building (engineering) firms, while the corresponding figure for Britain in 1905 was eight. Further, if we disaggregate a little we can see important divergencies between Germany and the USA, with a preponderance of heavy industry on the German side. Germany, for example, had only one sizeable oil firm, while eight of America's top 82 industrial firms in 1909 were petroleum refineries. On the other hand, energy production and iron and steel were interlocked in the German Ruhr to an extent obviously impossible between Texas and Oklahoma oil and Illinois, Ohio and Pennsylvania steel. Of Germany's top 80 industrial firms in 1907 31 were in iron and steel, compared to 25 of America's top 82 in 1909. Finally, while a large proportion of American (and French and British) engineering firms made machines for private consumption – bicycles, sewing-machines and, especially, motor cars – the majority of German engineering was heavy engineering, destined for productive consumption – shipbuilding, locomotives and diesel engines.

At the heart of German heavy industry was of course the iron and steel sector. Notwithstanding the railway-connected boom from 1851 to 1872, the German iron and steel industry was in these early years uncompetitive internationally. This was because the Bessemer process – which Krupp, for example, adopted in 1861 – was unable to make use of the low-grade phosphoric iron ore in German Lorraine. The patenting of the Gilchrist-Thomas process changed this. Germany overtook Britain in pig iron and steel production in 1900; from the late 1880s German basic steel became cheaper than elsewhere. From 1898 to 1903 exports doubled and almost reached British levels. Indeed, during many years of the same period, 25 per cent and more of finished iron and steel was exported. The formation of the iron and steel cartels in the mid-1890s was undertaken with the intention not so much of protectionism, but of keeping domestic prices high in order to sell more cheaply abroad.[4]

In 1887 Krupp was the largest German firm, with 20,000 employees and 40 million marks of share capital. Twenty years later it was still the country's number-one firm but now with 64,000 employees and 180 million marks of share capital. Moreover, contrary to Chandler's thesis that cartels are incompatible with the rational expansion of the firm, from 1887 to 1907 German iron and steel had cartelized *and* expanded through backward and forward integration, diversification and, perhaps most of all, through straightforward takeovers and mergers.[5] Most important, maybe, was backward integration, especially into coal mining. A great proportion of the capital for the enormous expansion of coal production from 1894 to 1913 was provided by backward integrating iron and steel firms. It has been estimated that in 1900 some 20 per cent of coal output was through these now 'mixed' metal-producing enterprises.[6] But forward integration was also important. Merchant profits in the late 1880s badly damaged iron and steel, as most firms at that point did not possess distribution outlets. The solution was to create syndicates for distribution of product lines of very high demand. Some firms also diversified downstream into machine building. For example, Krupp had made Essen a company town with his steel plant, machine shops, coal mines and large tracts of company housing; Gelsenkirchen was similarly dominated by the Schalker iron works.[7]

Now let us consider the 'new' industries.[8] Before 1860 there was little application of chemical processes to industry on any kind of scale in Germany.[9] France and Britain at that time were international leaders, using the traditional Leblanc process of soda manufacture which was the basis of many other inorganic chemical processes. Germany, however, pioneered the industrial application of *organic* chemical processes, first (in the commercial production of synthetic dyestuffs, in the late 1880s) to pharmaceuticals production at Hoechst and Bayer, but also to the manufacture of explosives and artificial fibres and many other products. Chemicals was the fastest-concentrating branch in German industry from 1887 to 1907 – represented in 1887 by 12 firms in the top 100, and in 1907 by 17 firms. The enormous capital needs of such rapid growth were provided through the involvement on a large scale of banks. This expansion did not involve the tremendous increases in share capital that was the case in the very largest firms in iron and steel and the electrical industry. Also in the 1880s chemicals was not highly diversified. The most marked improvements were in forward and backward integration, which took place partly through cartelization and quasi-cartelization. In 1887 the top chemicals firms had little distribution apparatus. In 1907 all the most important concerns had sales subsidiaries in the most important commodity market-places. The tertiarization of the workforce was far advanced in chemicals. The 'abstract–rational' pure-science training that was only available so widely in Germany paid off in this branch, in which research and development was of the utmost import. Only Germany – especially in comparison with France and Britain – offered the mass university training of chemists.[10]

The electrical industry, which in terms of its contribution to the national product was to become highly central only during the inter-war period, was nevertheless already significant during the decades leading up to the First World War.[11] In 1907 two of the five firms with the nation's largest share capital were electrical concerns – Siemens and Halske, and AEG (German General Electric) – and the other three were iron and steel manufacturers. Equally important was the role of the electrical industry in the transformation – through electrification – of German cities, and its creation of demand for associated industries. Germany was the world leader in this field. In the decade leading up to the First World War its exports of electrical equipment were three times greater than those of the United States, which was its greatest international competitor. Part of the reason for German growth here was the existence of a large number of big cities – more than Britain or France, and matched only by the USA – which provided markets for municipal lighting and transport. In 1902 one-half of the total European length of electric tramways was in Germany. In the next decade the growth in municipal demand was stimulated by the building of undergrounds, of inter-urban electric transport and of a very considerable number of large-scale central power stations.[12]

We have already noted that in certain industries cartels were of some importance in this period. There has been considerable debate on their role and significance in the development of German organized capitalism. The common wisdom expressed by Alfred Chandler was that the level of cartelization was extraordinarily high and that these cartels hindered the rational expansion of such capitalist firms.[13] Opponents of this viewpoint, such as Kocka, have argued that effective cartelization was never that pervasive before the First World War and where it did exist it in fact promoted rational expansion.[14] We will briefly consider the evidence here.

The most effective cartel during the pre-war period was in coal, where the Rhenish-Westphalian Coal Syndicate was particularly succcessful in promoting downstream integration and hence concentration through its distribution apparatus. However, the syndicate's function of maintaining domestic prices above their market value in the promotion of exports was in the end self-destructive. High domestic coal prices made it worthwhile for iron and steel to integrate backwards into coal production and to form 'mixed' concerns, which increased from seven in 1895 to 18 in 1902, when these 18 controlled 19 per cent of coal production. And the mines which the iron and steel firms had taken over were among the *larger* syndicate mines. The syndicate also appears to have changed the interests of the coal-producers in respect to iron ore. The syndicate companies owned a number of iron mines whose production they controlled in order to keep prices high. But this damaged the position of syndicate-owned iron mines in relation to non-syndicate mines, with the latter increasing their production by 100.5 per cent from 1893 to 1902 in comparison with the former's increase of 60.5 per cent. By 1902 the non-syndicate iron mines had surpassed the syndicate mines in production.[15]

The two other most prominent pre-war syndicates underwent not dissimilar experiences. One, however, the Rhenish-Westphalian Pig Iron Syndicate, was founded in the midst of economic expansion in 1896. During the cyclical downturns of 1901–2 and 1908 the syndicate was threatened by the ability of independents to undersell syndicate firms and the hesitancy of the large 'mixed' concerns to hold prices high, when they could produce more cheaply through selling to themselves. This was resolved in 1903 when independents were coerced into joining the syndicates, but the combination of outsiders and mixed concerns led to the cartel's dissolution in 1908.[16] The other syndicate, the Steel Manufacturers' Association, *Stahlwerksverband*, was founded in 1904 as a joint-stock company for the distribution of both heavy and light rolling-mill products. Shortly after the association's foundation it became clear that there was a conflict of interests between firms which produced only light products and those which were integrated backwards. During the downturn of 1908–9 it proved impossible to control the prices of light products for the backward-integrated firms, which again could sell to themselves more cheaply. Thus when the association's contract was renewed in 1912 the light products were no longer included. At this point, although the association controlled 80 per cent of the German market, it had, yet again and for similar reasons, difficulty controlling prices for even the heavy products.[17]

In summary, then, neither Chandler nor Kocka offer convincing evidence for their conflicting theses regarding the effects of cartels on the rational expansion of the firm in Germany. What seems clear though is that the highly vertically integrated and expanding firms – whether inside the heavy industry cartels or outside of cartels (such as Thyssen and the Siemens Martin-Werke in steel) – were inconsistent with the pricing policies of cartels. It was only after the First World War that heavy industry became pervasively cartelized; but at this point the dynamism of the coal and metal-producing firms had long since declined.[18]

Another common claim is the 'finance-capital' interpretation of German economic history. However, on closer examination the big banks were not the innovative industrial investors that they have often been purported to be. During, for example, the relatively stagnant years of the late 1870s and 1880s, the big Berlin banks were reluctant to provide regular services for heavy industry, services which were carried out by the provincial banks such as Essener Credit-Anstalt and Norddeutsche Bank and by private banks such as Oppenheim or Rothschild.[19] Again, when chemicals firms needed money for expansion in the 1880s, it was the local and private banks which handled the share issues on the Stock Exchange. Yet the Berlin banks were important in providing capital for the electrical industry and for a number of engineering firms. Their role with regard to heavy industry – despite the self-financing capacities of heavily capitalized firms like Krupp and Gelsenkirchen – was enhanced during the 1894–1913 period. However, it was industry rather than the banks which took the initiative. In several sectors, the firms which survived and thrived between 1887 and 1907 were the ones which integrated vertically and diversified, and for this capital was needed. And from the mid-1890s the big banks were most effective, not through the negotiation of substantial long-term loans, but through the extension of current account facilities to firms.[20] Further, a large proportion of the ownership by banks of industrial shares was the ownership of shares that the banks had themselves issued for an industrial concern. That is, after the bank issued the shares it would buy them up itself; it would then be in the bank's interest to sell the shares as soon as possible. This is hardly a picture of banks vying for controlling shareholdings in companies. To underline this point, in 1912, only one German bank had more than 3 per cent of its assets invested in industrial shares.[21]

Finally, as Hopt argues, the position of banks on industrial boards of directors was a complicated matter.[22] The banks tended to perceive their interests in terms of price and production stability and hence tended to opt for caution, rather than innovative investment, in their attitude towards industrial firms. In addition the increasing heterogeneity of interests on the boards of directors provided top management with a great deal of autonomy from the interests of any shareholding group, while in family firms like Siemens which were at the same time joint-stock companies, the banks could hardly expect to carry undue weight on the *Aufsichträte* (board). As Hopt shows, the most important functions of the banks' representatives on industrial boards were the contacts they provided external to the firm. Their representation on many boards as well as their desire for stability motivated them to pursue policies of cartelization, and a conservative cartelization at that.

We will now consider the role of the state in the structuring of German organized capitalism. First, the state, through its protectionist policies, promoted the organization of commodity markets and capital markets.[23] Most of the period of organized capitalism (apart from 1919 to 1927) were protectionist years. More precisely, during the period from 1873 to 1945, Germany was at its most protectionist, *ceteris paribus*, when heavy industry was uncompetitive internationally. Inefficient Prussian large landed agriculture was also always protectionist during this period. For the state to adopt such policies, these landed interests needed allies from heavy industry. The story of the quid pro quo in the 1870s between the state and Bismarck on the one hand and heavy industry on the other, whereby the industrialists sacrificed their liberal principles for their economic interests, is well known. It is worth remembering that the sacrifice of such universalistic values was a step in the direction of accepting the characteristic ideologies of organized capitalism. Second, the state organized markets through the promotion of cartels. It enacted legislation which facilitated cartel formation, and also imposed the formation of cartels in, for example, the marketing of potash. Cases such as this served as an incentive to firms to organize cartels 'independently' rather than submit to enforced state organization.[24] Third, the state promoted the concentration of industry through the creation of demand in sectors in which survival was only possible through vertical integration and mergers. Important in this connection was, initially, the demand that was created through state-owned railways and its effects on the expansion of heavy industry; and of particular importance was the demand created by the local state which acted as a catalyst for the electrical industry.[25]

The *personnel* of governing bodies is an interesting indicator of the changing relationship between state and capital during the development of organized capitalism. First, we should note the importance of the recruitment of government officials into leading industrial management positions. About one in three of top Ruhr industrial leaders, for example, had served and/or trained as government bureaucrats in the decades leading up to the First World War. Over 26 per cent of high-level entrepreneurs in Upper Silesian heavy industry during this same period were government officials at the same time as they were employed as top managers. Second, the experience of industrialists in the army and the bureaucracy led to their adoption of typically organized capitalist formal rules of organization in private enterprise. Third, though we should not underestimate their capacity for cynicism, the biographies of key Ruhr industrialists indicate that their development of private social welfare programmes for workers was partly motivated by a 'universalist' mentality which they had acquired as civil servants.[26]

Industrialists themselves only became elected memebers of municipal and *Land* (provincial) bodies on any kind of scale with the advent of organized capitalism. During liberal capitalism, professionals, notables, merchants and aristocrats filled these positions. Aristocrats continued to do so on a very significant scale well into organized capitalism, especially in commercial and administrative centres. In industrial towns – and many of them were not large enough to obtain municipal status and the creation of a city council until well into organized capitalism – the large entrepreneurs came to dominate.[27] For example, from 1852 to 1913, among leading Ruhr entrepreneurs, 24 per cent of top managers and 16 per cent of company owners were elected to municipal councils; *and* 13 per cent of managers and 12 per cent of owners were members of a comparable supra-regional body. Similarly, in Upper Silesia 16 per cent of owners were representatives in supra-regional bodies. Most of this membership, especially in the Ruhr, came in the later years (in particular after 1894) of this period, 1852–1913.

Most significant, perhaps, in this context is the relation of industrialists to non-elected, of at least not directly elected, officers of central and local government. The most important of these were the provincial and district governors, the *Landräte* and mayors. The governors were the Reich's representatives and had primary responsibility for the supervision of county and municipal government. There were, for example, three district governors in proximity to the Ruhr, as well as the provincial governors of the Rhineland and of Westphalia.[28] These governors were not from the local area. They differed from the industrialists in their noble backgrounds or aspirations; their education was in law, not in commercial or technical fields as was typical among industrialists. Politically, the bureaucrats were quite often Conservatives and the entrepreneurs National Liberals. Yet there was a great deal of personal and social contact between the governors and the businessmen, who were after all the local elite. The industrialists recruited retired civil servants or their relatives to their boards of directors in order to influence the government. Requests for contributions from the entrepreneurs to conservative and nationalist causes often came via the governors. And the governors paid in kind. For example, they helped the industrialists to evade Berlin's factory legislation – such as, the 1908 Bundesrat Order regarding shopfloor workbreaks in the iron and steel industry – by granting exceptions. Equally the governors, who if they excelled in their role could hope for a future ministerial post, were the conduit of information on strikes and other industrial matters, which was passed through them from the industrialists to Berlin.

In this, and in other ways, there was a shift away from bureaucratic universalism in this period towards an increasing entwinement of bureaucracy with the interests of big business, and a growing identification with the aspirations of the nobility.[29] It was government policy during the Wilhelmine period to use a system of effective quotas to ensure that the aristocracy of each of the various *Länder* was represented in the highest administrative offices. And not only in the very highest offices but in the next level too: some 62 per cent of the *Ländrate*, for example, were of aristrocratic background, as well as many of the provincial governors.

Organization at the bottom

The second stage of organized capitalism involves the development of organization at the bottom. It typically consists of welfare legislation, often the growth of some kind of 'corporate bias' or tripartism in labour relations, and various forms of government planning and regulation. This may take either a social democratic form (as in Sweden in the 1930s, or in Germany's Weimar Republic in the 1920s) or an authoritarian form (as in fascist Italy and Germany, or Vichy France).

In Germany and Germany alone was the substantial growth of the welfare state connected with organized capitalism's first stage, i.e. organization at the top. Thus using Flora's index of social insurance coverage, we see that the 'take-off' of German social insurance preceded that in Britain and Sweden (which took place just before the First World War) by some twenty years.[30] Another set of new advanced capitalist countries – Denmark, Norway, Finland and the USA – had their take-offs in the 1930s. Finally, Italy and France experienced qualitative lift-offs only in the post-war period. Whereas welfare legislation in Britain, Sweden and the USA around the time of the First World War was the work of liberal parties, and the advances after the Second World War were due to social-democratic and Christian democratic forces, the late ninteenth-century German legislation was organized by conservatives. Likewise in Germany, in contradistinction to most other countries, the take-off of a welfare state system was wholly detached from even the beginnings of a 'corporate bias'. Germany, then, was the only country in which the take-off of welfare was categorically from 'above'.

The first set of Acts were legislated from 1880 to 1883 and comprised accident, sickness and old-age insurance.[31] Curiously, some of the most important original supporters of Bismarck's legislation came from heavy industry, largely as a quid pro quo for Bismarck's protectionist legislation of 1879 but also – and this seemed to be the prime motive for Bismarck himself – as part of a package including repressive policies aimed at the Social Democrats (SPD). By the mid-1880s, however, when costs became apparent, heavy industry became more critical.[32] The second substantial improvement in the German welfare state came with the 1927 passage of unemployment insurance legislation. Neo-conservative 'overload' theorists[33] hence claim that the Social Democratic Party (SPD) acted too much like a trade union with its demands on unemployment insurance, and that it put the day-to-day interests of its constituents before the safeguarding of the democracy of the Weimar Republic. Weisbrod has, however, counterposed an effective case against this thesis.[34] He notes that the legislation called for a contribution to the unemployment fund of 3 per cent each from both labour-market partners, which was sufficient only to support 800,000 unemployed. The 1929 increases in job losses led the SPD to demand a 4 per cent increase in the contribution from both sides and the retention of guaranteed state loans to the unemployment fund. The German People's Party (DVP – the Weimar equivalent of the National Liberals) proposed however that from 1929 benefits be substantially reduced, to the extent that 60 per cent of the unemployed would have been dependent on a rate of benefits below the old public-aid level. Rejecting a compromise with labour (after the departure of Stresemann), the DVP – in whose ranks heavy industry had just begun to dominate – acted to push the SPD out of government. In this they succeeded in March 1930; it was a success which meant the end of parliamentary government in inter-war Germany.

Political sociologists have often made the connection between the problem of overloads and the growth of corporatism. There is considerable controversy as to how to interpret the Weimar Republic with respect to these issues.[35] Our view is that there were important corporatist developments in the Weimar Republic but that these should not be overemphasized.

The first of these developments was the agreement between the iron and steel industrialist Hugo Stinnes and the leader of the *Allgemeiner Deutscher Gewerkschaftsbund* (ADGB, General Confederation of German Trade Unions),

Carl Legien. In a series of negotiations carried out between October and November 1918, leaders of a coal, iron, steel, engineering and electro-technical industries agreed to an eight-hour working day and union recognition and bargaining rights. The Stinnes–Legien agreement led also to the creation of a quasi-corporatist institution, The *Zentralarbeitsgemeinschaft* (ZAG), whose intention was to avoid state control of the economy through agreements between industry and labour. The immediate achievement of the ZAG was to take demobilization out of the auspices of the *Reichswirtschaftsamt* (the Reich's economics office) and turn it over to a newly created demobilization office which was to work in close collaboration with the ZAG. The other proposed corporatist body was Wichard von Moellendorff's largely unimplemented *Gemeinwirtschaftsplan*, which was developed in the Reich's economics ministry in 1919. This was a plan which would have significantly strengthened the hand of the state in the economy, though it was based on self-governing bodies in industry. Though never completely clearly formulated by Moellendorff, who had formerly worked at the war office with Walther Rathenau, the plan envisaged considerable state control in the areas of production, prices and export controls. Its proposed central body was also, as opposed to the ZAG, to have executive as well as general economic and social policy formulating powers. The self-governing bodies were to include not only representatives from industry and labour, but also merchant and consumer delegates. Some heavy industrialists supported the Moellendorff idea, but only in the face of threats of revolution and socialization from below. The industrialists far preferred the ZAG, although the latter was based on a set of organs set up on the basis of parity between employers and workers. The ultimate goal of the industrialists, however, was to free themselves from the ZAG as well.[36]

Although these 'corporatist' institutions were not effective, and although heavy industry especially used them only tactically, at least the question of such institutions was placed on – and was central to – the political agenda. The only participants who were sympathetic to a corporatist solution – the German Democratic Party (the 'social–liberal' DDP) sympathizers who were involved in the drafting of the Weimar Republic's Constitution, some right-wing Social Democrats, and some leaders of the new industries, such as Siemens and Duisberg, who were more willing to go along with the eight-hour day and the establishment of bargaining structures with unions – were relatively marginal actors. The active driving forces, from the sides of both capital and labour, were basically unsympathetic to a corporatist compromise. The latter was also the case during the Weimar's 'good years' of 1924–9, which Maier has characterized as corporatist.

Nor were the latter years fully corporatist, in that the state was less a full partner in a tripartism than a referee between capital and labour. Equally there was too little trade union centralization to qualify these years as fully corporatist. Profitability had sunk too low at the expense of wage gains, and neither capital nor labour was opting for a compromise solution. Labour veered towards anarchism in its instrumental collectivism; and ADGB plans for an 'economic democracy' were more gradualist socialist than corporatist. Capital, and especially heavy industry – but more and more also the new industries – were cynical about collective bargaining and looked forward openly to the day when labour would be routed.[37] None the less, the relative stand-off between capital and labour from 1924 to 1929, with a social democratic state intervening as impartially as possible in industrial disputes, along with high growth rates and arguably relatively favourable wage gains, are clear indicators of organization at the bottom. Capital, especially heavy industry, was nostalgic for the days when organization was only at the top and a strong state coexisted with a large measure of independence for entrepreneurs. This is clear from the 1925 report of the Reich Association of German Industry's *Sonderausschuss für ein Wirtschaftsprogram.*[38] When the industrialists achieved their goal with the successful offensive against labour in 1929–30, the Depression deprived the moment of much satisfaction, and this was further diminished after the Nazi accession to power.

Germany: conclusions

The unique profile of Germany approaches the organized capitalist ideal type in that high levels of organization took place rather early on at both 'the top' and 'the bottom': in the economy and civil society, on the one hand, and in the state, on the other. At the top, and in the economy, no country matched German heavy industry in terms of concentration and forward and backward integration; only the USA matched German heavy industry and its new electrical and chemical industries in the development of modern management structures and in its overall strength. No major country boasted a comparative level, though its legacy was ambiguous, of cartel formation. In civil society, only Sweden was a match for the strength of the employers' associations. At the bottom few countries matched Germany at the turn of the century for the strength and militancy of working-class organization; no country came close for political working-class organization; precedents were set in the early development of a welfare state. Where Germany has deviated from the ideal type is in the *mode* of organization and especially the organization of the state; Germany in particular is deviant here in terms of *who* was the central agent of organization. In Germany it was *capital* which, in an unparalleled one-sided manner, was doing the organizing. The dominant classes were not only key in bringing about state organization through high levels of protectionism from the 1870s, but it was the 'top' itself which organized the 'bottom' in the Bismarckian social insurance legislation. This inordinate role of the dominant classes in the organization of the state was in large part due to the very strength and perceived threat of working-class organizations in civil society. The year 1918 began more than a decade of working-class militancy and perceived proletarian threat, in response to which the National Socialist organization (from the top) of the state – in terms of 'planning' and effective 'Keynesianism' – constituted a perceived solution. Even the initial post-war expansion of the welfare state in the 1950s and early 1960s came from the top – from Christian democracy – and not from social democracy.

We will now turn to the other prototypically *organized* capitalist society of the five nations under consideration here, that is, Sweden, in which organization at the bottom has been of unsurpassed strength.

SWEDEN: FROM FINANCE CAPITAL TO SOCIAL DEMOCRACY

One of the key elements in distinguishing differential national paths in the development of organized capitalism is the question of *who* is the organizing force: that is, the set of social or political actors or collective actors – whether a social class or class fraction, an interest association or political party – which takes on the primary role in bringing about the organization of a country's capitalism. Heavy industry, as we have seen, was crucial as the motor of organization at the top of German capitalism, while organization at the bottom and in particular the growth of the welfare state largely came about through initiatives also taken at the top. Sweden, whose profile as a highly organized society comes closest to resembling the German, could not have been more different in terms of its organizing forces. During the initial moment of development or organized capitalism in Sweden, in the decades spanning the turn of the century, it was not industrial but finance capital that was the main agency of organization. From the inter-war years by contrast, and allowing that Sweden had perhaps the most *organized* capitalism of any major western nation, it was the labour movement itself – first the Social Democrats and then the central trade union confederation, the Landsorganisationen (LO) – which provided the motor of organization.

Organization at the top

Organized capitalism developed rather later in Sweden than in Germany. In the period from 1893 to 1914 industrial capital was not particularly concentrated, and the state functioned more as a night-watchman state. Although from the 1930s Sweden has been the most highly organized of societies, this was not the case at the turn of the century. What explains this relative slowness to 'organize'? In chapter 1 we noted two general factors affecting the 'pace' of organization. The first is the extent to which pre-modern – especially feudal and guild – corporate forms survive intact into the capitalist period. The more pervasive these social and political residues are, the more they will facilitate the development of organized capitalism. On this point, Swedish capitalist organization would have been inhibited by the relative weakness of such corporate groupings in pre-modern Sweden. Feudal institutions stayed at a relatively rudimentary level partly because of Sweden's highly centralized absolutist state, in which the army's role was not at all dissimilar to that of Prussia. Also important were the lasting effects of a far-reaching eighteenth-century Swedish Enlightenment, which left the bourgeoisie far more consistently sympathetic to parliamentary politics and later to free-trade and the non-interventionist state than was the case in Germany. This was reinforced by the dominant role of merchant and export-oriented interests in the Swedish bourgeoisie.

The second general factor is lateness of industrialization. That is, the later a country industrializes, the more organized it must be (in terms of concentration and centralization of capital and so on) in order to compete with countries whose industrialization is already well underway. This factor is less applicable to the Swedish case in which development, at least initially, could take place free from direct competition, by exporting what other countries could not export. This was the case for Sweden's early iron and timber industries and later for its pulp and paper and new engineering industries. When direct competition was avoided by the export of specialized products, the economies of scale of the very large enterprise were less necessary, and hence Sweden's early development was not at very high leve's of capital concentration. The appropriate comparison here then – all the more so because of the importance of Swedish organization at the bottom – would not be with Germany but Britain.

Although Sweden did not develop high levels of capital concentration by the turn of the century, there was considerable economic growth, particularly between 1870 and 1914. The first upsurge in economic activity, occurred in the 1850s and was characterized by a substantial increase in the export of grain.[39] Up until 1830 Sweden had been a net grain importer. The reversal in the 1840s and 1850s was largely due to the role of the new mortgage banks, which borrowed through the issuance of bonds in Paris, Hamburg and Berlin and made long-term loans – up to 40-year mortgages – to large landowners who then rationalized grain production. The foreign bond liability of the mortgage societies had reached 52 million kronor by the end of 1858.[40] The remarkable economic expansion from 1870 to 1875 was associated with the very rapid growth of the Swedish railway network. Again, financial institutions played a crucial part. To finance the new railways the state depended on a very substantial bond issue. These bonds, through the mediation of Swedish financial institutions, were mostly issued abroad; this phenomenon was reflected in the fact that up until 1910 some 83 per cent of the state's bonded debt was to foreign creditors.[41] Privately-owned rail lines were also financed by bonds, issued mainly through the Stockholm Handelsbank, which again for the most part borrowed in foreign markets.[42]

The timber and the iron industries, unparalleled as exporters during Swedish liberal capitalism, maintained a strong position until after the Second World War. In the fourth quarter of the nineteenth century, the state and the large timber companies began to acquire most of the timber forests. The initiating entrepreneurs of the large companies were largely drawn from the wholesaling commercial houses. Swedish commercial enterprises which had begun by purchasing timber from small peasant concerns, ended up buying land and establishing tree-felling and sawmill operations that now took place at coastal sites prior to shipping. In the absence of institutional sources of finance, the merchant houses – mostly Swedish banks, but which often borrowed from foreign merchant houses – provided banking capital for the timber companies; this was mainly a matter of short-term credit against promissory notes in an industry whose fixed capital needs were, in any case, minimal.[43] In iron, initially, medium-sized producers and refiners integrated backwards into smelting on a large scale during the second and third quarters of the nineteenth century. This integration – although the industry kept the outmoded Lancashire process until near the end of the century – was financed again through the exporting merchant houses, themselves dependent on German, English and Dutch banks. Such dependency on pre-modern forms of finance capital was reinforced when open-hearth steel-making began in 1868. Yet this financial involvement was minimal, as we shall see, in comparison to the inter-war period in which commercial banking restructured and effectively controlled large sections of the iron and steel industry. Iron and steel export began to decline sharply as Sweden entered the epoch of organized capitalism, though much of this deficit was made good by the boom in the export of iron ore.[44]

It is difficult to overestimate the importance of the period from 1891 to the beginning of the First World War in the development of Sweden's economy. First, it was during this period that Sweden largely caught up with the major capitalist countries. Second, this was a period in which there were very strong increases in industrial growth. In 1891–5 there was, for example, a 44 per cent increase in the value of industrial output; in 1896–1900, a 49 per cent increase; and in 1901–5, a 29 per cent increase.[45] Third, this period witnessed the important development of the home market as a stimulus for industrial growth.[46] Thus from 1866 to 1890 export growth about matched industrial growth; from 1891 to 1910 export growth fluctuated at about only 40 per cent of industrial growth; from 1911 to 1940, despite wild fluctuations, industrial growth on balance approximated export growth; and from 1946 to the 1980s – partly due to disorganization at the top (i.e. the international decline of protectionism and the decline of industry relative to services in Sweden and internationally) – export growth has been far higher than industrial growth. Fourth, this period was also characterized by the flourishing of the 'new industries', in Sweden's case the pulp and paper industry and the mechnical and electrical engineering industries. This important shift marked the change from the dominance of capital goods production to one of consumer goods production, a periodization which is the reverse of the trend that most western countries have experienced.

The role of finance was again crucial for the new industries. Bank loans to industry increased fourfold in the 1890s. Stockholm's Enskilda Bank was particularly important in financing electrical and mechanical engineering in the early stages. Stockholm's Handelsbank was key in helping to set up production facilities abroad. The steady improvement of Swedish terms of trade (i.e. the ratio of export prices to import prices) from the mid-nineteenth century had put Sweden in the position of a net creditor country at the outset (the 1890s) of organized capitalism. Sweden, which – to its great benefit – had been more dependent on the import of capital than other nations, was now a net capital exporter. As a capital importer it was mainly local government and the state, and merchant and to a lesser extent commercial banks, which held the foreign liabilities; only 5 per cent of bonded foreign debt was owed by industry.[47]

For all of this dynamism and growth, Swedish industrial capital was surprisingly unconcentrated at the turn of the century, and fell somewhere between the highly concentrated German and American cases, on the one hand, and the rather unaggregated British case, on the other. Electrical engineering was very concentrated, but mechanical engineering does not correspond to the American and French examples of pre-war rationalization. Iron and steel was surprisingly scattered in ownership until the inter-war years. The ownership of the timber and even paper and pulp industries was similarly scattered.[48] We will now consider rather more systematically the role of credit markets and financial institutions in the development of Swedish organized capitalism.

We can speak of three stages in the development of the Swedish banking system. The first, from about 1820 until the beginning of the 1890s, was an epoch in which the main institutions – a national bank (the Riksbank), commercial banks, mortgage banks and savings banks – took shape. During this time there was almost no lending by these formal credit institutions to industry; the latter were dependent on non-institutional credit provided by the merchant houses. The second, from the 1890s through to the Second World War – and residually extending into the 1950s and 1960s – was a period of very strong involvement of the banks in industry. This period, which saw the commercial banks gain unchallenged hegemony of credit markets, was until the First World War marked by substantial increases in the extension of credit to industry and then during the inter-war years, by large numbers of bank takeovers of industrial firms. This proved to be temporary as the third, primarily post-war, stage saw banks divesting themselves of industrial ownership and – in the context of a now concentrated large industry with its own internally generated funds – diversifying their credit activity in the direction of non-industrial borrowers.[49]

It was only from the fourth quarter of the nineteenth century that the Swedish National Riksbank took on all the characteristic functions of a central bank, now making advances on real estate, shares and bonds, and, more importantly, providing borrowing and rediscounting facilities for other banks. Until then, one of the three most influential commercial banks, Stockholm's Enskilda Bank, had functioned as 'bankers' bank', becoming the bank at which other banks held their accounts. In this capacity the Enskilda Bank created a reliable system of information in which a network of contacts helped capital flow towards and between regions as the demand for credit shifted. In this early phase of Swedish banking, in which loans to industry played only a secondary role, among the 'big three' commercial banks the Enskilda Bank's industrial loans were largely to the sawmill and ironworking industries, the Skandinavbank's to domestic market-oriented industries and Stockholm's Handelsbank's to firms in the Stockholm area. The banks also arranged local authority and bond loans, not through the purchase of debentures but through the issue of them, often abroad. During Sweden's liberal capitalism, bank loans were typically short term, through current account overdrafts and discounted bills of exchange; with the shift to organized capitalism, long-term commercial banks loans began to catch up with and overtake short-term loans. Mortgage loans, a hangover from mid-nineteenth-century practices when most credit was extended to agriculture, were the predominant form of outstanding loan until the First World War. For industry these were long-term loans against the security of buildings, fixed capital and land owned by an industrial firm. In organized capitalism, however, industrial loans through the underwriting of shares came to play a substantial role as well.[50]

In the 1890s commercial banks established a clear position of dominance in the credit market and loans against the security of shares became more pervasive. Such loans filled, arguably, a functional gap in Swedish credit markets, given the absence of effective issuing banks and issuing houses as well as a conservative investing public with a reluctance to buy equities. But public opinion and government saw the development of such an equity market as fraught with danger. First, it was seen as encouraging speculation. The preference would have been for a system like that of Germany in which the advance of long-term bank credits would after an intervening period be followed by the issue of shares or bonds to the public, the proceeds of which would be used to repay the bank loans. Second, it was seen as opening the way for the undesirable development of bank ownership of industry. Legislation in 1911 in fact enabled banks not just to underwrite, but to acquire industrial shares, although numerous constraints and conditions continued to discourage such ownership. Indeed major change in commercial banking practice during the early years of the organized capitalist period was the banks' purchase of share-issuing institutions for security against industrial loans: this meant that industrial takeovers could be effected within the limits of the law; it also brought about the restructuring of the stock exchange.[51]

The story of Stockholm's Handelsbank – which from the inter-war period until the late 1980s has accounted for between one-fourth and one-third of Swedish commercial bank deposits – is instructive in this context.[52] The bank was founded in 1871 by a breakaway group of directors from the

Enskilda Bank with the intention of financing Stockholm's merchant houses. Concentration of Sweden's commercial banking only proceeded on any scale after 1910, the four largest banks controlling only 28 per cent of turnover in 1908, but 56 per cent in 1924. Such concentration was a condition for the risk diversification which became necessary to meet the increased demand for industrial loans. The crucial period of the Handelsbank's growth was under manging director Louis Fraenckel, when assets increased from 22 million kronor in 1893 to 150 million in 1911. The German-born Fraenckel ran the Handelsbank like a merchant bank, with deposits and advances being confined to his personal circle. Profitability was boosted by the fact that most deposits were on current account and most advances on high-interest overdraft. Soon, however, the massive volume of lending in the 1890s meant that additional bank borrowing was necessary – a matter which Fraenckel handled through the largely foreign issue of bank shares. Fraenckel handled bond issues abroad and at home for the government, for municipal public utilities and for private railway entrepreneurs. By 1912 he had done business with eight of ten of Sweden's largest industrial firms, many of whom he had served in an advisory capacity on industrial matters. The Handelsbank's role was greatest with several of the very large ironworking and forestry companies, but it was also prominent in copper, flour mills, sugar refining and breweries. Fraenckel organized L. M. Ericsson's creation of industrial subsidiaries in France and Hungary. After Fraenckel's death, the Handelsbank – partly because dividends on stocks and floating-share debentures had become costly – expanded its deposit liability by a series of bank acquisitions, geographically diversifying to take over large banks in Sweden's north, south and south-west, all of which also entailed a whole new set of industrial connections.

The inter-war period was marked by a steep increase in the concentration of industrial capital; this increase greatly contributed to Sweden's status by the end of the 1950s as boasting perhaps the highest level of concentration of any western country, over 50 per cent higher by one account than the United States.[53] We saw that before the First World War Sweden could compete internationally without particularly high levels of capital concentration, because of their specialization in exports of commodities which were scarce elsewhere. During the inter-war period and especially after the Second World War, Sweden's key sectors came to parallel those of other advanced capitalist countries. Sweden thus became engaged in direct competition with the large firms of the major capitalist nations and could only compete at very high levels of capital concentration.[54]

The banks played an important role in this increase in concentration, largely through their takeover of sizeable numbers of industrial firms. In many cases, takeovers were unwanted by, and not particularly profitable for, the commercial banks. As we saw above, the commercial banks came increasingly to issue and underwrite shares for industrial companies through special issuing subsidiaries that the banks themselves had created. Problems here arose in the sharp recession after the First World War, when the general public began to fail to take up such issues, and the shares remained with the banks' issuing subsidiaries. Once share prices on the stock exchange had fallen to the value at which the banks had underwritten the shares – in order to avoid further losses if the firms were forced to close and under heavy pressure from the state and public opinion not to contribute to a further swelling of unemployment – the banks had little choice but to purchase the shares themselves. These industrial failures led to heavy bank losses, but at the same time banks became the largest shareholders in many industrial enterprises. In 1913 there was scarcely a large industrial firm which was dependent on a commercial bank; by the end of the 1920s and especially in the mid-1930s, major firms in mining, engineering, iron and steel, paper-pulp and timber had become dependent. Banks forced into such *de facto* acquisitions responded by enforcing mergers and rationalization of these firms. But even so, when – often decades later – they in characteristically disorganized capitalist fashion divested themselves of the dependent firms, they rarely did so at a profit.[55]

Stockholm's Enskilda Bank (the 'House of Wallenberg') had systematic intentions regarding industrial takeovers. After the 1932 crash of Ivan Kreuger's industrial empire, the Wallenbergs reorganized and controlled major parts of Swedish industry including ASEA (almost from the company's origin), L. M. Ericsson, SKF, Store Koppaberg and what was to be Electrolux. Other banks were in contrast forced into such acquisitions. The Handelsbank, for example, in order to bail out borrowers merged and rationalized the sizeable Fagersta steel concern in the 1920s, and was only able to divest itself of these industrial shares from 1943 to 1946, barely breaking even in the process. In the pulp and paper industry the Handelsbank bailed out borrowers through the acquisition and re-aquisition of the Swedish Cellulose company (SCA), which it could only finally dispose of in 1950, again roughly breaking even.[56]

Social democracy and organization at the bottom

If Sweden is distinctive in so far as more than elsewhere finance capital was responsible for organizing its capitalism at the top, it is also distinctive for the role that social democracy and the working-class movement played in organizing its capitalism at the bottom. Alone of the countries discussed here the working-class movement provided the main impetus for the shift away from the *laissez-faire* state to one of some rationalized form of economic intervention, and the development of the welfare state. What we are claiming is that from the 1930s the labour movement was the motor for the organization of the *whole* of Swedish society; that it provided a set of norms, institutions and policies which were generalized not just to working-class Swedes, but to *all* of Swedish society. The key to grouping these socio-historical developments is the very *universalism* of the Swedish working-class movement. To speak of the development of abstract, general, impersonal and affectively neutral norms in contradistinction to concrete, particularist, personal and affectively charged norms is of course to speak of the process of modernization. In crucial respects the transition from liberal to organized capitalism is at the same time the continuation of the process of modernization. In most countries it was, as Marx had foreseen, the bourgeoisie who served as catalysts of the modernization process. In Sweden it was social democracy and the labour movement more generally, who in so serving, imparted to Swedish modernity and Swedish organized capitalism a very specific coloration. Let us then scrutinize this universalism of the Swedish labour movement.

Sweden's development is not as close to the Prussian model as one would be likely to suppose, and is in many respects instead rather a hybrid form between the Prussian/German and British cases. Like Britain, Sweden was characterized by first, a peasant/farmer class which was relatively independent from very early on; second, a class of industrial capitalists which was free-trading and less dogmatically paternalistic in the factory than was the case in Germany, as well as more sympathetic to the extension of suffrage; and third, like Prussia/Germany, Sweden had the embryo of a modern civil service from the middle seventeenth century, some 200 years before Britain.[57] These three factors are crucial in accounting for Swedish social-democratic universalism. A subsequent set of class alliances with the strongly organized farmers presented Swedish solid democracy from pursuing policies of working-class particularism. Neo-corporatist co-operation with a relatively congenial class of industrial capitalists encouraged the pursuit of policies in the 'general' and national interest. And the abstract normative apparatus of a mature state bureaucracy could be taken and wielded by social democracy itself.

In the sphere of institutional politics key to the later universalist role of the labour movement were the strength of the farmers and the lateness of parliamentary sovereignty. The traditional framework of Swedish political representation which endured until 1866 included *four* estates; the peasants' previous independent strength was reflected in their representation in an estate. In 1866 a bicameral parliament was established, in which the second chamber was in fact dominated by farmers who quite consciously represented the interests of farmers. Although their rural parliamentary fraction – in a shift anticipated too early from kingly accountability – refused to form a government when asked in 1867, the farmers' very strength was a phenomenon then unknown outside of Scandinavia. These powerfully organized agrarians were later responsible for the creation of the world's first universalist social benefits scheme – in other countries coverage was usually limited to manual workers – in the pensions legislation of 1913.[58] Later in parliamentary alliance with Social Democracy (the SAP, Sveriges Socialdemokratiske Arbetarparti), they would have similar policy effects. It was necessary that national organizations of political parties be established before there could be a decisive change towards parliamentary sovereignty. The first party to establish such an electoral organization was the SAP in 1889, though the party was at that time still essentially an extra-parliamentary party. Near universal male suffrage came only in 1909 and was first effective in the 1911 elections to the second chamber. When parliamentary accountability of ministers was initiated in 1917, the SAP were the party with the most deputies in the second chamber and had entered into coalition government with the Liberal Party.[59] The point, for the present argument, is that the universalization and modernization processes to which full (male) suffrage and parliamentary sovereignty are integral were associated – and more importantly publicly identified – with social democracy.

From the mid-nineteenth century right through the 1920s, the Swedish state was faithful to free-market policies, both in regard to foreign trade and home markets. Policy through these years was, as in Britain, governed by the desire to maintain the gold standard. Despite the strength of the Social Democrats such classical economic policies were continued.[60] The krona was realigned with gold immediately after the end of the First World War, and Sweden enjoyed economic growth which was matched by few in the twenties, though at the cost of seemingly permanent unemployment. This averaged 11 per cent from 1926 to 1930, but rocketed out of all proportion after the Depression hit Sweden in the summer of 1930. From 1931 to 1935 – with a peak of over 23 per cent in 1923 – a mean of 19 per cent were unemployed.

The Social Democrats came to power in 1932. Per Albin Hansson, party leader since 1928, became Prime Minister and the Keynesian Ernst Wigforss, Finance Minister. Sweden had already gone off the gold standard in 1931, but the simultaneous raising of the Bank Rate had at the time only reinforced the Depression. The new Social Democratic government pursued conscious deficit spending policies; they encouraged exports by not posing obstacles to the krona's devaluation; benefiting industrialists responded with an increased readiness to tolerate and compromise with a trade union organization. Their deficit spending included the creation of public works projects paid at market labour rates, and a general policy aimed at ending the crisis through the increase of purchasing power. In the absence of a parliamentary majority the SAP was dependent on Agrarian Party support and they had to abandon their international free-market principles and institute protectionist measures, especially in agriculture. Unemployment was additionally the object of policy through the (belated) establishment of unemployment insurance in 1934. The Social Democrats' guiding notion was a 'framework planning' which even the Liberals came to accept by the end of the thirties. This was associated with the birth of Swedish corporatism, marked by the 1938 agreement between the central manual workers' confederation, the LO, and the central employers' confederation, the SAF (Svenska Arbetsgivareförnigen), at Saltsjöbaden on procedures to regulate collective bargaining and strikes and lockouts. The stabilization of the thirties was indicated by the decline in enterprise failures as – surely largely brought about by international rearmament – unemployment was back down at 10 per cent in 1939.[61]

The most important change introduced in the 1930s was not in the level of welfare spending but in the ideological recasting of Swedish society. Especially important was Per Albin Hansson's notion of the 'peoples' home' (*folkshemspolitik*) which began to enter the everyday discourse of social democracy. As Therborn summarizes:[62]

> The Peoples' Home had an explicit connotation of 'family' – rather than 'house' – of family community and equality with 'no favourites or stepchildren'. It connoted common concern and caring for each other and had its focus on society rather than on the state and particular institutions. It is noteworthy and testifies to the tactical skill and success of the SAP, that the notion turned out quite compatible with a reaffirmation of classical working class demands in the fields of social policy.

Therborn thus emphasizes the universalism (in Beveridge's sense) of the *folkshem*; a universalism which contrasted with the working-class particularism and selective nature of most social insurance programmes in other countries; one which had first seen the light in Sweden in the Old Age Pension legislation in 1913.

Also very universalist and rationalist were other ideas discussed in Sweden at the same time. For example, the Myrdals' *Crisis in the Population Question*, published in 1934 made an enormous impact on public opinion at the time.[63] They encouraged welfare measures for the working classes in order to prop up the declining birth rate. They argued that an increase in the birth rate would be encouraged if women were not discriminated against in the labour market and if provision for child care was made a social right. Not nationalism, not keeping mothers in the home, but public guidance and the socialization of consumption would lead to renewed population growth. Partly in the same spirit was the sudden and pervasive appearance on the scene of modernist architecture. Catechized by the Stockholm Exhibition of 1930, the new architecture was functionalist and decidedly 'social' in its working-class orientation. Modernist ideas lay behind the building of Stockholm's Stadhus in 1923; and the *Folkets park* became more and more ubiquitous.[64]

Thus more than anywhere else social democracy and the working-class movement were responsible in engineering and giving shape to the 'second moment' of organized capitalism. But from what did this powerful working-class movement derive? There are a number of competing explanations of the early strength of the Swedish working class, and in particular of the high level of union density. The most influential account, put forward by Korpi, is that it stemmed from the ethnic and religious homogeneity and from the lack of serious political divisions among the Swedish labour movement.[65] This explanation can, however, be challenged. France has also been ethnically and religiously homogeneous. Equally the major political division in the French (and many other) labour movements came after the First World War, yet Sweden boasted comparatively high levels of union density *prior* to the formation of the Comintern.

Kjellberg has more recently argued that Sweden has high levels of union density because of, first, the strength of shopfloor organization and, second, the formidable resources national unions have at their disposal.[66] At first glance this explanation appears to be tautological; it is, however, worth closer consideration. Like British and American trade unions and unlike French and German organization, the Swedish local union was located, not outside the factory (i.e. the city central federations did not play a major role), but on the shopfloor. This meant that it was recognized by employers that it could more easily collect dues at work; that it could more easily recruit members at work; and that it could more easily be seen as defending workers' rights at work. Whereas in France and Germany union organization was mainly external to factory gates, such recruitment was difficult. Like Germany and France, but unlike the Anglo-Saxon countries, Swedish unionism was at the same time highly centralized. More important than the simple development of national unions is that of national-level collective bargaining. The United States and France, for example, had national unions well before the Swedes, but very little bargaining at the level of the national union – and this is significantly different from bargaining at the level of the company on a national scale, which became widespread in the United States – right up to the present day. National-level bargaining began in Sweden on a significant scale in the 1890s. A very early centralization of collection of strike funds in the purse of the nationals gave them an effective veto over strike action from the very start. The LO's founding convention produced a constitution which was strongly centralist and lodged considerable powers in the executive.[67] It is as if the part British, part German character of Swedish class/political relations were reflected in Swedish industrial relations and responsible for the high levels of union density. On the one hand, like the British, the independent farmer *mentalité* fostered a working-class orientation towards the establishment of shopfloor rights; and also as in Britain this was aided by an early industrial capitalist class of comparatively liberal coloration. And on the other hand, as in Germany, there was no distinct hostility to but a clear proclivity towards the creation of relatively bureaucratic and centralized organizational forms, whether of capital or labour.

This early and strong national and centralized character of the trade unions (together with the high level of commitment of the shopfloor) is part and parcel of the Swedish labour movement's universalism. Collective-action theorists have observed that when membership in an interest association becomes increasingly widespread, the nature of the benefits which the association seeks come to resemble 'public goods'. That is, narrowly based interest organizations, such as early craft unions, are more likely to have aimed for particularistic benefits, possibly at the expense of the wider public.[68] High levels of union density and national-level bargaining – partly because of their very visibility to the public – tend to discourage the pursuit of such particularistic benefits. Sweden of course has been the country *par excellence* of high union density and centralized bargaining. This early broad coverage of trade unions is largely explicable through the lateness of Swedish industrialization. Thus unskilled workers began to join unions on a large scale in the late 1880s, less than a decade after main craft unions were formed. Also, rather different from other countries in which a hiatus of 50 years or so was common between the formation of local unions and national unions, the first national unions got off the ground in Sweden in the early 1890s. Further, political parties are by their nature more universalistic than unions, and to a large extent organization of the unskilled was carried out by the Social Democrats (formed in 1889) which functioned as a *de facto* central confederation until the establishment of the LO in 1898.[69]

We will now consider a number of further aspects of the development of the Swedish welfare state. We can begin by noting some distinctive characteristics: its relative lateness of development; the extent to which benefits are funded out of the general taxation, as distinct from contributions of employees and employers; its early universalism, the extent to which the problem of unemployment has been dealt with, not by benefits, but by prevention through labour-market policies; the extent to which – in paradoxical coexistence with its universalism – it has taken in the post-war period a decidedly working-class structuring.

Partly due to relative lateness in industrialization, Sweden was the slowest of the Scandinavian countries to adopt social legislation. From very early on, however, this legislation was universalistic both in terms of the source of its funding and its coverage. Sweden thus emulated the New Zealand (non-contributory) model rather than the German (contributory) model of social security provision. From 1919 the state provided 47 per cent of the funding for old-age pensions; in the 1934 unemployment legislation the state provided 40 per cent of the funding; and in the 1953 Health Act, the state supplied 26 per cent.[70] It was importantly the presence of farmers on the social-insurance 'investigating committees' – which met from the 1880s until the successful pension legislation of 1913 – that led to the law's universalistic character. On the one hand, the farmers opposed substantial employers' contributions, and hence favoured state funding; on the other hand, the farmers themselves wanted to be covered.[71] Especially important in bringing about universal social entitlements in Sweden were progressive farmers, who understood themselves and virtually the whole of the population (minus leaders of big business) to be workers. The Social Democrats, influenced by the negative experience of the Austrian labour movement also supported universal entitlements. The irony in this is that whereas in most countries non-working-class forces had taken the initiative in the development of social insurance legislation whose coverage was class-specific to the working class, in Sweden where the labour movement itself played the greatest role in welfare state formation, the policies legislated were not class-specific but universalist.

Though Social Democratic leader Hjalmar Branting was an active member of the 1913 pension commission, social insurance was quite low on the list of SAP priorities until the middle 1920s. Provoked by soaring unemployment (unemployment insurance of any kind had yet to be adopted), the third Social-Democratic minority government of 1925–6 introduced a series of bills on health and unemployment insurance, bills whose propositions featured among the foremost of SAP campaign promises in the run-up to the 1928 election.[72] Swedish Social-Democratic universalism was reinforced upon the party's accession to power in the early 1930s. It was a conception on the left in the thirties and later which was not unassociated with class-alliance 'frontist' type strategies. In Sweden this was evoked – as described above – in the *folkshemmet* idea and the population crisis discussions of the Myrdals. Alva Myrdal, in fact, polemicized against the International Labor Organization (ILO)'s arguments for workers' insurance as late as 1944, invoking instead the universality principle. The new universalism was not so much any more a matter of individuals' social rights, as part and parcel of a *Weltanschauung* of national solidarity. It was, as Myrdal asserted, a matter no longer so much of social insurance as a question 'of social policy, as a productive social policy – as common investment by the nation in its future welfare – with its accentuation of family policy and of preventative measures'.[73] Such a typically Swedish project of a productive rather than an insurance-based welfare state is underlined by its labour-market policies, its housing policies and most of all by its disproportionate spending on education. From the early twenties the proportion of outlay on education of total social spending in Sweden was about double the proportion in Britain and Germany.[74] Such a mobilizing, universalist, and national version of the welfare state is crucial to our understanding of Swedish social democracy, both as reality and as symbol. Parliamentary sovereignty (and the onset of extended suffrage) in Sweden was at the same time social-democratic sovereignty in fact, and surely in the national collective memory. And Social Democratic government was, in fact, rooted in a series of party and class alliances, partly imposing universalism on proposed social legislation. Social Democracy was somehow and unmistakably – at the time when the 'social body' for the first time replaced the 'body' of the king as the locus of power – *volkisch*. But what an unusual *volkisch* party it was – identified with modernization, with abstract rationalism and with universalism, and which put the lie to the right-wing populism of contemporaneous fascism. It was a party and a movement which created a partly libertarian *folkhem* unsurpassed today on a large range of indicators of social benefits; a universalist and abstract–rationalist *folkhem* whose symbolism has largely entailed the destruction of symbol itself, and whose social costs may have been borne on the level of individual invention and creativity.

Some conclusions

The most distinctive feature of Swedish development has been its unusually powerful organization at the bottom. The shifts to substantial welfare state development, quasi-corporatist industrial relations, and a sort of Keynesian, rationalist approach to the economy were all based, first, on the early high Social Democratic vote, but second, and more importantly as time passed, on the unsurpassed high levels of union density and discipline of the unions and of the LO. The key point here in comparative perspective is that of our five countries only in Sweden is capitalism organized at the bottom almost solely *by* the bottom. It is the continued organization of Swedish collective agents at the base of the society (indicated by the high proportion of Social-Democratic vote, high levels of union density and, even recently, a continued high level of class voter alignment) that has kept Sweden from disorganizing more quickly at the bottom than would otherwise – given the changing occupational distribution – have been the case.

BRITAIN: THE *MAKLER* ECONOMY

Two aspects of British organized capitalism stand out in particularly bold relief in contrast with the German case. They are, first, that Britain organizes quite slowly at the top, but rather quickly at the bottom; and second, that when high levels of concentration of industrial capital were functional for rapid economic growth, British industrial capital was woefully unorganized. We will begin with an analysis of what turned out to be the 'phoney' organization of the British enterprise in the last decades of the nineteenth century; and then discuss the limited amount of organization associated with the rationalization movement of the inter-war years. We shall argue that the slowness to organize at the top is attributable to the existence of a *Makler* (middleman) economy in organized capitalist Britain, whose main characteristics were an overdevelopment of markets; a sectoral balance in which the weight of liberal–capitalist, or service, industries such as brewing, food, textile, tobacco, and the 'City' were overpreponderent and both heavy industry and the 'new industries' weak; and a very high profile for commercial firms, financial firms and overseas investment. Much of this *Makler* configuration is understandable in terms of premature British industrialization. We shall then go on to address the problem of capital markets and the state, partly by way of a sympathetic debate with Marxist arguments. Here our thematic claim is that such arguments overemphasize the destructive roles of the financial sector and the Bank of England, and that the role of both can be better grasped in the broader *Makler* framework.

The account of Britain's early and substantial organization at the bottom will be familiar to most readers. It is partly attributable to the absence of a bourgeois revolution which left intact a number of pre-modern corporate groupings. It also left intact an 'organicist' (one-nation) conservative political ideology which underpinned the Factory Acts and associated movements of the 1830s and 1840s and Disraeli's not insignificant welfare legislation of the 1870s. Britain's organization at the bottom included the enrolment of the unskilled in the 'new unions' of the 1880s, the Liberal-initiated national insurance legislation of 1906 and the development of a rudimentary corporatism in the tripartism of the First World War and the inter-war period.[75] Because these developments are well known, we will concentrate on organization at the top and our arguments concerning the *Makler* economy.

The critical point at which the British economy was overwhelmed by both the German and American economies was during the Kondratieff A-phase of rapid international growth from about 1893 until 1914. Between 1899 and 1913 in Britain real GDP increased only by 1.1 per cent per year.[76] It was at this time more than any other that a country's industry had to approach the organized capitalism ideal type in order to avoid economic stagnation. Britain's characteristic configuration was so different from this ideal type that a legacy was created from which nearly a century later Britain has never fully recovered. Britain departed from the ideal type, first, in the sense that the USA and Germany (but not Britain) were characterized before the First World War by the development of systems of shopfloor rules, the rudiments of scientific management, and organized capitalism's characteristically proletarianized working class. But also Britain was distinctive in that there was no real concentration of capital in this period, but rather the pervasion of loose federations of holding companies. Moreover, Britain was very weak in the two economic sectors necessary for healthy capital accumulation during the period of organized capitalism: heavy industry and the new industries. Britain's strength on the contrary lay in food and drink, insurance and banking, commerce, services. Britain, the workshop of the world in liberal capitalism, became in Hans Medick's words, 'the *Makler*' (broker, middleman) of the world in organized capitalism.[77]

Organization at the top

We will begin by considering the organization of industry in Britain. Alfred Chandler has spoken of a new type of managerial hierarchy which emerged on a considerable scale in Germany and the USA from 1890 to 1914; this he has termed the 'centralised, functionally-departmentalised' structure.[78] This means that after a merger, managerial functions are largely centralized at head office, so that the individual acquired or merged firms lose most of their autonomy. They and the larger branches are staffed by lower management while middle management staffs the centralized functional departments at head office. In this type of firm purchasing, sales, to a certain extent engineering, marketing and especially finance, become centralized in head office.

Unlike in the United States and Germany, the British merger wave of the two decades prior to the First World War did not bring about centralized functionally-departmentalized firms but rather loose federations, and these could not realize the economies of scale that German and American companies were able to realize. There was a notable absence of functional depart-mentalization in the largest firms in Britain's strongest industrial sectors at the turn of the century. For example, the two largest producers of spirits were loose federations. In textiles, which comprised nine of Britain's largest 52 firms in 1905, in the four largest textile combines at the turn of the century the average number of directors drawn from constituent firms was 41. These directors continued largely to represent the interests of the constituent firms.[79] Imperial Tobacco, Britain's number three firm in 1901, had no central office for executives whose responsibility was long-term strategy. Metal-making and metalworking, especially shipbuilding, did boast backward and forward integrated enterprises, but amazingly little by way of centralization in terms of purchasing, sales, research or even financial departments. In comparison with the USA, machinery and transport-equipment manufacturing were badly handicapped by the absence of forward integration into sales. In chemicals there was little integration backwards or forwards through the building of extensive buying and purchasing organizations. Even putatively thoroughly modern companies like Boots did not at the end of the First World War have a centralized, functionally-departmentalized managerial structure.[80]

Chandler has also introduced a useful further classification of types of management structures.[81] Firstly, he talks of the 'personal enterprise' in which the owner–manager has few other staff who are in a position of close personal relations with the owner. Secondly, the 'entrepreneurial enterprise' typically comprises some 20–50 managers, who stand in impersonal relation-ships to the owning family in whose hands company shares are still centralized; at this point the managing director is often from the family. Finally, the 'managerial enterprise' is characterized by scattered stock ownership and salaried managers in the very top positions. The striking fact here is that, while the USA and Germany at the turn of the century were moving towards 'managerial' forms in the largest companies, in Britain mergers of over 20 firms were typically perpetuating the 'personal enterprise'.[82]

British business history has witnessed three merger waves: the first from 1880 to 1918; the second during the 1920s; and the third during the 1960s. Mid-nineteenth-century legislation, which extended to manufacturing industry the right of quotation on the stock market and of limited liability, set the stage for the first of these merger waves. After a number of joint-stock limited liability failures – partly due to share prices being too high – Guinness and Coats textile firm carried off very successful flotations in 1886 and 1890 respectively. The tendency during this period, in which mergers were most frequent at peaks of economic activity (contrary to the Marxist devalorization hypothesis), was to merge and then immediately to form a public company. A high proportion of these mergers, it should be noted, were not (unlike the USA and Germany) in the key organized capitalist heavy industry and new industry sectors, but in two particular industries, textiles and brewing. Also, again unlike the USA and Germany, these mergers were not characterized by forward and/or backward integration and diversification; they were instead overwhelmingly horizontal mergers. The most important years of British firm 'disappearances', between 1896 and 1904, were impelled by large-scale mergers of 20 firms or more. This was in contrast with the 1920s boom, though even the latter comprised quite a number of mergers of five or more firms. The point is that these large-scale mergers produced, as noted above, federations of companies, whose boards comprised a significant number of family firm owners with considerable independent powers, and whose board meeting decisions tended to result in compromises which rather resembled government through a *Ständestaat* of feudal barons.[83] When the first wave terminated after 1906 it was substantially due to the visible failure of a number of the multi-firm consolidations; these failures were often a matter of managerial problems associated with the absence of centralization. We noted above that German organized capitalism was far less cartelized than commonly thought. British industry, by contrast, was riddled with *de facto* cartels, in these federated holding companies, but also in the salience of price-fixing associations, which were particularly common in the not heavily merged iron and steel sector.[84]

A further point to note is that the size of the merger wave was not very large by German and especially by American standards. In the USA the firm disappearance rate was proportionally far higher than in Britain during these years. In the period from 1896 to 1905 the largest 100 American corporations increased their size by a factor of four to gain control of about 40 per cent of US industrial production. Such a percentage was not reached in Britain until the inter-war years. The key corporations in the crucial organized capitalist sectors got off the ground in the USA and Germany in the 1890–1905 period, and were already in existence for some 25 to 30 years at the time of the formation of their British equivalents – a matter of great competitive disadvantage for Britain. Of Britain's largest 31 manufacturing concerns which had expanded by means of one major merger in 1848, only 13 were in existence at the turn of the century; of 63 such American firms 38 had their major merger prior to 1916.[85]

We have already described Britian's idiosyncratic sectoral balance in the years leading up to the First World War. Britain's weakness in heavy industry was particularly apparent after 1900; its new industries did not develop on any scale until some 30 years later than in the USA and Germany. In 1905 nine of Britian's top 52 firms were in textiles, and 18 of these firms in the downstream integrated brewing industry. Hannah deprecates the latter fact, pointing out how capitalization of these companies was artificially inflated by their ownership of public houses.[86] Hannah misses, however, the telling point, which is the relative absence of both heavy and new industry firms. Besides the growth in traditional sectors like food and drink and textiles – with less strategically central organized capitalist positions than heavy industry and the new industries – other elements of pre-war sectoral growth reinforce the shift towards the *Makler* economy during this period in Britain. From 1870 to 1914 British national product rose by 150 per cent; but the growth of the commercial sector and services during this period was much greater, and that of the insurance, banking and financial sector some 1100 per cent. Moreover, by 1914 overseas investment led to the accumulation of £4,000 million of capital outside of the domestic economy, a figure which came to one-third of the total value of British commodity exports.[87]

During the inter-war years, in spite of persistent unemployment, British growth rivalled that of other industrial nations, as GDP grew on average 2.3 per cent a year from 1924 to 1937. The new industries began to grow, especially chemicals, but also electro-technical and engineering and vehicle production. And the centralized, functionally-departmentalized firm and the managerial enterprise became common in several industrial sectors. In 1914, the three largest British firms were still J. & P. Coats in cotton, Imperial Tobacco, and Watney Combe Reid in brewing. In the twenties and thirties, the pace was set by ICI, Unilever, Dunlop and Courtaulds. Lever Brothers, ICI, Austin and Morris had shifted towards the functionally-departmentalized structure; Dunlop in the 1920s towards a multidivisional form. Equally, some of the holding companies moved towards departmentalization, and commercial firms such as Boots swiftly integrated backwards into production.[88]

A major feature of the inter-war period was a strong emphasis on rationalization. For example, during the First World War such rationaliza-tion was encouraged by the state, which insisted that industry should avoid excessive product differentiation, and, in the presence of a shortage of skilled labour, encouraged mass production. With unemployment remaining fairly high until the onset of the Second World War, there was some discrediting of the ideology of the market among industrialists, and this was replaced by a new enthusiasm for the application of scientific principles to the economy. This was not just a matter of the development of formal shopfloor rules and modified scientific principles, but included the favouring of certain forms of national planning and an ideology that favoured more extensive mergers. The 'corporatist bias' that this ideology comprised was popular among fairly large numbers of entrepreneurs, partly because it was bound up with a revived nationalism.[89] The explicit objective of a number of rationalization initiatives was to achieve economies of scale that would help British industry to catch up with American and German industry. Hence Imperial Tobacco was formed before the Second World War as a defence against the incursion of the

American Tobacco Company into British markets. Likewise ICI was consolidated in the inter-war years partly in reaction to I. G. Farben's attempt to acquire British Dyestuffs. Rationalization and product diversification helped Unilever establish a very favourable competitive position *vis-à-vis* American and German companies by the early 1930s.[90]

But this experience was on the whole unrepresentative of the state of British industry during the inter-war years. In terms of sectors, in 1930, 19 of the top 50 British firms were still to be found in food, drink and tobacco. Even in 1948, 25 per cent of Britain's top 200 firms were in food and allied areas.[91]

We will not consider the main sectors of British organized capitalism. In 1930 two of the three largest electrical machinery firms, formerly subsidiaries of General Electric and Westinghouse, were still controlled by US capital.[92] In the motor industry, although boards were dominated by British managers, two out of three of Britain's largest manufacturers, Ford and Vauxhall, were controlled in 1930 by American capital.[93] Also, although there was a pervasive ideology which favoured integration, iron and steel making was still not integrated with steel finishing; nor was there much integration of cotton spinning and weaving; in transport equipment, motor vehicle companies still had not generally acquired steel pressing and electrical components plants. This was partly due to the fact that disagreement on boards of federated companies sometimes could limit vertical integration and diversification. And indeed, most of the former holding companies still existed as loose federations. In 1948 Hawker-Siddeley, the second largest British transport equipment concern, continued to exist in its loose federational form. At the same time 60 per cent of the British top 200 firms had family board members: the founding families persisting with greatest strength in brewing, shipbuilding and the food industry.[94]

What thus appears to have happened in Britain is that because it was the first industrial nation, there was the emergence of extensive and systematic market mechanisms which made it unnecessary for any individual company to develop an enormously complex 'visible hand'. Companies could rely upon the 'invisible hand' which had served British companies so well during nineteenth-century liberal capitalism. Why integrate forwards and purchase a number of sales outlets when existing commercial firms operated more efficiently via the market? Why integrate backwards into raw materials production when the market mechanism was already highly developed? Why adopt expensive technologies with an abundance of skilled workers in the labour market? Geographical distances made such an effective market system inoperable in the USA, where vertical integration and hierarchy were the only viable strategies. But in places like Sheffield, where the costs of information and transaction were low, there seemed no need for vertical integration in metal-making. Besides, in Britain, unlike the USA, backward integration in the search for raw materials often meant integration overseas. Thus, what was rational for an individual British firm resulted in failures to develop the economies of scale and centralized research department which were in the medium term debilitating.

Understanding British development in terms of the *Makler* economy enables us to make better sense of the historical relationship between 'industrial/productive' capital on the one hand and 'banking/financial' capital on the other. In the past decade or so the following claims have become fairly widespread: (1) banking/finance capital has been of outsized importance in relation to industrial capital in the development of the British economy; (2) bank capital has concentrated on short-term loans to a variety of capital outlets, especially those overseas (particularly in the Empire), rather than in providing long-term loans to British industry; (3) bank capital has exercised an overwhelming influence upon British economic policy, especially through the institutional complex of the City of London–Bank of England–Treasury; and (4) the latter set of institutions has been especially important in maintaining the historical role of sterling, and this has particularly harmed British industrial capital which would have benefited from the pursuit of both more expansionist policies and of a greater willingness to devalue.[95]

Although we would accept all of these points, there are a number of clarifications which should be emphasised. First, the interpretation above puts undue stresses on the necessity of the role of the banks and minimizes the alternative sources of funds available to industry. We saw that German banks were also a relatively conservative force in industrial investment policies; and we will see below that most of the large characteristically organized capitalist American firms in fact expanded through internal finance and not from bank loans.[96] Second, the nature of even the larger British firms, which were loosely federated, unintegrated and technologically relatively undeveloped, meant that there was a fairly modest demand for external finance and hence for 'developing any special institutional devices for the provision of long-term capital to industry'.[97] And third, the banking/financial sector should be seen as part of the broader *Makler* economy which had developed on a very large scale indeed prior to the possible emergence of an organized British capitalism in the early years of this century. By then the sheer size of the City of London – in terms of capitalization and turnover – was to ensure its dominant role within the twentieth-century trajectory of British society.

To see banking/financial capital as part of the *Makler* economy is to view that capital rather differently from how it has been normally viewed. Ingham has recently argued that the importance of the City of London lies in its more general *commercial* (and not simply financial) role. He says:[98]

London's roles in the world system may be seen as the specialisation and near monopolisation of the commercial activities which are based on the existence of international economic exchanges...The City has not simply dealt with Britain's exchanges with other states, but has performed a wide range of functions for the world system as a whole.

These services include the financing of trade, the insurance of commodities, transport and trade agreements, and dealing in foreign exchange. Britain's 'exceptionalism' here, then, stemmed from its early, effective and centralized monopolization of these diverse services. Britain created at a very early stage the means for an extraordinarily extensive commercial capitalism based on what Weber referred to as 'the profit possibilities in continuous buying and selling on the market ("trade") with free exchange – that is, absence of formal or at least relative absence of substantive compulsion to effect any given exchange'.[99]

In establishing such conditions for the buying and selling of various 'services' the City organizations have almost exclusively acted as *intermediaries* between investors and borrowers. Most of the City's earnings have not stemmed from interest but from various kinds of fees or commission, in other words from a commercial profit derived from trading in multitudinous forms of investment capital. Thus, from the 1830s until the present, with the exception of the period between the late nineteenth century and 1914, the City's earnings from foreign exchange, money markets, freight and commodity brokerage, and insurance, have exceeded the income from overseas investments.[100] Morever, by contrast with American 'finance-capital', most overseas investment effected by and through the City has consisted of portfolio investment and this has resulted in part from the extraordinary importance of a secondary market for stocks and shares in London, namely, the stock exchange. At the same time much of the money-capital apparently 'exported' from the City itself derives from abroad. As Ingham says: 'London has been a commercial entrepôt for finance as well as commodities throughout its history.'[101]

Thus, although it is clear that investment funds have not been adequately channelled into British industry, this does not simply result from the dominance of a *finance* capital oriented to short-term and overseas profit; it is rather that the relative separation of 'finance' and 'industry' is itself based on the dominance of commercial practices within the financial system. As Ingham again writes, this time of Marx: 'he failed to envisage the extent to which a single nation-state could monopolise the general commercial (including international banking and wholesale banking) functions in the global circuit of capital.'[102] And we may add, as Britain's role as the central *Makler* economy became extended and developed throughout the nineteenth century, it did not depend particularly on the growth of the domestic economy, but on the unprecedented expansion of the world economy, and on a pre-established set of procedures and practices which were not strictly economic and certainly did not depend upon a thriving domestic industrial economy.

The consequence of this was, of course, that British capital markets were not as effective as those in Germany and the USA in channelling funds into investment in key industries. We are using the term 'capital market' in its very broadest sense, in which demand is from industry for investment in plant and machinery, and the supply of funds is from banks (through equities, debentures), from insurance companies (through internal industrial finance), and from the consumption funds of industrial firm owners and those close to such owners. Though the state and the Bank of England did play a role in making those markets less effective than they might have been, other factors were of greater importance, in particular problems of information and diversification.[103] British companies, publicly quoted and otherwise, appear to have been consistently more secretive than American and German companies, and obviously without information there was great disincentive to invest. Partly this was due to the relative absence of intermediaries who could provide information and a basis of trust for investors. This intermediary role was played in Germany by the investment banks who had considerable access to industrial information and issue securities to the public. In the United States banks have had more access to information than in Britain and, more importantly, security issuing houses have played an important intermediary role. In the absence of information, diversification has been the rational strategy. The investment of funds into technologically innovating industry has always contained very high elements of risk. Diversification – where the probability of all risks simultaneously failing approached zero – is sometimes the only way in which such risks will be taken by investors. And Britain has also been notoriously lacking in institutions for diversification.

In the late eighteenth and early nineteenth centuries, lending institutions evolved which were favourable for the early phases of industrialization, but less favourable for organized capitalism. Short-term lending dominated and was well suited to the needs of commerce and industry of, for example, the 1790s, at which point as much funding was necessary for inventories as for fixed capital formation. During the course of the nineteenth century British banks began to grant long-term loans to industry; these were mostly local banks which progressively came to be short on resources in comparison to the fast-growing industrial firms. A rash of mid-Victorian bank failures, however, led banks largely to cease long-term lending towards the end of the 1870s. The advent of limited liability meant that investors were more likely to entrust their savings to people they knew. An estimated 60–70 per cent of industrial capital formation in the last quarter of the nineteenth century came from investors lending to friends and acquaintances.[104]

Before the First World War, the London securities market was more concerned with government issues and foreign loans than it was with domestic industrial finance. Institutions for diversification, such as investment and finance trusts, also tended to choose the safer foreign issues, as did the great issuing houses, Rothschild, Lazard, Schroeder and Hambro. Insurance companies had the same type of information problems and similar investment patterns, shifting over to industrial investment on any scale only after the Second World War. Especially important in destroying confidence in the securities markets for industry were a series of disastrous new issues. These in particular damaged the chances for expansion of the new industries, electrical engineering and automobiles. An unsuccessful equities issue in 1882 gave electrical engineering a bad reputation on the stock exchange a decade later, when the industry began its rapid development internationally. And external funding was indeed necessary, given the fact that electrical engineering was often carried out by diversifying small to medium-sized mechanical engineering firms. The largest electro-technical firm of the 1880s (Brush) in fact could not sell sufficient equities to meet demand in the 1888 boom and had to rely on the less felicitous issue of debentures. Further failures from 1888 to 1890 created conditions in which British firms could not develop economies of scale nor had the technology to compete with American and German firms in the crucial period of buoyancy for electrical engineering from 1896 to 1903. Also, unlike their foreign rivals, British firms could not integrate forwards into electricity supply. Hence, from 1896 to 1904 foreign firms accounted for some two-thirds of the increase in fixed assets in Britain in the sector.[105] In automobiles the first British company was established in 1896 by individuals who already had a poor reputation on the London security market for their previous activity in the cycle industry. In the years leading to the First World War funds were difficult to raise for the industry through equity issue, and Ford had already begun to capture the popular market for motor cars.[106]

British industry, as we saw above, finally took on an organized capitalist complexion during the inter-war years; the same can be said for the financial sector. In 1911–13, 34 per cent of borrowing on the new issue market was for domestic industry; the corresponding figure by the mid-1930s was far more than 50 per cent. The boom of 1919–20 saw large issues by Lever Brothers and Dunlop and in automobiles and shipbuilding; there were large issues in the electro-technical sector in the 1924 upturn, and the 1927–9 boom saw investors rushing to place their savings, in a burst of speculation, in untried industries such as film and gramophone production. The next upturn of 1934–7 witnessed large-scale purchase of equities in heavy industry – coal, iron and steel – much of which was sunk into building more plants in the wake of the newly created tariff protection. This change was partly accounted for by newly instituted government controls on foreign investment, and partly by the fact that industry was attempting considerably more new issues, in as much as the main pre-war sources of finance were both insufficient and relatively exhausted.[107] The year 1918–19 witnessed a surge of bank mergers from which the British big five clearing banks emerged. High levels of lending to industry were recorded from 1918 to 1925. The return to the Gold Standard seems to have depressed the level of advances in the 1927–9 upturn; but a slow recovery of advances began once more in the mid-1930s. Bank advances were roughly equal to the new issues of stocks and debentures on the stock market in the good years of the inter-war period, and over twice as high as this – due to the difficulty of reducing outstanding loans – during the bad years. High volumes of loans were made especially to the textile sector, but also to iron and steel and food and drink.[108]

We will now turn briefly to the analysis of the British state and more specifically to economic policy. It would not be wholly misleading to conceive of British state economic policy during the period under discussion as a contest between forces favouring the structures of liberal capitalism and those favouring the characteristic forms of organized capitalism: the former winning the day before the First World War; the latter being triumphant during the inter-war years. The liberal capitalist state was not just some kind of non-existent 'night-watchman's state', nor was it somehow – as conventional wisdom would have it – 'there'; instead, as Max Weber stressed at many points in his work, it had to be created.[109] Four important components of such a form of state in Britain took shape in the 1830s and 1840s; these were the Reform Act of 1832, the contemporaneous shift towards a more codified system of private law, the repeal of the Corn Laws in 1846 and the Bank Act of 1844. The objective of the last of these was to check the undue expansion of credit. The Bank of England here became an instrument for the regulation of money supply through its control of the issue of notes which was based on the Bank's monopoly of British gold reserves. The condition of such regulation was the Gold Standard; that is, the state policy of free convertibility of sterling to gold. This, in conjunction with another 'liberal capitalist' state policy – a thoroughgoing anti-protectionism which included an absence of control on foreign investment – was of particular significance in facilitating the explosion of British investment abroad from 1880 to 1914, largely because of the stability which was guaranteed to the British currency. Two other factors reinforced the role of the Bank of England in this period. The first was that major increases in government spending and thus borrowing at the end of the nineteenth century made the Bank the effective regulator of the national debt. The second was that from the 1880s the Bank began to control the discount houses and thus the market interest rate – through controlling the interest rates at which Bank funds were available to discount houses. A further factor in helping to ensure an absence of long-term investment, and thus keep British organized capitalism liberal, was the Bank's policy of keeping up levels of dividend payments to Bank shareholders. This meant that gold reserves were small, and that even seemingly insignificant outflows of gold, given the Bank's prime objective of protecting the level of gold reserves, produced violent fluctuations of interest rates.[110]

It was not originally Keynesian rationalizers who were the main force behind bringing some organization to the British state, but rather conservative imperialists.[111] In the context of the first surfacing of unemployment as an economic problem and the rising to consciousness of German competition, these protectionists began to place their arguments in the context of an empire-based customs union. The consolidation after the First World War of an organized capitalist state was associated in a sort of *de facto* alliance between imperialists and the increasingly nationalist 'entrepreneurial rationalizers'. One reason for the restrictions on non-imperial investment and the beginnings of government's closer association with industry after the First World War was the objective of the wartime securing of consumer necessities and of weaponry. A second was to put government securities in a more favourable position. The movement towards organized capitalist political forms was also partly a matter of the unintended consequences of pursuing liberal–capitalist objectives. Hence, two key arguments for the shift away from free-market policies were: first, that revenues obtained from tariffs would help the state balance the budget; and second, that the regulation of investment in non-Empire countries would improve the exchange rate of sterling and protect the gold reserves. The former was one of Chamberlain's main arguments for the installation of the protectionist legislation of 1931. Whatever the objectives, the Bank of England was deprived of a number of powers from the First World War through the inter-war years. Though the Bank recaptured its control over interest rates and its note-issuing powers, (1) these were of less significance because of the increased importance of cheques in the monetary supply; (2) for all but six of the inter-war years sterling was off the Gold Standard; and (3) investment controls remained applicable throughout the period and tariffs on imported goods were instituted in 1932. The development of the British organized capitalist state, and its bringing together of believers in 'national destiny' with proponents of rationalization, was well marked in the 1920s by, for example, the formation of the BBC, the Central Electricity Board and the London Public Transport Board, all in the same year, 1926. Perhaps the best illustration of elective affinity between nationalism and organized capitalist rationalization was the formation and subsequent development of ICI, whose title, *Imperial* Chemical Industries, should be taken quite literally.[112]

Organization at the bottom

The paradox of the British case is that organized capitalism developed the wrong way round. Britain had an inter-war experience which was not wholly dissimilar to that of some other western countries; but prior to this British capitalism was already very strongly organized at the bottom, and at the same time British capitalism was beginning to organize only weakly at the top. The processes involved here are however fairly well known and we will just mention a few points.

The 1880s were crucial years. Though skilled labour had been in unions for some time, the mid-1880s saw masses of the unskilled flow into the 'new' general unions. Wage differentials began to diminish and the new unions in the following decade were to adopt an orientation more to the development of welfare legislation than to industrial struggle.[113] Workers began to constitute their own separate political resources (independent of the Liberal Party) with the advent of labour representation committees. At the same time, collectivist ideologies began to replace co-operativist notions. The state came to be understood as a bourgeois state, and public or national ownership – as distinct from ownership by workers' co-operatives – of the means of production, distribution and exchange was placed on organized labour's political agenda. In response to such mobilization, employers began to set up more substantial and formally structured organizations to supersede bodies created earlier, such as the Association of British Chambers of Commerce (1860) and the National Association of Federated Employers (1873). At a very early stage of capitalist development social classes were thus beginning to replace the individual as the political unit of society. That is, representative bodies came to represent individuals, no longer as citizens, but as members of interest groups, and in particular those two great interest groups of labour and capital. These collectivities – these *classes* as causal agents – began to have important effects on state policy-making and especially on the growth of the British welfare state.

The two main agents effecting the development were typically organized capitalist, that is, the male-based, working-class movement and the social–liberal bourgeoisie. Working-class agitation in favour of welfare legislation was particularly pervasive from the 1890s onwards. In 1894 reform of local government franchise brought working men as local councillors on to the boards of Poor Law Guardians; this helped catalyse manual-worker discontent with the Poor Law. At the same time, in the face of growing unemployment, the new unions increasingly turned to focus primarily on the objective of state welfare benefits. The immediate catalyst of the Liberal legislation was the activity of the National Committee of Organized Labour for Old Age Pensions, which gained mainstream labour support and campaigned in the 1906 election. But, according to Hennock, two further political considerations were also of major importance: 'One was a concern to protect the human resources of the nation at a time of international competition, both economic and military. The other was the need to reassure the citizen voter that he (sic) would not be allowed. . .to fall into the non-citizen class of paupers.'[114] The second of these reasons – and here the contrast with the German case could not be starker – was a universalist notion of social citizenship which was gaining currency among the capitalist and developing service classes. The equal and universalist benefits of national insurance were to succeed the benefits of the Poor Law. The public opinion which informed the former was based on a notion of social citizenship, which, as Dicey poignantly suggested, was foreign to the paternalist Tory grounding of the latter. Also important was the idea of national 'human resources'. Thus much middle-class justification of the proposed insurance legislation was in terms of instilling military-type 'discipline' into British workers to improve economic efficiency. This is related to Foucault's claim that such a notion of discipline, often associated with putatively social–liberal reform, has been most importantly interlinked with mobilizing, recruiting and normalizing human resources for the benefit of 'the social' or the nation.[115]

For Foucault, this is the basic characteristic of the 'modern' period which he dates from the beginning of the nineteenth century. We think though that it was more characteristic – in Britain, in American Progressivism, and elsewhere – of *organized* capitalism that began towards the end of this century, which in Britain began at the bottom rather than at the top.

3

The development of
organized capitalism (2)

In Germany and Sweden the most revealing sociological factor to be considered was *who* was the main agent of organization. This was the operant question in both countries to explain successes in economic growth in the framework of highly organized national capitalisms. In Britain and France, to the contrary, the issue with the most purchase on comparative social development is what it is that can account for the characteristically *retarded* pace of organization in the era of organized capitalism. In respect to Britain we put further a set of explanatory arguments via the notion of the *Makler* economy. We shall argue below that the slow pace of organization in France is explicable by a dislocation or disarticulation of the French economy. We shall show that this slow and dislocated organization was marked, on the one hand, by an exaggerated case of the 'British disease' of a premature industrialization and, on the other, by an almost Third World-like absence of national economic integration, between production and consumption of both capital goods and consumer commodities.[1]

France thus was in many ways a liberal capitalist nation during the 'first moment' of organized capitalism. During the second moment of organized capitalism it emerged as one of the most highly organized countries. How can this reversal be explained? The absence of such a propensity of capital, as a collective actor, to organize French capitalism in the economy, and at the top was, we shall see, belatedly compensated for during and after the Second World War by the state. In a not wholly dissimilar manner, the lack of propensity of *workers* to organize in civil society meant that French capitalism was also organized at the bottom, in terms of *inter alia* social spending and collective bargaining frameworks, largely through the agency of the state.

Economic 'forwardness'

France has for some time now been considered to be the case which confounds Gerschenkron's 'economic-backwardness' thesis.[2] If France has been more backward than Britain, then it should have quickly achieved higher levels of capital concentration, both on enterprise and plant level; it should have had an initial spurt of growth which was faster than Britain's; and it should have quickly moved into production on a large scale of producer commodities. However, France did none of these. We may therefore wonder whether this proves Gerschenkron's thesis to be false, or whether he just got the facts wrong and that France instead was economically 'forward'. We want indeed to argue that France was a case of 'economic forwardness', that France was more like Britain than Britain, to explain not France's successes, but France's failure.

(1) To be economically 'forward' is to have high levels of secondary sector production at an early date. Up until 1875 the absolute value of secondary sector production remained larger in France than in Britain.[3]

(2) To be economically forward, indeed the common wisdom as to the quintessentially 'British syndrome', was to have a labour force disproportionately top-heavy with highly skilled workers. France had a higher proportion of wage-earners in workshops - in comparison with industry - than any nation discussed in this book. In 1896, 36 per cent of French manufacturing manual workers were in *ateliers* (workshops).[4] As late as 1906 the mean number of wage-earners per French textile enterprise was 5.4, in comparison with 68 in the USA; in French iron and steel the French and American figures were 8.1 and 60.2 respectively. Until the 1890s secondary sector labour productivity was higher in France than in Britain because of the skills of the French *atelier* sector. From 1905 to 1913 French productivity in building, and skilled production processes in textiles and food gave the country comparative advantage over Britain. Problems began to emerge however in the 'great depression' of 1870–96. French secondary sector output, which grew 2.3 per cent per year from 1820 to 1870 and at 2.5 per cent per year from 1896 to 1929, increased at a rate of only 1.6 per cent per year during this period. During these years also, Britain came from well behind to overtake France for overall industrial productivity per worker.[5] When French productivity once again received a boost in the first decade of the twentieth century, it was largely due to gains in the new industries and a largely renovated metallurgy.

(3) Economic backwardness was further characterized by the early shift into production of semi-finished goods; thus Germany, the USA and for example, Russia specialized quite early in the production of 'means of production'. At a point at which even Britain was, via mechanized production, turning out semi-finished goods, in textiles, in iron and steel, in coal, France

was producing high quality goods in workshops for direct consumption by households. Particularly in the clothing industry, France avoided standardization – with the goal of a *production raffinée* for a *clientèle fantaisiste* – until well into the twentieth century. Indeed, French–British trade, even more in 1905 than in the mid-nineteenth century, was characterized by the British export of raw materials and intermediate goods in exchange for finished industrial products from France.[6]

(4) To be economically forward was to industrialize with relatively low levels of concentration at both the enterprise and plant levels. That may well have been functional for labour productivity during liberal capitalism, but was dysfunctional during the period in which other economies were becoming organized. In France very low levels of concentration at the enterprise level persisted well into the twentieth century.[7] Kindleberger notes that the level of *establishment* concentration, as measured by workers per productive unit, changed very little between 1896 and 1936.[8] France's much delayed movement towards concentration was characterized by a disinclination of industrialists to utilize the financial resources necessary for horizontal integration. Caron has observed in fact a tendency *away* from diversification and towards narrower specialization in the first part of the twentieth century in France, in the framework of what were in fact protected markets.[9] Lorraine steel and iron did not, for example, sufficiently integrate backwards into the coal industry of the north (which has been France's liberal capitalist growth leader in textiles and in coal) nor integrate forwards into engineering.

(5) Economic forwardness was also characterized by the localization of product markets. We discussed above the comparative retardedness of Britain in comparison with Germany, the USA and Sweden in this context. And France's markets were far more localized even than Britain's. This was partly due to a deficiency of transport resources – a notable scarcity of canals in the canal age and of railroad lines, apart from the Paris-centric system finally achieved in 1870. A large portion of France's high quality workshop goods were produced, not in Paris and/or for export, but in provincial *ateliers* for a very geographically circumscribed local clientele.[10]

(6) Economic backwardness in Gerschenkron's influential hypothesis was characterized by a concerted working together of industry and the banks. In this context France seems to have been an even more extreme case of economic forwardness than Britain. This was partly explicable by the marked disinclination of industrialists to borrow, due to the very strong sense of independence and dynastic continuity which were central to the identities of French entrepreneurs. Large companies like Wendel and Sidelor, for instance, managed fully to avoid capital markets until the first decade of the twentieth century.[11]

An economically forward economy was one which was particularly orientated to foreign markets and hence was in a sense internally 'disarticulated'. It has thus been ironically observed that the industrial revolution passed *through* France rather than being simply based in and developed within

France. Hence, French engineers in particular and French capital more generally were liberally sprinkled through the rest of the world economy and especially through Europe. Overseas capital investment was indeed extensive. Between 1878 and 1911, for example, the interest earned on bonded foreign investment was one-third higher than that earned on bonds sold in France.[12] The *Société Générale d'Entreprises* (SGE), for instance, a leader in France's electricity industry, had in 1913 about half its labour force employed on foreign construction sites. Its public works and electrification projects, often operating through SGE-organized syndicates, were divided between several Central Eastern European countries. Schneider et Cie, the Creusot metallurgy and engineering giant, in the aftermath of the First World War invested heavily in Czechoslovakia and Austria.[13] First operating through French banks and later using London capital markets, by the mid-twenties, these Central European production facilities were comparable in size to Schneider's French operation itself.

Other forms of disarticulation in the French economy were similar to current Third World countries. Thus the highly developed Nord (in coal, textiles, metallurgy) was importantly orientated, not just to France, but to close-by Belgium. And Lorraine iron ore and metallurgy was as closely articulated with German industry as with the French. What external articulation meant was domestic dislocation. The same can be said in terms of the chasm between peasant agriculture and the secondary sector. Very slow gains in productivity of the former nullified peasant purchasing power of industrial goods. Carré and his collaborators claim that weak agricultural purchasing power was the most important cause of the very slow French growth from 1870–96; equally, the subsequent upturn of the *Belle Époque* was, Caron observed, due largely to demand increase in *urban* consumer markets.[14]

Another symptom of dislocation is that alongside the non-rationalized industrial sectors and backwards peasantry was the presence in management of a *highly rationalizing* corps of engineers. France probably boasted the world's best-educated top management; in 1912 some 75 per cent of higher managers in the 30 largest quoted industrial firms had graduated from tertiary education; in 1939 this had risen to 93 per cent. The groundwork for their presence lay in the creation of the *grandes écoles* of engineering (see chapter 4). Until the 1880s, the boards of French companies were largely comprised of bankers and large merchants; from then onwards there was a significant replacement by the technically qualified. More importantly, key companies in the new industries were founded in the period up to just after the First World War by the generation which had graduated from the *grandes écoles* in about 1900; these included such durable giants as Citroën, Pechiney, Kuhlmann, L'Union d'Électricité, Alsthom and the Compagnie française des petroles.[15]

We have paid attention to capital concentration above. We will now emphasize in some detail the inordinate retardation of 'real' capital concentration in

France over the first half of this century. Measuring concentration by workers per firm, Kindelberger noted that by 1954 British companies in metal-production were almost twice as large as the French; in textiles some 50 per cent larger.[16] There had nevertheless been some increases in the size of firms in France. In 1912, 31 per cent of French employees worked in firms which numbered among the top 5 per cent (in labour force terms); in 1936 this proportion had increased to 40 per cent; and in 1952 to 50 per cent. Yet, in terms of the per cent of total assets of Bourse-quoted firms, there was a fall in capital concentration. The proportion of the assets of the top 100 firms of total assets in France was 71 per cent in 1912, 59 per cent in 1936 and 58 per cent in 1952; that of the largest 50 of these firms was 52 per cent in 1912, 42 per cent in 1936 and 43 per cent in 1952.[17] And even where mergers did take place, they mostly consisted of forming holding companies, particularly to save small businesses and to keep prices high.[18] The structure of production remained unconcentrated, and vertical integration (through merger or acquisition) was especially rare. The type of real concentration in significant sectors of British industry in the inter-war period – and American and German industry much earlier – was only achieved in France during the merger wave of 1950–4, when French industrialists began to accept outside finance and to restructure through diversification. What is entailed was a decline of the dominance in France of technical management and of the engineer, and the rise in influence of executives in finance and sales in more decentralized managerial structures.[19]

We will now briefly consider the main industrial sectors during this pre-war period where we find, more than in other countries, very old-fashioned production and managerial arrangements coexisting with the very new. In outline, we should note, first, that in 1913 just about one-half of France's industrial labour force (minus building workers) were employed in (broadly speaking) textiles, clothing and leather[20] (engineering only surpassed textiles as France's biggest sector of industrial employment in the 1950s). Second, whereas from 1865 to 1894 the growth rate was higher in consumer goods than capital goods industries, from 1895 onwards this tendency was reversed.[21] Third, French organized capitalism falls into three periods: one of growth and development, 1896–1929; the slump, 1929–49; and a much more rapid growth period from 1949. It was only the new industries, petroleum products, chemicals and electricity, that continued to expand during the 1912–49 middle period. Over the whole period from the 1890s to the 1960s it was the new industries, electricity and chemicals, which unsurprisingly registered the greatest gains in labour productivity.[22]

French steel – mostly because of the dearness of coal, but also due to the industry's lack of integrated concentration – had little success in competing on world markets, except in the areas of armaments and special alloys. During the 1920s, in metal producing and working, there was the near-disappearance of the conservative ententes (which had become rather a tradition in the sector), the French takeover of the German companies in Lorraine and a certain measure of vertical integration through acquisitions. After the Second World War a number of new holding companies and 'super-groups' with interlocking shareholding and control were formed, Yet the amount of real concentration involved was doubtful; in the event, in 1912, 14 companies in the sector controlled 61 per cent of assets, while in 1952 the figures had scarcely changed, with 15 companies controlling 77 per cent of assets. Real rationalization came with the large-scale merger wave of the 1950s, in which, under the whip of the *Communauté européene du charbon et de l'acier* (CECA), such soon-to-be-famous companies as Usinor and Sidelor were established.[23]

At the turn of the century France was the world's centre of technical innovation in automobile production, even after being overtaken in output by the USA. It was toolmakers such as Panhard and Levasseur and bicycle producers such as Peugeot who got the industry off the ground. France boasted Europe's largest output in automobiles during the *Belle Époque*; and cars were a key export, some one-third of French production from 1902 to 1905 being exported to Britain. It is argued that France's early success in this branch was due to the country's long tradition of practical engineering, its excellent road system, its tradition of producing quality goods for a luxury market and the fact that cars were at first easy to manufacture in France's characteristically small firms.[24] The most modern among France's rationalizing industrial leaders were in the electrical industry.[25] For example, in 1957 when 1.6 per cent of French citizens over the age of 14 possessed a diploma in higher education the figure for top industrialists was 72 per cent and for leaders in the electrical industry was 87 per cent. Of all characteristically organized capitalist industries, electricity has had the greatest need for capital resources. Thus the industry formed in holding companies which from the 1890s had strong links to the Paris banks, who were important on the boards of directors of such leading electrical sector holdings as Parisienne Électrique and Thomson-Houston. Towards the end of the 1930s there came to be a greater reliance on internal finance and banker–industrialists declined in number.

Finance

Turning to the role of the banks in the French economy, we find once again the phenomenon of disarticulation. We will see that, not unlike the British case, the comparatively close connections of banks with domestic industry during the nineteenth century became very thin indeed during the crucial early decades of organized capitalism; and that such connections were only re-established on any kind of substantial scale around the time for the Second World War.[26] Modern banking really began in France with the formation of the joint-stock banks during the Second Empire, the most important of such being the Crédit Mobilier founded by the Péreire brothers in 1853. The Péreires, as Saint Simonians, articulated a two-sided ideology and *politique bancaire* which propounded (1) the centralization of money capital through the spread of popular branch banking, and (2) money capital's entry into the productive classes in the shape of industrial finance. In 1847 the five largest Parisian *caisses* had assets varying between 2 and 17 million francs. The Crédit Mobilier started business in 1853 with assets of 56.5 million francs in 1864. By 1865 France's 'big four' deposit banks and two largest regional banks had together resources of 493 million francs; two decades later this figure had approximately trebled to 1694 million francs.[27]

Bank involvement with productive capital underwent a qualitative increase from the 1830s, but now received another more substantial boost from the joint-stock banks. From its founding, Crédit Mobilier helped get the stalled French railroad network off the ground, though even here the state had to guarantee Crédit Mobilier-underwritten bonds. The state also borrowed from the joint-stock banks for (non-industrial, yet secondary sector and 'productive') public works and especially for urban construction in, pre-eminently, the rebuilding of Paris which began under Baron Haussmann's prefecture.[28] Right from the start, and often playing an originating role, the joint-stock banks founded in the Second Empire had not just merchants and representatives from the private banks, but industrialists on their boards. Bank involvement in industry here often took the form, not of long-term loans nor underwriting of securities, but of shareholding in the industries themselves. Société Générale, for example, was thus involved in metallurgy, and the 'groupe bancaire' Crédit Lyonnais held controlling shares in the Société lyonnaise de constructeurs mécaniques et de lumières èlectriques. Because such finance often went to the industrialists who sat on the banks' boards does not negate the fact that industrial finance indeed did take place.

But these days of industrial involvement were already shown to be numbered during liberal capitalism itself. One cause of what was to be the growing separation of banks and industry (events that duplicated those taking place in Britain at the same time) was a considerable number of industrial failures. Thus Crédit Lyonnais survived a disaster of the Las Fuchsine dyestuffs company, while Union Générale did not survive a failed Balkan railway project in 1879. In the event, from the end of the 1870s, Crédit Lyonnais led the way towards the separation of the banks from industry, which involved at the same time the functional differentiation of the joint-stock banks into deposit banks (the big four here were Crédit Lyonnais, Société Générale, Comptoir National d'Escomte de Paris and Crédit Industriel et Commercial (CIC)) and 'banques d'affaires' (the leaders here were the Paribas, the Banque de l'Union Parisienne and the Banque d'Indochine).[29] During the first decades of organized capitalism, this tendency towards the separation of banks and industry – with the exception of some of the regional banks – was exacerbated, both because it became more explicitly bank policy not to lend to industry and because overseas investments proliferated. Such investment trebled in the years from 1880 to 1913, when it stood at some 8.3 billion dollars.[30]

Foreign investment became concentrated in the more peripheral countries during these years, in particular in Russia, Bulgaria, and the Ottoman Empire, as well as Italy.[31]

The inter-war years were particularly marked by an increase in importance of public institutions of finance capital, whose resources were being put increasingly to productive use.[32] In 1913 72 per cent of such resources were placed in state bonds, in 1938 52 per cent, and in 1965 only 5.8 per cent. There was some growth in the involvement of the banques d'affaires in industry. Paribas, for example, was instrumental in the creation of the Groupement de constructions électriques in 1919-20; the banques d'affaires increased medium-term industrial lending in general in the 1920s and particularly to the auto industry; more and more industrialists came to sit on the boards of these banks. Equally the big four deposit banks became more active in underwriting securities, especially for the electrical industry. Also in the late 1920s there was a highly significant increase in foreign investment in industry in France. However, the largest of the banques d'affaires' 'finance capital' combinations was shattered in 1921 by the split between Schneider and the Banque de l'Union Parisienne. Most important, the crisis in deposits from 1930 onwards precluded any longer-range intervention of French banks and industry, and was related to the rapid foreign disinvestment in French industry.[33]

The nationalizations of 1945–6 can be seen in part as further increasing the importance of public financial institutions and regulation. The big four deposit banks, but not the banques d'affaires, came under public ownership, as did the largest insurance companies. Private capital assets were excluded from the Banque de France and the National Credit Council was established, extending public regulation over the banques d'affaires. This legislation, however, changed little, the deposit banks continuing to function like private banks; for example, they resisted the extension of credit to nationalized industry because of their disapproval of its public expropriation.[34] Change, however, did subsequently come in the shift back to the mixed bank and the increase in industrial investment which began in the 1950s and continued to grow right through to the end of the 1970s. Not only during these years was there an increase in the ratio of gross capital formation to net national product but, Patat has shown, also an increase in the proportion of gross capital formation accounted for by the financial resources of the banks.[35]

The state and organization at the bottom

We have so far seen that French capital was, comparatively speaking, quite slow in its economic organization. By contrast, we shall see the French state developed very considerable levels of organization, in a sort of 'bipartite' corporatism which excluded labour as an organized interest. This political configuration, which spanned the 1940s, 1950s and 1960s, accounted, not just for the success of French planning,[36] but also for the particular nature of France's welfare state.

Prior to the First World War the French economy was reasonably close to the standard *laissez-faire* pattern. Divergencies from the latter were present, however, in the existence of a large state bureaucracy; in intermittent protectionist policies; and in the tendency of industrialists to form defensive ententes.[37] Elements of planning during the First World War were introduced by the Radical Minister of Commerce and Industry, Etienne Clémental, who established 'consortiums' for the purchase and distribution of major raw materials. Consortium officers (in contact with French trade associations) were to decide on the quantity of given raw material needed; the state would then function as purchasing agent for imports; and the consortium members would then distribute the raw material to individual enterprises with the proviso that no more than 6 per cent profits were made on the investment.[38] After the war employers effectively opposed the continuation of such a budding corporatism, and a return to liberalism followed. In the 1920s consumer interests dominated state policy, and particularly the interest of middle-class rentiers (Weber's famous *Besitzklassen*). Raymond Poincaré in the mid-1920s, like Gustav Stresemann in Germany, struggled with some success against the hawkish post-war diplomatic objectives of the producer interests (*Erwerbsklassen*) of the metallurgy employers' federation, the *Comité des Forges*. The latter proposed significant stock cessions (to themselves) and guaranteed deliveries of Ruhr coal. But otherwise the producer interests seemed to have subscribed to the hegemonic conceptions of the *Bestizklassen* themselves. Central industrialists such as François de Wendel, for example, served as regents of the Banque de France, which was a prime mover in the legal fixing of the franc in 1928. Unlike the German industrialists who pushed post-war inflation and therefore benefited, the French industrial *patronat* (employers) seemed to share the middle-class objective of guaranteed savings and a stable currency. This was partially matched on the left, in which the *Section française de l'Internationale Ouvrière* (SFIO) (socialist party) endorsed similarly 'monetarist' (though mildly redistributive) policies.[39]

The French state in the 1930s employed effectively counter-cyclical measures to a substantially lesser degree than any other country considered in this book. Yet post-liberal political-economic *ideologies* were beginning to take shape in this period, in particular on the moderate left. Non-Marxists in the Confédération générale du travail (CGT) were influenced by the conceptions of Belgian socialist, Henri De Man. The idea in the French context was a very gradualist, mixed-economy transition to socialism. The alliance of the productive classes was to be an array against finance capital, price-fixing and Malthusian monopoly capital. Credit would be nationalized, loans to middle-class businesses facilitated, and private interests excluded from the regents of the Bank of France. A tripartite corporatist economic council with wide-ranging powers would be created which would be responsible for producing an annual plan. The idea was not so much of long-term growth as of counter-cyclical exit from the depression. It rested on an underconsumptionist explanation of the crisis, whose solution lay in the redistributive build-up of purchasing power.[40]

During the Second World War, the basic groundwork of French post-war planning was lain. Ideological input into the Vichy regime came from Clémental's First World War, neo-liberal conceptions and from social democratic De Man-type 'planism'. The latter tendency was most markedly represented by Reñe Belin, one-time heir apparent to leader Léon Jouhaux at the CGT, who became the first minister of labour and production under the Vichy regime. Belin was the senior figure behind the drafting of August 1940 legislation which created the framework of Vichy state-corporatist industrial structure. The legislation abolished the largest repesentative groups of producer interests, including the CGT and the *Confédération générale du patronat français* (CGPF). In their stead *Comités d'Organisation* (COs) were set up in each sector; these were corporate bodies which proposed price schedules and regulated competition. In industries in which pre-war CGPF trade associations were strong they continued to wield significant coporate power; the *Comité des Forges*, for example, evolved into the CO for the iron and steel industry. Corporatism in this context, however, was the corporatism of private business and thus excluded labour. Belin chose the CO leaders mostly from among the modernizing large business leaders who retained their private managerial positions.[41] Yet a number of innovations (besides the CO) which prefigured post-war planning were established in Vichy. State control over the banks was tightened and the collection of economic statistics was reformed. The *Tranche de Demarrage*, developed in 1944 for the immediate post-war period, featured the provision of a much higher investment to GDP ratio which was to be a prime characteristic of post-war planning.

Planist ideologies in the Resistance did not diverge very markedly from those of Vichy. Resistance Socialists pushed for strong corporatist bodies (with full workers' participation) which would play a dominant mediating role in what would be left of the private sector.[42] What these Socialists seemed to want was a gradual transition to socialism via a corporatism in which labour played an important part. Even Resistance neo-liberals and Gaullists who eventually put French planning on the ground originally advocated a tripartite basis. What happened in practice was a Vichy-like removal of labour from involvement. In other words, planning via a tripartite corporatism had by 1947 or so turned into planning via a bipartite corporatism. How and why this happened will be examined in chapter 8 when we outline a structural account of the decline of corporatism and neo-corporatism.[43]

The bipartite corporatism – which excluded labour – in conjunction with the influence of Catholic interest and the demographic obsession of French nationalism, can also account for the specific nature of the French welfare state. French social spending thus has been characterized by a disproportionate place for social transfer and family allowances, and a strong workplace linkage of social security. Fully 20 per cent of French GNP was devoted to social transfers in 1975, second only to the Netherlands in the West. At this time Sweden devoted only 16.6 per cent of GNP to social transfers; West Germany 16.7 per cent; Britain 11.1 per cent; and the USA 10.4 per cent.[44] In terms of total social spending as a proportion of GDP France has done less well: 22.7 per cent in France in 1975 compared with 27.9 per cent in West Germany. It should be noted that despite the absence of left governments in the Fifth Republic and, relative to other countries, the less rapid growth of social spending, the French welfare state continued to grow strongly in absolute terms. Thus social transfers as a proportion of GNP amounted to 11.3 per cent in 1950, grew to 13.2 per cent in 1959, and from 1961 to 1975 steadily increased from 13.5 to 20 per cent.[45]

In 1975 the proportion of spending on family allowances of all social spending amounted to 19.6 per cent in France, in comparison to 10.6 per cent in Britain and 10.2 per cent in Germany.[46] Generally it should be noted that in countries with a majority Catholic population, family allowances have consistently figured more prominently in social spending than in Protestant countries. Equally, in Catholic countries the struggle for family allowances has often been quite separate from the labour-movement inspired struggle for other social benefits. In France the family allowance issue was also intertwined with the 'demographic panics' of the nineteenth and especially the twentieth centuries, and with the rise and pervasion of French nationalism. The notion of social welfare spending as functional for the demographic health of the 'social body' was, we noted, also central to the development of the Swedish welfare state. The importance of this issue is highlighted by Foucault, for whom an important objective of modernity is the expanded demographic reproduction of the social.[47] In the Swedish and in the French cases there were a cluster of interarticulated ideological/political notions revolving around the modern, the social, demography, and nationalism. The comparative point here is that, whereas in Sweden this ideological constellation – especially in regard to the demographic question – found its elective affinity with Social Democracy and the working class, in France the class agents of 'modernization' were petits bourgeois and often Catholic and on the right. Thus in 1899 employees in parts of the public sector were awarded salary bonuses for large families, a practice which was extended in 1913. The heavy death toll of the First World War brought about the birth-rate bonuses of 1918 and other child-rearing subsidies of the following year, as well as the reform of public assistance to families of 1923. Another demographic panic – given impending hostilities – brought about the fixing of large family compensation for all employers at a significantly higher level in 1938, and at a yet higher level the following year by the *Haut Comité de la Population*. The CGT and the left opposed these enactments in the inter-war period on the grounds that they were divisive of the working class.[48]

A further distinctive characteristic of French social spending has been the extent to which it has been linked to the workplace. Thus perhaps the main function of the post-war *comités d'entreprise* has been the management of social security funds. When unemployment benefits finally – more than two decades later than in most other countries – came on to the agenda they did so not through legislation nor executive order but through a national collective bargaining agreement. This was the 1958 *accord* which created the *Association pour l'emploi dans l'industrie et le commerce* (ASSEDIC). These associations, with union and employer representatives on their boards, managed the insurance funds which covered all employees in commerce and industry.[49] This is again illustrative of policy-making via a bipartite corporatism excluding labour as an organized interest in that (1) the *comités d'entreprise* have inhibited, and arguably were designed to inhibit, labour from constituting a presence on the shopfloor; and (2) the most important interest organizations of labour have typically not been participants in national bargaining agreements.

In France the economy and civil society – partly due to its very economic forwardness, that is, its gentle industrialization and long-enduring overly large class of urban and rural petits bourgeois – were extraordinarily under-organized. We explored this underorganization in the economy in some detail above. In civil society it was most strikingly and significantly instantiated in the low membership density and instability of the trade unions. If – like Germany – the ideology *and the practice* of class struggle were pervasive from the turn of the century until into the 1970s, then – unlike Germany – the ideology and practice of collective organization were absent. This American-like small property owner's individualism was, however, unlike in the USA, paralleled by a renowned tradition of statism. Thus – as we saw above – the absence of the propensity of capitalists to organize French capitalism in the economy and at the top, was belatedly compensated for after the Second World War by the state. In a not wholly dissimilar manner, the lack of propensity of *workers* to organize in civil society meant that French capitalism was also organized at the bottom, and in particular here we refer to the post-war growth in social spending, largely through the agency of the (in no way working-class) state.

UNITED STATES: INSTRUMENTALISM AND PROGRESSIVISM

More than any of the other societies under investigation, the United States approximates the crude 'state-monopoly capitalist' ideal type in that it seems to demonstrate both an extraordinary fusion of banks and industry and a state which is the clear instrument of the economically dominant class. In the early part of this century, for example, the largest industrial firm was controlled by the same man as the second largest commercial bank, and the largest commercial bank was controlled by the same man as the second largest industrial firm. And instrumentalism was demonstrated in the same period in the day-to-day contact between the president and top industrialists, the domination of industrial interests on various regulatory commissions, and the quasi-governmental role assumed by major business leaders in the First World War.

To come to any understanding, we shall see, of the American state under organized capitalism, it is necessary to analyse the elusive phenomenon of 'progressivism'. It is in the Progressive era, from 1900 to 1920, that the American state became more instrumentalist than did the state in any society under consideration in this book. It is at the same time largely due to the input of a number of Progressives and a transformed progressivist ideology that the state during the 1930s New Deal gained considerable autonomy from capital. Further, the Progressive movement and later the Progressive ethos had figured as important inputs into the development of the American welfare state.

Organization at the top

Two centrally significant issues to be analysed here are, first, the role of banking capital in the development of American organized capitalism; and second, the degree, forms and effects of the concentration of industrial capital. We will deal with these issues in that order.

The main financial institution in the USA was the investment bank, which had typically begun as commercial capital operations in dry goods and clothing. Investment banks were not involved in industrial loans until the organized capitalist 1890s, but previously floated securities mostly abroad for railroads and state and local governments. They were also the primary creditors of American railroads. When in the early 1890s – due to asset stripping and ruinous competition – some one-half of railway assets came to belong to bankrupt companies, these assets passed into the receivership of the investment bankers, foremost among whom was J. P. Morgan.[50]

The cartel formation and mergers in industry of the 1880s were mainly carried out in oil, meatpacking and other agricultural products industries without the involvement of financial institutions. The much larger merger wave of 1898–1903, that saw the creation of such firms as United States Steel, American Tobacco, International Harvester and Du Pont, was largely the result of the financial institutions. From 1895 to 1904, American firms disappeared at an average rate of 301 per year.[51] As a prelude to this avalanche of mergers, J. P. Morgan oversaw the crucial joining of Edison Electric Company and the Thomson-Houston Company to become General Electric in 1892, with the resulting placement of two Morgan partners on the new company's board of directors. Morgan also oversaw the largest merger ever in America, in the formation of United States Steel in 1901; US Steel was formed out of what had originally been 138 companies, and controlled 62 per cent of the market at its creation. In the economically central and technologically advanced agricultural machinery sector the McCormick and Deere companies merged in 1902 – overseen by George Perkins again of the House of Morgan – to form International Harvester; in 1918 Harvester controlled some 65 to 90 per cent of the product market in the company's main lines of binders, mowers and harvesters. Bell Telephone Company (the precursor of American Telephone and Telegraph (AT & T), who were the precursor of International Telephone and Telegraph Corporation (ITT)), had a monopoly over telephones and lines from 1877–9 until 1894 when their patent expired. With competition now entering, Morgan, Bell's premier financier, aided in the establishment of long-distance lines between cities. From 1907 AT & T's capital needs catapulted Morgan into a controlling position where he engineered a policy of merger with the independent companies.[52]

The seemingly ubiquitous House of Morgan were not the only financiers forming industrial capital out of these mergers. John D. Rockefeller created a financial group through the profits of Standard Oil, and thus came to dominate the (commercial) City Bank of New York, later to become the National City Bank. Through the latter, Rockefeller was able to control the predecessors of both the Anaconda Copper Co. and Commonwealth Edison and able to back E. H. Harriman's (at times Morgan's greatest competitor) railroad ventures. Also at this time the banking business was undergoing a process of change. First, financiers began to take over the major life insurance companies; for example, by 1910, Morgan had control of the nation's three largest insurance companies: Equitable, Mutual and New York Life. More important was the shift towards the domination of the commercial banks. The Morgan group went into an alliance with, and then took control of, the First National Bank of New York, and through allowances and interlocks were connected with a number of other major commercial banks. These, however, were pure-type commercial banks as debtors only; as creditors they took on investment banking functions.[53]

What explains the turn of the century merger wave? A comparison with the smaller cluster of mergers of the 1880s is instructive. The motives for this wave in the 1880s in which trade associations were quickly replaced by relatively integrated companies were (1) to stabilize markets in which there existed destructive competition, and (2) to realize economies of scale through integration. Because of the nature of the industries involved the intervention of finance capital was unnecessary. Moreover, the investment banks had then been occupied with railway activities. By contrast, the qualitatively larger turn of the century wave took place in a different set of conditions. First and foremost, with the decline of opportunity for railway investment, industry was the only logical place for the investment banks to go for investment opportunities. Second, most of the industries then important, because of the high ratio of initial capital layout to initial sales, needed external finance in order to expand. Third, US corporation laws were liberalized in the late 1880s and the 1890s and this made it easier to grant corporate charters, to raise the limit on authorized capitalization and for one corporation to own shares of another.[54]

In the event, the investment banks went about their merger activity in much the same style as they did in the railways, that is, through the issue of a large proportion of 'watered stock', which represented the costs of merger and the anticipation of future earnings. With the watered stock, the total value of stock issued was often set at about twice the value of the firm's capital assets. This enabled the investment banks, through stock-holding, to be in a position of control over the firm. But whereas this watering strategy may have been – at least temporarily – successful on the railways, in industry it was disastrous. In industry the heavy fixed interest and dividend payments, which such capitalization entailed, brought down profits and made merged companies non-competitive with independents, who quickly increased their share of product markets. Equally, economies of scale were not realized because these horizontally-merged firms did not integrate, either horizontally or vertically, but often (the prime example is US Steel) persisted as holding companies.[55]

In the 1920s there were a number of significant changes in American capital markets. First, automobiles and chemicals, the 'new industries' which attained a special primacy in the 1920s, grew mainly out of internally generated profits, as did a number of the industries which expanded enormously from automobile-created demand. Second, for the first time individual investors – as distinct from financial institutions (stockbroking firms are not financial institutions) – came to play a pervasive role on security exchanges. At the same time, towards the end of the twenties, stock issues began to raise more capital for industry than bonds. Third, new investment banks began to challenge the old on security exchanges, where they were joined by a new institution, the investment trust, which (unlike the investment banks) issued its own stocks and bonds and then invested itself in other securities. Fourth, commercial banks took on new functions. Originally drawing on the wealthy and on corporations for deposits, new West Coast banks like the Bank of America also attracted small depositors as creditors. Also in the 1920s commercial banks began to form security affiliates which (as Swedish and German banks did) underwrote and held securities. After the First World War, the USA became for the first time a net creditor nation and New York became the world's banking centre, with the Federal Reserve, created in 1913, taking on the functions of the bankers' bank. The houses of Morgan and Rockefeller also prospered. The expansion of utilities in the twenties necessitated large issues of new securities. Great public utility holding companies in electric light and power were created, the two largest of which were controlled by the Morgan group from 1921; to these firms the Morgan group added control-ling interests in RCA and Kennecott Copper by the late twenties. The Rockefeller group began at this point to operate mainly through the Chase

Manhattan Bank, and also obtained control of the Metropolitan and the Equitable Life Insurance companies.[56]

Overall, although banks and industry have been very significantly interconnected in American organized capitalism, the main power of banks has been its veto and not one of determining investment strategies.[57] For considering the development of particular industries it is useful to divide the history of modern US industry into four periods which are at the same time four successive modes of capital concentration: the first, of largely horizontal integration in the 1880s; the second, of (a) the unproductive mergers and (b) subsequent successful vertical integration of the 1890s to 1920s; the third of diversification and the creation of multidivisional enterprises which began in the 1920s; and fourth, the 1960s formation of conglomerates, in which industrial capital, in effect, takes on the role of finance capital.

During the 1880s horizontal combination took place especially through the form of trusts in the refining and distilling industries. In several of these (petroleum, cotton-seed oil, whiskey, sugar refining) in which technologies were available for economies of scale, genuine concentration of production took place in fewer, larger firms which were more optimally located with regard to markets. The case of Standard Oil is instructive in this context.[58] To stabilize prices in petroleum refinery, John D. Rockefeller took the lead in creating a cartel in the 1870s. To inhibit the continuing entry of 'wildcat' refiners, Rockefeller put the cartel in a monopoly position in terms of reduced transport rates from the railroads. Trading securities with cartel members, Rockefeller was able to acquire over 50 per cent of the total stocks and bonds of cartel members by 1880. This horizontal integration permitted rationalization when the introduction of the long-distance crude-oil pipeline enabled the relocation of refining capacity nearer to markets and in larger units.[59]

In the food-processing industry vertical integration began on a very large scale.[60] The key to this was successful forward integration into wholesaling and sometimes retailing. In meatpacking, where little advance in production technology was possible, integral to expansion were sales and transport, and in particular the ability to shift meat from the Midwest to markets in the eastern cities. The Swift Company was the first to develop in this, using not just refrigerated railway cars, but building refrigerated storage facilities near the main cities. The company, incorporated in 1885, then, in the early 1890s, developed a sizeable purchasing department to organize systematically the buying of cattle. Swift was thus one of the first of the functionally-integrated industrial firms, with substantial purchasing and sales departments. By 1905 they and four other meatpackers controlled 35 per cent of the market in the industry. In machinery manufacture concentration through horizontal integration was unnecessary for reasons of finance because reasonable levels of sales were possible without a large initial capital outlay. Crucial though was the sales and servicing of equipment that was difficult to use. Thus, paid staff instead of commissioned agents came to be used in wholesaling. Important also was the development of franchised dealers for advertising, final sales and service. Most successful firms in mechanical engineering grew through such vertical (downstream) integration.

German industry, as we noted above, concentrated and took on similar management patterns at about the same time as the USA;[61] America, however, underwent this process on a far wider scale. The major explanatory factor operating here, we believe, was the existence of mass consumer markets. Germany developed modern managerial structures in industries – coal, iron and steel, electro-technical, chemicals – which sold either on capital goods markets, and/or to the (central or local) state. The first genuine burst of American concentration took place in oil, food processing, agricultural machinery, and sewing machines. Apart from oil (which was a massive exporter of its central product, kerosene, before 1900) this concentration, either through the production of standardized machinery and/or the creation of a rationalized sales apparatus, was only possible because of the existence of well-paid urban and rural popular classes. It has been estimated that in 1905 German real wages were only 42 per cent, British real wages 56 per cent, and Swedish real wages 47 per cent of the American figures. In 1930 the corresponding proportions were 40 per cent for German, 51 per cent for British and 60 per cent for Swedish industrial workers.[62]

In organized capitalism, then, capital typically undergoes concentration, first, through horizontal and vertical integration, which yields to development of functionally-departmentalized managerial structures. The second wave of concentration takes place through diversification and leads to the development of the multidivisional company. The difference between a functionally-departmentalized and multidivisional structure is that the latter is composed of a number of divisions – based on product or geographical lines – each one of which has various staff departments.[63] In the USA both renewed concentration and transformation of managerial structures were catalysed by the mass consumption of motor cars. This brought about the total reorientation and expansion of the oil industry, the quick concentration of the rubber industry, and the transformation of the steel industry. Three American firms to move very early to multidivisional structures were Du Pont, General Motors (GM) and Standard Oil of New Jersey. The two former became multidivisional through diversification, and thus their divisions were along product lines. The 1920–1 post-war economic crisis led to Du Pont and GM restructuring as multidivisional firms. In the case of Du Pont, as it was much later to be elsewhere, the unfavourably high ratio of financial resources to narrow and collapsed markets forced diversification.[64] There were two main necessary conditions for such managerial restructuring, both of which had functional equivalents in Germany, though neither had functional equivalents in Britain or Sweden. The first was simply that the firms possessed the economic resources for such rationalized restructuring. We remember in Sweden that, in the absence of such resources, it was the banks that had to control and oversee rationalization in response to the same recession. In Britain it was a catalyst not to the development of multidivisional structures – or to insufficient diversification – but instead to the adoption of the (already tried in several countries) structure of functional departmentalization. The other condition was on the level of what Bendix some time ago came to characterize as managerial ideologies. If in Germany such rationalizing ideologies had their origins in the military or state bureaucracy, in the United States the origins were arguably in the engineering school. This explains not just American development of Taylorist-type shopfloor arrangements; it also explains the growth of managerial hierarchies. Three members of the du Pont family, trained at the Massachusetts Institute of Technology (MIT),had brought about such radical restructuring of company management in the two decades before 1920 that when diversification came, the managerial structure was already on the ground that could effortlessly adopt the multidivisional form. And it was Pierre du Pont himself who, after acquiring GM in the crisis, laid the groundwork for the multidivisional structure of this already diversified firm. As for Standard Oil of New Jersey, it was the enormously rapid expansion of markets for petrol for motor cars, in conjunction with the geographical scatteredness of sources of crude oil and the expense of transporting refined gasoline to areas of final consumption, which made a geographically-based multidivisional structure necessary.[65]

Let us then attempt to analyse the state in organized capitalist America via the phenomenon of 'progressivism'. The Progressive movement began before 1900, essentially as a response of certain 'middle-class' elements to the problems caused by industrialization. Progressives aimed at a number of reforms regarding labour, capital and the state: labour, in regard to their early efforts to improve the quality of life in the slums and support of workmen's compensation; capital, in their push for limitation and regulation of monopolies, including the restriction of big business access to political power; and the state, in their programmes for municipal ownership of utilities and for a more general reform of urban machine-dominated politics. The Progressive era is normally said to have commenced in 1901 with the Theodore Roosevelt presidency. Though not a member of the Progressive Movement, Roosevelt had, as Governor of New York just before the turn of the century, imposed taxes on corporation franchises. As President from 1901 he gained a 'Progressive' reputation due to putative regulation of the 'trusts' through his resurrection and use of the Sherman Anti-Trust Act.[66]

On closer examination, however, it is clear that the large corporations not only acquiesced in, but in part co-directed, their own regulation. Furthermore, the stiffest use of the Sherman Anti-Trust Act in the Supreme Court decisions of 1877 and 1899 had the effect of discouraging pools and cartel-like agreements and instead encouraged the largest merger waves in American history, and thus, as we mentioned above, reinforced the power of the largest corporations. The most renowned use that Roosevelt made of the Sherman Act was in his ordering of a successful suit again the Northern Securities Company in 1902. This seemed to strike at J. P. Morgan railroad interests: it banned the formal device of the holding company, yet the *de facto* holding company continued to exist. Roosevelt's relation to Morgan interests was to say the least problematic. George Perkins, a Morgan partner, was key in the drafting of Roosevelt's regulation legislation. Probably the most universally recognized contravention of the Sherman Law was the receipt of railroad rebates by the trusts. Yet when it became apparent that the Morgan-controlled International Harvester was receiving rebates from a Morgan railroad in 1904, no such litigation took place. Further, Elihu Root, long deeply involved with Morgan interests, became Secretary of State in the second Roosevelt administration in 1905.

Perhaps the most striking and widely publicized failure of Roosevelt trust-busting involved the Morgan-financed US Steel. Progressive supporters of Roosevelt, and organized small business, expected litigation when the company extended further its market dominance through the purchase of Tennessee Coal and Iron in 1907. Roosevelt refused litigation on the shaky grounds that such acquisition was necessary to save an investment firm which held the shares of the Tennessee company as collateral. Finally, as a kind of bad joke mocking the Northern Securities decision, in the last two years of Roosevelt's administration, Morgan was permitted to become owner of the majority of assets of New England's railroad system.[67]

Counter-factual explanation is a thorny business. It is, however, likely that the large corporations would not have pushed for their *own* regulation in the absence of the Sherman Act. It is clear that the movement for the establishment of regulatory agencies by big business came only after the passage of Sherman. Equally, most efforts by big business to promote such regulatory agencies was apparently in reaction to the unpredictability which entered business life because of the intermittent, and seemingly arbitrary, use of Sherman suits. Thus, the instrumentalist interpretation of the American state, though arguably valid on counts of the consequences of state policy and the frequency of contact between big business and state personnel, is less valid on the count of business intentions and state policy.

At this point we should note the contemporaneous balance of political forces in the USA. Large-scale industrial capital had formed the National Civic Federation (NCF) in 1900, in direct response to Sherman litigation; the NCF grew out of a conference on the regulation of trusts in Chicago in 1899. Morgan interests were very strongly represented on the NCF; much of the federation's legislative effort spearheaded by George Perkins, a Morgan partner, who consistently had access to Roosevelt's ear. The NCF was relatively liberal on trade-union matters, conceding that a broad reading of the Sherman Act would protect unions as well as the large firms from litigation. Smaller business men were organized in the National Association of Manufacturers (NAM), vociferously hostile to trade unions, whose sympathy for trust-busting and a narrow reading of Sherman made them the awkward political bedfellows of the Progressive movement. Samuel Gompers of the American Federation of Labour entered into 'quasi-corporatist' relations with the NCF and the government, thus isolating the left-wing unionists and socialists, who found a number of interests in common with the Progressives. Roosevelt himself was closely aligned with the views of the NCF, endorsing litigation only against unreasonable constraints of trade, and friendly to the notion of socially responsible 'trusts' and conservative trade unions.[68]

Original business uncertainty in the face of law suits under the Sherman Act led to pressure which ended in the creation of a regulatory agency, the Bureau of Corporations in 1903. When this turned out to be toothless, and regulation by litigation persisted, the NCF pressed again this time for an effective agency. A number of Congressmen then asked the NCF itself to exercise the drafting of a bill, a subsequent version of which became law in 1914 and created the Federal Trade Commission.[69]

Just as the Progressives and small business, occupying opposite poles on the spectrum of 'respectable' politics, took similar positions *vis-à-vis* trust-busting, so was there a functional similarity of their politics with respect to the local state. Both wanted, and to a large extent succeeded, to replace local government of corrupt political machines by apolitical government by technocrats. Before the turn of the century, local capital had been antagonistic to Progressives and other more radical urban reformers, and had preferred the old 'machine' politics. What persuaded the small capitalists of the need for urban reform was the requirement for a modern municipal infrastructure. This was to be provided with the greatest efficiency and the smallest amount of waste, on the principle, many were to propound, of 'one-man management'. To bring this about meant the dismantling of partisan politics, and this was the aim of the city commission and manager movements. The means to accomplish this end was local government, no longer through 'political' aldermen and mayor, but through the direct election of (many fewer) non-partisan 'commissioners'.[70] Commission government first spread widely in American towns and cities from 1900 to the First World War. The effect was an increase of the political influence of business, as working-class aldermen lost their seats and commissioners came to work particularly closely with chambers of commerce. Yet the means to this end was the Progressive idea of rationalized local government. Indeed prominent Progressives either did not effectively oppose, or even played an active role in, the introduction of the government by commission plan.[71]

We should distinguish at this point between the Progressive era discussed above, the Progressive movement, the various incarnations of the Progressive Party, and the ideology or ethos of progressivism. The Progressive movement began about a decade before the turn of the century, and by 1910 was led by Robert La Follette, governor of Wisconsin, who had transformed

Progressive ideology into legislative reality, through the institution of direct primaries, tax reform and railroad rate control. The Progressive Party grew out of a league that the genuinely radical La Follette had created inside the Republican Party. It was subsequently captured by NCF and business interest, making use of Theodore Roosevelt's progressive credentials in order to launch his presidential candidacy in 1912. Woodrow Wilson, victorious in the election, shared Roosevelt's type of progressivism. These politics were partly a response to a sort of progressivist tendency (not strongly linked to the movement itself, but an outgrowth of 1890s populism) in the Democratic Party – the largely rural-based southern and western followers of William Jennings Bryan. After 1916 Wilson's (limited) social legislation, in conjunction with a general shift to the right of the American political spectrum, meant that the Progressive movement was finished and the Progressive era over. But the Progressive ethos was still deeply imbued in several strata of the American population. It resurfaced in the 5 million electoral vote performance of La Follette's second incarnation of the Progressive Party in the 1924 presidential election, and it resurfaced again, in a radically transfigured form, as we shall immediately see, in the New Deal.[72]

The Franklin D. Roosevelt presidency (1933–45) surely signalled, in comparison with times past, a relative autonomy of the American state. Ellis Hawley has identified three sets of political actors during the New Deal, which vied with one another to determine policy; all had roots in one form or another of progressivism.[73] These were, firstly, those who stood in a principled opposition to monopolies, and favoured most of all initiatives towards political or economic decentralization. This group saw state spending, as distinct from state planning, in a positive light. It promoted state anti-trust activity to enhance economic competition. These 'anti-trusters' harked back to progressivism's populist origins.[74] The second group of political actors were the 'planners', who included the classic New Deal liberal left, who had roots in more mainstream progressivism, associated with the rationalization of urban government. They were less hostile to big business than were the anti-trusters, but considered that effective state planning was necessary in order to keep business in line. The third group, whose slightly more suspect progressivism derived from Theodore Roosevelt, were the proponents of a 'business commonwealth', favouring trade associations in which the various industrial sectors would effectively act in the public interest through a process of 'business self-control'. The second and third groups could both be termed 'corporatists', the difference between them being that the public-interest tripartism of the 'planners' assumed significant powers for labour and especially the state, whereas the vision of the 'business rationalizers' could only accept very minor roles for the latter two groups. Their project actually propounded an even more instrumentalist American state in as much as business would take on quasi-state powers.[75]

Prior to the New Deal, departures from *laissez-faire* policies were almost invariably associated with the third group of Progressives, the 'business rationalizers'.[76] During the First World War a group of interventionist bodies, in which big business came to play a quasi-state role, were created, including the Food Administration and the War Finance Corporation. The most central of these however was the War Industries Board (WIB) which was established partly due to strong lobbying by the US Chamber of Commerce. The WIB was less significant in its ineffectual practices of industrial pricing and resource allocation, than in its symbolic role and in its production of administrators who were to figure as business rationalizers in the New Deal. Perhaps as important was the new role of the Federal Reserve Board and the fledgling trade associations that developed in the 1920s.[77] Prior to the New Deal the Federal Reserve became encharged with increasing powers of national monetary co-ordination. Its break from traditional Gold Standard practices, in an attempt to intervene rationally in money markets, unfortunately helped bring on the crash of 1929. Herbert Hoover, as Secretary of Commerce from 1921-9, was instrumental in fostering in response to the recession of 1921 the 'cooperative associationalism' of the 1920s. Hoover expanded the Department of Commerce but supported the use of moral suasion only to prevent competitive abuses by the flourishing trade associations. As President, though, he opposed Robert Wagner's bill for federal relief to the unemployed and the expansion of the money supply; he yielded to farmers' pressure in 1929 to institute a government grain-buying programme, and to business pressure for the creation in 1932 of the Reconstruction Finance Corporation.

The Franklin Roosevelt presidency can be broken down into three periods. The first was 1933-5, and involved the National Industrial Recovery Act's (NIRA) attempted institution of a 'business commonwealth'. The second was 1935 and 1939, in which the idea of planning through business self-control was abandoned, and during which Roosevelt and the leading figures of his Administration saw themselves as governing *against* oligopolistic power. Finallly, there was the war period, in which policy objectives were intended to and succeeded in reincorporating big business in the (changed) status quo.

Skocpol has argued against an instrumentalist Marxist reading of particularly the 'first' New Deal of the National Industrial Recovery Act (NIRA).[78] Her case largely rests on four (difficult to dispute) pieces of evidence: that capital was far less cohesive after the First World War than during the heyday of J. P. Morgan and the National Civic Federation; that only a minority of the most prominent business leaders were notably active in pushing for the trade-associational components of NIRA; that organized business opposed the union security provisions of the Act; and that business displeasure with the operation of the National Recovery Administration (NRA) which the Act created, often on grounds of creeping socialization, was commonplace.

However, it would seem that Skocpol has in part overstated her case. First, Title I of the Act prescribed that there should be codes regulating government-backed industrial cartels but the codes for each sector themselves were in fact written by representatives from the leading firms *in that sector*. Secondly, when the government proved incapable of finding administrators for the codes, business itself provided the state-employed administrators. Third, the codes, much like in the WIB, provided for business self-control, the government being able to use only moral suasion and capable of no sanctions with any teeth whatsoever. Fourth, Section 7a, supposedly guaranteeing a measure of trade union security, did not prove of much direct help to labour, and businesses in the various sectors evaded its provisions whenever possible. Fifth, the codes as written consisted of a victory for the third group of Progressives mentioned above, the 'business rationalizers'.[79]

Some business leaders genuinely believed that the codes were a 'business-commonwealth' path out of the depression. Many industrialists it seems were originally induced to co-operate at least minimally with the Act for more cynical reasons, that is, for a *quid pro quo* in which anti-trust constraints would be lifted in return for the granting of minimal rights to the state and labour. The point is that in granting to big business an important bundle of quasi-state procedural and substantive rights, as well as offering on a plate the possibility of guaranteed profits through anti-trust immunity – and all this in return for very little – the NIRA offered the possibility of an almost unprecedented degree of control on the implementation of state policy. As a result virtually all (small business, farmers, unions, pro-planning middle classes) of the constituent parts of the New Deal coalition were unhappy with the NRA because of what they saw as business domination, and the effect of the Act was to foster 'restricted output, higher prices, reduced purchasing power and scarcity profits'.[80]

However, from the Schechter decision midway through 1935, which declared Title I of the NIRA to be unconstitutional, to the end of the Roosevelt Administration in 1945, the American state attained a degree of autonomy, power and influence separate from the interests of large capital – an autonomy that it had not possessed for nearly a century. This is clearly indicated by analysing the legitimating arguments put forward by government in defence of the New Deal. In 1933–4, the main such legitimating argument was two-pronged: first, government spokespersons hailed New Deal policy as 'bold experimentation' in contrast to the negative, inactive approach of the old regime; and second – quite clearly the defence of Title I of the NRA was in question here – not statism but 'co-operation' between businessmen, between labour and capital, between industry and agriculture, was counterposed to a discredited individualism.[81] Not far into the life of the NRA, when Roosevelt began to suspect big business of being anything but co-operative, 'co-operative action' came to refer to state action. And from the beginning of 1935 the discourse of 'neighbourliness' was replaced increasingly by an anti-business rhetoric. The new legitimating argument was two-sided. On one side, and this was to persist especially from 1936 until entry into the war, was a set of utterances in condemnation of 'vested interests', a revival of the slogans of the Progressive era which invoked the opposition of the 'people' to the 'interests'. Especially during the 1936 re-election campaign, Roosevelt spoke of 'economic autocrats' and 'captains of finance'. On the other side was a discourse of a new individualism which was also for the weak, which would be guaranteed by government and was crystallized in the 1940s in Roosevelt's call for the famous 'four freedoms' (of speech, of worship, from want, from fear), and an 'economic bill of rights'.[82] It is at this point that we should turn to whether and in what form American capitalism came to be organized at the bottom as well.

Organization at the bottom: little and late

If the codes of the National Recovery Administration were conceived with the idea of turning big business into quasi-governmental organizations, then New Deal policy from 1935 illustrated the state's relative autonomy through what Hawley has called 'counterorganizational planning', through anti-trust activities, and through unintended – and then conscious – deficit spending.[83] The planners' subsequent approach to state rationalization of the economy was rather piecemeal, and consisted mainly of promoting the organization of scattered groups whose influence in organizing markets (in comparison to the oligopolistic firms) was weak. Thus they focused their efforts at promoting labour organization through the Wagner Act, the interests of the unemployed and pensioners through social security legislation, and the interests of farmers. These 'counter-organizers' also were able to procure government aid for inefficient, sick sectors of the economy such as bituminous coal and the retail trades. The point at issue is not just that these are indicators of 'relative autonomy', but that the state itself was a key agent in promoting the organization of American capitalism at the bottom. At the same time a number of successful initiatives were launched against the perceived interests of the meso-economic companies. The Securities and Exchange legislation of 1934 which, in the face of Wall Street opposition to its attempt to counteract the concentration of investment banking, led to the stabilization of the securities markets. The late 1935 utilities regulation, which – in, for example, the Holding Company Act – was in effect an attempt to break the domination of the electrical 'power trust'. In the same vein can be seen Roosevelt's undistributed profits tax of 1936, and the appointment of activist Thurman Arnold to head the moribund Antitrust Division of the Department of Justice.[84] In 1938 the planners, who had become quite directly influenced by Keynes, and the anti-trusters entered into an alliance against the business-oriented, budget-balancing conservative Democrats.

During the Second World War the state's autonomy was reconfirmed on the level of 'civil society', by gains made by subordinate collective actors. Unemployment diminished rapidly in 1940–1 and had virtually disappeared by 1943. Working-class income improved, both absolutely and relatively. The share of the top 5 per cent of national income declined from 23.7 per cent in 1939 to 16.8 per cent in 1944. Organized labour succeeded, taking advantage of the National Labor Relations Board (created by the Wagner Act) and a tight labour market, to increase trade union membership from 9 million in 1939 to some 15 million in 1945. The moderate wing of the civil rights movement got underway, marked by A. Philip Randolph's march on Washington of 1941 and the subsequent establishment of the Fair Employment Practices Committee.[85] In the apparatus of the state itself, however – largely in exchange for support for the war effort – the power of big business began to reassert itself. Though the Congress of Industrial Organizations (CIO) proposed to contribute to the organization of war production through the creation of Industrial Councils, labour was effectively excluded from economic decision-making. The Office of Production Management was headed by William Knudsen, former General Motors president. Notwithstanding this, only with the attack on Pearl Harbor was government able to halt automobile production, and through contracts shift activity into aircraft parts, tanks and other armaments. The War Production Board, established in 1942, offered virtually no decision-making power to labour; instead a market military presence on the board was complemented by the dominance of key posts by 'one-dollar-a-year' men on loan from the largest companies. Finally – in the face of small business protests aimed at a quick restoration of competition – meso-economic power proved capable of stalling reconversion virtually until VE Day.[86]

Given the weight of the middle classes and progressivist conceptions in the development of the American welfare state – from Jane Adams' turn of the century settlement-house movement in the urban slums through the New Deal – it has come to take on a number of distinctive features. First, we should note its slowness of development. It is indeed striking that American pension insurance and other forms of social insurance followed most other countries by a generation, and that the USA is still without a federal system of family allowances and a universal system of health provision. Second, the extent and level of welfare state provision has remained inordinately low. As late as 1966 the proportion of GNP accounted for by social insurance spending was about half that in France, the Federal Republic of Germany (FRG), Sweden and the UK.[87] Partly as a corollary the ratio of social assistance to social insurance has been substantially higher in the USA than in Europe, indicating that in America welfare spending often means exclusion from, rather than inclusion into, citizenship. Having said this, it should be noted that the per capita provision of welfare resources in America is unmatched anywhere. There is a higher consumption of welfare state-*type* resources in the USA than in any other country; for example, by 1975 the percentage of national product spent on health care (not to mention absolute spending per capita on health care) was highest in the USA, while the standard of living for over 90 per cent of Aemrican pensioners has been superior to that of most European pensioners.[88]

In analysing a given welfare state it is necessary to consider whether services are provided publicly or privately, who are the recipients of welfare resources (particularly whether the distribution is two-tiered), and whether the consumption is positively or negatively redistributive. In the USA an absolutely and relatively great quantity of welfare resources have tended to be, on the one hand, privately provided, and on the other, selectively and regressively consumed. Perhaps the crucial area, in terms of the early, largely private and largely regressive provision of welfare resources in the USA, has been in education. Put plainly, the United States was about one generation behind Western Europe in the provision of social insurance legislation, but one generation ahead in the expansion of the education system. Secondary and tertiary education began their explosive expansion in the USA at about the time that Germany, the education 'leader' until the 1880s, introduced its social insurance legislation. In 1890 6.7 per cent of Americans aged 14 to 17 were already enrolled full-time in school; by 1920 this proportion had burgeoned to 32.3 per cent.[89] The explanation for this must be sought in the peculiarly American understanding of the pursuit of society's welfare and equality goals not via social insurance, but through education.[90] This American 'reading' of welfare and equality was associated with a notion of equality largely equated with social mobility and the possibility of everybody, or at least a large proportion of almost everybody's acquaintances, becoming or being in some sense, 'middle' class.

Americans believed in such a notion of equality for a number of reasons, some of which were causes, others justifications. First, the absence of a strong organized political working-class movement meant that no alternative, more collective interpretation of equality was made available to them and so they focused on equality, not of opportunity, but condition. Second, only in the United States was the existence of a large, independent farmer class so quickly superseded by the establishment of massive numbers in the service class, and in white-collar occupations more generally. It must be remembered in this context that the premature expansion of American secondary and tertiary education was a crucial condition of the early expansion of the service class, who then came to have ideal and material interests in the valuation of higher education itself and the credentialism to which it lent legitimation.[91]

In any event, what is America's *differentia specifica* is the inordinate role of social–liberal elements of the service class in the development of its welfare policy.[92] The crucial distinguishing characteristic of American organized capitalism, more generally speaking, was the existence of a strong and well-mobilized capitalist class and strong and well-mobilized middle classes; in the context of the absence of a substantial working-class movement, capital in America was organized at a very early date: financial and industrial wings were strong and interarticulated. The service class, whose condition of existence was the quick burgeoning of American higher education (see chapter 6 below), achieved a presence in the inter-war period that was not matched in Europe until the 1960s. And these new middle classes were eminently well organized. From its beginnings American political history, it might be suggested, could be conceived in terms of a succession of experiences of 'aristocracy' and 'democracy', all of course within the framework of a capitalist polity. During phases of 'aristocracy' – and this holds true for liberal, organized and disorganized capitalism – what state policy there is tends to be rather immediately aligned with the interests of the strongest groups among big business; that is, the state is highly instrumentalist. During phases of 'democracy' – the Jefferson and Jackson administration in liberal capitalism; the New Deal and arguably the Wilson administration in organized capitalism; the Kennedy and early Johnson years of disorganized capitalism – the state assumes a greater autonomy.[93] What is crucial here is that periods of 'democracy', and even periods where democratic movements unsuccessfully challenge 'aristocratic' state power, are brought about through the mobilization of political resources by the *middle* classes: first, until the turn of the century by the traditional, largely agrarian, petite bourgeoisie, and then (in organized and disorganized capitalism) by the service class and the new petite bourgeoisie. Elsewhere, the democratic challenge and the creation of state autonomy finds its relevant vehicle in organized capitalism in the working class; and only in disorganized capitalism does the service class play a comparable role. What we are arguing, then, is that 'American exceptionalism' is explicable not just through an ethnically divided and ideologically weak labour movement, but also through the existence as a political force of a prematurely sizeable service class, which at the same time as providing the most important source of opposition to the naked power of capital, functioned to spread a transformed and characteristically organized capitalist ideology of achievement and expertise which had its effects in large part at the expense of the American labour movement.

Some cross-national conclusions

In these two chapters, we have tried to sketch a panorama of the cross-national development of organized capitalism. We have attempted to establish the most significant cross-national distinction by asking the 'who?, the 'how much?', the 'where?' (top or bottom, state or civil society) and the 'why?', of the development of organized capitalism within five major western societies. In Germany and Sweden, countries which became strongly organized both at the top and the bottom, we asked the question who was the salient agent of organization. The answer was that heavy industry played a role in Germany comparable to finance in Sweden. In Britain and France we asked the question of why so little organization, and so late. This led us to discussion of how Britain was in some important ways a *Makler*, a broker or middleman, economy, and how France was slow to organize because on a number of counts it was less, and not more, economically backward than England. The USA, in contrast, became strongly organized at the top but only weakly at the bottom. The early decades of German and Swedish organized capitalism were dominated by capital goods industry, in Britain and France by consumer goods sectors, only in the USA, with its large popular markets was there a balance of the two. American banks, more than German banks, helped lay down the conditions for successful industrial capital concentration. The American national state – partly due to the absence of an étatist tradition – more than the German state, was an effective 'instrument' of business interests.

Perhaps more telling in foreshadowing comparative profiles of capitalist *dis*organization, the subject of much of the remainder of this volume, is the matter of organization at the bottom. In Germany and France it was the top itself that in a very important sense helped organize – in the development of welfare legislation and in the departure from *laissez-faire* economic policies – the bottom. In Britain it was a combination of top and bottom. In Sweden, social democracy and the trade-union movement took on these modernizing tasks, and in the USA, it was neither capital nor labour, but a set of political actors and forces drawn from the prematurely expanding service class who played a key activist role in welfare development and the partial shift from *laissez-faire*.

Probably more important is the 'how much?' and 'when?' of organization at the bottom, and here our argument is a sort of sophisticated version of Marx's famous *de te fabula narratur*. Whereas other countries became, at the bottom, organized very early on and have begun to disorganize only quite recently, the United States became organized at the bottom quite late, and not very much later at all began to disorganize. In terms of trade union membership, welfare state legislation and departure from *laissez-faire*, the USA can be said to organize no earlier than the mid-1930s. And already by the late 1940s and early 1950s – in terms of for example class voting, percentage of manual workers in trade unions, percentage of core working class among the economically active, suburbanization of working-class residence patterns – the process of disorganization seems to have begun to set in. We are not claiming simplistically that other countries will follow the American path. We maintain indeed that nations with longer and more developed periods of organization will not only disorganize more gradually than the USA, but that disorganized capitalism in these nations will remain marked by the institutional characteristics specific to each nation's previous experience of organized capitalism. We do think however that social and economic change in the United States, not because it has been the most developed *organized* capitalist nation but because it has been the least developed organized capitalist nation, does merit a good deal of scrutiny – and not least by the left – by those in other western countries.

4

Economic change and spatial restructuring (1)

We have so far described the main differences between liberal and organized capitalism in the five societies under consideration. Implicit in the change to organized capitalism were substantial transformations in the manner in which these societies were 'spatially' organized, transformations which in turn have affected the further patterning of social relations. In this and the next chapter we shall consider this issue directly, particularly as the change from organized to disorganized capitalism has brought about substantial spatial (and temporal) transformations. Our argument here is both the general one that there is in the spatial an aspect of social relationships which has been inadequately explored, and the specific one that there are particular spatial patterns associated with *each* of these phases of capitalist development. However, as we noted in chapter 1, it is also part of our objective to elucidate what it is like to be 'modern', to live in a modern age. In particular, we will examine some of the extraordinary spatial and temporal transformations in the location of work and of people, and in patterns of mobility from day to day, season to season and year to year, that substantially organize our experience of modern social life.[1]

The investigation of time and space intrudes at three different levels in any social analysis. First, empirical events are distributed *in* time–space. This is true both of the relatively routine features of everyday life and of distinct and unique social events. Second, any particular social entity (relations of production, the state, civil society, classes, etc.) is built around a particular temporal and spatial structuring. For example, the modern state is highly centralized and contains spatially and temporally transformed means of surveillance over its subject–citizens. Capitalist relations, to take another example, have become dramatically more extended. The conveyance of information and decisions and the maintenance of control whose efficiency depended on spatial proximity, has been transformed by the development of electronically transmitted information. This has enabled capitalist relations to be spatially transformed, with a functional separation of offices from workplaces and of different workplaces from each other in terms of the different labour-forces and labour processes that are employed. And third, social entities are temporally and spatially interrelated with each other, interrelationships which change over time and across space. A crucial example here concerns the changing profile of capitalist relations of production. Although the development of such relations involves the progressive commodification of space, there is an increased distance between capitalist production *per se* and civil society within parts of the disorganizing capitalist societies. In other words, capitalist production is progressively deepened and yet spatially concentrated.[2]

So, time–space occupies complex and variable relations in an appropriate analysis: first, 'empirical events' are distributed in time–space; second, social entities with causal powers are structured in terms of time–space; and third, the relationships *between* such entities are structured temporally–spatially. In short, the social world comprises a number of temporally and spatially interdependent, mutually modifying, four-dimensional time–space entities, which constitute a particularly complex 'open system', separate in part at least from physical time–space.

So far, we have not distinguished between the 'temporal' and the 'spatial', and in this we have followed post-relativity physics. However, within the analysis of the 'time–space' constitution of social systems, it is important to consider the *relative* significance of time *and* space. Marx argued that the development of capitalist relations had the effect of overcoming all spatial barriers; hence to 'annihilate space with time'.[3] Now, although this is a fundamental *objective* of capitalist production, what Marx (and some other Marxists) ignored is that this annihilation can only be achieved through the production of new, fixed and relatively immobile spatial configurations. As Harvey puts it, 'spatial organisation is necessary to overcome space'.[4] Now some of these new spatial configurations are exceptionally significant and result in the constant revolutionizing of the spatial constraints on production, or more generally, on social life and even on the distribution of 'knowledge'.[5] Such new spatial configurations, following the contradictory tendencies of 'differentiation' and 'equalization', involve three interconnected processes:

1   The tendency for capital to see-saw from place to place seeking locational advantage, resembling a plague of locusts, settling on one place, devouring it, moving on to a new place while the old restores itself for another attack.[6]
2   The tendency for capital progressively to become spatially indifferent, through reducing its dependence upon particular raw materials, markets, sources of energy, areas of the city, supplies of skilled labour, and so forth.[7]

3   The tendency for certain characteristics of labour-power (skills, cost, supply, organization, reliability) to become of heightened importance because labour-power, unlike the physical means of production, cannot be produced capitalistically and hence is not subject to the same process of geographical levelling or homogenization.[8]

The interconnections between these processes do not reduce the importance of space and place, for a number of reasons. First, relations within space are always highly constrained, since while an infinity of objects may occupy a 'point' in time, no two objects can occupy the same point in space. Although the objective of capitalist production is to annihilate space with time it cannot literally be done because new sets of social relations have to be physically extended across space and cannot simply be concentrated within a single point in space. Those new spatial configurations will in turn structure and channel emergent patterns of social life. Moreover, the effect of heightened spatial indifference has profound effects upon particular places and upon the forms of life that can be sustained within them – contemporary developments may well be heightening the salience of such localities. Also, it is important not to over-emphasize the mobility of capital. Undoubtedly labour is far less mobile than capital, but it is also clear that certain forms of managerial control depend upon there being fairly long-established patterns of social life sedimented within particular places, and that people's commitment to those particular spaces are part of the conditions under which the forms of control by capital are sustained.[9]

We have so far made out a fairly general case for the importance of the analysis of space. It is now necessary to examine the interconnections between the social and the spatial more carefully.[10] It is useful to begin here by making the distinction between, on the one hand, those relations between social phenomena which are external to one another and which are therefore 'contingent' and, on the other hand, those relations which are necessary and hence internal to the phenomenon in question.[11] The former consist of those relations where the objects in question do not stand in any necessary relationship with each other, and where they can exist independent of each and of the relationship between them. The latter, by contrast, consist of those relations which are necessary for the very existence of the objects; such objects cannot exist without such relations. An example of the former would be the employment by a firm of workers from one particular town; an example of the latter would be the relations between landlord and tenant, neither 'object' being able to exist without those connecting relations. What then of 'space'? How does space relate to this distinction between necessary and contingent relations?

We will begin here with capitalist relations of production, which can be summarized as follows:

1   There are capitalist relations of production which are *necessary* or internal and which operate on diverse spatial scales.

2 There are particular agents who happen *contingently* to bear one function or the other.

3 Given that particular agents will function as labour-power or as capital, then it is *necessary* for these agents to be spatially proximate.

4 No necessary spatial division of labour will develop since industrial and commercial capital appropriates space in different ways; which develops is partly *contingent* on location of raw materials, physical constraints, relative transport costs, changes in labour supply, skill, and organizational levels, etc., and on the changing importance of these different factors.

5 There are *necessary* laws of the capitalist economy which constrain the possible form taken by the spatial division of labour; but the recent development of these necessary laws means that it is a relatively *contingent* matter as to where capitalist relations will in fact be found and hence which particular labourers in which particular localities will be employed by capital.

6 Since it is *necessarily* the case that individual sellers of labour-power act as subjects possessing a consciousness or a will, there have to be social practices within which those subjectivities are developed and sustained.

7 It is *necessarily* the case that these practices are structured by the commodity relations generated from the overarching capitalist relations; but the form taken by those practices depends upon various *contingencies*, such as the degree to which pre-capitalist associations and structures persist, the location and nature of the housing stock, the struggles by individuals and groups to extend or protect those practices, the relations of gender domination and racial oppression, etc.

In order to account for the social structure of a given society, the inter-connections between these various necessary and contingent relations must be deciphered: a project which so far has not been realized. A starting-point for analysis is given by Massey when she argues that 'the social and economic structure of any given local area will be a complex result of the combination of that area's succession of roles within the series of wider, national and international divisions of labour.'[12] In the following we take it that the social and economic structure of a society is the complex result of the combination of that society's succession of roles within the series of wider, national and international divisions of labour; of the combination of spatial–temporal relations which characterize 'civil society' and the 'state'; and of the spatial–temporal relations between these diverse social objects, each of which is spatially–temporally structured. We will initially consider six important forms taken by the spatial divisions of labour.[13]

1 *Regional specialization*: up to the inter-war period many industrial sectors were characterized by a high degree of specialization within particular regions (in Britain, for example, cotton textiles and textile machinery within

Lancashire; mining and shipbuilding within the north-east; woollen manufacture within West Yorkshire, and so on.

2   *Regional dispersal*: other sectors are characterized by a high degree of dispersal with relatively little concentration in specific regions. Obviously 'consumer services' mostly take this form, as well as some 'producer services' and certain manufacturing industries such as food-processing, shoe production, etc. Labour reductions in this case will take the form of 'intensification', that is, relatively uniform cutbacks spread throughout the different regions.

3   *Functional separation* between management/research and development in the 'centre', skilled labour in old manufacturing centres, and unskilled labour in the 'periphery'.

4   *Functional separation* between management/research and development in the 'centre', and semiskilled and unskilled labour in the 'periphery' (this example is found in the electrical engineering and electronics industry).

5   *Functional separation* between management/research and development and skilled labour in a 'central' economy, and unskilled labour in a 'peripheral' economy.

6   *Division* between one or more areas which are characterized by investment, technical change and expansion, and other areas where unchanged and progressively less competitive production continues with resulting job losses. The former may involve the development of new products as well as new means of producing existing products.

As already noted, we should not analyse a given area purely as the product of a single form of the spatial division of labour. To do so, as Sayer points out, is to 'collapse all the historical results of several interacting "spatial divisions of labour" into the rather misleading term which suggests some simple unitary empirical trend'.[14] Rather, any such area is 'economically' the overlapping and interdependent product of a number of these spatial divisions of labour and attendant forms of industrial restructuring.

In analysing such transformations it is clear that a centrally important change has concerned the growth of very large corporations. Indeed although we will see that one important feature of modern disorganized capitalism has been a tendency both for average plant size to decline and for some increase in the number of small enterprises, this does not mean that large enterprises are not increasingly significant for the overall organization of western capitalism. In order, though, to understand the mechanisms involved here, it is necessary to present an ideal-typical representation of the way that firms develop in the three stages of capitalist society.[15] This is set out diagrammatically in figure 4.1.

In the first stage (A), liberal capitalism, all firms were small and there were high birth and death rates of companies. Firms operated at the local or at most at the regional level. There was only one pattern of corporate development.

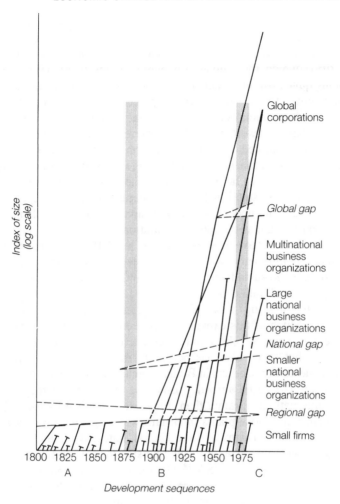

Figure 4.1   Growth paths of firms in different stages of capitalist development
Source: Taylor and Thrift, 'Models of Corporate Development', p. 24

In the second stage (B), organized capitalism, three kinds of enterprise had developed: the small firm, which statistically was unlikely to grow into one much larger; the regional national company, which sometimes developed multinationally; and the multinational company, which expanded 'mono-centrically' so that the parent company kept tight control over foreign subsidiaries and branches (normally known as a mother–daughter relationship). In each case capital was nationally owned and clearly tied into the fortunes of the country in which it was owned and to which it was indissolubly bound.

In the third stage (C), disorganized capitalism, a further kind of enterprise is to be found. This results from some developing a 'polycentric' structure as their subsidiaries operate more independently and a multidivisional organizational pattern emerges. Certain of these polycentric multinationals develop into the crucially important 'global corporations' as they take over other firms which themselves are operating multinationally, firms often producing quite different products and based on different industrial processes. The attachment to any single economy becomes more tentative, as capital expands (and contracts) on a global basis. A much more complex spatial division of labour develops in which different parts of different production processes are separated off and develop within different national economies, depending, in part at least, on relative wage rates and worker organization. The spatial division of labour, which in the earlier phases results from the unplanned patterns established by a considerable number of legally separated enterprises, becomes under disorganized capitalism a largely planned development *internal* to the vast global corporation.

The changes here have been momentous. In 1950, 76 per cent of the leading 180 American multinationals and 86 per cent of the leading 135 European multinationals had subsidiary networks in only six countries or less. By 1970 these figures had fallen to 5 per cent and 23 per cent respectively, as corporations pursuing a world-wide strategy expanded into dozens of countries.[16] Much of this expansion has been into other western economies as there has been a substantial interpenetration of capital across those economies, but much also has been into the Third World. By 1980, for example, one million workers in British manufacturing industry were employed by multinationals based abroad.[17] Likewise the recent strategy of ICI (now dubbed 'International', rather than 'Imperial' Chemical Industries) has been to rationalize and close plants in Britain while opening up new productive capacity in West Germany and the United States. By 1985, 60 per cent of ICI's world-wide assets were located outside the UK and 20 per cent of its shares were owned in the USA.[18] The massive expansion of the new international division of labour has partly stemmed from the establishment of 'world-market factories' in various 'free production zones' offering all sorts of exemptions, reliefs, preferential rates, tax holidays and the like.[19] Partly also it has stemmed from the more general attractiveness of low-cost production possibilities in a wide range of Third World countries. For example, Phillips' employment outside Western Europe and the USA rose from zero in 1964 to 13 per cent in 1970 and 19 per cent in 1976.[20] More generally, between 1972 and 1977 there was a marked increase in overseas production by the largest 200 multinationals: the proportion rose from 25.3 per cent to 30.7 per cent as what Lipietz terms 'peripheral Fordism' became established on a wide scale.[21] Clarke shows that by 1980 over 50 per cent of employment in the international chemicals industry was accounted for by global rather than merely multinational corporations.[22] The development of globalization of production adds a major new element in the structuring of capitalist production, and is a crucial source of its disorganization.

Turning now to civil society, this can be analysed in terms of a number of different dimensions, each of which has implications for its spatial structuring. The following are some of the relevant dimensions.

(1) The degree to which the existing *built environment* can be transformed. The given environment represents a freezing of the past, as both capitalism's 'crowning glory' and its 'prison'. The construction of a new 'built environment' (such as nineteenth-century towns, new towns, suburbanization, etc.) permits a restructuring of civil society. The development of new 'created spaces' will allow novel civil societies to emerge which are freed from ties to particular 'localities'. A good example of this was the development in the USA after 1890, of suburbs away from the 'facts of production', signalling a move towards the Arcadian ideal of ruralized living on the edge of the city.[23] This was an indication of class weakness on the part of the bourgeoisie, who were unable to enforce a system for controlling industry and the working class other than by constructing a new 'created space' on the margins of the existing frozen past. At the same time, however, suburbs have been actively developed because of their small scale, their social and political independence, and their ability to confer heightened status.

(2) The degree to which there is *integration* of the social relations of civil society into the wider capitalist economy, depending in particular on the distinctive mode of consumption characterizing particular classes, nations or other social groupings. To take one example, there is variation in the extent to which the domestic property market assumes a 'capitalistic' character. Agnew suggests that in Britain the 'home' is mainly regarded as a use-value and not as an investment with potential exchange-value.[24] This is in contrast to the USA, where the high levels of geographical mobility, the pronouncements of state agencies, the emphasis within popular culture, and the lack of regional land-use planning laws, all reinforce the notion that the home (the cell-form of civil society) is a capitalist commodity to be acquired and disposed of in a manner broadly similar to any other commodity.

(3) The degree to which more generally the social relations within civil society are based on the *local community* rather than on either commodity relations or the state. Where the local community is the basis, this involves sets of social relations which are multiplex (neighbours who are workmates who are leisure-time companions etc.), where 'everyone knows everyone else' and where these sets are organized into a locally structured and delimited system. Such community supports faster bonds of trust, friendship and reciprocity within that local civil society, even if this is a 'mutuality of the oppressed'. Market transactions within such a place-bound community are indelibly suffused by considerations of long-term reciprocity and community. Interactions occur within a given physical setting, and one's living space is necessarily personalized, particularized and non-directly commodifiable. Such a community-based civil society, described here in its ideal-typical form, is

based upon mutuality and reciprocity, locally derived criteria of power and status (such as patriarchy), and non-maximizing economic behaviour. It provides a considerable insulation from the commodity relations of a capitalist economy and from the 'capitalist production of a mode of consumption'.[25]

(4) The degree to which there is a *heterogeneity* of class experiences based upon the distinctive characteristics of particular communities, places of work or kinship relations. Cox, however, argues that mass education and the mass media have both undermined such class heterogeneity; Seabrook argues that there is increased homogenization across classes: 'The consciousness of many young people. . .has been fashioned, not by work, not by place, not by kinship, but by a homogeneous culture of shops, images and *réclame*. . . .A freely chosen sameness?'[26]

(5) The degree of *spatial concentration* of different social classes or other social forces. In Italy, for example, Paci points out that the working-class concentration in the north is higher than in almost any other area in Europe and may explain why Italy has one of the strongest communist parties in the West.[27] One important development, especially in the past few decades, has been the shift of both employment and of the population out of the formerly heavily industrialized urban conurbations. The movement of population has been permitted by the growth of widespread private transport and by the development of cities as labour pools, as particular, localized civil societies. As a consequence, individual households of at least the 'central' working class are able to choose where their labour-power is to be reproduced. One important dimension within civil society has been a return to 'nature', a desire to get closer to the 'natural', and this is in part reflected in the urbanization of the rural.

(6) The degree to which either local or national civil societies are *vertically* organized; that is, when diverse social groupings and voluntary and informal associations are specific to particular classes and there are relatively few independent organizations.[28] By contrast, civil society can be said to be horizontally organized when there are a large number of social grouping and other social practices which are non-class-specific and which generate relatively autonomous forms of organization and representation.

(7) The degree to which local civil societies are *long established*, with inter-generationally reproduced and sedimented patterns of life and cultural forms. This will obviously be undermined by a range of factors, including certain forms of economic restructuring as already described, and by the related transformations of civil society through rapid in- or out-migration.

These spatial (and partly temporal) structurings of the division of labour and of the civil society in a given nation-state have profound effects upon the capacities of different social groups to enter into and to sustain forms of collective action. To illustrate our argument, the following are the minimal conditions necessary for a working class in one of the western nations to be organized as a class-for-itself.

1   There are a number of spatially-specific but overlapping and class-based 'collectivities-in-struggle' in which there are shared and long-established experiences at work and/or through residential propinquity and/or through kinship, which facilitate the establishment of 'dialogue', so that workers are able to express, to debate, and to form collective identities that would minimize the costs of engaging in collective action.[29]

2   The spatially separated experiences of different groups of workers can each be viewed as representing the experiences of the whole class within a given nation-state. This depends upon a wide number of local 'civil societies' (often within a region) being structured by class division between capital and labour rather than by more complex class/status divisions or by the division between the people versus the state. Minimally in each locality this implies that (a) there is a degree of residential differentiation between classes and (b) those residentially differentiated classes are nevertheless spatially adjacent.

3   Other collectivities within local 'civil societies' are organized in ways which either reinforce these class divisions or are at least central to them. Collective action is thus more likely the more that civil society is organized on a 'vertical' basis in which there are few social groupings and other social practices which are non-class-specific.

4   Gains and benefits (such as higher incomes, lower prices, increased educational and other opportunities, improved housing, better conditions of work, and so on) are thought to be, and in fact are, unavailable except through collective action of a broadly class-based sort. This condition will be more likely to be met where social inequalities result from a nationally based system of class relations, in which in a clear sense class relations *produce* the major divisions of social inequality.

5   A substantial proportion of workers within a variety of spatial locations conclude that class actions *can* be successful and are therefore worth pursuing even if they do not immediately produce successful results. They conclude also, that residential and work patterns are such that levels of participation and the sustaining of the class's cultural resources mean that success is not to be judged in quantitative terms.

BRITAIN

We will now consider how these changes were reflected in the temporal and spatial restructuring of British society. In conducting such an analysis it is important not to suggest that there was anything like an unchanging 'traditional' society which was then simply transformed by industrial and urban developments. However, Bairoch shows that before industrialization levels of inequality both between regions and between different countries were very limited. He suggests that the income gap between the poorest and richest countries was certainly smaller than the ratio of 1:2 and was probably more like 1:1.5.[30] That was soon to change dramatically as a result of the transformations which were initiated in Britain.

The growth of industrial workshops and later of factories initially occurred in Britain outside London in previously rural areas and in smaller settlements: in Lancashire, the West Riding of Yorkshire, the 'Black Country', Northumberland and Durham, the East Midlands, Kent, South Wales and so on. Indeed, increased rural prosperity in the eighteenth century also combined to reverse a centuries-long process of urban population concentration in the largest cities. What has been called the 'new urbanization' of 1750–1800 was disproportionately the result of the growth of smaller cities and the addition of new cities to the system.[31] This new urbanization was thus an urban growth from below which produced the first concentrated wave of new city formation since the thirteenth century. De Vries[32] summarizes these developments:

> many smaller cities with resource-based industries such as metallurgy grew as a consequence of technological innovation, and many rural places that had grown thick with people as protoindustrial textile production spread in the preceding era broke through to become industrial cities as technological change encouraged factory organization.

Clearly, then, in many rural areas there was both an extensive process of proto-industrialization and of the growth of a widespread 'proletariat' which did not primarily work in agriculture.[33] Tilly concludes that in Britain, just as in much of Europe, there was a 'substantial industrialization through the multiplication of small producing units and modest capital concentrations over the territory of rural regions'.[34] There was, then, a substantial process of rural industrialization prior to 1800 and this occurred mainly through the employment of rural labour. What then happened was a process of de-industrialization within some rural areas as industry (especially factories) became concentrated in certain smaller towns that grew very rapidly. In those regions which did not experience nineteenth-century industrialization, they were ironically *more* agriculturally based in 1900 than they had been in the previous couple of centuries.[35]

The industrialization in the nineteenth century produced a massive urbanization in Britain. In 1801 one-fifth of the population lived in towns; by 1901 four-fifths did. Apart from London, which grew from 1 million to 7 million over the course of the century, most of this expansion occurred in the Midlands, the north, Wales and Scotland. London was important, not in housing much of this growing industry, nor in financing it, but in providing a major and rapidly expanding market. The German economist, Friedrich List, noted in the nineteenth century that London was a centre for an internationalized cosmopolitan mercantile capitalism and as such had little interest in the national industry-based economy.[36]

As a result of this unique development, of incredibly rapid urban growth of an unprecedented sort, there were extremely high levels of poverty, over-crowding and ill-health to be found within the new towns.[37] In Liverpool, for example, one-sixth of the population lived in 'underground cellars'; elsewhere back-to-back housing was common. There were no public spaces of parks, squares and gardens, and rivers were used as open sewers (hence London's Great Stink in 1858). These cities grew up with very little planning, before the growth of nationally organized professional experts, of sanitary engineers, medical inspectors of health, civil engineers, social workers, town planners and so on. Builders, interested in short-term profit maximization, constructed as many dwellings as possible on each acre of building land, which were not conducive to effective communications and other infrastructural services.

Most of the housing in the typical 'Coketown' (as in Dickens' *Hard Times*) followed the distribution of new workshops and factories, and as a result there was a fairly high degree of residential segregation by class. This pattern was well summarized in *The Economist*[38] in 1857:

> Society is tending more and more to spread into classes – and not merely classes but localised classes, class colonies . . . It is not in London merely, nor as a matter of business and in consequence of the 'division of labour' that this happens . . . there is a much deeper social principle involved in the present increasing tendency to class colonies. It is the disposition to associate with equals – in some measure with those who have similar practical *interests*, in still greater measure with those who have similar tastes and culture, most of all with those with whom we judge ourselves on a moral equality, whatever our real standard may be.

In Birmingham, for example, the strongly working-class area of Ladywood grew very rapidly, from under 10,000 in 1841 to over 40,000 in 1871, while adjacent to it was Edgbaston, sometimes known as 'Birmingham's Belgravia', which was described in the *Edgbastonian* as the 'favourite place of residence for the professional man, merchants and traders of the busy town which it adjoins'.[39] It is important to note further in Birmingham that there was a substantial residentially separated 'merchant class' which partly blurred the class divisions between employers and workers. In Sheffield, by contrast, there was a much smaller merchant class, although there was considerable residential segregation between employers and workers.[40] This pattern of segregation was also to be found in mid-Victorian Liverpool and Merthyr, although Leeds appears to have been less residentially segregated.[41]

One of the central features of liberal capitalism was that both enterprises and individuals were distributed through space by the workings of a relatively unorganized set of market processes. The distributions of both industry and population were unorganized. Towns and cities grew at incredibly fast rates and out of control. Local structures of regulation and direction were unable to cope. As Calhoun argues, the liberal capitalism of late eighteenth- and early nineteenth-century Britain involved 'the breakdown of the structure of hierarchical incorporation which knit local communities into the society as a whole'.[42] this was because the existing patterns of political and social control had been appropriate to agrarian capitalism, and to small-scale commodity production. Such political and social organization had been organized through networks of clients, kin and friends, and focused on the country houses of the aristocracy.[43] It was quite unable to cope with the massive growth of industry and particularly the development of enormous towns and cities. Visitors to Manchester, for example, constantly remarked on the vast noisy crowds whether going to and from work, shopping, or celebrating some public event. There was a general concern for establishing new forms of order and discipline. Although the aristocracy often owned large tracts of land in the new urban/industrial areas, these were not amenable to the same patterns of direction and control which had been possible in the 'old corruption' of rural society. As early as 1851 the urban population had overtaken that to be found in rural areas and social and political power came to be exercised by dissenting manufacturers, by national bodies of professional experts, and initially by groups of the newly urbanized working class.

Thus, one of the effects of economic, demographic and spatial transformation was to produce 'self-regulating working-class communities' in the newly developing urban/industrial centres, communities which were relatively autonomous of either the old or new incorporating institutions of the wider society. In the early part of the century there were two main forms taken by such communities. First, there were the relatively small, homogeneous villages or small towns where propinquity ensured frequent interaction, and the small size led to a high density and multiplexity of bonds; and second, there were the communities of urban artisans in which common craft and workplace relations sustained community sentiment.[44] Calhoun argues that the populations that were able to mobilize for collective action in early nineteenth-century England were these locally based communities organized around the village, the town, or the craft. Collective action involved the defence of these communities against the threat implied by the processes of economic and social change. Calhoun argues that collective action was more likely in those towns based on small pre-industrial communities, with more male, better-paid workers fairly evenly divided between spinning and weaving, and working in smaller factories.[45] Smith argues in his comparative study of Sheffield and Birmingham that it was in the former that the craft unions were able to maintain a much higher degree of artisan autonomy and strength.[46] The craft unions established self-regulating working-class communities that were much better at resisting the increasingly significant activities of 'modern' national organizations of an organized capitalism. By the election of 1885, Sheffield had developed a clear voting pattern based on the class composition of different housing areas; and this was the first case of political difference resulting from residentially segregated housing patterns based on class.[47]

We saw in chapter 2 that in certain respects organized capitalism in Britain did not develop at the top until the inter-war period. Until then industry remained dominated by relatively small family firms; real mergers were infrequent and holding companies more common; there was little growth of financial institutions investing in British manufacturing industry; managerial hierarchies and new managerial practices developed relatively little; and multi-plant firms were fairly uncommon.[48] Until the inter-war period, British capitalism remained relatively unorganized; the visible hand of organization and management had not yet replaced the invisible hand of the market. Moreover, the rapid growth of towns in Britain seems to have reinforced this concentration of market processes and led to further urban development as more 'distributional' functions (as well as infrastructural features such as gas works and telephone exchanges) came to be concentrated within the large and expanding urban agglomerations.[49] Four general points should be noted:

1 Since British industrial capitalism developed after a long period of mercantile capitalism, there was already available widespread marketing expertise and systems of organization.
2 When industrial capitalism did develop, it did so in a spatially concentrated form which permitted the further development of efficient marketing arrangements.
3 Market mechanisms within these agglomerations remained relatively successful at co-ordinating resources, either for local sales or for export to the closed markets of the Empire.
4 Firms did not need to merge and to form complex administrative structures – they remained as single units based in particular urban centres and it was the invisible hand that effected co-ordination.

By the time that organized capitalism at the top developed in Britain there were a number of important features of its spatial organization. First, a fairly clear set of regional economies had developed based upon particular products: cotton textiles and textile machinery in the north-west; coalmining and steelmaking in South Wales; agriculture in East Anglia; mining, shipbuilding and related heavy industry in the north; and so on. Most regions had a fairly significant coefficient of specialization of around 0.2 (complete specialization is given by a figure of 1.0 and complete diversification by 0).[50] For example, while agriculture only employed 7.8 per cent of the labour force nationally, its share was two to four times as high in East Anglia, Northern Ireland and the south-west. Nationally, just over one-third of all jobs were in manufacturing, while its share was nearly one-half in the north-west, West Midlands and Yorkshire. These economic differences in turn helped to generate distinctive political cultures in some regions. For example, there was a set of interdependent economic, social and political processes which served to produce and to reinforce distinctively 'radical regions', such as that of South Wales, while other regions seem to have developed distinctively conservative or deferential political cultures.[51] As a result of the increasingly class-organized character of different regions, considerable spatial variation in the voting patterns for different political parties came to develop. Hobson, referring to the 1910 general election, concluded:[52]

> A line drawn across Great Britain along the Mersey and the Trent shows an overwhelming majority of Liberal and Labour seats in the northern section, an almost equally overwhelming majority of Unionist seats in the southern section, if Wales be left out of the account.

In the case of the northern section, he explained[53] that

> Where industrialism is most highly organised and most concentrated, upon the great coalfields of Lancashire and Yorkshire, Derbyshire, Northumberland and Durham, not to mention South Wales, the greatest intensity of Liberalism and Labourism prevails. The textile, machine-making and mining constituencies yielded almost the largest Liberal majorities, infecting with their views even most of the semi-agricultural constituencies in their near neighbourhood...The Liberalism and Labourism of the North is mainly dependent on the feelings and opinions of this upper grade of the wage-earners...this artisan element.

A further feature of organized capitalism was the accelerating physical expansion of large towns and their increasing influence over the adjacent countryside.[54] Over 4 million houses were built between the wars and by 1939 one-third of all British houses were less than 20 years old. There was also a slowdown in the increase of population in the industrial areas of the north of England, Scotland and Wales. Towns and cities in the southern half of the country increased in population, while many of the industrial towns outside that region showed relative or absolute falls in population. Partly, this resulted from migration. Between 1921 and 1951, for example, the south-east gained more than an extra million people through migration from other parts of Britain. In the same period northern England lost about one million. The areas around London grew considerably in population throughout the inter-war period. They also had higher proportions of managerial and pro-fessional jobs than other parts of the country. This was a period in which there was a widespread growth of suburbs, although most employment remained concentrated in city centres. As a result, there was an increased separation between the place of work and the home. This led to the develop-ment of widespread commuting, of the importance of improved public transport and of increased isolation for the homebound housewife.

Finally, one of the major effects of the development of organized capitalism was to bring about a growing conflict between the local and national levels. This can be seen in the case of locally organized municipalities, which were increasingly subjected to nationally organized professions and bureaucratic structures;[55] and it was also true of much locally based plant bargaining that became increasingly governed by regional and national bargaining procedures.

We will now turn to consider the spatial transformations which begin in Britain in the 1960s. It is from that decade that one can note an array of inter-connected processes which disorganize or literally deconstruct social and political life in modern Britain. Clearly, one major factor lying behind these changes has been the collapse of employment in manufacturing industry – this fell from 8 million in 1971 to 5.5 million in 1984.[56] Between 1979 and 1981 an extraordinary 1 million such jobs disappeared. Since 1970, while most economies experienced a pattern of job-less growth in manufacturing industry, Britain first experienced a similar period of job-less growth, then one of job-destroying zero growth, and finally one of job-destroying industrial decline. Manufacturing has become less and less significant in the total of economic activity in Britain; by 1980 manufacturing output represented only 26 per cent of GDP.[57]

At the same time, service employment has grown considerably, from 11.3 million in 1971 to 13.3 million in 1984: a considerable increase but 1 million less than the fall in manufacturing employment over the same period.[58] There has also been a considerable increase in part-time working in service industry. By 1984 about half of all women in service industry worked part-time, this figure having increased from 45 per cent in 1980.[59]

At the same time as there have been these very general developments, there have been extensive changes in the location of population. The most significant feature here is that the population in the major cities was either static or growing slightly during the 1950s, but then began to decline during the 1960s and 1970s. Britain by 1971, 'was amongst the most advanced of these nations experiencing decentralization and deconcentration', and this tendency con-tinued during the 1970s.[60] The development of counter-urbanization has, in part, offset the long-established drift to the south, which had been a feature of demographic change in Britain since the 1920s. Although some of the regions in the south (East Anglia, the south-west) have grown rapidly, the popula-tion in the south-east region itself fell between 1971 and 1981.[61] This resulted particularly from the dramatic decline in the population of London – that in inner London fell by 17.7 per cent, while some boroughs lost more than 20 per cent of their 1971 population. Elsewhere, Manchester and Liverpool lost 17 per cent and 16 per cent respectively. Other very large losses were suffered by Birmingham, Bristol, Hull, Leeds, Newcastle, Nottingham, Portsmouth, Sheffield and Southampton. Between 1961 and 1981 the popula-tion of the six largest conurbations fell by 2 million. This was not however a process which only affected the inner cities, since many suburban areas in these large cities also suffered considerable population loss (for example, outer London, the suburbs, lost 5 per cent, 1971–81). And this pattern of population loss also affected many smaller cities and towns, such as Middlesborough, Brighton, Preston, Reading and York.

Since there was also a small increase in population nationally between 1971 and 1981, there were substantial gains in areas outside the cities. The strongest gains were recorded in a wide arc of districts stretching from the Wash to the Solent, in almost all of East Anglia, in the south-west, in rural and north Wales, in the non-conurbation parts of Yorkshire and in the less urbanized areas of Scotland. There was thus a centrifugal movement from cities to surrounding satellite towns and rural areas. There has indeed been a spectacular renaissance of rural areas, beginning, it seems, between 1966 and 1971.[62] Growing population rather than 'rural depopulation' is now a general feature of such areas.

This relates to the shift in the location of industry in Britain. Fothergill and Gudgin argue that recent patterns of employment change in Britain do not reflect the simple shift from north to south, nor does it reflect the industrial structure of different regions, since for them, 'industrial structure has become more or less irrelevant as an explanation of disparities in regional growth'.[63] Rather, they emphasize the fact that all the areas experiencing major employment loss between 1959 and 1975 contained a major conurbation, while many of the areas that gained employment in the same period were 'rural'. This pattern was particularly marked in the case of manufacturing industry.

Table 4.1 indicates the contrasting experience of different regions, showing that the more 'rural' the region, the greater the gain in manufacturing employment between the 1950s and the 1970s. The percentages should be treated with some caution because of the relatively small numbers employed in the regions of East Anglia and the south-west. However, two points are important to note.

Table 4.1 Manufacturing employment change by region 1952–79

Region	Percentage
East Anglia	+ 70.3
South-west	+ 25.7
Wales	+ 17.5
East Midlands	+ 11.4
North	+ 7.8
West Midlands	− 7.8
South-east	− 9.9
Yorkshire & Humberside	− 13.7
Scotland	− 18.4
North-west	− 24.5
Northern Ireland	− 27.4
UK	− 7.8

Source: Fothergill and Gudgin, Unequal Growth, p. 17.

First, there is a very dramatic change in direction in the location of manufacturing industry away from the pattern which was characteristic of organized
capitalism. Second, the investigation of the experience of sub-regions reveals
a similar patterning of employment change, namely an inverse relationship
between the size of settlement and growth in manufacturing employment. The
greater the settlement size, the faster the decline in employment, especially
in manufacturing industry. This is connected with the fact that the larger the
city, the higher the rate of plant closure and of losses through plant contraction,
and the lower the rates of new firm formation, of expansion of surviving firms
and of profitability. These relationships appear to hold irrespective of corporate
status. Table 4.2 summarizes the main features.[64]

Table 4.2   Manufacturing employment change by type of area 1959–75

Type of area	Percentage
London	− 37.8
Conurbations	− 15.9
Free-standing cities	+ 4.8
Industrial towns	+ 16.3
County towns	+ 28.8
Rural areas	+ 77.2
Britain	− 5.2

Source: Fothergill and Gudgin, Unequal Growth, p. 22.

It is also clear that in the 1970s this tendency has characterized all the major
economies in Western Europe, particularly the EEC countries, although this
appears to be more marked for manufacturing output than for manufacturing
employment.[65] Moreover, this pattern is not explicable in simple 'structural'
terms. Keeble, Owens and Thompson note that it is far from the case that
it is the highly urbanized regions which exhibit an historic bias towards older,
declining industries.[66] Rather, it is these very regions which stand out as
enjoying the most favourable structures, with a marked absolute and relative
bias towards more modern industries. And yet it is those which have declined
the fastest.

The changing spatial distribution of both industry and population in the
UK since the 1960s reflect a number of interrelated processes, partly involving
changes in the 'spatial division of labour', partly resulting from a variety of
state policies, and partly derived from a restructuring of civil society.[67]
These processes include:

1   The increased geographical mobility of firms enabling them to spread more
    widely as goods have become less bulky, less dependent on the location

of raw material/energy sources, and transport has radically improved and transport costs have fallen relatively.

2 An increased ability of firms to subdivide their operations and to situate them in different places, often in different countries, so taking advantage of relatively small differences in the characteristics of different locations.

3 The existence of rural labour reserves in both the First and Third World with few other competitors for labour, and where the labour will be relatively 'green' and not strongly unionized.

4 Limitations on the possibilities of expanding plants in existing urban areas, because of the structure of old buildings, congestion, inappropriate transport, labour organization etc. This factor is particularly heightened by increased capital-intensity of production.

5 The policy of 'urban containment', especially as stipulated in the 1947 Town and Country Planning Act. The expansion of urban areas in the 1930s was considered undesirable, and it was thought necessary to restrict the growth of cities and to disperse populations into various new towns. At the same time, many of the inner-city slums were knocked down and so in a sense a proportion of the growing post-war population was obliged to move out of the central urban areas.

6 A strong emphasis placed on the development of owner-occupation, particularly by the Conservative Party. This resulted in the doubling of owner-occupied houses between 1947 and 1973. However, there was relatively little housing available for purchase within inner city areas, especially as the desirable parts of the central areas of cities were 'redeveloped' generally for offices.

7 The Labour Party's housing policy emphasized the development of council estates, generally on the edge of cities or within the various new towns where land was much cheaper. The population of council housing rose from 13 per cent to 31 per cent between 1947 and 1973.

8 The widespread growth of private transport, which has enabled men in particular to commute substantial distances to their places of work.

9 A very strong emphasis has been placed upon the desirability of living in suburban or semi-rural contexts, particularly because they appeared to provide a more desirable environment away from the areas of high crime, racial tension, high accident risks etc.[68]

Thus, for a number of reasons there have been some marked tendencies towards decentralization of industry, employment and population out of major urban centres and urbanized areas. Scott summarizes the processes as follows:[69]

the mutually reinforcing multiplier effect whereby the decentralization of industry helps to beget the decentralization of population has proceeded very far indeed, and nowhere more so, it seems, than in the large British conurbations.

We noted above that a key feature of organized capitalism was the development of distinct regional economies and identifiable regional civil societies. To some extent, those regionally-generated entities have remained of some importance in terms of a regional social consciousness, at least in relatively deprived areas like the north-east.[70] But in terms of recent demographic change and patterns of spatial restructuring, processes are now much less obviously organized *within* regions, and this is for a number of interconnected reasons:

(1) Around the time of the First World War, most regions were economically fairly specialized, particularly Northern Ireland, the north, Wales and East Anglia. But by the 1970s all regions had become more diversified, with relatively low concentrations of particular industrial sectors. There has been a considerable decline in the degree to which circuits of capital are focused upon particular regional economies; some sections of capital are able to take advantage of local variations in the price, supply, skills and organizations of each local labour force although they are not necessarily footloose.[71]

(2)   Local variations have become much more significant in explaining long-term employment change; according to Fothergill and Gudgin, 'there are much greater contrasts within any region than between the regions themselves'.[72] Even in 1966 only two regions appeared to possess a regional industrial structure; and yet in the case of one of them, the north-west, there were extraordinary variations in a number of centrally significant economic indicators: unemployment rates, the ratio of male:female employment, percentage changes in male/female employment, and so on.[73]

(3) Recent population trends show a similar pattern; as Kennett notes, the 'intra-regional shifts of population have been shown to overwhelm inter-regional contrasts'.[74] The centrifugal movement from cities has spilled across relatively arbitrary regional boundaries. Demographic change is not the result of regional patterns, or even of the simple contrast between northern and southern regions.

(4) The massive growth of service employment within the total employment pattern which is fairly evenly distributed has undermined the distinctiveness of particular regional economies, except in the case of the south-east, in which two-fifths of all UK service employment is to be found.[75]

(5) Processes of de-industrialization have affected all manufacturing sectors and all regions and this had had the effect that 'Previous differences between growing and declining industries, and hence between growing and declining regions, have narrowed considerably, if not disappeared.'[76]

We will now consider some of the main effects of these developments on the organization of individual enterprises in Britain. Firstly, we have already noted how the modern multinational corporation possesses a larger number of individual manufacturing plants. Prais notes that the 100 largest enterprises in Britain averaged 27 plants in 1958, and this had risen to 72 in 1972.[77] At the same time, the average number of employees per plant fell from 750 in 1958 to 430 in 1972.[78] Over the same period there has been an increase in the number of enterprises employing under 100 workers. (Table 4.3.)

Table 4.3   Number of establishments in UK manufacturing industry employing over 1000 and under 100 workers

Year	No. of plants	
	employing more than 1000 workers	employing less than 100 workers
1958	1128	78676
1968	1198	77793
1970	1233	75041
1975	1087	92795
1978	1049	97223
1981	776[a]	99303

[a] This figure is based on the 1980 Standard Industrial Classification.
Sources: Historical Record of Census of Production 1907–1970 Census of Production 1978, 1981. Compiled by the Business Statistics Office. Further information: telephone 0633–81 2973.

The growth in the number of smaller plants reverses the patterning found during the period of organized capitalism in Britain. The Bolton Committee on small firms reported that the number of manufacturing enterprises employing under 2000 employees fell from 135,000 in 1935 to 60,000 in 1963.[79] But here too there has been a reversal. Since the early 1970s it has been found, for example by Fothergill and Gudgin in the East Midlands and by Storey in northern England, that employment in manufacturing firms, many of which were new, grew during the 1970s.[80] One obvious reason for the increased employment significance of small firms in the national economy has been the massive job loss experienced by large plants. But there have also it seems been increases in the rate of *new* firms formation (although this often also occurs in recessions). To assess this, one can examine the registrations of all types of firm for the payment of value-added tax (VAT). The number of firms still registered at the end of each year has risen from 1,158,156 in 1973 to 1,241,325 in 1978, to 1,375,866 in 1981.[81] Likewise the number of new company registrations rose from 40,000 in 1971 to over 85,000 in 1982. There are two main factors explaining spatial variations in the formation of the new small firms in manufacturing: a high proportion of manufacturing employment already in such small firms, and a high proportion of the population in non-manual occupations. This has had the effect of increasing the rate of new small-firm formation in the south and east, and hence of further reducing the employment opportunities in the north and west of Britain, and this spatial bias is particularly true of high-technology firms.[82] It should also be noted that there has recently been a marked increase in the number of self-employed in Britain. Between 1981 and 1984 self-employment grew almost half a million, by 20 per cent.[83]

At the same time, the shift towards service employment itself produced an increase in self-employment, and in the number of smaller plants and firms in the economy. Moreover, there has been in part an increase in the number of small firms in the service sector, and this has resulted from the development of many new 'producer services' firms, which have been hived off or 'unbundled' from the bundle of activities previously carried out by a single organization.[84] Indeed in recent years there is considerable evidence of the increased importance of such 'unbundling' in generating separate service and manufacturing plants and firms, and in the development of commodities like software that are really neither one nor the other. Lloyd[85] summarizes the overall impact of this process of 'unbundling':

> Unbundling is best regarded as an example of a more general disintegrative process at work in modern industry which also includes such phenomena as 'de-mergers' and 'management buy-outs'. Together they represent the lumps of rock tumbling down the industrial mountainside, dislodged by the growing power of the technological earthquake. . . Nowhere is this process of industrial disintegration more evident than in the high-technology industries. Unbundling is taking place there on a grand scale.

One technological development which has threatened the 'dinosaurs' of organized capitalism has been the growth of local technologies. World technologies provide the bases for standardized products or are of universal application; local technologies, by contrast, are specifically developed and are usable in a 'local' system to meet specific local needs (such as in agro-food, printing, solar energy, aqua-farming, waste-disposal etc.).[86]

But even in those industries where there is a world of non-local technology, it is not the case that all parts of the labour process are necessarily located, or bundled together, within a given plant. The 1971 Census showed that 1.5 million people work at or from home, and, of course, a sizeable minority constitute the major employment category of manual homeworkers who appear to be employed in a wide variety of different industrial sectors.[87] It had previously been thought that homeworking was an anachronistic and declining form of labour organization. But it now appears that neither 'factorization' nor 'technology' precludes some of the work being done as outwork in the home. As Rubery and Wilkinson point out, the techniques of production most suitable for outwork are usually fragmented or fragmentable, so that individuals or small teams can work independently – examples of such industries being cutlery, construction, clothing, packing, maintenance, catering, cleaning, delivery, typesetting etc.[88] They concluded that 'the ease with which we have found examples of outwork in a wide range of industries and in a wide range of tasks suggests that it is of considerable importance'.[89] As there is a decline in the importance and profitability of mass production in industrial sectors, so there is the development of older craft-based technologies and forms of labour organization as well as new forms.[90]

One industry where outworking, small plants and small firms have been particularly important is that of clothing. It is not that there are no large firms, but rather each large firm, normally a retailer like Marks and Spencer, is surrounded by a huge array of small subcontracting suppliers.[91] These competing suppliers have maintained Marks and Spencer's flexibility, particularly through ensuring multiple sources of most of the products being sold. Some evidence suggests that there is increased importance of subcontracting relationships in other non-service industries in Britain, such as steel, automobiles, and construction.[92] In 1981 Sir Adrian Cadbury[93] well summarized the progressive capitalist's conception of the disorganizing of contemporary British capitalism:

> We will want, in future, to break these organizations down into their separate business units and to give those units freedom to compete in their particular markets. Large companies will become more like federations of small enterprises – not because 'small is beautiful' but because big is expensive and inflexible...I would expect tomorrow's companies...to concentrate on the core activities of their business, relying for everything else on specialised suppliers who would compete for their custom.

One crucial consequence of these developments has been to transform the spatial distribution of social classes, away from the inner cities, out of the conurbations and large cities and away from the previously dominant extractive/ manufacturing industry.[94] This can be clearly seen from the changing location of British trade unionism. In the immediate post-war period, at the height of organized capitalism, union membership was concentrated in the cities, the coalfields and the regions of industrial concentration.[95] Many unions were highly concentrated in a few parts of the country. Moreover, this was not only true of the unions which organized particular industrial sectors (the Association of Textile Workers, for example), but was also the case for the large general unions. Union strength was concentrated in the 'heartlands' of industrial Britain.

However, the recent decline in union membership in Britain (2.25 million since the late 1970s) has particularly affected the old bases in these very industrial heartlands. There has been a flattening out of membership between different areas.[96] For example, in 1951 the Amalgamated Union of Engineering Workers (AUEW) had 3500 more members in its old base areas (London, Lancashire, Birmingham/Coventry, South Wales, Glasgow/Paisley) than in the rest of the country. But by 1979 these 'central' areas had 120,000 *fewer* members than the remaining areas.[97] Total membership had fallen by 17 per cent over the same period. This pattern of spatial dispersal has also affected unions which were initially more widely distributed. For example, between 1951 and 1983, the National and Local Government Officers' Association (NALGO) mainly contracted in those areas in which 10 per cent or more of its membership had been concentrated at the beginning of the period.[98] Likewise, in the National Union of Public Employees (NUPE) the share of membership made up of the union's periphery (north, south-west and Wales) increased from 7 per cent to over 20 per cent between 1971 and 1983.[99] Moreover, the increasing relative importance of public-sector and white-collar unions, which have been more spatially even in their distribution, has itself served to effect an increased spatial levelling of British trade unionism overall.

These processes are in turn connected with the decline in the employment significance of the 'city'. Lane summarizes[100] how cities have been singularly important for British trade unionism:

> What the city has provided has been quick and easy communication via an elaborate network of informal meeting places and formal organisations. The city, too, has a large and diverse population and this bestows on the individual a certain social invisibility, an immunity from the sort of scrutiny and social censorship that is more evident in the small town. The city...has provided both a range of organisation and a high degree of personal 'protection'.

With the locational changes noted above, the plants remaining in the larger cities will be those which are less likely to be centres of militant trade unionism; while the plants established in the smaller towns and cities, although unionized, will be unlikely to develop as centres of militancy. This is partly because of the employment of a 'green' labour force, but also because of the distance from the previous centres of militancy in that union, the difficulties of worker organization in a large number of spatially dispersed plants, and the general lack of a radical culture in many smaller towns and cities in Britain.[101] Moreover, the associated increase in the number of smaller plants will also discourage strike activity. Daniel and Milward show that among manual workers in establishments with 1000 or more employed, 67 per cent had gone on strike in the previous year; while among those employed in plants with under 10 employees, a tiny 2 per cent had struck in the previous year.[102]

Moreover, at the same time, the development of multinational and global corporations have made the workforce increasingly hard to organize.

1 It is very difficult for local shop stewards to discover how their company is, in fact, organized and the real financial standing of different plants.
2 There may be a fairly high degree of financial autonomy (between divisions or even plants) which sets one group of workers against another.

3 Companies now produce an enormous range of different products and workers are again divided in terms of the different labour process involved in different product lines.

4 The spatial redistribution of plants, even within a single country, has made the process of organizing a section of the labour force very hard to achieve, requiring considerable travel and financial resources. It is small wonder that the attempts to develop combine committees have been beset with difficulties.[103]

As a result of these various considerations, there are important spatial differences in strike activity. In the later 1970s, for example, the incidence rates of industrial disputes were two or three times as high in the north, Yorkshire and Humberside, the West Midlands, and Scotland, compared with East Anglia, the south-east and the south-west.[104] The shifts in population and employment noted above will clearly affect the impact of such patterns, but strike activity will not itself disappear. This is because one feature of disorganized capitalism is the breakdown of the *national* structures which organize labour. Since the later 1950s there has been a marked increase in shopfloor organization, especially within some sectors of manufacturing, but within parts of service employment as well. Cronin talks of the 'extensive character of organization on the shop floor'.[105] This process has increased the tendencies to sectionalism within British trade unionism; Lane argues however that although 'working people themselves are trapped into sectionalism, they find it deeply unattractive'.[106] So long as collective bargaining was industry-wide or national, the pursuit of sectional interest could be partly held in check. With the growth in plant-level bargaining, itself a very clear response to the growth of massive *multi*-plant corporations, sectional competitiveness has become far more marked.

Thus, disorganization does not mean that the British working class has been simply dissolved. This can be seen by considering the historical patterning of British strike-rates; there have been five waves of strikes in this century: 1910–13, 1919–22, 1957–62, 1968–72, and 1979–81.[107] These waves have tended to affect most of the major industries, although not to anything like the same degree. It is important to note that these waves have, roughly speaking, characterized the periods of transition: the first two from the liberal to the retarded organized phase, and the last three from the organized to the disorganized phase. There was no major wave of strikes during the main period of British organized capitalism, between the 1920s and the later 1950s, except of course for the 1926 General Strike. The onset of disorganized capitalism has led to some considerable development of plant-based industrial conflict, particularly between the late 1960s and the mid-1970s. However, since then there has been a major decline of industrial conflict within manufacturing industry (now less than 50 per cent of recorded stoppages, compared with 60/70 per cent previously). Moreover, in the past, waves of strikes were associated with increasing union membership. With falling membership and its changing spatial distribution, industrial conflict will still occur but whether massive waves of strikes will take place is much more doubtful. In chapters 6 and 7 we will examine some more general features of British politics consequent upon these various patterns of spatial restructuring.

THE UNITED STATES

Processes of spatial change have been even more advanced in the USA, which has in many ways led the way in the processes of spatial decentralization. Indeed, decentralization out of urban areas began almost immediately after the USA had become an urban industrial society.

Up to the end of the nineteenth century, the USA was a predominantly rural society. Indeed, between the end of the seventeenth and the end of the eighteenth centuries the proportion of the population living in the substantial colonial cities actually fell, from 9 per cent to 5.1 per cent, partly because the British Crown strictly controlled the granting of town charters.[108] With Independence, however, there was an explosive growth of the urban population, rising from one-twentieth to one-fifth of the American population between 1790 and 1860.[109] This massive growth was particularly found in the major ports: New York, Boston, Baltimore and Philadelphia. Such cities developed in an extremely haphazard fashion, with very little residential segregation. Many different occupational groups lived and worked in intimate, intermingling and heterogeneous contiguity.[110] Until industrial development took place, the expansion of commerce simply led to new occupational groups entering the city and attempting to find a location for residence and for work as close to the wharves as possible. There was an intense public life, at least for men, as they engaged in various forms of trading relationships. The close proximity of various groups with differing levels of income and wealth had the effect of producing considerable popular protest during the 1820s and 1830s, for example.[111]

However, even by 1840, nearly two-thirds of the workforce were still employed in agriculture and only 10 per cent lived in urban areas.[112] The commercial cities which did exist contained a growing number of industrial workshops, but the main early development of factories occurred in various smaller towns, particularly along the rivers in New England, in places like Fall River, Lawrence, Lowell, Lynn and Waltham. By the 1870s or so there was a substantial expansion of industrial production and of an industrial workforce in many of the larger commercial centres. There was a massive growth of American cities. Between 1860 and 1910, while the total American population doubled, the urban population grew nearly sixfold.[113] Likewise the number of industrial wage-workers increased fivefold and the product of manufacturing industries twelvefold over the same period. As Pred summarizes:[114]

In short, in the decades after 1860, the economy completed its transition from an agricultural and commercial–mercantilistic base to an industrial–capitalistic one. Concomitantly, the top of the urban hierarchy became characterized more and more by industrial, multifunctional cities, and less and less by cities dominated by mercantilistic wholesaling and trading functions.

These massive industrial cities exhibited a number of characteristic features:

1   The concentration of substantial factories in central areas generally near to the railroad and the river.[115]
2   Major concentrations of the working class in cramped housing built close to the factories so that the mainly male workers could walk to work.[116]
3   The emergence of working-class communities based on the relationships established within the factories and in which leisure activities depended upon the character and rhythms of work – particularly important was the lodge and the saloon for sustaining male working-class communities.[117]
4   Different crafts appear to have been established in relatively segregated areas so that clear, well-defined, and thriving occupational communities grew up with numerous leisure activities for wives and children as well as for the male workers.[118]
5   Newly arrived immigrant groups forming distinctive communities based around the extended family, the home, the courtyard, fraternal lodges, friendly societies, and the saloon in the case of men.[119]
6   The growth of middle- and upper-class housing away from the centre – for example, in Boston from the 1880s, partly because of the street railroad there was a growing pattern of suburbanization as more affluent families moved away from the centre.[120]
7   Very high turnover of population as the less 'successful' individuals and families who owned little or no property moved to other cities, particularly in the west.[121]
8   The central significance for male working-class culture of the peer group saloon or tavern which provided a non-work space for fellowship, industrial organization and political discussion.[122]

One significant consequence of these developments was to produce changes in the rates and location of industrial strikes and other workers' struggles. During the 1870s most labour unrest took place in small towns, in the mines, and along the railroads. Strikes at this time particularly occurred in the smaller towns and cities as workers gained some support from sections of the middle class where the lesser industrialists had failed to legitimize their power and influence locally.[123] By the 1880s and 1890s there was a large increase both in the strike-rate and in the number of workers involved in strikes.[124] In Lynn, for example, the unions were particularly strong during this period; Cumbler says they were 'vigorously independent and militant, and were built upon local conditions and community interactions.[125] Such militant *localized* unionism also on occasions embraced immigrant and women workers. Nevertheless, it also seems that there was some considerable increase in the organization of workers and the frequency of strikes in the larger cities. This is indicated by the fact that almost two-thirds of strikes during this period around the turn of the century took place in just three states – Illinois, Pennsylvania and New York – in which most major American cities were then found.[126]

One of the reasons for such militancy during this period was that there was often a fair degree of localized support. In the Gilded Age such support, especially from the middle classes, was invaluable.[127] This was expressed through sympathetic national guards, local militias and sheriffs, pro-workers juries, a sympathetic local press, credit from shopkeepers, attacks on strikebreakers etc. Such support resulted in part because local business leaders resented the influx of regional or national industrial or financial interests and were often willing to join forces especially with skilled workers in defence of the particularities of the local 'community'. There was also some hostility shown to the increasing powers of nationally organized 'professionals', a process well summarized by Warren:[128]

> Various parts of the community – its education system, its recreation, its economic units, its government functions, its religious units, its health and welfare agencies, and its voluntary associations – have become increasingly oriented towards district, state, regional, or national offices and less and less oriented toward each other.

As we shall see later, one result of this was to produce in the American Federation of Labor (AFL) an extreme hostility to anything 'professional', to anything which developed out of the Progressive movement in the early years of this century. As Lash has written:[129]

> The Federation was unsurpassed in its enmity towards reform-minded intellectuals
> . . . The AFL was four-square opposed to all that was Protestant, anti-corruption,
> suffragettist, prohibitionist and pacifist.

By the inter-war period the AFL, through its renunciation of class alliances, had helped to secure a substantial industrial presence for the American working class – and we will now consider various forms of spatial restructuring which reduced the size, organization and effectiveness of the very industrial proletariat which the AFL had sought exclusively to mobilize.

Organized capitalism characterizes the USA from around the turn of the century to the post-war period. There was a massive reduction in employment in the primary sector (a fall from 37.6 per cent to 17.6 per cent between 1900 and 1940), a slight increase in the proportion in the secondary sector, and a 50 per cent increase in the proportion in tertiary employment.[130] Manufacturing industry developed new forms of work organization during a period in which there was a major increase in industrial concentration (even between 1896 and 1905 the 100 largest corporations quadrupled in size and by 1905 controlled 40 per cent of American manufacturing industry).[131]

These increasingly large and powerful corporations developed networks of foreign subsidiaries; began to implement assembly-line production following its 'invention' in 1913;[132] and began to decentralize from the centres of the large cities very much earlier than was occurring elsewhere. For example, right at the beginning of this period, between 1899 and 1909, central city manufacturing employment increased by only 41 per cent, while that in the suburban rings increased by almost 100 per cent.[133] At the same time completely new manufacturing towns were constructed beyond the limits of existing cities (Gary, Indiana, for example). A contemporary commentator, Graham Taylor, noted 'the sudden investment of large sums of capital in establishing suburban plants'.[134] After the First World War the widespread use of the truck/lorry was very important in decentralizing industry, while throughout the period two other factors were centrally significant: the growing militancy of workers in the centres of the existing cities; and the widespread availability of cheap and convenient land away from the high rents in the centre. This growing militancy was explicitly referred to by a number of industrialists. The president of a contracting firm claimed[135] as early as the US Industrial Commission held between 1900 and 1902 that:

> all these controversies and strikes that we have had here for some years have...prevented outsiders from coming in here and investing their capital...It has discouraged capital at home...It has drawn the manufacturers away from the city, because they are afraid their men will get into trouble and get into strikes...The result is, all around Chicago for forty or fifty miles, the smaller towns are getting these manufacturing plants.

Another industrialist claimed[136] that:

> Chicago today is the hotbed of trades unionism...If it were not for the high investment (manufacturers) have in their machines and plants, many of them would leave Chicago at once, because of the labor trouble that exists here...In fact, in Chicago within the last two months we have lost some of the very largest corporations that operated here.

While the chairman of the New York State Board of Mediation and Arbitration asked of a leading industrialist:[137]

> Q: Do you find that isolated plants, away from the great centers of population are more apt to have non-union shops than in a city?
> Answer: Yes.

Q: Do you know of cases in the State where they do isolate plants to be free...from unionism?
Answer: They have been located with that end in view.

One particular reason for decentralizing was that industrial disputes in the city centres could be 'contagious' and spread from plant to plant. Gordon quotes Graham Taylor's account from 1915:[138]

> In an eastern city which recently experienced the throes of a turbulent street-car strike, the superintendent of a large industrial establishment frankly said that every time the strikers paraded past his plant a veritable fever seemed to spread among the employees in all his work rooms. He thought that if the plants were moved out to the suburbs, the workingmen would not be so frequently inoculated with infection.

It was generally thought at the time, moreover, that unions were far less successful when they tried to organize workers outside the central city districts.[139] At the same time, however, the very large corporations which developed during and after the First World War increasingly began to separate their administrative headquarters from the directly productive plants and to locate them within a few of the major American cities. So while workers began to be 'quarantined', management became increasingly organized into central business districts which facilitated the contagiousness of capital. By 1929 50 per cent of national corporations had located their headquarters in New York or Chicago.[140] The headquarters of such corporations were far more unevenly distributed than nineteenth-century industrial establishments had been. As a result, many towns and cities lacked a central business district, and with the dispersal of manufacturing employment, they became highly dispersed, developing into what Fogelson termed the fragmented metropolis.[141] In this process of fragmentation the increasing availability of trucks/lorries enabled many different centres of manufacturing to develop, since they no longer had to be all close to railway termini. At the level of a single city spatial variations in the cost of transporting industrial commodities had mostly disappeared by the inter-war period; as a result there was the beginning of a 'massive decentralization of economic activities in large metropolitan areas',[142] and this was occurring while the other societies were still developing into organized capitalist societies.

Organized capitalism in the USA involved a considerable decentralization of population as especially various middle-class groups, and particularly the service class, moved out of the central areas of cities and began the process of suburbanization. What was in part involved here was, as Walker puts it, 'an effort to "banish the facts of production" from the landscape, i.e. pollution, noise, crime, the threat and misery of the working class'.[143] At the fringes of the cities it was easier to fashion areas, in part at least, consistent with the

'Arcadian ideal of ruralized living', bearing in mind that at the turn of the century the industrial landscape was itself an exceptionally recent phenomenon. At first suburbs were 'middle class', but this was not simply because that was where such groups lived; rather the middle class lived there because the suburbs could be *made* middle class.[144]

By the end of the Second World War the USA was economically, politically and militarily dominant. In 1945 it possessed more than half of the world's usable industrial capacity, it was the banker to most of its former allies and enemies in the war, and it possessed the only still powerful military machine.[145] That kind of dominance had not been seen since the turn of the century when British pre-eminence engendered the shift of its competitors into organized capitalist development. In the case of the USA, its world-wide dominance spread capitalist relations throughout the world economy, particularly into the hundred or so countries which had previously been part of various imperial blocs, each linked into one or other of the organized capitalist societies. That in turn led in the 1970s to a number of disorganizing tendencies in the world economy which reproduced many of those features found in the USA since the late 1940s.

America's 'organization' of the global economy between 1945 and the 1970s was secured through, firstly, the establishment of the dollar as the principal reserve currency at the 1944 Bretton Woods Conference; secondly, the extensive pattern of loans, particularly Marshall Aid, to Western Europe; and thirdly, the enormous investment by American companies throughout the global economy.[146] On the last point, General Electric, for example, increased its overseas capacity from 21 foreign plants in 1949 to 82 in 1969. By the early 1970s nearly one-third of US automobile investment was being made abroad, and yet it has been 'guesstimated' that one in six of all *Americans* still owed their job to the existence of the private car.[147]

There has also been an increase in the concentration ratios for some sectors of American industry in the early part of the post-war period: for example, between 1947 and 1972 the four largest American producers increased their percentage of domestic sales from 79 per cent to 90 per cent in the case of breakfast foods; 32 per cent to 78 per cent in the case of carpets and rugs; from 46 per cent to 57 per cent in the case of semi-conductors; from 61 per cent to 74 per cent in the case of photographic equipment etc.[148] At the same time, there have been enormously important waves of mergers, particularly during 1949–55, 1964–8 and the late 1970s.[149]

However, there are three further points to note here. First, these mergers generally increased the heterogeneity of particular companies and did not increase their domination of particular markets. Second, these ratios of concentration refer only to domestic markets and ignore the role of imports. In most American markets there have been considerable increases in the size and effectiveness of foreign competition – the best examples being the competition in automobile production from especially Nissan and Toyota. The merchandise trade balance in the USA was $4.9 billion in credit in 1960; yet by 1980 it was $25.3 billion in deficit.[150] Third, although individual companies have grown greatly in size, their individual plants have not. In table 4.4 it can be seen that between the late 1960s and late 1970s large increases were recorded in the number of plants employing below 1000 employees, particularly those employing less than 250 workers.

Table 4.4 Number of manufacturing establishments by employee size in the USA: 1967, 1977

Year	<20	20–99	100–249	250–99	>1000
			Employee size		
1967	199,000	74,000	20,000	11,000	2000
1977	237,000	78,000	22,000	12,000	2000

Sources: adapted from *Statistical Abstract of the United States*, (1971), table 1143; (1982–3), table 1387.

This is also supported by the fact that by the end of the 1970s four-fifths of net growth was occurring in plants with less than 100 employees.[151]. Fourth, *overseas* operations are now of extraordinary importance for American corporations. By 1978 one-third of the overall profits of the 100 largest corporations and banks were derived from operations located in other countries.[152] Indeed, between half and three-quarters of American trade now consists of transactions *within* corporations rather than between them.[153] These transactions depend upon the establishment of new forms of communication and transportation technology which significantly bypass existing *national* systems of post, telephone and transport.

At the same time as new forms of the international spatial division of labour have developed, so too has there been a spatial restructuring within the USA. In particular, there has been a further substantial suburbanization of American industry. One important reason for this in the post-war period stems from the fact that, while central city areas have a comparative advantage for labour-intensive activities, out-of-centre areas have a distinct advantage for capital-intensive activities that require extensive land. As many manufacturing and service-sector enterprises have become more capital-intensive, they have moved further and further away from the city centre.[154] This tendency was more developed in the USA by comparison with the countries of Western Europe because American industry was far more capital-intensive in the inter-war period. Industry in the USA also took up a great deal of land so that more than one acre of land was used for every 10 employees in the immediate post-war period, and this figure was four times that of the previous generation.[155]

Partly as a result of this, 'a preponderant majority of the new net jobs created in the United States recently have been located in the nation's suburbs'.[156] By the 1970s only about 25 per cent of suburban dwellers commuted to central city jobs. Between 1960 and 1970 nearly 1 million jobs were lost from the central areas in America's 15 largest cities, while over 3 million were created in the suburbs.[157] In Chicago,[158] for example:

> Dispersal of manufacturing activity from the inner zones of the central city was the dominant trend in plant location throughout the United States in 1950–1960. In Chicago, typically, the greatest gains in activity took place in an arc ten to fifteen miles from the central business district. The greatest losses occurred within five miles of the core. Warehouses, in particular, moved from inner zones to the periphery, situating themselves close to areas of population growth and expanded manufacturing activity.

A second and related pattern of disorganization has been the suburbanization not of employment but of the population. Table 4.5 indicates that since the 1930s it is the suburbs (the 'metropolitan balance') which have become the most important sites of population growth. Between half and three-quarters of all such growth since 1930 has been concentrated in the suburbs. Willbern summarizes the overall pattern:[159]

> the greatest concentration of metropolitan population inside central cities occurred between 1920 and 1930. Until 1920 the central cities were growing faster than their metropolitan rings; beginning with the census of 1930, the fringe growth has been faster than the central growth and the gap widens with each census.

In 1950 one-quarter of Americans lived in the suburbs; by 1970 nearly two-fifths; and by 1980 well over two-fifths.[160]

Very many workers have participated in this process of suburbanization, particularly after the Second World War. This was encouraged by the Federal Housing Administration loans to veterans, which particularly encouraged the movement of workers out of the city centres.[161] This movement was not necessarily to new suburbs, but to inner suburbs; the more affluent residents of those suburbs then moved out to new housing as the standard of their original communities gradually lowered.[162] Suburbanization was also encouraged by urban renewal programmes that occurred following the Federal Housing Act of 1949.[163] Tens of thousands of acres in inner cities were redeveloped as slum housing was demolished and middle- and high-income housing, schools, libraries, parks and so on took its place. Poorer families were simply forced to seek housing and employment elsewhere. This pattern was integrally related to the massive expansion in car ownership. In 1945 there was one car for every four people of driving age; by 1970 this had jumped to one for every 1.4 persons.[164] One interesting effect of the movement of white Americans

Table 4.5 Population growth rate, in central cities, metropolitan balance, and non-metropolitan areas: 1900 to 1980 (Average annual rate per 1,000 population)

Period[a]	United States total	Central cities	Metropolitan balance	Differential between balance and central-city growth	Non-metropolitan areas
1900 to 1910	19.3	29.3	32.8	3.5	15.4
1910 to 1920	14.3	23.1	28.6	5.5	9.4
1920 to 1930	14.6	19.6	35.6	16.0	7.4
1930 to 1940	7.0	5.0	14.1	9.1	6.3
1940 to 1950	13.5	13.0	30.4	17.4	5.8
1950 to 1960	16.9	10.2	39.5	29.3	7.6
1960 to 1970	12.5	6.2	23.7	17.5	11.7
1970 to 1980	10.8	-0.1	16.6	16.7	14.4

[a] Data for 1910 through 1940 are for metropolitan districts as officially defined at each ending census date.
Data for 1950 through 1970 are for standard metropolitan statistical areas (SMSA) as defined at each ending census date.
Data for the 1970–80 period for SMSA's as defined on January 1, 1980.

out to the suburbs was to allow most union offices in a south Chicago steelworks to be taken by Slav workers who did not become suburbanized and had preserved strong neighbourhood networks.[165]

It is important to note that in the 1970s there was the development of an even more marked pattern of population deconcentration: there was an absolute decline in the number of people living in the main American cities. By 1980 the proportion of the population living in the central cities had fallen to below 30 per cent, a figure comparable to that in the 1920s. The towns that did grow in size were mainly the smaller urban centres. Thus, Long argues:[166]

> As a result of the faster growth of smaller metropolitan areas, the system of metropolitan areas is itself deconcentrating, as well as losing population to non-metropolitan areas.

At the same time, there have been major changes in the regional distribution of the American population which are summarized in table 4.6. Long summarizes the recent demographic history of the USA:[167]

> higher rates of population growth are associated with the South and West, smaller places, rural areas, and suburban and non-metropolitan counties. The highest rates of decline are in Northern cities of over 100,000; the fastest growing populations are in the South and West in places of less than 25,000 or areas outside of places altogether.

Because of these overlapping patterns of population decentralization, it is incorrect to see these changes as merely involving the rise and decline of particular large-scale regions. The contemporary pattern of demographic and economic change in the USA can be described as a 'mosaic of unevenness'.[168] In 1979, for example, while the national unemployment rate was 5.8 per cent, county unemployment rates varied from 40 per cent in Menominee County, Wisconsin, to less than 1 per cent in Sioux County, Nebraska. These massive local variations in economic experience make a regional basis of union organization difficult to establish and sustain.

A further important shift in the economic structure has been the changing balance between different employment sectors. Secondary industry, including mining and quarrying, has never employed more than just over one-third of the employed population. Increases in that proportion occurred in the years up to the inter-war period; but since then, although absolute numbers rose until the 1960s, the proportion stabilized until the 1960s when it began to fall back.[169] However, the most spectacular change has been increased employment in the service sector. By the inter-war period it accounted for almost half of the employed population and since then it has continued to increase until in 1986 it accounted for seven-tenths of the workforce. This recent increase is the result of the considerable expansion in employment in 'producer services' and in 'government and government enterprises', which have particularly drawn women into the labour force.[170]

Table 4.6 US Population by region: 1790 to 1980 (in millions)

Year	North-east	North Central	South	West
1790	2.0	—	2.0	—
1800	2.6	—	2.6	—
1810	3.5	0.3	3.5	—
1820	4.4	0.9	4.4	—
1830	5.5	1.6	5.7	—
1840	6.8	3.4	7.0	—
1850	8.6	5.4	9.0	—
1860	10.6	9.1	11.1	0.6
1870	12.3	13.0	12.3	1.0
1880	14.5	17.4	16.5	1.8
1890	17.4	22.4	20.0	3.1
1900	21.0	26.3	24.5	4.3
1910	25.9	29.9	29.4	7.1
1920	29.7	34.0	33.1	9.2
1930	34.4	38.6	37.9	12.3
1940	36.0	40.1	41.7	14.4
1950	39.5	44.5	47.2	20.2
1960	44.7	51.6	55.0	28.1
1970	49.0	56.6	62.8	34.8
1980	49.1	58.9	75.3	43.2

Source: Long, Population Deconcentration, p. 38.

At the same time there has been a similar shift in the American occupational structure as shown in table 4.7. The proportion of manual workers (outside agriculture) has always been well under half, reaching a peak of about two-fifths in the inter-war period. The proportion of white-collar workers has continued to increase in steady fashion from then until 1986, when they constituted over half of the 1980 labour force. It is important to note that white-collar workers in both manufacturing and tertiary industry tend to have low rates of unionization in the USA.[171]

These structural shifts in the economy have been particularly well reflected in comparative strike rates in different industries. For example, in the period 1950–61, the number of workers involved in strikes per 1000 employees varied between 427 in rubber; 307, steelmaking; 292, motor vehicle manufacture; 113, building; and down to 2.1 (personal) services; and 0.8, government.[172] Similar differentials can be found for the next decade when rates varied between 50 and 250 per 1000 employees for almost all of manufacturing industry, while the rate for government was 10.5 and services only 2.2.[173] By 1973

Table 4.7 Percentage of the employed labour force in major occupation groups

Occupation groups	1900	1910	1920	1930	1940	1950	1960	1970	1980
White-collar workers	17.6	211.3	24.9	29.4	31.1	36.6	42.0	46.7	52.2
Manual workers (except farm and mineworkers)	35.8	38.2	40.2	39.6	39.8	41.1	37.5	36.3	31.7
Service workers	9.0	9.6	7.8	9.8	11.7	10.5	12.6	12.4	13.3
Farm and mineworkers	37.5	30.9	27.0	21.2	17.4	11.8	7.9	4.6	2.8

Sources: J. Hollingsworth and E. Hollingsworth, Dimensions in Urban History (University of Wisconsin Press, Madison, 1979, p. 25); Statistical Abstract of the United States (1982–3), p. 386.

the average number of workers involved in strikes per 1000 non-agricultural employees had fallen to considerably less than half that found in the late 1940s.[174]

A further factor contributing to these changes has been the growth of employment and population in the sunbelt states in the south and west.[175] In part this shift can be attributed to the low wages of the southern labour force. However, this does not explain all of the shift, since even in 1960 only 40 per cent of manufacturing employment in the south did in fact consist of low wage industry. Indeed, it was the high wage, high technology industry which, even between 1940 and 1960, was increasingly located in the south and west.[176] Once these areas did begin to industrialize, they were able to use the backlog of existing technologies that had been initially developed by firms in the so-called Frostbelt (north and east). The turning point was the inter-war period and particularly the period between 1930 and 1940. This can be seen from table 4.8. After 1930 New England and the Middle Atlantic both began a fairly steep decline in their relative per capita income, while the per capita incomes in the South Atlantic, East South Central and West South Central all began to rise. The development of the sunbelt, then, is a phenomenon dating back to, and constituting an integral part of, the premature and lengthy disorganization of contemporary America. As a consequence of the flow of black migrants to the north and of the expansion of white workers within the south, a massive modernization of southern agriculture, the great increase in manufacturing industry in the south, and a corresponding expansion of service employment, overall regional differences had become far less marked in 1975 compared with, say, 1940 (standard deviation fell from 29.2 in 1940 to 10.8 in 1975). Indeed, in terms of one particular aspect of sunbelt develop-ment, the expansion of population in the south, Leven argues that this has been occurring since 1940 and if anything is weaker in the 1980s than it used to be.[177] It is also important to note that sunbelt growth is highly selective and it is necessary to consider *intra*-regional variations which, as in the case of Britain, have increased in importance.[178]

Finally, here, we will briefly note some political correlates of economic and spatial transformations. The changing balance of political forces is well indicated by the following observation from Richard Nixon in 1973.[179] He said to his counsel:

> the basic thing is the Establishment. The Establishment is dying, and so they've got to show that despite the successes we have had in foreign policy and in the election, they've got to show that it is just wrong, just because of this [Watergate]. They are trying to use this as the whole thing.

In other words, the American President considered himself an outsider, opposed to the establishment in the USA. For Nixon this establishment was something based in the north and east of the country, the world of New York, Chicago,

Table 4.8 Per capita income as percentage of US total; by regions: 1900–75

Year	USA total	New England	Middle Atlantic	East North Central	West North Central	South Atlantic	East South Central	West South Central	Mountain	Pacific
1900	100	134	139	100	97	45	49	61	139	163
1920	100	124	134	108	87	59	52	72	100	135
1930	100	129	140	111	82	56	48	61	83	130
1940	100	121	124	112	84	69	55	70	92	138
1950	100	106	116	112	94	74	63	81	96	121
1960	100	109	116	107	93	77	67	83	95	118
1965	100	108	114	108	95	81	71	83	90	115
1970	100	108	113	105	95	86	74	85	90	110
1975	100	108	108	104	98	90	79	91	92	111

Source: W. Rostow, 'Regional change in the fifth Kondratieff cycle', in *Rise of the Sunbelt Cities*, ed. Perry and Watkins, pp. 83–103, p. 85.

Philadelphia, and Boston: the 'world of great wealth, high culture, nurtured traditions, industrial power, and political aristocracies, the world of "soft heads" and "the media", the "liberal elite" and "impudent snobs" – "the enemy"'.[180] Nixon by contrast saw himself as representative of a new kind of economic, social and political force in the USA rooted in the newly emergent wealth and power of the 'southern rim'. It was his task as he saw it to challenge the north-eastern establishment which until the Second World War dominated economic, political, and social life in the USA.

Apart from the demographic changes already noted, the most significant transformations have occurred through the massive growth in the six basic industries of what is termed the 'cowboy' economy: agribusiness, defence, advanced technology, oil and natural-gas, real estate and construction, and tourism and leisure.[181] As these industries have grown at colossal rates and have created a veritable culture devoted to 'growth', so there has been a corresponding growth of political influence of the south. This has been particularly marked on the right and includes the takeover of the Republican Party, particularly from 1964 onwards.[182] The success of Nixon (until Watergate) and Reagan best represents the coming to power of the southern rim, the true conquest of the 'cowboys'.

5

Economic change and spatial restructuring (2)

Charles Tilly has drawn an interesting analogy between using the river Seine as the basis for finding one's way around Paris and the supposed general character of industrialization.[1] Just as it is inappropriate to straighten out the Seine in one's imagination in order to work out how to proceed from A to B in Paris, so is it incorrect to presume a straight-line model of industrialization, from agriculture to handicraft to full-scale industry. Yet if Tilly's argument is correct in general then it is especially applicable to the French case. We have already seen that in the nineteenth century France was 'economically forward'. In the following we will see that more generally France has been characterized by exceptional degrees of uneven development, economically, socially and spatially.

One particularly effective indicator of this unevenness can be seen from the fact that even after the Second World War there were 35 per cent more men employed in agriculture, forestry and fishing than there were in manufacturing industry.[2] For most of the twentieth century, there were among men considerably more agricultural than manufacturing workers. Similarly there have been more women workers in agriculture than in manufacturing until after the Second World War. Furthermore, the number of service workers in France has remained smaller than that of agriculture over much of this century.

Corresponding to this 'pre-industrial' pattern of employment has been a distinct trajectory of socio-spatial development, a particular combination of very 'modern' or 'progressive' characteristics together with some very backward 'pre-industrial' patterns. For example, the Napoleonic period endowed France with a number of institutional changes which, it could be suggested, were conditions necessary for and perhaps sufficient to induce rapid capitalist accumulation. These changes included the introduction of the metric system; the elimination of internal tolls and tariffs; the rationalization of local administration; the establishment of a legal system in which all citizens were equal before the law; the eradication of the restrictive guilds and more generally of all forms of economic coalition; the abolition of feudal rights and the establishment of equal inheritance; the general state encouragement of innovative manufacturing, of the 'practical arts', through the provision of medals, prizes and loans; and the establishment of advanced education in the form of the *lycée*, the *écoles d'arts et metiers*, and the first of the *grandes écoles*.[3] It was not for nothing that Napoleon has been described as Hegel's 'World-soul on horseback'. However, these developments did not produce the expected take-off into widespread and sustained capitalist accumulation. In the decade after 1789 the output of textiles fell by over one-half; metallurgy, even with an increase in demand for arms, also seems to have declined; pig iron increased relatively little over the Napoleonic period.[4] While isolated sections of the French economy developed fast, much of the rest underwent what Crouzet terms a process of pastoralization from which it took over a century and a half to recover. It seems that many French entrepreneurs almost self-consciously invested in the less efficient technologies then available.[5] The Napoleonic wars had the effect of disrupting access both to new technologies and the growing international markets. As a result British industry had surged ahead of the French by the end of the Napoleonic period.

Developments in the nineteenth century can be analysed as follows. First, the destruction of all feudal title deeds had the effect of transforming the French peasantry into a peasant freeholding class with firm rights of tenure in land and free of the financial burdens which it had previously borne. This land settlement produced a freezing of the layout of fields and villages; in many places the open field system remained. Farms were small and there was little incentive to effect any radical changes in farming methods – *petite culture* prevailed.[6] Many millions of men and women remained dependent on their family plot, although Lefebvre has shown that the middling peasantry gained most from the Napoleonic land settlement.[7] Agriculture, then, was a massive sector making low profits, employing old technology, marginally involved in the market economy, and showing relatively low increases in productivity throughout the nineteenth century.[8] The French peasantry remained throughout the nineteenth century as determinedly localized as in 1789. The peasant family was tied to its plot of land even if the size of this was reduced through the equal inheritance law and the gradually increasing population. By 1862, for example, there were 2.5 million farms of less than 10 hectares.[9]

The uneven pattern of development can also be seen in the case of French industry in the nineteenth century. Even by 1789 there were a number of very advanced capitalist plants in France, particularly in coalmining and textiles. For example, the cotton giant, Richard-Lenoir, consisted of 39 establishments and 15,000 employees.[10] However, such firms remained the exception rather than the rule and they do not seem to have generated more *widespread* industrial development. Even in textile manufacture, which does not require massive investment, French industry often failed to use the best available technology. French development has been characterized as *'industries de pointe'*.[11] Although there were centres or points of advanced industry, such as the cotton metropolis of Mulhouse or the woollen capital of Roubaix, these were unusual. In the 1840s, for example, while one half of all French power looms were found in Mulhouse, handlooms remained the most common type of loom in the woollen industry right up to 1914. Crouzet summarizes: the *industries de pointe* remained 'heavily outnumbered within economies which, in their bulk, were still traditional'.[12]

By comparison with Britain, advanced technology in a given sector in France was more highly concentrated within single towns; while the traditionally organized sectors of that industry were to be found throughout much of the rest of France.[13] The largest of the major cotton centres was in Normandy, but this was also the most backward; in Britain the largest concentrations of textile industry were in those places which were also the most advanced.

One reason for the spatial division of labour in textile manufacture was the segmentation and location of the markets for these various products. French production began with high quality consumption items and only subsequently moved upstream into more basic sectors. Luxury production, however, remained particularly important both because of the restricted buying power of the French peasantry and because the French population failed to grow very much. Between 1850/1 and 1910/11 the population grew by only 11 per cent, while that of both the UK and Germany more or less doubled over the same period.[14] As a result, French industry remained dependent upon the market for various luxury goods demanded by the capitalist, professional and landed classes.

We have already noted the size of the backward textile industry in Normandy. One reason why it nevertheless remained of importance was its convenient location near to the market provided by Paris, particularly for luxury products. Indeed, Paris has been particularly significant in the spatial structuring of the French economy and society. Kindleberger notes[15] that:

> Blame for the dominance of Paris has been variously ascribed to Louis XIV for assembling the court in Versailles, to the departmental system of Napoleon I, and to the beautification of the city of Louis Napoleon and Haussmann.

Particularly rapid growth of the Parisian population occurred between 1871 and the First World War. While the French population remained more or less static, there was considerable migration from the countryside into Paris, which grew by 1.8 per cent per annum.[16] Paris became a rapidly congested and very unhealthy city with very dense concentrations of population.[17] Typhus and cholera, poverty and starvation were commonplace and provided the background in which Baron Haussmann organized the rebuilding of Paris after he was appointed Prefect in 1853 by Napoleon III.[18] Broad straight avenues were laid out partly to facilitate the fast movement of cavalry. Many public buildings were built around the Notre-Dame cathedral, as a great deal of working-class housing was demolished. Paris was 'disembowelled' with the construction of the *grands boulevards*. Haussmann demolished the old medieval city and constructed the first modern capital city. Berman summarizes the changes:[19]

> The Napoleon–Haussmann boulevards created new bases – economic, social, aesthetic – for bringing enormous numbers of people together...These cafes...soom came to be seen all over the world as symbols of *la vie parisienne*...Great sweeping vistas were designed, with monuments at the boulevards' ends, so that each walk led toward a dramatic climax.

Berman also points out how this modernization of the public urban space transformed how people felt and experienced personal relationships. The boulevards, cafes and public spaces provided a context for the very modern experience of romance, of friendship and love apart from the restrictions of family, church and community. Part of the appeal of the modernized Paris was to permit people to be 'private in public'.

Three further points, though, need to be made about this extraordinary transformation of the urban landscape. First, much of the Parisian working class forced out of the Ville de Paris had to find increasingly wretched accommodation in the outlying areas. Suburban Paris became an 'unspeakable collection of rabbit hutches of which any other capital city would be ashamed'.[20] Second, the boulevards were the first place in the world in which fast-moving urban traffic was to be experienced. For as Baudelaire commented: 'I was crossing the boulevard, in a great hurry, in the midst of a moving chaos, with death galloping at me from every side.'[21] At the same time, though, the ability to move very fast through the city represented a previously unexperienced freedom, one that was to be so extraordinarily heightened in the twentieth-century development of the motor car and its transformations of time and space. And third, although 'Haussmannization' did occur in a number of other French cities, there was a general heightened inequality within France between the modern, modernized Paris and 'the provinces'.[22] Paris was an extraordinarily modern city within a largely pre-industrial, economically undynamic, primarily agricultural society.[23]

Moreover, in the mid-nineteenth century, the provinces consisted of a series of relatively localized and separate economies. France was in no sense a national or nationalized economy: prices, for example, varied by 200 per cent between different regions. One important consequence of this highly localized socio-spatial structure was that the growing working-class movement was unable to forge any kind of regional or national alliance.[24] In certain urban centres, such as Toulouse, there was a substantial artisan population which, threatened by proletarianization, was able to provide political leadership of working-class organizations (especially through political clubs, newspapers, electoral organizations, cafes, taverns etc.). This was assisted by the weakness of the ties of patronage the aristocracy were able to mobilize in some urban areas. Republican control of some municipal governments in urban areas also strengthened working-class capacities. However, in 1870–1, the major insitutions of state power remained subject to bourgeois and aristocratic political control (although note this was often local), while the small French working class failed in any way to transcend its own local bases of organization. Aminzade summarizes the explanation of this:[25]

> The central weakness of French working-class politics at this time, which was reflected in the defeats of the revolutionary communes, was the inability of dispersed revolutionary forces to effectively coordinate local revolutionary struggles. The French working class failed to transcend its local basis of organization in 1870–71 for a variety of reasons, including the persistence of a localized artisanal economy of small-scale production,.a relatively poorly developed national system of transportation and communication, and the absence of a national working-class political party. The persistence of handicraft production was thus a contradictory phenomenon. Although the struggles of artisans to preserve handicraft production relations made it difficult for the bourgeoisie to consolidate its rule, working-class insurgency was also weakened, and ultimately unable to effectively wage political struggles at a national level, because of the survival of such relations.

It must also be noted that republicanism and socialism have not been confined to apparently 'urban' areas in France, although, of course, most French workers were not even unionized right up to 1914.[26] Judt has analysed the social geography of the French left in the nineteenth century, and in particular the social bases of radicalism in the Var.[27] He argues that it was not simply the independence of the small peasant *per se* that was important in generating radicalism; it was rather the fact that in the Var the kinds of labour process involved had the effect of forcing the peasantry into collective patterns of organizing work. This had the effect both of blocking tendencies to economic individualism, and of reinforcing an independence from local notables and authorities. The shortage of landless labourers encouraged the peasantry to work for each other, while the poor soil had encouraged the collective purchase of fertilizers. Judt also argues that the typical left-producing community was the large village where many workers were part peasant and part industrial worker, especially in fairly small artisan workshops. Brustein has reinforced and broadened this interpretation by arguing that the general pattern of left voting found in Mediterranean France was the result of a complex of conditions: of a market-oriented economic activity; small owner–cultivator land tenure; a closely interdependent workforce; intense town–country interaction; and the relative absence/ineffectiveness of local elites.[28] Likewise he adduces evidence which shows that the right voting in western France was the product of a subsistence economy; medium-sized tenancies; isolated hamlets, dispersed population; and strong church-based and other social elites.[29]

The increasing significance of the Parisian populace within the total French population has already been noted. One important reason for this during the second half of the nineteenth century was the extensive migration of farm-workers from the countryside. For example, 820,000 people migrated from the farms to the towns between 1876 and 1881.[30] Much of this migration was to Paris, so that in the four decades after 1870 the Paris region had an annual growth rate of 1.8 per cent while the rest of the country remained virtually stationary. This was partly because the new railway system was designed in the form of spokes which all radiated out from Paris. The First World War, too, fostered the growth of numerous industries in various cities. In Paris there was rapid development of armaments, metal construction, and metal-working. Service employment in France was in this period even more concentrated than that of most industrial sectors. Following the First World War, nearly one-half of all employment in banking, insurance and financial services was to be found in Paris, as well as 46 per cent of all university students.[31] In the inter-war period Parisian industry continued to expand. By 1931 the rapidly growing automobile industry employed over 100,000 workers in the Paris region, while aeronautical, radio-electrical and other advanced industrial sectors all expanded considerably. This was partly because of the market provided by the state, and partly because of the concentration of research laboratories in the capital.[32]

Again what we see here is a particularly marked pattern of uneven develop-ment. Side by side with the growth of sophisticated modern industry much of France changed relatively little and hence in a sense regressed. Kindleberger summarizes through comparison:[33]

> Enlargement of markets, specialization, mergers and competition went much less distance in France than in England. *Exceptions existed especially in the modern industries*...But the period from perhaps 1870 to 1939, *except for steel, automobiles, electricity, chemicals,* was characterized by local markets, produc-tion to order, and emphasis on quality. Haunted by the fear of overproduction and collapse of prices, producers held back output and maintained markups.

French development up to the Second World War was not, therefore, of a national economy but was particularly localized in Paris, Alsace, and parts of the Nord. Trebilcock talks of 'its pronounced parochialism, its liability to splinter into isolated local systems of rural consumers and petty capitalists, unsophisticated and largely self-contained industrial domains, contending with one another to withhold capital and labour from the modern sector'.[34] At the same time, however, French development up to the Second World War in certain senses was 'international'. It possessed the most sophisticated 'modern' capital city; it was the centre of western culture and design; its engineering and scientific institutes were internationally renowned; and French banks and financial institutions were second only to the City of London for their orientation to the internationalization of capital. Trebilcock points out that:[35]

> In this sense the international industrial revolution passed *through* France, leaving strong domestic pockets of manufacturing, but mobilizing men (sic) and money for a wider, transcontinental task. Arguably, the French industrial revolution was more forceful in its international than in its homespun aspects.

Although organized capitalism developed before the Second World War, French development in the post-war period was distinctive. One important indicator of this post-war 'organization' was an exceptional increase in the French population, from 40.5 million in 1946 to 50 million in 1968 and 52.3 million in 1974.[36] This was a far faster rate of increase than had been achieved in any previous quarter century. In this brief period, France became a complete industrial economy. The proportion of the labour force in agriculture fell by over a half – a faster rate than was found in any other industrializing country. Most urban and industrial economies increased in population, sometimes very quickly, while rural areas and older industrial zones both lost population. France became an urban society almost overnight.

We have seen that organized capitalism in France was particularly developed through the active role and intervention of the state in the post-war settlement. This was in part necessitated by the tremendous destruction brought about in the war: one-third of all railway stations were damaged; one-third of all cars destroyed; 91,000 factories rendered inoperative; and 2 million buildings destroyed.[37] Prior to the war, the French state was an active partner in preserving stability; after the war its role became much more that of *L'État Entrepreneur*.[38] The French state began to pursue a national economic policy, particularly through attempting to increase exports. Substantial government subsidiaries were channelled through the state-dominated banking network to support research and development and technological education.[39] Within the context of the newly developed national economic planning a number of privately-owned industries were nationalized (coal, electricity, gas, banks, insurance, Air France, Renault etc.), and a number of other companies reorganized multinationally, as in automobiles, tyres and aluminium.[40]

If the early years of the post-war period were characterized by previously unsurpassed levels of economic and spatial organization, by the early 1970s a number of clear indicators began to show that major changes of a broadly disorganizing character were beginning to take place. There was a marked change in the relationship between settlement size and net migration (this is shown in figure 5.1). In the 1950s urbanization was clearly dominant and

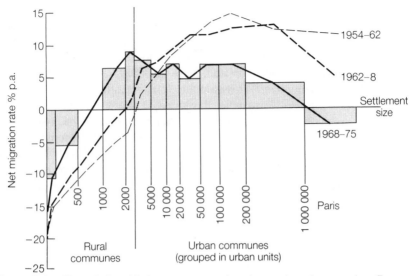

Figure 5.1 The relationship between net migration and settlement size, France 1954–75
Source: A. J. Fielding, 'Counterurbanisation in Western Europe', *Progress in Planning* 17 (1982), pp. 1–52, p. 11.

rural depopulation was wide-ranging. The smaller the settlement size, the faster the population loss. The greater the size of settlement, the greater the population gain. Paris, Lyons and Marseilles all increased in population to a considerable extent. In the 1960s, by contrast, the rates of rural migration were somewhat lower while the industrial regions of Nord and Lorraine suffered population losses. The rate of increase of the Paris population slowed down considerably. In the 1970s the transition was complete with only very small rural communities suffering population losses, while small and medium-sized towns in rural areas experienced considerable population increases. Cities over 1 million began to lose population and Paris, for the first time, experienced a significant net loss (but not the Paris basin). There was the first reversal of the pattern of migration to Paris from the rest of the country that had begun in the previous century.[41] Many rural departments grew in population, while massive net losses were experienced by the Nord and Lorraine. In 1975 rural communes made up 27 per cent of the population but 35 per cent of new housing starts.[42] Overall, then, by the 1970s an inverse relationship between net migration and settlement size had become well-established, although unlike Britain and Germany, the proportion of the population living in settlements above 10,000 increased slightly between 1970 and 1980.[43] That the urban population did not increase considerably in size over the post-war period is particularly surprising considering the dramatic decline in employment in French agriculture.[44] The number of farms fell by three-quarters of a million between 1955 and 1970, while the number of farm workers declined by 40 per cent over the same period, as France rapidly became an industrial economy drawing in many ex-agricultural workers from Mediterranean Europe. Damette and Poncet point out that in the 1960s, while most regions had similar rates by which new jobs were being created, there was great variation in the rates at which jobs were being lost.[45] It was in the principal agricultural regions like Pays de la Loire, Basse-Normandie, Burgoyne, Poitou-Charentes, Aquitaine, Auvergne, Midi-Pyrenees and Bretagne, that the greatest job losses were recorded; yet it was also some of these very regions that demonstrated the most substantial increases in population in the period 1960–80.[46] Aydalot argues that from 1968–75 onwards there was an inverse correlation established between migration movements and net levels of regional income per capita and there was more or less no relationship between migration movements and regional unemployment levels.[47]

One obvious consequence of the period of rapid population growth up to the 1960s was a fairly considerable house-building programme. This, of course, was also necessitated by the wartime destruction noted earlier. Some towns, such as Le Havre or Boulogne, were completely remodelled in the post-war reconstruction, while in others there was a substantial building programme of suburban high-rise flats. In these *grands ensembles* no particular provision was made for shops, schools or social centres. In Paris a massive programme of suburban housing was carried out throughout the 1950s and 1960s. In the few years between 1962 and 1968, for example, the outer *departements* of Val d'Oise, Yvelines and Essonne increased in population by 29 per cent while the population in central Paris fell by 7 per cent.[48] The *grands ensembles* built around Paris have been singularly problematic – the largest one, Sarcelles, having given rise to the disease *Sarcellitis*. Little employment was to be found in these suburbs and so the typical suburban worker had to commute into central Paris. Moreover, the suburbs were generally built beyond the limits of the Metro system.[49] At the same time as this building was taking place, however, the housing densities in central Paris remained extremely high and much of the accommodation remains overcrowded and lacking in basic amenities. The central area lost 220,000 inhabitants between 1975 and 1982.[50]

One reason for the continuing importance of the Paris region relates to the extreme concentration of the headquarters of major companies within it. Thus in the mid-1970s four-fifths of the head offices of the major French manufacturing firms were located there.[51] This was in contrast to Britain, where about one-half of the headquarters of comparable companies were located in London. Likewise, about 60 per cent of 'research activities' have been centralized in Paris.[52] These spatial inequalities are reflected in the patterns of inter-regional dependence in France. Briguel shows that the Île de France has virtually no dependence upon any other region.[53] Only a tiny 3 per cent of industrial employment related to companies that were controlled outside that region. Yet, by contrast, a massive 40 per cent of all industrial employment in France was controlled by Paris-based companies. Furthermore, in 1971 over half of all industrial investment outside Paris was undertaken by firms with headquarters in the Île de la France.

At the same time, however, there has been a fairly extensive decentralization of industrial production in France over the past decade or two.[54] This has occurred partly through various conventional regional policy initiatives (training schemes, tax incentives, favourable energy prices, investment grants etc.); partly through the direct establishment of eight 'growth poles' with some decentralization of service employment; and partly because of the new forms of the spatial division of labour. Aydalot reports that half the moves between urban areas are over more than 200 km; the areas to the west and south acquired considerable inward investment.[55] However, the moves were of establishments and not of headquarters and many of the moves from the older industrial areas were in fact to the Paris Basin.[56] Aydalot notes that the pattern of de-industrialization is one involved in the 'de-industrialisation of urban zones, favouring the more peripheral districts and bringing about the industrial demise of the more central districts'.[57] Indeed, he suggests that spatial concentration today is about the same level as it was in 1850; although that previous dispersion coincided with highly dispersed capital while today's decentralized pattern reflects a high concentration of capital.[58]

A further reason for the reduced spatial concentration of industry has been the rapid change in the employment structure of France. In 1946 only one-third of the labour force was employed in services, while the figure was over 45 per cent in the UK. By 1970 the figure for France had risen to 48 per cent and by 1982 it was 57 per cent.[59] This was somewhat unequally distributed, with the Île de France having a location quotient based on population of 1.47, while all other regions varied between 0.78 (Nord–Pas de Calais) and 1.17 (Baissin Parisien).[60] Service employment between 1972 and 1984 increased from under 10.5 million to just under 12 million: one of the fastest rates of increase of any European country apart from Italy. At the same time the numbers employed in manufacturing employment fell from 8.25 million in 1972 to 7.25 million in 1982, a considerable decline but not nearly as fast as that of the UK.[61]

Although this period a number of French multinationals came to be of considerable importance in the French economy; there was also a sizeable increase in the number of establishments generally, and particularly of those which are very small. Table 5.1 presents the size distribution of French establishments in 1971 and 1982. Unfortunately the data do not enable us to assess the changes in the numbers of large establishments with over 1000 employees. Aydalot concludes that 'in France, as in the United States, overall manpower decreased in large firms while, on the contrary, the increasing dynamism of small firms stimulated their employment possibilities'.[62]

Table 5.1   Size distribution of French establishments 1971, 1982

		No. of establishments 1971			No. of establishments 1982
Employees	0–5	1,670,910	Employees	0–5	2,680,052
	6–49	211,552		6–49	338,734
	50–199	25,191		50–99	25,975
	200–999	6,041		100–199	13,196
	1000 plus	599		200 plus	10,978
TOTAL		1,914,293	TOTAL		3,068,935

Source: adapted from INSEE, *Annuaire Statistique de la France* (INSEE, Paris, 1975), p. 604 and (1982), p. 242.

One reason for this has been the extraordinary resilience of the family-organized firm in the French economy. As Landes argued:[63]

> Such economic unity exists because of the profound social ties of family with firm. The business is not an end in itself, nor is its purpose to be found in any such independent ideal as production or service. It exists by and for the family . . . The word *maison* has retained business connotations long since lost by our word 'house'. It is this bond that accounts for the astonishing solidarity shown by French families when the integrity or the stability is imperilled.

The relatively unlimited power of the typical *patron* accounts for aspects of the social relations between capital and labour which have never become institutionalized. French employers have retained their traditional rights to determine unilaterally both the terms of payment and the organization of work within the firm.[64] Representatives of the labour force have always been given minimal influence over decision-making. In some industries this resulted in a paternalist relationship which overall resulted in low levels of union density and organization in France (25 per cent by the 1960s).[65] However, some French workers have sustained singularly high levels of work grievance and militant organization – a class consciousness which meant that grievances could not be locally confined but were generalized to the national level. In some years this resulted in very high levels of strike action. In 1948, for example, over 6.5 million workers were involved in strikes; in 1957, nearly 3 million. In 1947 22.5 million working days were lost in strikes; nearly 12 million in 1950; nearly 10 million in 1953; nearly 6 million in 1963; over 4 million in 1967, and so on.[66] The contrast with West Germany is shown in Table 5.2.

As in the case of Britain, the thesis of 'disorganization' is not one of simply working-class decomposition. Indeed, France has some interestingly distinctive

Table 5.2 Industrial disputes in France and West Germany in the 1960s

| Year | France | | | West Germany | | |
	No.	Workers involved (1000s)	Days lost (1000s)	No.	Workers involved (1000s)	Days lost (1000s)
1960	1,494	1,072	1,070	28	17	38
1961	1,963	2,552	2,601	119	20	61
1962	1,884	1,472	1,901	195	79	451
1963	2,382	2,646	5,991	187	316	1,846
1964	2,281	2,603	2,497	34	6	17
1965	1,674	1,237	980	20	6	49
1966	1,711	3,341	1,523	205	196	27
1967	1,675	2,824	4,204	742	60	390
1968	...	...	...	36	25	25
1969	2,480	...	2,224	86	90	249

Source: adapted from Mitchell, *European Historical Statistics*, p. 179.

patterns of strikes and militancy which are worth noting. First, the larger cities tended to have higher rates of strike activity when faster growing cities had lower rates.[67] These larger cities were clustered in particular regions and account for the noticeably regional clustering of strike activity. Second, the larger plants have not been particularly militant in France; as Shorter and Tilly argue, 'the small shop, with its emotional rivalries and natural benefits to worker cohesiveness, was a much superior incubator of solidarity.'[68] The First World War provided an interesting watershed: before 1914 the large plants were highly unionized for the period, while after 1918 the large plants de-unionized while the smaller plants increased their unionization and strike rates. Third, the massive wave of strikes in 1967 and 1968, particularly the sit-down strikes of May–June 1968, were the largest mobilization of workers in French history.[69] They involved very considerable numbers of white-collar and service-sector workers, and the mobilization was highly 'disorganized'. Generally, it consisted of local unions which took command in disregard of, and partly in opposition to, the wishes of the national federations and confederations of labour. To some degree, therefore, it represented a highly disorganized pattern of labour-based politics, although its concentration in Paris made it more characteristic of an organized pattern. What we have already suggested is that between the late 1960s and about 1980 there was a period of transition from organized to disorganized capitalism in France, a process somewhat lengthy and producing a great deal of conflict partly because of the relatively recent establishment of organized capitalism.

GERMANY

Much greater than in any of the other countries being considered, have been the changes in the territory understood to comprise Germany over the past century and a half. Although we shall refer to a single entity *Germany*, careful notice has to be paid to the changing geographical boundary of this entity; especially, of course, to the fact that in the post-war period we shall deal only with the Federal Republic of Germany.[70] Nevertheless, partly because of this, the concept of the unified German nation, and more generally of 'nationhood', has been particularly influential. Even one of Germany's most gifted 'liberal' thinkers, Max Weber, built his political convictions upon the notion that the 'national' was in a sense central, that national state power was the essential point of reference for political action at least within Germany.[71] This concern for establishing and sustaining the German nation-state arose for a number of reasons: first, because Germany enjoyed little in the way of natural boundaries and therefore always had a problem in determining its boundaries with its many neighbours; second, because unification was only achieved in 1871 and partly through military struggle; and third, because the newly formed German state contained a number of very powerful centrifugal forces, politically between its various constituent sovereign states, and economically between Berlin in the east and the Ruhr in the west.

The extremely rapid growth of German industry in the last decade or so of the nineteenth century has already been noted. This posed particular problems for the unity and effectiveness of the variety of succeeding German states, the Wilhelmine state, the Weimar Republic, the Nazi state and so on. The social structure of the first of these has been characterized as an 'industrial feudal society' in which governance was achieved through an 'authoritarian welfare state'.[72]

This development of an industrial economy was clearly reflected in the changing demographic pattern in Germany. Although urbanization had begun around the middle of the century it really gathered pace between unification in 1871 and the First World War. Thus, while in 1871 less than one-quarter of the population lived in towns with more than 5000 inhabitants, by 1910 this had doubled to just under one-half.[73] Particularly notable was the increase in population living in cities with over 100,000 inhabitants. In 1871 less than one-twentieth lived in these large cities; by 1910 this had risen to over one-fifth of the German population.[74] The number of these large cities had risen from 8 in 1871 to 48 in 1910.[75]

Considerable differences by region were to be found in these developments. In the Rhine province by 1910 almost three-quarters lived in towns and over half lived in large cities. Indeed, in 1910 in just the three areas of Saxony, the Rhine province and Westphalia, there were more urban dwellers than the total population had been in the whole of Germany in 1871.[76] Saxony and the Rhine developed very large cities, while much of the expansion of Westphalia was in small and medium-sized urban settlements.[77] East Prussia, which in 1871 had had the third largest population of the seven areas constituting the German Reich, grew most slowly of all, having only half a million urban dwellers in 1910, compared with over 2.5 million in Westphalia, nearly 3 million in Saxony, and nearly 5 million in the Rhine province.[78] The extraordinary growth in some urban centres (Gelsenkirchen's population trebled in size, 1868–71)[79] and in certain regions resulted from complex processes of internal migration, particularly from surrounding rural hinterlands and from the rural regions of the south and the west.[80] Also, though, the urban population was itself not permanently established since many towns exhibited very high rates of population turnover, particularly some of those in the Ruhr.

Among the cities which grew rapidly the importance of Berlin must, of course, be recognized: its population doubled between 1871 and 1890 as it drew population from both east and west Prussia.[81] Indeed, these regions became ever more agricultural during this period as population, industry and employment became more concentrated in Berlin – a process aided by the communications pattern in the east which was focused on Berlin. After 1871 Berlin had become the capital of the newly established German Reich; and it quickly became the commercial and financial centre as well.[82] Berlin took over part at least of the role of the older trading and banking centres, such as Frankfurt-am-Main, Hamburg and Leipzig, although it did not achieve such a prominent position within the national urban system as did Paris or London because of a traditionally strong regionalism reflected in the powerful position of various regional capitals.[83] Nevertheless, Berlin expanded in size, particularly under inspiration of the Hobrecht plan which led to extensive peripheral growth beyond the old city walls.

Clearly the context in which this expansion occurred was the massive sectoral transformation of the German economy at the end of the nineteenth century. In 1882 half the working population in Germany was employed in agriculture with less than a third in industry (this included mining, manufacturing, construction and transportation).[84] Just 25 years later (in 1907) the proportion employed in agriculture had fallen to 35.2 per cent while that in industry had risen to 42.7 per cent – only Britain having anything like the same rate of manufacturing employment during this period.[85] The decline in agricultural employment resulted from very substantial increases in agricultural productivity – increases far greater than those achieved by any of the corresponding European societies.

Much, but not all, of the expansion in agricultural production and productivity occurred in the eastern parts of Germany. Here the disintegration of the manorial economy had given rise to the Junkers, who were bound together through kinship, neighbourly traditions, and common interests in undermining the peasantry and in protecting their large estates.[86] Between 1800 and 1860, for example, 2.5 million acres of peasant land were appropriated by the Junkers; by 1907 over 40 per cent of the agricultural area east of the Elbe was made up of farms of over 100 hectares.[87] The economic and political power of the Junker class was particularly reinforced through the Bismarck constitution of the German Reich (1871), since it was Prussia that ruled the Reich and it was the Junkers who predominated in Prussia,[88] even when, in the case of Caprivi, there was a chancellor who did not immediately recognize that the interests of the large estate owners were paramount.[89] Thus Weber could, without undue exaggeration, claim:[90]

> With us, the broad strata of the bourgeoisie are still excluded from power by that feudalism which rules ministers and factory owners and makes them accept aristocratic titles.

The industrialization in Germany during the later part of the nineteenth and early years of the twentieth centuries occurred in an atmosphere pervaded by the political and ideological coloration of the Junker class; German society, according to Dahrendorf, remained quasi-feudal.[91]

One important reason for this was the pattern of industrialization in Germany. Throughout most of the nineteenth century industry was far more dispersed throughout the countryside than was the case in Britain. This was for a number of reasons: the continued reliance on water rather than steam power; the greater importance of metalworking and mining rather than textiles which were more dependent on the location of raw materials; and the increased importance of putting-out at least in the areas to the east of the Elbe where rural labour remained extremely cheap.[92] It was only by the 1880s that this dispersed and spatially relatively undifferentiated pattern had substantially changed, particularly under the influence of Bismarckian policy designed to effect German economic and social unification. Developments here included currency reform, the establishment of a central bank, the substantial nationalization of the railways, protectionism, imperialism and welfarism.[93]

As a result, a degree of regional specialization began to develop. By 1882 one-half of the German population lived in regions which significantly diverged from the national average structure.[94] Half of these lived in overwhelmingly industrial regions where this sector employed between 40–60 per cent of the labour force (Saxony, Westphalia, Rhineland). In the case of both Rhineland and Westphalia development up to the middle of the century was dispersed in many small locations. The most significant development in the next 30 years was the spectacular growth in the specific subregion of the Ruhr. It very quickly outpaced the other areas in Rhineland and Westphalia, particularly in the metals industries.[95] Tipton summarizes:[96]

> Metal products were sensitive to the location of coal resources because of the bulkiness and weight loss of coal used for fuel. In the Ruhr mining and heavy metals grew together. Mining employment increased from one hundred eighty to three hundred seventeen thousand workers between 1895 and 1907, and employment in metals from one hundred sixty-seven to three hundred seven thousand.

There were a number of critically significant consequences of this extraordinary development, one which occurred largely in opposition to the Junker-dominated Prussian influence in the post-1871 German Reich. First of all, agriculture in the Ruhr was substantially harmed by the high levels of smoke and ash in the atmosphere and by the indiscriminate sinking and regular collapse of mines.[97] Secondly, the rapid growth of metalworking and mining industries led to the final end of state supervision of working conditions in 1865 – and as a result work rules were changed and increases occurred in the length of the working day.[98] This was particularly important in the case of the coal-mining industry which had previously been organized with miners as members of a 'corporate body' with a recognized status in German society.[99] With the removal of the state's supervision of coal-mining operations, miners ceased to be guild-like workers attached to a particular mine and became much more subject to conventional capitalist rationality.[100] (Coalminers were not apparently involved in the events of 1848; but by 1872 18,000 miners went on strike and in 1889 81,000 miners in the Ruhr alone went on strike.)[101]

Thirdly, the rapid growth in towns and cities meant that many of the 'community' ties connecting employer and workers collapsed in this period. This was particularly true for those workers who had migrated to the Ruhr from rural areas, especially those to the east of the Elbe. The new towns and cities saw a very great turnover of population – so much so that movement had become the norm.[102] Fourthly, many new entrepreneurs were recruited into industry and a lot of these operated without particular patterns of obligation to their employees, particularly with the removal of much of the protective legislation.[103] Partly, this resulted because there was a very strong social gulf between the industrial elite in the Ruhr towns and the workforce, and there was little or no chance of workers themselves becoming small-scale entrepreneurs.[104] Often this was because many of the new industrial capitalists were 'outsiders' to the towns themselves, to some extent opposed to the existing *mittelstand* of small-scale property-owners.[105] In Bochum this antagonism remained of importance for many decades. Finally, the rapid growth of especially heavy industry in the Ruhr produced a local industrial bourgeoisie which was 'illegitimate' and which was unable to run 'their' local town or city as they would have wished. One effect of this was that employers controlled their enterprises as 'virtually separate communities over which they could exercise a far more complete dominion'.[106]

A consequence was extensive, albeit uneven, social protest, particularly in the Ruhr in the period before the First World War. Over 1 million German workers went on strike in the single year 1912.[107] There are a number of points that need to be made here:

1   It was the more secure and especially the more skilled workers who were likely to be union members and to participate frequently in strikes.[108]
2   It was workers in the largest concerns who were less likely to be union members and to go on strike,[109] although it should be noted that unions were organized, as in France, only outside the workplace.
3   It was workers in more homogeneous working-class industries and communities that were able to sustain greater solidarity and militancy – miners, for example, as opposed to metalworkers, who were 'utterly fractured along several lines of potential cleavage: religious, national, economic, political'.[110]
4   In many cases workers were provided with company housing and this tied workers to their employers and seems to have made them less militant.[111]
5   The actions of the state, particularly the exceptional law against socialists which was in operation between 1878 and 1890, which turned the social democratic movement in a militant and partially Marxist direction, especially as both the Junkers and the industrialists were at least united in their implacable hostility to socialism.[112]
6   The very recent formation of the German middle class which meant that it had to compete immediately with the massively expanding and exceptionally

powerful industrial proletariat and this seemed to have heightened antagonism.[113]

7   The high turnover in many plants made it difficult to organize workers, especially in the large, very rapidly expanding Ruhr cities.[114]

8   The organization of unions and of the Social Democratic Party covered many different aspects of the lives of their members. The SPD, for instance, published over 70 newspapers and ran choral societies, gymnastic and cycling clubs, pubs and clubs, insurance schemes etc.: it constituted in a sense a whole alternative subculture, a mechanism of 'negative integration'.[115]

9   There was considerable antagonism on the part of many unions to the attempt to make them more centralized and hence governed by full-time national officials. This opposition was particularly marked in the case of metalworking and building unions which were organized in distinct localities and bitterly resented the growth of national structures.[116]

Compared with Britain, the militancy of this period was successful in generating the first mass socialist movement, but extraordinarily unsuccessful in that there was very little development of collective agreements between workers and employers. In 1913 82 coalminers were so covered in Germany, compared with 900,000 in Britain in 1910.[117]

Organized capitalism was further consolidated at the bottom during the First World War by a very large extension of such collective agreements. The best data relating the industrial/occupational structure relate nevertheless to 1907; table 5.3 summarizes the basic divisions. Barrington Moore, on the basis of

Table 5.3 Industrial/occupational structure of Germany 1907

Occupations		No. of workers (in 1000s)
Agriculture and forestry		9,883
Industry and mining		11,256
Made up of:		
independent proprietors	1,977	
office workers	686	
workers and helpers	8,593	
Commerce and transportation		3,478
Miscellaneous including servants		472
Free professions		1,087
No occupation reported		3,405
Rentiers		1,792
Not in the labour force		31,000[a]
TOTAL		62,373

[a] Approximate figure.
Source: adapted from Moore, Injustice, p. 175.

the figures in this table and elsewhere, points out the relatively small size of the German proletariat in this period. Only about 8 million out of 62 million were industrial workers. Moreover, he says that if we were to consider only those working in *new* industries and living in medium and large cities as really proletarian, then there were perhaps 1 million or so workers, or 4 million household members, who could be deemed members of an industrial urban proletariat.[118]

There were very significant changes in the composition of this industrial labour force during the First World War. For example, the Krupp works in Essen grew from 34,000 in 1913 to more than 100,000 in 1918; another major establishment gained 28,000 workers during the war but lost 21,000. It was reported by the Factory Inspection Service that each worker spent no more than one year in any single job.[119] One important consequence of this was that many individuals in the labour force who before the war had favoured social stability were no longer clearly and unambiguously entrenched in key positions. Barrington Moore argues:[120]

> The chaos, confusion, moving about, rise and fall in individual fortunes that characterized the fate of the German working classes in general during the war appear to have been especially intense in the Ruhr.

And in particular there were major changes in the typical workplace and the typical labour process in this period. Tampke summarizes changes in the Ruhr:[121]

> Where before the war the small workshop and the medium-sized factory... [were] the chief source[s] of employment, now the bulk of the German labour force was found in the *Grossbetrieb* with its mechanised assembly lines. The type of worker also changed. Skilled craftsmen made way for semi-skilled factory workers. Huge plants arose...

We will not detail the social conditions which underpinned the revolutionary events at the end of the war, nor indeed the events themselves. Rather we will consider the main economic and social features of German organized capitalism.

The first point to note is the relative importance in Germany compared with elsewhere of the new industries; electrics and chemicals. The leading firms included Siemens, Bosch (electrical); Degussa, Hoechst, Bayer, Agfa (chemicals). All of these companies were by 1914 manufacturing in a number of western economies. By 1929 there were about 150 German manufacturing subsidiaries established throughout the world.[122] Part of the reason for this tendency to export manufacturing capacity abroad was the somewhat different structure of demand for industrial products in Germany as compared with the USA and UK which reflected the income distribution in Germany throughout the period of organized capitalism. In 1913, for example, the middle income families in Germany (the fortieth to eightieth percentiles) received only 27 per cent of the national income, compared with 36 per cent in the USA (in 1918).[123] This, it is suggested, resulted in the typical pattern of German industry which involved either the satisfying of demand for mass products (the Volkswagen Beetle, for example), or the production for a luxury market (Daimler, Benz), with relatively less production for the market inbetween.[124]

During the inter-war period there were significant regional variations which are broadly indicated in table 5.4. The proportion of workers in agriculture fell and that in tertiary employment increased in all regions. In the case of industrial employment different patterns can be observed in different areas. Certain of the less industrialized regions (Südost, Südwest) increased in industrial employment, while this fell a little in the most industrialized areas (west, centre). The main point to note is that the regional differences established before the First World War remained broadly the same for the next few decades and that distinct regional economies were thus to be found in Germany during the first half of this century. Dahrendorf suggests that these differences were in part responsible for explaining variations in the degree of voting for parties of the extreme right.[125] In the Reichstag elections in November 1932, 31.3 per cent of the Berlin electorate, 37.2 per cent of what is now the German Federal Republic, 45.1 per cent of what is now the German Democratic Republic, and 61.6 per cent of the eastern territories now part of Poland and the USSR, voted for the National Socialist and other extreme right parties.

Over the first half of this century there was a marked increase in the average size of establishments in German industry. Between 1907 and 1950 the proportion of the labour force employed in establishments with 5 workers or less fell from 31.2 per cent to 16.2 per cent; while that proportion with over 200 workers increased from 16.7 per cent to 19.6 per cent; and that with over 1000 increased from 4.9 per cent to 13.5 per cent.[126] These tendencies have occurred steadily over the period except for 1933, when there was a sizeable increase in the proportion of the labour force employed in small firms (explained as a 'flight into self-employment' during the Depression) and a reduction in the proportion of workers in large firms (explained by the fact that mass redundancies principally occurred among larger firms).

The most distinctive features of the development of West Germany after the immense devastation of the Second World War were, firstly, its organization as a decentralized federal state, and secondly, its extremely rapid economic growth.[127] Conservative commentators have linked the two features noting the extremely strong emphasis on *laissez-faire* economic policies, such policies being seen as the natural accompaniment of a minimal central government. Until the 1960s this policy of *Sozialmarktwirtschaft* (social market economy) was at one level fairly vigorously pursued. However, other aspects of post-war policy designed to 'disorganize' the centralized structures of the Nazi period were less successful. The attempt to prevent any 'reconcentration' of

Table 5.4 Regional distribution of the working population in Germany 1907, 1925, 1939 (in %)

	Year	East	North-west	Centre	West	South-west	South-east	Total
Agriculture	1907	39.2	35.0	24.9	27.2	44.0	52.0	35.5
	1925	33.4	30.9	21.9	22.8	39.2	45.0	30.5
	1939	28.3	26.3	18.5	20.2	31.4	38.4	25.9
Industry	1907	36.8	37.6	54.5	52.3	39.0	30.0	43.0
	1925	35.5	34.3	52.6	48.7	39.4	32.5	42.1
	1939	36.2	35.6	52.1	48.5	42.9	34.0	42.2
Tertiary	1907	24.0	27.4	20.6	20.5	17.0	18.0	21.5
	1925	31.1	34.8	25.5	28.5	21.4	22.7	27.4
	1939	35.4	38.1	29.4	31.3	25.7	27.6	31.9

Source: D. Petzina, W. Abelhauser and A. Faust, *Sozialgeschichtliches Arbeitsbuch III* (C. H. Beck, Munich, 1978), p. 56.

nation-wide bank power by, for example, confining the branches of a given bank to a single *Land*, broke down as early as 1950, when two of the three big banks had regained control of all their branch banks.[128] A further force aiming for 'reorganized' capitalism in the post-war period was the re-establishment of the German industrial association and especially the central body, the *Bundesverband der Deutschen Industrie*. This was set up in 1949 and was based on 39 national industrial federations which were essentially taken over from the Nazi period.[129] These associations were structured very hierarchically – in the Nazi era the system of associations modelled by Krupp was organized like an industrial *army* (with *captains* of industry).[130] In the post-war period there was still a very strong tendency for firms to collaborate, to plan and organize with each other, especially guided or aided by the banks. Shonfield suggests that the situation described by Alfred Marshall still applies to the post-war period:[131]

> Each of the great banks has representatives on several other banks and on a vast number of industrial enterprises. . . Representatives of banks have exercised, for two generations at least, a strong control on industrial businesses which they support.

Indeed, since we have seen that bank control was less effective in the inter-war period than has been previously argued, there was considerable continuity between the pre- and post-war period. There was also extensive representation by the banks on the boards of companies, particularly on the *Aufsichsräte*, or supervisory boards, and this encouraged German companies to engage in long-term forecasting and planning, especially within the context of national income data.[132] Furthermore, for all the West German rhetoric about the free market, the federal government, even in the 1950s, actively intervened in the economy discriminating between industries through the offering of special tax benefits, large depreciation allowances, tax remissions for exporters, subsidies, cheap loans etc.[133] The main aspects in which there was less 'organization' were, first, the disappearance of cartels, and second, the reduced importance of heavy industry, which were typically the most 'organized' sectors.

Apart from these characteristics of a continuing 'organized capitalism' at the top during the 1950s and 1960s, a further factor which contributed to the West German economic miracle was the massive migration during the post-war period.[134] At first this came mainly from East Germany, but then from Italy, Greece, Turkey and Yugoslavia. The movement of the latter, the *Gastarbeiter*, assumed staggering proportions: by 1973 there were almost 4 million.[135] This helped to produce a sizeable increase in population in West Germany in the post-war period, although both death and birth rates have continued to decline.

The distribution of this population also changed. At the end of the war the population was fairly widely distributed. This was because of, firstly, the still considerable proportion of the population employed in agriculture; secondly, the large number of refugees from the east who settled in the more easterly (more rural) parts of West Germany; and thirdly, the wholesale destruction of urban areas during the war. It has been calculated that in the large cities over half the housing stock was destroyed, in medium-sized towns one-third, and in small towns one quarter.[136] Over the next 20 years there was an enormous rebuilding programme much organized and financed by the separate *Länder*. The physical size of towns grew considerably, partly because of the confused conditions in the bombed out inner cities, and partly because of the belief dating back to Weimar that workplaces, residences and leisure activities should be physically separated.[137] During this period also the West German population grew more urbanized with a number of major urban centres replacing the previously dominant Berlin. Big cities, at least in the 1950s, grew in population, while rural areas declined.[138] The west and the south-west also benefited from population gains. In the 1960s some cities, such as Munich, Frankfurt, Wiesbaden and Koln/Bonn, continued to grow in population, while much of the Ruhr, other Rhineland areas, and the eastern rural areas lost population. In the 1970s those areas containing large cities tended to show net migration loss, except in the case of Bonn and Munich, although much of the expansion of these was due to the growth of surrounding smaller towns. The Ruhr continues to lose population in the 1980s, while there has been expansion in population for the more rural parts of northern Germany. By the late 1970s there was general evidence of 'counter-urbanization', although it was less marked than in some of the other societies we have examined. This is partly because West Germany already constituted the extreme case of the decentralization of all its leading urban functions.[139]

The decline in the population of the Ruhr reflects the economic changes it has experienced in the post-war period. For the first 100 years or so of German development the Ruhr was the very centre of the economy, but since the late 1950s its pre-eminence has been challenged as industry has developed elsewhere.[140] There has in fact been a general shift in the balance of industrial power away from the northern cities, such as Essen, Dortmund, Duisburg and Brunswick, to southern cities such as Munich, Frankfurt, Karlsruhe, Nuremberg, and Stuttgart. This shift has stemmed from a number of factors. First, there have been dramatic changes in the sources of energy employed in West Germany. In 1960 coal provided three-quarters of German energy; by 1972 this had fallen to one-third.[141] Even by 1960 oil was competing with coal within the Ruhr, but in that period it mainly reinforced existing patterns of industrial production. But the more rural *Länder*, especially in the south, soon realized that oil could spearhead industrial development in alternative areas. The first strategy involved extending North Sea oil pipelines further south and the construction of a huge refinery near Frankfurt. More radical than this, however, was the linking of certain German cities to terminals on the Mediterranean coast. Pipelines connected Marseilles with Karlsruhe and Mannheim, and Genoa and Trieste with Ingolstadt. By 1968 every *Land* except West Berlin (not strictly a *Land*) had its own refinery and associated growth areas.[142] By the early 1970s German industry had become dependent upon world-determined oil prices and experienced a massive decline in the coal-mining industry (there was no longer a single productive pit in Bochum, for example). Certain efforts were made to support the coal industry, partly because around 1970 30 per cent of the population still lived in Nordrhein-Westfalen and 80 per cent voted for the SPD.[143]

The iron and steel and chemical industries in Germany have lagged behind the high technology and consumer goods industries like electronics and vehicle manufacture.[144] Partly this was because the Allies forced upon West German industry a policy of decartelization, to break up the massive companies of organized capitalism in pre-war Germany. One of the consequences of this policy was to diversify the major industrial companies whose interests have thus become very broadly based.[145] Krupp, for example, more or less abandoned basic iron and steel production and became a large and varied engineering company. A somewhat different pattern was to be found in the case of the chemical industry. During the Third Reich the German chemical industry had been dominant. After the war the allies prevented the German companies from manufacturing most of its basic products, such as synthetic rubber and oil.[146] Instead, however, the industry developed a completely new range of products, mostly based on oil, but also including a range of artificial fibres and textiles, to some extent away from the older, smaller centres.

The German automobile industry has likewise shifted location. In the 1950s production was primarily concentrated in Wolfsburg in the north-east (Volkswagen), and in the Rhine-Main area (Opel and Ford).[147] Since then a disproportionate amount of growth in the industry has occurred in Bavaria and Baden-Wurtemberg. Volkswagen, Opel and Ford established assembly plants in the south because of the availability of cheaper, less organized labour; while BMW in Munich was the fastest growing motor vehicle firm in the 1960s. In the electrical industry Siemens used Munich as a base in order to expand into nine smaller towns within a radius of 100 km of the city.[148]

So far we have considered only single very large German companies. What is the more general recent pattern of employment within different regions in West Germany? First of all, the headquarters of German firms are strongly concentrated in a small number of central agglomerations. Of the largest industrial enterprises in West Germany, 42 per cent have their headquarters in the Rhine-Ruhr area;[149] of the largest 500 companies, 80 per cent are found in one of the eleven largest agglomerations. Or, to put it rather differently, if we consider the five largest agglomerations (Hamburg, Rhine-Ruhr, Rhine-Main, Stuttgart, Munich), in 1971 they contained only 17.6 per cent of all industrial plants, but 43 per cent of all headquarters (out of a sample of 716 firms).[150]

Thus headquarters have become more centralized in Germany, and at the same time production plants in more central areas have a higher proportion of 'non-production' workers. However, industrial *employment* has become not more concentrated, but more dispersed within these large industrial companies. Bade summarizes:[151]

> Most characteristics worsen when moving from centres towards other agglomerated and non-agglomerated areas and then on to the peripheral regions of the FRG. In respect, however, to employment growth the picture is the reverse. While in the period 1970–80 most locations, especially those in central areas, suffered losses, the peripheral locations increased their employment... Whereas the employment in central locations fell between 1970–80 by 3.9%, the peripheral locations *increased* by 1.9%.

Three other points should be noted. First, for all industrial plants employment fell in central areas of the agglomerations by 20.4 per cent between 1970 and 1980, while in peripheral areas the decline was only 6.8 per cent. Second, large firms, rather than 'industry as a whole', did significantly better in employment terms in peripheral areas over this same period.[152] And third, there has been some levelling out in the characteristics and fortunes of different regions in West Germany: those with the higher per capita incomes in 1950 losing ground (Hamburg, Nordrhein-Westfalen, Bremen) and those with the lower per capita incomes gaining ground by 1970 (Bayern, Rheinland-Pfalz, Lower Saxony, Schleswig-Holstein).[153] Keeble, Owens and Thompson argue that there has been some tendency for the more rural areas to gain in output and employment, while the more urbanized the area the greater the tendency for output and employment to fall; this is shown in table 5.5.[154] Furthermore they show that this urban–rural shift in West Germany (as in the rest of Western Europe) is not confined to particular types of industry but characterizes a fairly wide spectrum in all sectors, and has occurred from all the major urban centres.[155] However, interestingly, the more rural areas tend to possess a higher proportion of those manufacturing industries which are declining faster in Europe overall, while the particularly urbanized regions possess a more favourable industrial structure. Given this discrepancy the urban–rural shift is then even more surprising and suggests that there has been quite a marked dispersal to rural areas of older labour-intensive industries as part of a general process of capitalist restructuring, although this occurred more noticeably in the late 1960s and early 1970s than more recently.[156]

We will now consider the role that small firms appear to play in the contemporary German economy. Certainly until the 1970s, they provided a declining proportion of German employment. In manufacturing the percentage distribution of employment provided by firms employing less than 10 people fell from about one-quarter in 1950 to one-tenth in 1970.[157] However, more recent evidence suggests that this has changed and that the smaller firm is

Table 5.5 Urban–rural shift in industrial output and employment in West Germany 1970–9

Region	Manufacturing employment		Gross value-added at market prices: industry, energy, construction	
	% Share 1973	Change[a] 1973–9	% Share 1970	Change[b] 1970–7
Highly urbanized	30.9	− 1.8	36.3	− 2.7
Urbanized	28.2	+ 0.3	26.8	+ 0.1
Less urbanized	18.7	+ 0.9	19.4	+ 1.4
Rural	22.2	+ 0.6	17.4	+ 1.3

[a] 1979 % share minus 1973 % share.
[b] 1977 % share minus 1970 % share.
Source: Keeble, Owens, Thompson, 'The urban–rural manufacturing shift', p. 412.

again growing in importance in West Germany. Friedrich and Spitznagel investigated 844 manufacturing firms in the 1970s and concluded that large firms were not an important motor of growth: the growing firms were predominantly those with less than 200 employees.[158] A further study by *Infratest* showed that between 1973 and 1980 there was an almost unbroken trend of employment growth in firms employing fewer than 10 persons – they increased employment by 50 per cent.[159] Firms with 10–99 employees increased employment by 13 per cent, while employment in firms with 100–999 employees fell by 6 per cent and those with over 1000 by 12 per cent.

This shift in turn reflects some decline in manufacturing employment in West Germany in recent years. Thus in 1973 there were 9.25 million workers in manufacturing industry, but by 1977 this had fallen to 8.3 million, and by 1982 the number was a little over 7.75 million.[160] Service employment rose continuously over this period, from 10.25 million in 1973 to 10.75 million in 1977 to 11.5 million in 1982.[161] Furthermore, unlike all the other societies analysed here, service employment is not distributed in a particularly spatially uneven manner:[162] it is less concentrated than employment in general in those larger *Länder* where most employment is found. There is no evidence of domination by any single region. The highest relative concentrations of service employment are to be found in the smaller *Länder*, such as Bremen, Hamburg, Schleswig-Holstein and West Berlin, in some cases at least because of the importance of public sector employment. But in, for example, those *Länder* where there is high public employment (Rheinland Pfalz, Schleswig-Holstein, West Berlin) there is relatively low employment in financial services, and vice versa.[163]

We will now briefly consider the degree to which contemporary West Germany has been disorganized through the growth of new forms of the spatial division of labour which have become known as the 'new international division of labour'. By 1971 West Germany had already become a major exporter of productive capital. There were then 666 foreign manufacturing subsidiaries of West German firms – this compares with 3756 from the USA (1968 figures), 2160 from the UK, 376 from France and 157 from Sweden.[164] The West German subsidiaries were more concentrated into particular sectors than were the subsidiaries of those other countries. Thus 46 per cent were in 'Chemicals and Drugs' and 18 per cent in 'Electrical (including Office Equipment and Computers)'. Over 40 per cent of these subsidiaries were based in other 'developed' parts of Western Europe, including especially the Low Countries and the UK.[165]

However, what is most distinctive about the present period has been a considerable shift in the siting of new productive capital. In recent years investment abroad by West German companies has exceeded the investment in Germany by foreign companies.[166] In particular, there has been a marked increase in investment in the Third World since a number of conditions (inexhaustible supply of cheap labour particularly because of agricultural innovations;

subdivisions of the production process; new techniques of transportation and communication) have conspired to produce a world-wide labour market and a world market for industrial sites. Fröbel, Heinrichs and Kreye illustrate this by noting that between 1966 and 1974/5 the German textile and garment industry more than doubled its foreign employment, while its domestic employment decreased by a quarter, although the proportion of white-collar and skilled workers increased.[167] By 1974/5 some 30,000 employees in the Third World were employed in the foreign production facilities of the West German textile and garment industries as the less skilled, more manual work, was exported. More generally the number of workers *directly* employed by West German manufacturing companies in foreign countries amounted to 20 per cent of the total domestic labour force in the mid-1970s.[168] And at the same time, there was a substantial increase in international subcontracting in which a number of producers were contracted to perform particular parts of the overall production process, producers who were bound to the West German company through subcontracting arrangements.[169] One-seventh of all clothing imports into West Germany now result from such subcontracted production. The following quotation from the *Greiling* group of Mannheim ('Felina')[170] well illustrates many of these developments:

> Felina's current aim is to maintain the present level of output in its German plants and secure increases in output by the use of contract plants abroad. The sole reason for this is the wage difference between the company's own plants in Germany, and the finishing carried out under contract in Yugoslavia, Hungary, Czechoslovakia and Italy, which produce up to a third more cheaply for Felina. At the present time 55% of the pieces are still produced in Federal German plants, with 45% coming from the Felina works in Austria and from subcontracting. Subcontracting abroad is constantly being expanded...The group's general profit situation has improved following the extensive cost-cutting measures of recent years which have stabilised the work-force at 1000 at home and 300 abroad.

Finally, we can note some features of labour organization in Germany. We saw in the previous section that post-war strike rates in West Germany have been substantially lower than in France and indeed the UK. At the same time, however, the proportion of the labour force that has been unionized has always been higher than in France (and the USA) but lower than in the UK or Sweden. Throughout the post-war period about 30 per cent of the total labour force has been unionized, while the proportion of 'non-agricultural wage and salary workers' fell from 44 per cent to 37 per cent between 1950 and 1970.[171] White-collar workers have not been particularly unionized in comparison with, say, Sweden or, to a lesser extent, the UK.

SWEDEN

Swedish organized capitalism we have seen resulted from the separate influences of finance capital and social democracy. This development occurred over a relatively short period. Towards the end of the nineteenth century, Sweden was still an essentially rural, agricultural country with a fairly small population and few major industrially based cities. This began to change fairly dramatically in the period before and just after the First World War. Jorberg states that 'Sweden's industrial development, indeed, probably occurred more swiftly than any other European country's at that time'.[172] The organized pattern once established became more entrenched and less subject to disorganization than in all the other countries under examination.

Before the nineteenth century Sweden was characterized by a highly traditional agriculture based on grain; the importance of an extensive woodland for both timber and hunting; the widespread proliferation of home crafts; a predominantly rural population apart from the 50,000 or so who lived in Stockholm; and a relatively small population of around 1 million.[173] Swedish development was strongly influenced by those processes affecting the peasantry. In 1680 what is known as the *reduktion* occurred and as a result half the lands of the nobility were alienated and either kept by the Crown or were handed over to the peasantry.[174] The *reduktion* saved the peasantry as a class but it also facilitated its ultimate dissolution. The process of redistribution encouraged the commercialization of agriculture and the increased differentiation of the peasantry.

During the nineteenth century the population grew considerably, from 2.4 million in 1800, to 3.5 million in 1850, to 5.5 million in 1910.[175] Nevertheless, the population remained firmly wedded to agriculture, the numbers employed in 'agriculture, forestry and fishing' increasing in absolute terms until 1920. There were at that time twice as many employed in that sector than in manufacturing industry,[176] as well as many rail workers.[177]

There was some urbanization during the nineteenth century. In 1860 one in nine of the population lived in towns and this had increased to one-quarter in 1910. There was considerable internal migration, particularly to the relatively small-scale urban communities with populations between 5,000 and 10,000. Indeed, by 1930 only five Swedish towns were larger than 50,000 and even in 1963 there were only three with populations greater than 100,000.[178] The migration to these modest-sized settlements was made possible by the processes of internal differentiation within the countryside which had been taking place since 1700 or so. This resulted from the *reduktion*, from the substantial increases in rural population which had outstripped the tendency for the subdivision of the land, and from a widespread enclosure movement. As Samuelsson says of the beginning of the nineteenth century, a 'large increase in the number of proprietor peasants occurred concurrently with a large increase in the number of those who owned nothing'.[179] Between 1760 and 1850 the landless and semi-landless agrarian population rose fourfold, making up 40 per cent of the total population; by 1870 over 70 per cent of the rural population were landless or semi-landless.[180] This differentiation in the countryside also led to the massive emigration to the USA of over 1 million Swedes between 1800 and 1910, particularly of young men.[181]

This in turn contributed to the relatively slow rate of urbanization in nineteenth-century Sweden, although two other factors were also of significance. First, there was the very high death rates in Stockholm and in the other major cities; these were astonishing given that they were by no means large towns by European standards.[182] Rates of infantile mortality were also prodigious with half the children dying before the age of one.[183] Second, the spatial divisions of labour in the main Swedish industries of iron, coal, forestry and textiles were all moderately decentralized. Small plants grew up close to the raw materials and this led to the growth of the small industrial communities that we noted above. In the mining of iron ore this produced the development known in Sweden as the 'bruks' – essentially mining villages controlled by a single family who owned the mines, the land and the employees' houses. 'Bruks' were, according to Scase, 'significant in that they avoided the class conflicts elsewhere characteristic of the early period of capitalist industrialisation'.[184] Timber, too, was decentralized. Two kinds of settlement were found: first, the saw-mill communities on the rivers in southern Norrland where some of the plants were relatively substantial; and second, conglomerations of small carpentry workshops. There was in places a fairly dense concentration of such timber workings; however, neither pattern of development resulted in large settlements. In 1890 one of the largest had a population of only 13,215.[185] In the case of textiles, high quality products had been produced by skilled craftsmen located in urban centres and protected by guild restrictions (such as Norkoping).[186] The growth of factories transformed this urbanized pattern and expansion took place in regions where there was little resistance to factory work from existing craftsmen but where there were potential supplies of rural textile workers. Although very large urban centres did not develop in this period the average standard of housing was extremely poor with rows of barracks or shanties, and with considerable segregation between permanent and casual labour, the latter often being female.[187]

The Swedish economy grew very rapidly in the quarter century up to 1914. Berend and Ranki suggest that the growth rate in productivity was the highest in Europe.[188] Industrial production grew 15.25 per cent every decade. Sweden went from having in 1860 a per capita GNP 28 per cent under the average for 13 of the countries in the European periphery, to a situation in 1910 when Swedish per capita GNP was 19 per cent higher than the average.[189] Nevertheless, despite the concentration and centralization of industry after 1880, Duncan notes that:[190]

the landscape by 1900 was not fully urbanised in the usual sense of concentration into a few large conurbation and industrial areas. The remnants of peasant production continued while commercial agriculture favoured the retention of a landless labour force in specialised agricultural areas. Many industrial enterprises were located in industrial villages while some enterprises still profited from the existence of a rural reserve army.

A number of further points should be noted here about the organization of civil society in Sweden by the time of the First World War:

1   There was a considerable degree of class segregation in the developing urban settlements.[191]
2   There was a less marked development of the long-established (multi-generational) traditional working-class community (as compared with Britain): most Swedes are either migrants or children of migrants.[192]
3   There was little development of craft-based unionism but an early and influential growth of industrial unionism.[193]
4   These industrial unions came together in the *Lansorganisationen* as early as 1898 – this combined with the forming of the employers confederation (the Svenska Arbetsgivareföreningen) in 1902 leads Samuelsson to conclude that the ' "organizing" of society, which culminated after World War II, had begun'.[194]
5   Combined with this high degree of organization was marked privatization of personal life which in part resulted from the predominantly individualistic character of Swedish agriculture and rural social relations.[195]

Overall, then, between the mid-nineteenth century and the beginning of the First World War, there was a rapid and extensive development of both industrial capital and of labour and this occurred without significant limitations imposed by earlier social forms. Swedish capital emerged without control by either a landed class or by foreign capital. Labour likewise emerged without strong control by a labour aristocracy and this was one condition which facilitated the early development of industrial unionism and especially of the LO.

Between 1850 and 1980 the Swedish population grew from 3.5 million to 8.2 million.[196] Up to 1940, the natural increase was greatest in rural areas, while there was considerable migration from the countryside. From the 1920s to the 1970s the total rural population fell because this out-migration exceeded natural growth. In 1850 the population living in places with more than 200 people represented only 10 per cent of the total population; by 1975 it was 82 per cent. This urban growth was most marked in the 1930s and 1940s (2–3 per cent per annum),[197] and particularly involved migration to places dominated by metal, textile, rubber, and chemical industries, as well as to the suburbs around Stockholm. Three clear consequences of this urban growth have been the increased importance of commuting to places of work; a rapid ageing of the rural population; and the heightened importance of the 'housewife' role in the 1940s to 1960s.[198] The last of these developments was bound up with the fact that Sweden only became an urban society fairly late and this meant that most housing in which people lived was modern, 75 per cent being built after 1940. Much of this was in the form of 'neighbourhood units' aimed at sustaining communities and preventing urban sprawl. These communities, containing between 3000 and 10,000 families mostly with children, were constructed as exclusively residential – this reinforced the gender and spatial split between paid and unpaid work. Built into these neighbourhood units was a distinctive view of the family and of women's work. The aim was to make work in the home more visible and hence more valued, while at the same time providing collective facilities which would minimize at least some of the more routine and tedious of such tasks. In 1944 there was even established the *Hemmens forskningsinstitut* (Institute for Research into Homelife). At the same time, although the home was very much seen as the sphere of women, this did not imply that women should be confined to the home. They were encouraged to participate as citizens in the emerging urban industrial Swedish economy. Franzen nevertheless maintains[199] that the crucial feature of the Swedish neighbourhood system was

> a more family-centred life-style, the three cornerstones of which were love (as the basis of the couple), parenthood and the home. The neighbourhood unit strengthened this orientation. There were, for example, no pubs to be found in such a unit, thus making home-based activities easier. The unit was, as its originator, Perry, remarked 'a scheme of arrangement for the family life community'.

Before this development, what towns and cities there were had been based on an extremely busy 'street life' in which small shops faced on to the street, all intermingled with private houses, small workshops and industries. The town was fairly socially segregated but the scale was small and very much based on the pedestrian and not the car.

The period of the neighbourhood unit in the 1940s and 1950s is known as the era of the 'housewife' in Sweden. The main occupational changes hence affected men – and these are shown in figure 5.3. Thus by 1960 the number of male salaried workers was about half the number of manual workers. The increase in female employment occurred in the 1960s and this was especially marked among married women. In the 1950s 14 per cent of married women were economically active; by 1975 this had risen to 58 per cent.[200]

We will turn now to recent changes in Sweden, showing that there has been some modest disorganization of the previous patterns. It has been noted that the urban population grew very rapidly during the high point of organized capitalism. However, since around 1970 there has been some reversal of these

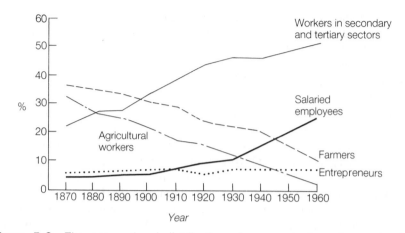

Figure 5.3 The occupational distribution of economically active males in Sweden, 1870–1960
Source: W. Korpi, *The Working Class in Welfare Capitalism* (Routledge, London, 1978), p. 57.

growth trends. First of all, Stockholm's population itself declined from 1,035,000 to 989,000 between 1970 and 1980.[201] Second, the population of cities with a size between 50,000 and 10,000 declined from 1,041,000 to 931,000 between 1975 and 1980. Third the largest growth rate was found among towns sized between 2,000 and 10,000: their proportion of total Swedish population rose from 16.7 per cent in 1970 to 19.1 per cent in 1975. Fourth, there has been a marked increase in commuting from these smaller settlements to the larger cities. The possible reasons for this are summarized by Warneryd,[202] who describes the 1970s as 'the decade of small urban places':

> The decline in the population of the larger urban places did not come as a complete surprise. The difficulties which the urban communities have in satisfying the demand for small houses, villas or terraced houses . . . is one reason. However, the right to deduct journey-to-work costs from taxes, the better possibilities of financing a small house . . . , changed views on the environment . . . have all contributed to the settlement sprawl.

A further reason, however, why commuting (especially by car) has become so important in modern Sweden is because there is less evidence of the kind of 'ruralization' of industry which has to some extent characterized all the other societies being investigated here. This is for a number of reasons: first, public sector employment is so important in Sweden and this is concentrated in the major urban centres (numbers more than doubled 1960–75);[203] second, private sector employment in many of Sweden's main industries, steel, pulp and paper, brewing, baking, food processing etc., is to be found in fairly large plants which it is believed are dependent upon considerable economies of agglomeration;[204] and third, much of this concentration of employment occurs in towns with a population smaller than 50,000, that is, towns that in the other countries would count as small but which are medium-sized in Sweden.[205]

However, there have been *some* changes in industrial location over the recent past. In the survey conducted by the Federation of Swedish Industries they found that the areas where manufacturing decline has been most marked have been the highly urbanized centres of Stockholm, Göteborg and Malmö.[206] Especially marked reductions in industrial employment were also found in the central areas of Sweden. The northernmost counties, of Jamtlands, Vasterbottens and Norrbottens, all showed marked increases,[207] although many northern municipalities still had fewer than 5 or 10 per cent employed in mining and manufacturing in 1979. The industries which have expanded in the northern areas are mining, food processing, textiles (in marked contrast with extensive decline in the centre and south), finished wood products, rubber and plastics, iron and steel, metal products (although some areas in the south also expanded employment), machinery, electrical and electronics (although this expanded and contracted in both north and south and, because of its large plants, is spatially highly concentrated), and transport apart from shipbuilding. Broadly speaking, those industries which were once the most concentrated, either because there were relatively few large plants or because there were very many small plants, have become less spatially concentrated.

This expansion of some industries in the north has been encouraged by Swedish regional policy which was only developed on a comprehensive basis in the 1960s. It was designed to cope with the structural imbalance caused in some of the northern counties by the rapidly diminishing employment in agriculture and forestry: these sectors provided 15 per cent of total Swedish employment in 1960, 7 per cent in 1970 and 3 per cent in 1980.[208] In the 1960s seven northern counties had a population loss of more than 10,000 people a year. The development of regional policy combined with the development of new geographically differentiated spatial divisions of labour of some industrial and service sectors meant that by 1980 there was 'a regional population stability',[209] although it should also be noted that there were some considerable imbalances in levels of underemployment of both men and women in most of the northern counties.

Three other points are relevant here. First, the international recession and the development of cheaper producers elsewhere in the world have had particularly severe effects on Sweden's 'traditional' industries, of mining, steel, shipbuilding, and pulp and paper. Second, many towns and cities have historically been dominated by a single industry with one or perhaps a handful of employers. When these industries have collapsed, the consequences on the employment structure and social fabric of such towns is devastating, especially where the next major settlement is many miles distant. Third, even as early as the 1960s there was a rapid increase in the export of Swedish capital. For example, foreign investments increased 80 per cent between 1960 and 1965: the total employees of Swedish-owned foreign firms grew four times faster than the growth rate of domestic employment.[210] Much of this increase in foreign employment occurred in the centrally significant industries of engineering and chemicals and through involvement in the export of some of the more labour-intensive parts of the enterprise.

The processes of restructuring in manufacturing industry in the period 1975–80 have recently been examined in detail. Håkanson and Danielsson show that although all 276 municipalities experienced manufacturing employment loss over this period, the larger the municipality, the greater the proportionate employment loss. Hence, those municipalities with less than 3000 people gainfully employed lost only 0.9 per cent of manufacturing employment; those with 5000–10,000, 4.7 per cent; those with 30,000–100,000, 9.1 per cent; and those with over 100,000 a massive 12.9 per cent.[211] They further subjected these changes to shift/share analysis. This shows that the relative weakness of the larger settlements was not a function of the pre-existing industrial structure. Indeed, municipalities with 20,000–100,000 gainfully employed workers had easily the most favourable industrial structure, and yet their actual performance in employment terms was among the worst. Their existing firms failed to grow, some shut down entirely, and new plants did not move into the municipality. This pattern of differential performance between municipalities very clearly showed a pattern of decentralization. Håkanson and Danielsson conclusively show that since 1975 there has been:[212]

> an ongoing process of deconcentration both nationally and within the metropolitan areas. Thus, large parts of the traditional 'heartland' of Swedish manufacturing industry, including for example the Lake Mälaren region, the Stockholm Metropolitan Region and old time industrial centres such as Norrköping, Linköping and Jönköping, record large differential losses. In contrast, more peripheral locations, particularly in the Regional Aid Areas but also in some of the southern counties . . . have had a relatively favourable development.

It is important to note that there has been decentralization from larger urban areas to smaller areas with a *less* favourable industrial structure. It is shown that this process of decentralization is at least connected with the diseconomies connected with large concentrations of industry, namely, congestion, rising land values, lack of floor space and higher costs of housing and transportation, and the fact that there was a greater availability of cheaper, less organized labour, particularly female, in the peripheral areas.

The 'de-industrialization' of Sweden, as measured by the numbers employed in manufacturing, began in the mid-1960s. Manufacturing employment had risen to a peak of 1,157,000 in 1965, but has declined since then reaching 937,221 in 1980.[213] At the same time the numbers employed in services (public, private and commerce) have risen from 1.25 million in 1960 to over 2 million in 1980.[214] Within the total employed in manufacturing there has been some decline in the numbers employed in the larger enterprises. The peak seems to have been reached in the mid-1970s. In 1975 there were 967,000 employed in manufacturing enterprises employing 500 or more workers; by 1981 this had fallen to 916,000.[215] Taking employment as a whole over the same period there was an increase in the number of workers employed in such large enterprises, from 1,644,000 in 1975 to 1,947,000 in 1981.[216] However, this was entirely accounted for by the massive increase in 'community, social and personal services' from 583,000 in 1975 to 935,000 in 1981 (in 500-plus enterprises). Overall, there was no significant increase in the numbers working in medium-sized enterprises employing between 50 and 500, but there was modest expansion in the numbers working in enterprises employing under 50. The areas of employment where small firms have relatively prospered have been in accountancy (especially subcontracting), advertising, law, engineering, chemicals, retailing and transport.[217] Generally, though, small firms have not been so successful in Sweden as in the other societies under investigation; and in manufacturing there has been a rapid decline in the number of new establishments per year, from 1700 in 1971 to about 1000 in 1980.[218] Two tendencies which have partly offset this are, first, the increasing numbers of the self-employed which rose from 157,000 in 175 to 195,000 in 1981,[219] and second, the rising numbers of employee-owned firms, especially in the late-1970s.[220]

In general, then, large firms still dominate the Swedish economy – and this is even more appreciated when it is realized that most smaller firms function as fairly closely supervised subcontractors. Thus, for example, the Swedish Association of Metalworking Industries found that 57 per cent of firms having fewer than 25 employees sold more than half of their turnover to other manufacturing firms.[221] Likewise it has been shown that two out of three small firms in metal and engineering operated as subcontractors. This has been particularly important in the car industry where Volvo, for example, uses more than 1300 subcontractors of which more than 700 are Swedish, many located in Gnosjö.[222]

Recent commentators on Sweden have very clearly shown that there has been a substantial increase in the number of wage-earners – in 1940 they constituted 74 per cent of the population of working age, but by 1970 this had risen to 91 per cent.[223] Nevertheless, there has been a marked decline in the industrial working class – beginning in the 1950s when they constituted 40 per cent of those gainfully employed. By 1975 industrial workers made up only 28 per cent of those employed: Ahrne, Lundberg and Himmelstrand suggest that this will fall to 10 per cent by 2000.[224] We have already noted that this declining industrial working class is progressively less concentrated in the older industrial centres and what has been remarkable about the recent period has been the growth of white-collar employees, especially in the public sector.

Using different definitions, Ahrne and Wright suggest that there are distinct differences between the class structures of the USA and Sweden (see table 5.6).

Table 5.6 Class structures of the USA and Sweden

Occupations	USA %	Sweden %
Managers	16.9	14.3
Supervisors	12.8	6.8
Total managerial	(29.7)	(21.1)
Semi-autonomous employees	9.5	17.4
Workers	46.2	50.7
Petty bourgeoisie	6.9	5.4
Small employers and bourgeoisie	7.8	5.5

Source: G. Ahrne and E. O. Wright, 'Classes in the United States and Sweden: a comparison', Acta Sociologica 26 (1983), pp. 311–35.

Two points should be noted: first, the much higher proportion of managerial staff in the USA; and second, the higher proportion of 'semi-autonomous' employees in Sweden. In the following chapter we will examine such differences in detail, to explain why in the USA an extraordinarily powerful managerial class developed in the early years of this century and how this is to be conceptualized as the making of the American 'service class'. By contrast, we will see how in Sweden a particularly important role has been played by a public-sector service class. In both cases these developments further serve to disorganize the class-versus-class pattern characteristic of organized capitalism.

6

The service class: its emergence and some consequences

In the previous two chapters we have shown that with respect to a variety of spatial and economic processes important changes of a broadly 'disorganizing' sort have occurred in all five societies being investigated. However, we have also noted that these changes have occurred in different forms and at different rates. Moreover, we shall see in the following chapters that there are further processes which are serving to disorganize contemporary capitalism, processes concerned with the financing of modern economies; political changes particularly in the relations between social class and political practice and state policy; and a variety of cultural changes. In this chapter we will consider in some detail one particular transformation in the social structure of western societies, a development in part noted by many commentators but one whose significance has been inadequately analysed.

In chapter 1 it was noted that one feature of 'organized capitalism' was the growth of substantial occupational groups located between capital and labour. Hence, although such societies are pervasively structured in terms of the social relations of class versus class, an increasing proportion of the employed population are only marginally either 'capital' or 'labour'. Much theoretical labour has been expended on trying to 'reduce' these emergent groups either to the side of capital through conceptualizing them as functionaries of capital necessitated by its depersonalization, and/or to the side of labour through seeing them as experiencing proletarianization.[1]

We would not want to deny these analyses but would maintain that these emergent groups cannot be explained without investigating the way in which a causally powerful 'third force', the service class, is generated and developed within the interstices of organized capitalism, in particular *out of* the relationship between capital and labour. Once attaining a certain threshold of development and mobilization, this new class itself begins to have a dislocating effect on the relationship between capital and labour and an irredeemably disorganizing effect on capitalist society in general.

There are five central points to note about this 'service class':[2]

1   It consists of those dominant positions or places within the social division of labour which do not principally involve the ownership of capital, land or buildings.

2   Those places are located within a set of interlocking social institutions that 'service' capital through meeting three functions: to conceptualize the labour process; to control the entry and exercise of labour-power within the workplace; and to orchestrate the non-household forms under which labour-power is produced and regulated.

3   Those places enjoy superior work and market situations: incumbents thus exercise authority within each institution; typically enjoy well-defined 'careers' in which work and market situations improve side by side; and enjoy medium to high levels of trust and discretion often stemming from forms of professional control and closure.

4   Entry into such places is generally regulated by the differential possession of credentials, which are either organization-specific or are general. Such credentials serve as the main demarcation between the service class and 'deskilled white-collar workers', although changes occur in exactly where the demarcation is to be found.

5   The relative size, the power, and the composition (male/female, public/private) of the service class vary substantially, depending upon class conflicts between capital and labour; gender conflicts, particularly over attempts to professionalize/masculinize occupations; struggles to extend educational credentialism; attempts to 'professionalize' particular sets of work tasks; conflicts over the size, functions and organization of the state; sectoral changes in the national economy, and so on.

Clearly in our emphasis upon the importance of a service class and hence in 'knowledge, education and science', our argument bears some superficial similarity with theories of 'post-industrialism'.[3] There are, though, a number of general deficiencies in that position, particularly revolving around the significance and explanation of service production in such supposedly 'post-industrial' societies. However, the main problem for us here in that approach lies in the failure to explain just why 'knowledge, education and science' come to occupy a particular importance in modern western societies and especially why they are more important in certain periods in some societies rather than others.

In the following analysis we shall try to show that an absolutely central development in twentieth-century capitalism concerns the growth of modern, scientific, rational 'management' and that such a development was not something that was simply inevitable, resulting either from the logic of capitalist accumulation or the imperatives of modern technology. It was, of course, very much bound up with the social relations between capital and labour in particular societies, but it is not to be reduced to that relation. The rise of modern management involved a substantial break in the logic of capitalist development, and was by no means inevitable. Until it emerged employers had employed a variety of other means of control over their workforces. It was in the USA that there was a major shift in these techniques with the growth of modern management. Indeed there was in effect something of a 'class struggle' in American society around the turn of the century, and that we shall show was a struggle *between* existing capital and 'modern management'. In that struggle existing capital lost. Complex managerial hierarchies developed in many American companies and this led to the extensive growth of white-collar employment. Such processes helped in turn to produce an interlocking complex of new institutional developments, of colleges and universities, of private foundations, of professionalizing occupations in both the private and public sector, and large corporate and state bureaucracies. They developed and extended themselves between labour and capital, constituting a kind of wedge or third force in American society. There was then a process of 'the making of the American service class', a process beginning with the initial development of modern management in the years before the First World War. Paradoxically then what is understood as the archetypal capitalist society, the USA, is that in which its structure has been most transformed by the development of an influential third force apart from those of capital and labour. It is the growth of this American service class which in part accounts for the particularly capitalistic character of American society. In the following section we will consider the contrasting socio-political trajectories in the European societies under analysis here.

THE AMERICAN SERVICE CLASS

It is now commonplace to note that the growth of the factory had a profound effect in changing people's work habits and experiences. There was some shift from an orientation to task towards an orientation to time.[4] However, it is also clear that the growth of the factory did not result in a direct increase in the social control that capital exercised over labour. What Marx called the 'real subsumption' of the labourer was not simply brought about by the factory system. Prior to the development of 'scientific management' in its various forms the labourer was not generally placed under conditions of real subsumption by *capital*. There were three alternative bases of control found in the USA: first, that exercised by skilled craft workers – as Nelson says, 'the factory of 1880 (in the USA) remained a congeries of craftsmen's shops rather than an integrated plant';[5] second, that effected by 'foremen', especially through 'driving' the workers via authoritarian rule and physical compulsion;[6] and third, that produced through 'internal contracting' by which contractors hired and fired their own employees, set their wages, disciplined them and determined the production methods to be used.[7] Internal contracting was important in the period up to 1914 in the following industries: iron and steel, foundries, coal, engineering, armaments, potteries, glass, newspaper printing and clothing – and was more common in the traditional industrial areas on the East Coast, often structured along lines of ethnic division as waves of immigrants settled in the USA beginning in the east.[8] Inside-contracting was an important non-bureaucratic form of control since the contractor 'did production work as well as supervision, there were no set qualifications, no levels of authority, essentially no written documents or files were kept, and there were no codified rules (or very few rules)'.[9] For the growth of 'management' and hence of managerial bureaucracies, this power of the inside contractor had to be substantially broken.

We will now consider the effect of the growth of early twentieth-century scientific management. F. W. Taylor realized that workers generally controlled the details of their work and so long as workers knew more than their managers, then management would have to cajole the workers to co-operate.[10] This could be clearly seen in relationship to piece-work. Since management did not know how long in fact it took to do each piece of work, it was rational for workers to engage in 'systematic soldiering' and hence to restrict output. Taylor realized that the only long-term solution to this from the viewpoint of capital was to devise a new system of capitalist control that would over-come the rational tendency for workers to restrict output. And this could only be achieved by transforming the very form of knowledge possessed by workers. In particular, it was necessary to create the separate category of 'management', which had until then enjoyed only a somewhat protean existence, based upon a necessary 'mental revolution'.[11]

According to Taylor, the first stage in this process was for the management to learn what its workers already knew. 'The managers assume . . . the burden of gathering together all of the traditional knowledge, which in the past has been possessed by the workmen.'[12] The second stage was for management to 'take over all of the work for which they are better fitted than the workman; almost every act of the workman should be preceded by various preparatory acts' of the management.[13] As a result there would have to be a vast growth in the bureaucratization of industry since Taylor advocated the creation of a 'planning room' where there should be a concentration of the 'brain-work' which had been removed from the shopfloor. Thus in the third stage of the process, management had to specify in advance precisely what each worker was required to do. And, although these tasks might have been similar to those which had been previously done, they were now to be determined within the 'planning room', or more generally within the bureaucratic structure. Taylor refers to the almost equal division of the actual work of the establishment between the workman, on the one hand, and the management, on the other. Under the old system, practically the whole problem was left to the workman, while under scientific management there were two divisions, and one of these divisions was deliberately handed over to the side of the management.[14] The Taylor system, then, involved an enormous expansion in what Taylor himself called 'non-producers'.

This new form of control was necessary because of the deskilling of the labour process which is entailed in scientific management. There are a number of different aspects here: the maximized fragmentation of work into its simplest constituents; the divorce of planning and execution; the separation of indirect and direct labour; the minimization of skill requirements and job-learning time; and the employment of scientific 'planning' to co-ordinate the entire process of production.[15]

There is much controversy about the degree to which Taylorist scientific management was to be found in American industry by, say, 1920. Overall it seems that the fully-fledged system was only implemented in about 140 enterprises and these were primarily concentrated in small-scale precision production industries mainly located in the north-eastern states.[16] However, considered much more generally, the basic principles of scientific management had been very widely accepted by the 1920s. These principles included the centralized planning and integrating of the successive stages of production; the systematic analysis of each distinct operation; the detailed instruction and supervision of each worker in the performance of each discrete task; and the designing of wage payments to induce workers to do what they were told. Moreover, these principles became generally applicable – as Merkle argues of Taylorism:[17]

> Evolving beyond its technical and national origins, it became an important component of the philosophical outlook of modern industrial civilization, defining virtue as efficiency, establishing a new role for experts in production, and setting parameters for new patterns of social distribution...the mental revolution that had been so deeply embedded in the structure of industrial society that it was a social philosophy that no longer could be casually abandoned.

There were a number of conditions which facilitated the development of scientific management in the USA:

(1) Technological changes which outstripped the capacity of craftsmen trained in traditional techniques to organize production in the way they had in the past. Particularly important effects of such technological innovations were upon the organization of the railways, which required increasingly elaborate systems of control to manage their enormous extensions. Other technological innovations of importance included the development of continuous process methods in certain refining, distilling, chemical and food-

processing industries; of undercutting machinery in the coal industry; and a little later of mass production techniques in both metalmaking and metal-working industries.[18]

(2) Growth in the size of both enterprises and plants in the period after 1865, particularly with the declining rate of profit from the 1880s onwards. Especially important here was the vertical integration of different components of production, distribution, marketing, so that by 1900 there were high concentration levels in many industries, particularly because of widespread mergers.[19] Also, by 1900, plants employing thousands rather than hundreds of workers had become fairly common (there were 1500). By 1914 such plants accounted for 18 per cent of manufacturing employment.[20]

(3) Dramatic expansion of immigration into the USA, especially from 1897 onwards. Immigrants were normally single males, often illiterate, coming from southern and eastern Europe and working in the old industrial areas of the north-east.[21] By 1913 over half of the workers in many industries were immigrants (for example, 58 per cent in iron and steel, 72 per cent in cotton textiles, 83 per cent in clothing etc.).[22] Such immigration had a number of important effects: (a) extraordinarily high turnover rates among semi- and unskilled workers – by 1913 it was on average 100 per cent per annum;[23] (b) the generation of a wide social/ethnic gap between workers and management enabling the latter to treat the former as an object of supposedly 'scientific' study, based on appropriate racial stereotypes;[24] (c) both continuous problems and extraordinary opportunities for management if they could adapt the illiterate, unskilled, 'pre-factory' labour force to industrial conditions;[25] (d) ethnic segregation of neighbourhoods which distanced the immigrant workers especially from skilled workers until after the First World War – a tendency which was reinforced by the associations and community associations of the immigrants which were often organized into secret societies;[26] (e) readily available strikebreakers which caused the failure of strikes in textiles, mining, iron and steel, and the railways;[27] (f) segregated and fragmented labour force of primary and secondary components, where in the case of the latter the skill and knowledge required for labour was embodied within the socio-technical organization of the factory and not within the mainly immigrant workers themselves.[28]

(4) The growing strength of the working-class movement, especially from the 1894 Pullman strike up to the 'holocaust' of strikes and unrest of 1919 and the perceived need to deal with this. Adams writes:[29]

Regardless of cause, geographic location, type of industry or ethnic grouping, turbulence in industrial relations flared all over the United States. It rocked large cities and small towns, manufacturing areas and agrarian communities. Industrialization had outdistanced American social attitudes and institutions. In many cases this led to a collapse of civil authority, to near anarchy and to military rule...Americans on the eve of World War I lived in an age of industrial violence.

This strength was also indicated by the exceptional growth in trade union membership, which rose from under 500,000 in 1897 to over 5 million in 1920, and by the emergence of political socialism as an effective presence during this period up to 1920 or so.[30]

(5) The impact of the First World War, which had a number of effects: a marked increase in union membership and strikes; an extension of scientific management to government enterprises, especially the arsenals; extension of state contracts for an enormous volume of *standardized* products which greatly facilitated the introduction of machinery and systematic management techniques; increases in managerial and white-collar employment (so much so that the term 'white-collar' derives from the wartime period); and a more co-operative managerial ideology which laid greater emphasis on the virtues of work and of at least a limited degree of worker consultation since labour organizations were clearly set to stay.[31]

(6) The growth in the numbers and influence of industrial engineers (although this is obviously also partly an effect). By 1900 engineering was the largest profession in the USA (except for teachers) and in the next 30 years it multiplied fivefold, especially in the areas of electrical and chemical engineering. Engineers were overwhelmingly male; three-quarters had middle-class professional social origins; they generally had a college education; and most became managers within large corporations.[32] There was a symbiotic process: the monopolization of 'scientific engineering' by professional engineers was the reverse side of the monopolization of such engineers by the large science-based corporations. Noble summarizes:[33]

> the big corporations, because of their control over patents, had combined their capacity to command the industrial application of science with their exclusive legal right to do so. The industrial corporation as it emerged as the locus of modern technology in America, became at the same time the habitat of the professional engineer.

Noble demonstrates that the profession of modern engineering was from the very beginning in the USA (1860s onwards) integrated with that of corporate capital, even to the extent of attempting to foster appropriate working practices and social habits among the manual labour force.

(7) The growth of progressivism during the period 1890–1920.[34] In chapter 3 we noted the importance of this broad multi-class movement of intellectuals, politicians, professionals, farmers and small-scale capitalists who exposed the limitations of the democratic system (with arguments for the referendum, for example); who argued for increased government intervention in the economy; who sought to improve the provision of housing, social services and welfare; and who sought to promote the growth of efficiency through the use of science. The development of the movement for efficiency had a number of aspects: personally, it emphasized hard work and denigrated

feeling and emotion; mechanically, it involved estimating and maximizing the energy input–output ratio of a machine; financially, it implied calculating and optimizing the commercial effectiveness of the enterprise; and sociologically, it signified the pursuit of social harmony among all components of the society and leadership by the most competent. One ideology and practice connected with this general movement of rationalization was the movement for scientific or systematic management. The key figures in this were Taylor, the founder of 'scientific management'; the Gilbreths and their time-and-motion studies; C. Barth, who introduced the slide rule to the shopfloor; C. B. Thompson, whose speeches and articles served to popularize the new creed of efficiency; and various cost-accountants and production controllers.[35] Haber well summarizes the Progressive character of Taylor's system of rationalization:[36]

> He proposed a neat, understandable world in the factory, an organization of men whose acts would be planned, coordinated and controlled under continuous expert direction. His system had some of the inevitableness and objectivity of science and technology. A Taylor plant became one of those places where an important segment of the American intelligentsia saw the future – and saw it worked.

One important feature of the movement for scientific management was that it was self-consciously organized. The viewpoint was represented particularly in the *Engineering Magazine* and the *Transactions of the American Society of Mechanical Engineers*, and various organizations were formed, such as the Efficiency Society, the Taylor Society and the Society for the Promotion of Scientific Management.[37] Crucial meetings were held, especially one in 1903 when Taylor read his paper on 'Shop management' to the American Society of Mechanical Engineers. And although the movement was characterized by considerable discussion (for example, over the importance of 'motion' studies), by 1912 and the Congress hearings there was widespread public awareness, and some acceptance, of the broad objectives of this new class of 'management'.[38]

This was also in part connected with the development of new managerial structures among some of the leading companies of the time. We noted in chapter 3 the shift from functionally organized companies to those which were based on a multidivisional structure. In the case of the latter, each division, which may have been based on either a product or a geographical location, would have a number of functional departments associated with it; and the head office itself would have a number of functional departments (such as legal, finance, research and development, industrial relations, marketing, etc.).[39] Leading American companies which adopted this structure were Du Pont, General Motors and Standard Oil of New Jersey. In each case there was a substantially more rationalized system of management which developed with head and divisional offices each containing a number of functional divisions.

Thus far we have seen that a number of conditions in the USA conspired to provide the *basis* for the growth of new forms of management in the early years of this century. In order, however, for that development really to work through the society management would have to overcome resistance from both labour *and* capital. In other words, as Stark puts it: 'the occupants of the new positions did not simply "fill in" a set of "empty places" created by forces completely detached from their own activity, but actually participated, within a constellation of struggling classes, in the creation of these positions themselves.'[40]

Workers in general showed great ingenuity in opposing, outwitting, and defeating the agents of scientific management before, during and after the 'appropriation of knowledge'. However, up to about 1910 there was relatively little organized union opposition to 'scientific management', partly because it had not been introduced into strongly unionized plants. However, for the next ten years or so, there was widespread opposition, which was initially organized through the American Federation of Labor, who particularly attempted to protect the 'secrets of the craft'.[41] Samuel Gompers clearly appreciated how scientific management would 'reduce the number of skilled workers to the barest minimum',[42] and the costs for labour were strongly emphasized in Professor Hoxie's report on scientific management prepared for the US Commission on Industrial Relations.[43] Apart from the opposition at the Watertown Arsenal, perhaps the most impressive opposition of labour to new forms of management was to be seen in the Illinois Central and Harriman lines Railroad Carmen's Strike which lasted for nearly four years and involved about 30,000 workers.[44] The carmen maintained an extraordinarily determined opposition to the transformation of their skilled trades which resulted from the attempt to introduce piece-work and bonus systems, speed-ups, and time-and-motion studies. In the course of the strike, 533 strikers were jailed, 91 per cent of strikers were forced to move to cheaper housing, and 16 men committed suicide.

However, for all the sustained and militant opposition of some groups of craft workers to scientific management, such workers were generally unwilling to develop broad-based industrial alliances with semi- and unskilled workers, especially immigrants, blacks or women workers. Benenson suggests that where the very earliest industrial unions were established, these were to be found in industries where skilled workers were not threatened by displacement by the less skilled.[45] The organization of labour during this period was not, then, simply the result of craft workers responding to the degradation of skill (as in Braverman's analysis), but was much more varied, geographically, industrially and historically. Such struggles involved differing and complex alliances of workers, not only struggling against specific 'deskilling', but much more generally over the forms of control within the workplace and the community. Many such struggles were directed as much against other workers, particularly immigrants, blacks and women, as they were directed against capital.

By 1919–20 the opposition of labour to scientific management had partly subsided, although as Palmer points out this was much more true of the official union leadership than of all groups of workers.[46] This stemmed from a number of conditions. First, there were various semi-corporatist arrangements established in wartime, which ensured, as Person put it, 'labor's interest in good management and increased productivity'.[47] Second, there was the more conciliatory and accommodating attitude of the engineers themselves; thus, in 1917, C. B. Thompson argued that 'scientific managers have been freely advised to recognize more fully the necessity of cooperation with the unions'.[48] And third, after 1919 and the following years when up to 20 per cent of the American labour force went on strike, labour was decimated in the early 1920s. One and a half million members were lost and the AFL advocated a new doctrine of labour–management co-operation.[49]

We will now consider scientific management's other struggle, from capital and pre-existing management. The starting point here is to recognize Burawoy's claim that 'one cannot *assume* the existence of a cohesive managerial and capitalist class that automatically recognises its true interests'.[50] Veblen, in the early years of this century, laid particular emphasis upon the progressive role of engineers whose interests, he argued, were contrary to those of capital. Especially significant were mechanical engineers and in some ways Taylorism represented a manifesto in favour of engineers controlling production, and hence a partial substitution of the engineers' technical definition of efficiency for a purely commercial one.[51] As Taylor himself said:[52]

> Personally my experience has been so unsatisfactory with financiers that I never want to work for any of them...As a rule, financiers are looking merely for a turnover. They want to get in and out of their business quickly, and they have absolutely *no pride of manufacture*.

Opposition from existing employers and managers was, not surprisingly, extremely widespread.[53] In Bethlehem Steel there was a management counter-attack on Taylor and ultimately they dispensed with Taylor's services. Thompson, a well-known publicist for scientific management, described it as a 'veritable storm-center', while H. Person talked of the general reluctance of most managements to undertake theoretically 'revolutionary improvements', preferring to continue existing opportunistic practices which were, according to Litterer, 'increasingly chaotic, confused and wasteful'.[54] Taylor himself stated in his testimony in 1912 to the Special House Committee to Investigate the Taylor and Other Systems of Shop Management that:[55]

> nine-tenths of our trouble has been to 'bring' those on the management's side to do their fair share of the work and only one-tenth of our trouble has come on the workman's side. Invariably we find very great opposition on the part of those on the management's side to do their new duties...

This is confirmed in Nelson's survey of 29 Taylorized plants where he found that opposition came from foremen and supervisors and more generally from management. He concluded that 'the experts encountered more opposition from managers than workers'.[56] For example:[57]

> Gantt encountered serious opposition from the management at the Sayles Bleachery and Joseph Bancroft & Sons, and less formidable problems at the Canadian Pacific shops; Barth antagonized his employers at the S. L. Moore Company and lost the confidence of the Yale & Towne officers; Gilbreth alienated the managers of the Herrmann, Aukam Company; C. B. Thompson complained bitterly of the opposition he encountered from the supervisors at the Eaton, Crane & Pike Company; Cooke reported a similar experience at Forbes Lithograph; Sanford Thompson noted the suspicions of the managers at Eastern Manufacturing; Evans faced substantial opposition from certain superiors and many foremen; and the experts who worked at the Pimpton Press and Lewis Manufacturing Company found Kendall, Taylor's friend and admirer, a highly critical observer of their work.

One reason for the opposition of existing management was that Taylor attempted, as he put it himself to substitute 'exact scientific investigation and knowledge for the old individual judgement or opinion, either of the workman or the boss'.[58] This involved giving considerable autonomy to the industrial engineer. Layton argues: 'Taylor has opened the possibility of an independent role for engineers in an area in which their position had been that of bureaucratic subordinates'.[59] Meiskins, furthermore, argues that the reason why the industrial engineers partly opposed capital was because they had become transformed into wage-labourers and their opposition to capital was in part *structured* by the basic class divisions of any capitalist society.[60] But there are two further points to note. Firstly, the growth of new managerial forms became gradually 'domesticated', as Meiskins puts it, and as such highly functional for the general domination of the world economy by American capital. In other words, the struggle between management and capital resulted in transformations of American capital of a broadly 'functional' sort. Secondly, the development of scientific management and more generally of complex managerial hierarchies produced a substantial restructuring of American society. In analysing this latter point we will begin with the occupational structure.

Not only was there a considerable growth in the number of engineers, from 7000 in 1880 to 136,000 in 1920,[61] but there were crucially important more general changes. The growth of new managerial systems transformed the occupational structure of American manufacturing industry, particularly because Taylorism was built upon verbalization, or co-ordination through *written* work orders. The increase in white-collar or administrative workers is shown in table 6.1. There was also a substantial rise in various kinds of service employment, increasingly organized in complex hierarchies, and this

Table 6.1 Administrative/production employees in American manufacturing industry, 1899–1929

Year	Administrative employees[a]	Production employees	Ratio of administrative: production employees %
1899	348,000	4,496,000	7.7
1909	750,000	6,256,000	12.0
1923	1,280,000	8,187,000	15.6
1929	1,496,000	8,361,000	17.9

[a] Excludes owners and top executives.
Source: Bendix, adapted from *Work and Authority*, p. 214.

was partly the cause of the changing sectoral composition of the labour force. By 1900 a third of the labour force was employed in the tertiary sector of industry (services) and this increased to almost one-half by 1930, mainly at the expense of primary industry (agriculture/mining/quarrying); see table 6.2.

Table 6.2 Sectoral distribution of the American labour force, 1900–30

	Employment in different industrial sectors (%)		
Year	Primary industry	Secondary industry	Tertiary industry
1900	37.6	30.1	32.3
1910	31.6	31.6	36.8
1920	27.4	34.4	38.2
1930	22.0	31.1	46.9

Source: Y. Sabolo, *The Service Industries* (ILO, Geneva, 1975), p. 9.

Furthermore, the growth of engineers, and of scientific management more generally, was crucially interconnected with the development of corporate capital.[62] Particularly important were the innovations involved in the growth of the chemicals and electrical industries which formed the vanguard of modern technology in twentieth-century USA. Their development fostered the gradual 'electrification' and 'chemicalization' of older, craft-based industries which rapidly acquired 'scientistic' features, partly through the recruitment of chemical and electrical engineers. This led to the growth of technical education, which was well summarized by Professor J. B. Turner's call to replace the 'laborious thinkers' produced by the classical colleges by the 'thinking labourers' necessary for industry.[63] The emergent, technically trained, electrical and chemical engineers were predominantly employed within large corporations and promotion consisted of movement within the corporation's labour market into management. Professional advancement consisted of promotion within the corporate hierarchies of the science-based industries. Professional engineers were particularly significant in directly producing a number of major changes in the USA in the period 1860–1930: standardizing weights and measurements; modernizing patent-law in favour of science-based industrial corporations; developing large industrial research laboratories with a heightened division of labour; integrating industrial and university-based research, ensuring an appropriate industry-based curriculum within the dramatically expanding university system; and encouraging the general development of modern management, cost accounting and related techniques.[64]

Of particular importance was the way in which the growth of engineers/ managers helped to weld science and technology into the growing corporate structure and this had the effect of further separating engineers/managers off from the directly productive workers. This was partly because their growth served to generate an 'ideology of technical expertise' which then served other occupations as they systematized cognitive categories and developed new organizational forms in, as Stark puts it, 'their attempts to define and maintain their privileged position over and against the working class and struggled to increase their autonomy from the capitalist class in the schools, the universities, and the state'.[65] This led, among other developments, to the very early establishment of schools of management or business administration in the USA, beginning with the Wharton School of Finance and Commerce in 1881, with others at Berkeley and Chicago following in 1898, at Dartmouth and New York University in 1900, and at Harvard as early as 1908.[66] Rapid innovative developments in engineering education occurred in Cincinnati, Massachusetts Institute of Technology, Pittsburg, Case, Harvard, New York University, etc.[67]

Both the industrial managers and engineers provided a model of how education and industry should be integrated over the course of the twentieth century. One occupation after another sought to strengthen its market-power by connecting together the production of knowledge with the production of the producers via the modern university. There was a structural linkage effected between two sets of elements, specific bodies of theoretical knowledge, on the one hand, and markets for skilled services or labour, on the other. By contrast with, say, nineteenth-century Britain, higher education became the means for bringing about professionalization and for the substantial transformation of the restructuring of social inequality. Merkle maintains that the subconscious lesson of Taylorism was that it demonstrated 'the strategy of creating and monopolizing bodies of knowledge as a means of perpetuating and expanding professional job opportunities'.[68] Or as Noble puts it, 'the integration of formal education into the industrial structure weakened the traditional link between work experience and advancement, driving a wedge between managers and managed and separating the two by the college campus'.[69] He goes on to note that in emphasizing the role of formal education as a vital aspect of their professional identity, engineers at the same time laid the foundations for the educationally based system of occupational stratification that has characterized the USA for the past half-a-dozen decades. The very process of professionalization contributed to the restructuring of the patterning of social inequality; to a system based on the salience of occupation; to legitimation via achievement of socially recognized expertise; and to a heightened concentration upon education and the possession of credentials. Jarausch summarizes these developments in the USA which were initiated by the industrial engineers and scientific managers:[70]

> Ultimately professionalization and academization fed on each other by continually upgrading entrance requirements (i.e. demanding more formal secondary schooling), making the curriculum content and teaching style more scientific...and by increasing academic demands for the various certifying examinations.

These interconnected developments of (1) standardized tasks and techniques in various white-collar 'managerial' occupations, and (2) increased certification requirements in an increasingly varied set of professionalizing occupations, produced an extraordinary expansion of higher education in the USA after 1880. In that year there were 118,000 students enrolled in American higher education (teacher and other colleges, professional schools and universities). By 1900 this had doubled and by 1928 it had increased tenfold.[71] In 1880 3.4 per cent of whites aged 18–21 went to 'college'. By 1928 it was 15 per cent and the USA possessed more institutions of higher education than France possessed academic personnel.[72] Indeed the college population of the USA was many times larger than the secondary school population of France. The American system developed on a highly diversified and differentiated pattern with private and public institutions developing in one state after another. This particularly stemmed from the 1819 decision of the Supreme Court in the case of Dartmouth College.[73] It was determined that colleges and universities should be protected from government interference and that *laissez-faire* should be the national policy in questions of business and higher education. This was in contrast with the position in France and Germany where there was increasing state regulation of higher education. In the USA private enterprise was encouraged to develop new colleges and universities independent of public regulation and control, and in a federal political system independent in particular of direction from Washington. Indeed, the absence of a central state bureaucracy meant the impossibility of enforcing rigorous standards on higher education, leaving the multiplying assortment of denominational and other private and public (municipal and state) colleges to expand rapidly through competition. Further, the fact that public servants themselves were often elected made the imposition of uniform educational achievement on office-holders difficult. Judges and other public servants were, however, expected by the public to possess higher degrees; these were often obtained through night schools and city colleges, which fostered in turn the expansion of the latter. Some time after the initial expansion of American higher education a process of centralization in regard to the determination of permissible credentials did take place. Credentializing power here, however, became lodged, not in the state, but in the service class (and to some extent directly in the capitalist class) itself. That is, a model of accreditation in higher education developed which was operated by educators in close conjunction with professional organizations – of doctors, lawyers, social workers, engineers – and in contact with the needs of employers and managers in industry.

One important reason for the development of a large number of occupations all pursuing a similar programme of professionalization via accreditation through the university was that the development of industrial engineering had raised but left in part unanswered a whole series of questions and issues concerned with the nature of work and the workers. Bendix summarizes the situation:[74]

> When Taylor and his followers proposed that the selection and training of workers be put on a scientific basis, they opened the way not to the promotion of industrial harmony on the basis of scientific findings, but to the involvement of industrialists in intellectual debates for which their training and interests had not prepared them.

During especially the 1920s and 1930s a large-scale debate developed concerning what workers were really like and how they could be appropriately motivated. A resulting battery of tests and testers emerged so as to investigate their typical attitudes and aptitudes. This was associated with the more general bureaucratization of industry and the realization by management that the exercise of control would ideally involve the elaboration of rules, the delegation of authority, the specialization of administrative functions and the development of complex systems of personnel investigation and management. Each of these developments presupposed new occupations, especially various branches of organizational psychology and sociology, which literally became in Baritz's term 'servants of power' and which copied the professionalization strategy employed by the industrial engineers.[75] This was part of a general movement summarized by Wiebe:[76]

> the specialized needs of an urban-industrial system came as a godsend to a middle stratum in the cities. Identification by way of their skills gave them the deference of their neighbours while opening natural avenues into the nation at large. Increasingly formal entry requirements into their occupations protected their prestige through exclusiveness.

He also points out that each of these groups, making up a 'service class', appeared first in the older, larger and more industrially developed cities in the north-east. Wiebe talks of the development of 'an aggressive, optimistic, new middle class' sweeping all before it from about 1900 onwards. Nevertheless, such professions were not autonomous since, as Lasch argues, we should not ignore 'the connection between the rise of modern professionalism and the rise of professional management'; or more critically, 'American professionalism has been corrupted by the managerial capitalism with which it is so closely allied'.[77] Lasch points out the considerable similarities between the appropriation of knowledge, centralization and deskilling in the industrial and in the non-industrial spheres of social activity, especially within the American health service.

Among the crucially important agents of this transformation of American medicine were the massive private foundations such as Carnegie, Ford, Gates and Rockefeller. These were key instruments in early efforts to rationalize the social services, public health and medical care under the control of specially trained managers in these various fields.[78] Particular emphasis was placed upon the development of a properly non-social technological 'scientific medicine' which in part obscured and minimized the role of structural and other environmental causes of illness and disease. The foundations were (and indeed still are) powerful bases through which corporate institutions, acting through creative and loyal managers, came to influence and direct universities, medical schools and the professions. Before the Second World War, when there was little federal state expenditure on medical care, the foundations acted as a substitute 'state'. Brown summarizes these developments:[79]

> Out of an earlier mercantilist philanthropy grew a new corporate philanthropy, intended not to ameliorate the lot of industrial capitalism's victims but to shape and guide social institutions...New occupations, like engineering and social work, and old ones, like law and medicine, gained elevated professional status in return for becoming the new order's managers of production or social relations. Medicine's almost fantastic transformation from rank ignominy to Olympian heights of status...

In the development of social work, a particularly important role was played by the settlement house movement, in as much as it was here that social workers first came to see themselves, not as charity workers, but as social reformers, and because of the vital role that the movement played in a developing progressivism. The settlement house residents 'were members of the first sizeable generation of American college graduates, men and women who came to maturity in an industrial or commercial society in which there was no clearly defined place for them. With big business at the top and organized labour at the bottom, many felt alienated from the society into which they had been born.'[80] These young people, often from Midwest Protestant backgrounds, struggled to bring about the great disinternment of the masses through what was in effect their own internment – in the settlement houses. The first of these was opened in 1888; some years later, the most influential – Chiacgo's Hull House – was opened. By 1900 there were 100 settlement houses; by 1910 some 400. The idea behind the settlement house movement was that of neighbourhood, of the reconstruction of a creative and optimistic *Gemeinschaft* among the ethnic (and often immigrant) big-city poor, to which end the reformers set up kindergartens, men's clubs, gymnasiums, courses in arts and crafts and music halls. But more important for the purpose of our argument was the organizational and legislative role of settlement house residents, particularly of women members. Jane Addams of Hull House was prominent in the Chicago Civic Federation and president of the National Conference of Charities and Correction; as a publicist and spokesperson, she was instrumental in persuading Theodore Roosevelt to support the enactment of child labour legislation. Julia Lathrop, also a Hull House resident, led the offensive for the founding of the first juvenile court in Cook County, Illinois, in 1903; two decades later she was prime mover fostering the passage of the Sheppard-Towner Act, which established the conditions for the creation of some 3000 child and maternal health centres. Yet another Hull House resident, Mary McDowell, was from 1899 the leading organizer of the National Consumers League and from 1903 of the National Women's Trade Union League.[81] This movement then fed into the development of social security during the New Deal, the growth of which in turn enhanced the expansion of substantial federal and state welfare bureaucracies. The further expansion of these during the 1960s led many commentators to argue that there was a 'new class' in American society, made up of educationalists, scientists, technologists, social workers, public-sector lawyers and doctors, government bureaucrats, etc.[82]

So far, then, we have seen that there have been a number of interconnected developments which have given a particular structuring to the trajectory of American society in the twentieth century. We are not, of course, claiming that this has been the only powerful determinant of that society. But we would claim that the strength of American capital, particularly on a world-wide scale, the weakness of American labour and the growth of credentialism and more generally of an education-based system of stratification, all stem from the making of the American 'service class'. This class possesses considerable 'causal powers' and by comparison with France and the UK, these have been substantially realized in the USA. What then are these causal powers? They are to restructure capitalist societies so as to maximize the divorce between conception and execution and to ensure the elaboration of highly differentiated and specific structures within which knowledge and science can be developed and sustained. These powers thus involve the deskilling of productive labourers; the maximizing of the educational requirements of places within the social division of labour and the minimizing of non-educational/non-achievement criteria for recruitment to such places; and the enhancement of the resources and income devoted to education and science (whether this is privately or publicly funded).

In the USA the service class began to realize these powers with the move to scientize management at the turn of the century. This then produced an interlocking complex of institutional developments: of universities and colleges throughout each state; of private foundations; of professionalizing occupations; and of large corporate and state bureaucracies, which have developed and extended themselves between labour and capital, weakening the former, transforming the latter, and in part producing new lines of social conflict, between capital and the service class. As Stark says more generally:[83]

> In attempting to defend their claims to technical expertise or to maintain the currency value of their certified degrees, the members of these new occupations stand not with one foot in the working class and one foot in the capitalist class but with one foot in a professional association and one foot in a bureaucratic (corporate or state) organization. The constellation of relations of conflict and alliance between these associations and other organizations arising from work, community and political life must be the object of study in the analysis of class relations in the current period.

THE SERVICE CLASS IN EUROPE

Britain

We shall now consider what is almost the exact opposite of these developments, namely the British case. Here scientific management did not develop to anything like the same degree in the period before the First World War; when it did emerge it was in an attenuated form in rather different, less modernizing industrial sectors at a time of economic depression; and nothing like the same interlocking institutional complex emerged by which the British service class could make itself. First, then, although some changes did occur in the period up to 1914 (development of piece-work and other bonus systems, the gradual and variable replacement of internal contractors with a directly employed supervision system, and revived forms of paternalism),[84] systematic schemes of scientific management aroused little or no interest among engineers and managers in this period and were very rarely implemented. Charles Maier summarizes:[85]

> Not merely did this reflect an industrial leadership set in its ways; an underlying satisfaction with decentralized production, with the premises of a liberal regime in a country where the middle classes felt little anxiety about the social order, postponed real interest until the economic difficulties of the 1920s and 1930s.

The journal *Engineer* in 1911 objected to American notions of scientific management with the comments that 'there are fair and unfair ways of diminishing labour costs...We do not hesitate to say that Taylorism is inhuman'.[86] Urwick summarized the reaction of capital by claiming that only a few employers in Britain had given serious attention to Taylor's work and this was because the industrial milieu presented an infertile soil in its scepticism and apathy. There was a startling inability to understand that anything other than 'technology' made any difference to industrial output.[87] He further suggests that where employers did take up aspects of Taylor's work (even during and after the First World War) they tended to over-emphasize one particular aspect (such as 'Welfare and Psychology on Costing or Technical Research'), and so their 'business suffered the usual penalties of lack of balance' and in consequence they 'revised scientific methods, when what they needed was more science'.[88]

Other contemporary commentators reinforced this interpretation. A. Shadwell, for example, the author of the monumental *Industrial Efficiency*, maintained in 1916 that in British industry:[89]

Very often there is no planning at all; it is left to the operative and rule of thumb. Generally there is planning of a rough and ready kind, but some of the most famous workers in the country are in such a state of chaos that the stuff seems to be turned out by accident.

Similar critical comments were developed by J. A. Hobson in *Incentives in the New Industrial Order*, and Sidney Webb in *The Works Manager Today*, while Edward Cadbury pointed to the potential dehumanizing consequences of the implementation of scientific management.[90] Levine details the specific lack of attention devoted to Taylor's seminal papers in the British engineering journals; for example, that entitled 'Shop management' was ignored by all four of the major British engineering journals.[91] Levine identifies three aspects of the reaction to scientific management: the humanitarian, as in the quote from *The Engineer* above; the economic, as in the claim that scientific management was unnecessary in Britain because labour costs were lower; and the anti-scientistic, as in another leader from *The Engineer* in which it was claimed that 'too much science...is likely to lead to a decrease of efficiency rather than an increase',[92] or as in E. T. Elbourne's view that 'golden rules' or organization *per se* 'can never be a substitute for good men'.[93]

Finally, in C. B. Thompson's survey in 1917, of the 201 factories where Taylorist schemes of management had been introduced world-wide, only four were to be found in Britain.[94] Likewise Levine, in his survey of the related development in mass production, maintains that there were very few traces of this in Britain in the period up to the First World War, particularly because of the failure to develop the characteristics of specialization, standardization and interchangeability of parts.[95]

There is some controversy as to when any widespread implementation of scientific management did occur in Britain. Certain commentators have seen the period of the First World War as marking some kind of watershed. Burgess, following Pollard, maintains that it 'was one of the major long-term effects of the War that it marked the widespread implementation in Britain of the methods of "scientific management"'.[96] However, he cites no contemporary evidence for this and it seems more plausible to suggest that while the war did produce a number of significant effects, such as increased standardization, advances in mass production techniques in government arsenals, and some erosion of skill differentials, the most important innovations in Britain did not take place until considerably later.[97] Moreover, these developments cannot be understood without considering in detail the Bedaux system which was the most significant managerial innovation in Britain in the inter-war years.[98]

The Bedaux consultancy firm had been started in 1918 in Cleveland, and within a few years Bedaux himself was the owner of two networks of consultants, one American and one international. He enjoyed extraordinarily rapid financial success which seems to have been particularly due to his salesmanship. Littler points out that while Taylor was keen to justify his system intellectually, Bedaux simply set out to sell himself and his system to engineers and managers.[99] Moreover, while Taylor's system took both a long time and was difficult to install, Bedaux's was quick and easy and involved relatively little change to the existing management structure. Indeed, the main innovation of Bedaux was to appear to have solved the problem the solution to which had eluded Taylor, namely the nature of the relationship between work and fatigue.[100] Bedaux claimed to be able to determine the exact proportions of the two necessary for the fulfilment of any task. Once that was achieved, it was then possible to compare all the different tasks within the factory, in terms of their variable combinations of work and rest. They could all be reduced to the same measuring grid and hence subject to a systematic control and monitoring system. At the same time, Bedaux built a fairly crude reward system late into his proposals:[101]

> If a man earned £3 a week for producing 40 articles, Bedaux offered him £4 a week if he produced 80. Put in these terms, the confidence trick is too obvious, but the logic was confused by jargon...For instance, Bedaux always started from the premise that the man should have been producing 60 articles for his £3, and thus if he produced a third more – 80 – he got a third more pay – £4. What could be fairer.

Another investigation of the Bedaux system by the *American Federation of Labor* concluded that underneath its pseudo-scientific jargon it was essentially a means of speeding up work with little consideration being paid to other aspects of good and efficient management.[102] In other words, it enhanced the *existing* power of management at the expense of the workers and it gave those managers an illusory sense of being able to understand and control efficiency. Indeed, Bedaux was frequently criticized for not doing enough to improve methods of working and organizing tasks and for thrusting all the burden for increasing output on to the workers. The Taylor Society itself, fearful of the charge that *they* were merely concerned to 'speed up' the work process, actively tried to dissociate itself from the Bedaux system.[103]

Nevertheless, the Bedaux system was in fact widely adopted in Britain. In 1937, of the 1100 or so firms using it worldwide, over 200 were British (and 150 French). The firms involved in Britain included many of those which were relatively new and expanding in the 1930s: in food processing (Huntley and Palmers), light engineering (GEC (Coventry)), motor components (British Goodrich Rubber Co. Ltd), chemicals (Boots Pure Drug Co.), and services (Vernons Ltd), as well as certain older industries, particularly textiles (Wolsey Ltd).[104] Two important aspects of the implementation of the Bedaux system in Britain should be noted. First, its introduction rarely involved the destruction of some long-established craft skill. Most of the industries in which it was introduced depended on semi- or unskilled labour, not on craft labour. Even where some craft deskilling was involved, this occurred *before* the implementation of the Bedaux system.[105] Second, the introduction of this system activated considerable opposition and antagonism from the workforce. This was both because it brought about increases in unemployment during periods of already very high national and local unemployment, and because of the obvious resentments about being spied upon and about the speeding-up of work. Nevertheless, much of the opposition was unsuccessful and strike action quickly evaporated.[106] Interestingly, the effect of such resistance was that the unions often became *active* participants in creating and sustaining effort norms, a process reflected in the generally accommodative response of the national unions and the TUC to Bedaux by the 1930s.[107]

These developments during the 1930s did not involve a simple pattern of craft deskilling within a given organization. Rather, to the extent that there was deskilling of certain crafts, this occurred in a 'non-confrontational' manner via changes in the occupational/industrial structure, such as the growth of new industries; the emergence of new firms with different technologies; the development of new production processes; and the spatial relocation of industries, firms and plants both within the UK and abroad.[108] The introduction of Bedaux mainly occurred *within* these new industries and firms where there were not well-established craft skills waiting to be 'deskilled'. Changes were then nevertheless brought about in a 'confrontational' manner but these did not involve the simple destruction of craft skills – indeed the main effects of Bedaux were to 'legitimize' the speeding of work and the introduction of new forms of control and payment, but not to 'restructure' management and its relationship with labour in anything like the way in which this was effected in the USA.

There were a number of reasons why there was this restricted and attenuated uptake of scientific management in Britain. Already noted are the following features of the economic structure of late nineteenth-century Britain: first, market mechanisms remained relatively efficient and this militated against the growth of large *internal* hierarchies; second, family firms remained more significant in Britain than the USA and there was little tendency for ownership and control to become divorced; third, there was relatively little increase in the overall level of industrial concentration until after the First World War when the 1920s merger booms brought about substantial increases; fourth, even in the industries where increases in industrial concentration did take place, the owners did not attempt to construct an integrated and centralized administrative system; and finally, there was an extraordinarily high rate of capital export in the years up to 1914, so much so that in that year British investments accounted for over one-half of the world's total.[109] As a result of these features industry remained relatively unchanged and subject to continuing forms of familial or decentralized control. Alfred Marshall wrote in 1903 that '[Many] of the sons of manufacturers [were] content to follow mechanically the lead given by their fathers. They worked shorter hours, and they exerted themselves less to obtain new practical ideas than their fathers had done.'[110] At the same time there was an expanding and increasingly profitable development of finance capital. The latter, as opposed to industrial capital, 'was decidedly richer, more powerful, and possessed of a more distinguished historical pedigree... the City, with its centuries-old traditions, its location near the hearts of upper-class England, and its gradually woven, closely knit ties to the aristocracy and gentry, enjoyed a social cachet that evaded industry.'[111] As a result, the financial institutions within the City did not greatly contribute to the financing of British industry, especially of the new industries of electrical engineering and automobile production which in the USA were particularly significant sites for the implementation of Taylorism and Fordism. Moreover, the enormous rewards from such overseas investment and the secure imperial markets cushioned the British economy so that the pressures to restructure management were less intense.[112]

The effects of these processes were particularly important because Britain had been the first to industrialize and broadly speaking its capital stock was of an older vintage compared with the other economies apart from France.[113] New schemes of management would have been more likely to have been introduced either where the latest technology was to be found, or where new capital investment was about to be implemented. Two examples where this restriction seems to have been an important factor preventing the development of new management structures in the UK were, first, the high levels of existing investment in steam and gas which militated against the widespread growth of electrification and hence of electrical engineering; and second, that existing investments in iron and steel were so enormous that this in itself constituted a formidable barrier to change. This problem was furthermore enhanced because of the essentially 'interconnected' nature of industrial organization so that it was impossible to introduce any particular innovation without in effect restructuring the whole industry. This was a particular problem in Britain for two reasons: first, because of the highly fragmented pattern of ownership in most of the leading industries; and second, because, unlike the USA, Britain was a national social and political entity which meant that it was much more difficult for new investments to be developed hundreds of miles away from those already established.[114]

It has also been widely claimed that the level of wages was not high enough in Britain for it to provide a major incentive to introduce new management schemes. The share of wages, for example, fell steadily from a peak in 1893 so that by 1913 wages constituted a smaller share than in the 1890s. Moreover, both money and real wages rose more slowly in Britain than in the other advanced economies after 1890 and real wages fell in Britain between 1895 and 1913.[115] However, Levine convincingly shows that this is not a sufficient explanation of the failure to introduce new schemes of management. A further reason for this failure, according to Burgess, was the 'substantial evidence to support the argument for increasing working-class "solidification" since the late 1870s, both at the workplace and in the community'.[116] This was related to the exceptional growth in trade union membership, from 1 million in 1889 to 4 million in 1913. If labour did resist it was therefore much more difficult to invest elsewhere in Britain in a non-unionized plant. Moreover, employers in Britain were normally unwilling to encourage their workers to *share* in the productivity gains that would result from a transformed managerial structure.[117] British capital simply sought to keep wages as low as possible rather than to develop a high wage and high productivity economy. As a result it is not very surprising that the rapidly unionizing, community-organized, labour movement was able to mount fairly effective and sustained opposition to most attempts to effect substantial managerial restructuring.

This was also true for another reason. As Hobson argued, the country's 'great business men' appear to have carved out their niche in the world without science or 'trained brains in others'. He pointed out their 'contemptuous scepticism of science and all that science stands for'.[118] Alfred Marshall likewise maintained that England could not 'maintain her position in the world, unless she calls science to her aid in a much more thorough way than hitherto'.[119] Particular deficiencies were noted with the failure to apply the fruits of scientific knowledge, especially within the field of chemical engineering. There was nothing like the same 'progressivism' which characterized the United States in the early years of this century. Maier notes that 'Rationalization in Europe, therefore, was only a stunted offspring of the American productive vision as originally conceived.'[120] Indeed, the USA provided a very distinctive negative example around the turn of the century. Disparagement of the American way of life – one centred on idolizing technology and wealth – became commonplace. Wiener suggests that the industrial revolution itself became redefined as a characteristically unEnglish event.[121]

This in turn was related to the development of two preferred 'agents of management' within British industry, agents that stood in opposition to the scientific rationalizers in the United States and Germany. These two agents were the 'educated amateur' or the 'gentleman', and the 'practical man'; their distinction from American management style was even considered to be reflected in leisure pursuits, the amateurish game of rugby union as opposed to the extraordinarily 'scientific', 'planned' game of American football.[122] The 'practical man' model was in effect the defensive ideal of those who were excluded from functioning as the 'gentleman', especially in the absence of an elite education. For those who favoured this model, training on the job was central and they disparaged the value of education or formal training for their work. The twin cults of the two models, the educated amateur and the practical man mutually reinforced opposition within management and industry to science, technology and to formal technical education. Coleman notes that 'Economics, management techniques, industrial psychology: all were frequently looked upon with grave suspicion, for they represented attempts to professionalize an activity long carried on jointly by "practical men" and gentlemanly amateurs.'[123] Management in Britain was not regarded as something to be pursued simply for its own sake, but rather more as the *means* to something else: to politics, land-ownership, culture, or a position in the City.[124]

Overall, then, in Britain 'management' did not really develop and then activate in British society the further transformations which were found in the USA. No really powerful service class emerged producing an institutional complex between labour and capital which characterized American society in the first half of this century. No British 'service class' formed itself until arguably the 1960s.

This has had a number of profoundly significant consequences for the trajectory of British society in the twentieth century. We will deal briefly with a range of interconnected developments which meant that by the mid-twentieth century British society was structured rather differently from the USA. First of all, there was a much slower growth of 'non-productive' white-collar workers in British industry compared with the American. By 1930, for example, while the ratio of non-productive:productive workers was 17.9 per cent in American manufacturing industry, it was only 11.3 per cent in Britain.[125]

Second, the rapid development of the professions occurred before the growth of scientific management and thus much more under the sway of the landed aristocratic class. Hence, British professions followed the gentry model of 'status professionalism' rather than the bourgeois one of 'occupational professionalism'.[126] Rubinstein summarizes the case in Britain,[127] particularly noting the spatial significance of London in this process of status professionalization which affected not only the old professions but newer ones as well, such as engineering:

> The process of incorporation, acquisition of an expensive and palatial head-quarters in central London, establishment of an apprenticeship system, limitations on entries, and scheduling of fees, are all manifestly designed to 'gentrify' the profession and make it acceptable to society. This aspect of professionalization is profoundly anti-capitalist, and hence at odds with much of the rest of nineteenth-century British society.

At the same time, however, the vast majority of British managers did not become professionalized. Even by the 1960s Nichols[128] concluded that managers

> cannot be regarded as professionals. They lack professional management qualifications and were seldom members of professional bodies. They have a low level of participation in such bodies. And, most important, they deny the legitimacy of such bodies and very rarely accept even the *existence* of a body of management theory.

Moreover, of those few managers identifying themselves as professionals, none of them considered that they were professional *managers*. This has particularly resulted from the relatively small role that educational qualifications played in British industry. There has been only a limited and late development of institutions concerned with higher management education. Business management in Britain 'has not been recognized in the past as a technically based profession like medicine, engineering, law...in Britain, entry to senior management posts has rarely depended much upon the posses-sion of higher education qualifications.'[129] Although this was challenged in the 1920s and 1930s by a small group of management intellectuals, the British 'management movement' which argued in favour of management education, they received very little support from either business, on the one hand, or from universities and the state, on the other. The members of this management movement found that they were preaching to an overwhelmingly unreceptive audience. Whitley, Thomas and Marceau neatly concluded that: 'The meta-morphosis of the ugly duckling of the management craft into the majestic craft of the management profession seemed as far away at the outbreak of the Second World War as it had at that of the First.'[130] This only changed after the Second World War with Sir Frederick Hooper's *Management Survey*, published in 1948; the foundation of the British Institute of Management in 1947 and the National Scheme for Management Studies in 1949; the establishment of business courses in a few universities; the setting up of the Administrative Staff College at Henley just after the war; and finally the Franks Report of 1963 from which followed the establishment of the London and Manchester Business Schools.[131]

However, higher education had not only been relatively free of management education but had also remained far more tied into the pre-industrial elite structures characterized by a 'sponsored' rather than by a 'contest' pattern of recruitment. British higher education was intimately connected with the landed aristocracy, with the established church, with the developing civil service, and with the traditional professions.[132] The contrast with the USA, where there were far fewer obstacles placed in the path of expansion and change, could hardly be more marked. In the UK the effects of social class on education are well summarized by Gowing.[133] She notes that it is

> strange that a country which had experienced such swift social mobility in the eighteenth and nineteenth centuries, and which had much admired its self-made industrial and engineering heroes, was so dominated by class and so reluctant to accord social prestige to science and technology. In some other European nations class divisions were as rigid, and in France much more bitter. In no other Western country did the class differences prevent scientific and technical education from permeating national life.

This was only to change to some degree in the 1960s, although when the British service class began to form itself in that decade, it did so heavily under the sway of what Bernice Martin calls the expressive professionals, mainly employees within the state and concerned with extending and protecting the welfare services.[134] Such employees in Britain gave a particular direction to the British service class and made it less obviously tied into private capital, private foundations and private educational institutions. When the British service class did develop it was very much something that was state-sponsored and occurred during the period in which British political culture was peculiarly 'progressivist' and when the long post-war boom ensured fairly high levels of welfare expenditure. In chapter 9 we will examine some of the very significant cultural correlates of the British service class and of the institutions with which it is connected.[135]

We have so far dealt with the way in which the growth of scientific management has directly 'activated' the causal powers of the 'service class' in the USA and how such an activation did not occur in the UK. We have also noted that this has had more indirect effects on the forms of occupational professionalization, bureaucratization and stratification via educational credentials in the USA. We will now much more briefly consider the situation in Germany, Sweden and France.

Germany

The country which most rapidly copied American innovations was Germany. According to Kocka, 'scientific management' first appeared in the workshops of large enterprises at the turn of the century.[136] Partly this stemmed from the fact that German entrepreneurs and managers took study trips to the USA in order to investigate the Taylor system at first hand and that 'Shop management' was translated into German very soon after publication. But it also derived from pre-existing features of German society, namely the bureaucratic tradition which led to written instructions, precision, punctuality, and formalization within organizational structures. Taylorism therefore did not appear to be unGerman in the way in which it seemed to be decidedly unEnglish. Indeed, Kocka maintains that in many German engineering works there was already to be found a clear division between the preparations for and control of production on the one side, and the execution of production on the other.[137] Already in Germany there had been the widespread growth of offices including paperwork and card index systems; some standardization of production; the reduction in the power of foremen; the growth of organizational specialists; and an increased devotion to science, technology and technical training. Such developments were also given a heightened impetus during the First World War, one result of which was a very rapid growth of administrative employees in German industry from 4.8 per cent of the labour force in 1895 to 14 per cent in 1933.[138] These white-collar workers in general occupied a separate stratum as *Angestellte*, and the higher echelons formally categorized as 'Leitende Angestellten', with command functions and special prerogatives derived from pre-industrial structures of hierarchy, deference, and bureaucracy.[139] According to an extensive survey by Gustav Winter (*Der Taylorismus*) published in 1920, many industrial sectors had already been 'rationalized' and subject to Taylorist-type reorganization.[140]

Kocka shows in a case-study of Siemens and Halske that fundamental changes had occurred as early as the 1890s.[141] Functions that had previously been carried out 'personally' were institutionalized, when written reports on routine matters began to appear and when detailed work regulations were issued for both workers and salaried employees. Especially important in this transformation were technical workers. Up to the 1880s the only technical personnel were the works managers, but after that date there was a massive expansion in their numbers, particularly for projecting, calculating and installing electrical equipment. From the 1890s onwards there was a much clearer process of standardized education and professional organization of various types of technical and engineering worker. Torstendahl maintains that Kocka's study shows that there was no contradiction between professionalization and bureaucratization; that is to say German engineers and technicians appeared to have been able to maintain loyalty to their 'profession' while at the same time demonstrating allegiance to their particular large company.[142]

Not surprisingly these developments had some influence over higher education in Germany during this period. There was a qualitative increase in student numbers, from 14,000 in 1870 to 34,000 in 1900; there were attempts by business to increase industry-related research, but the greatest rises were in fact recorded in the philosophical faculties; university education remained centrally unimportant for the allocation of status within German society; universities became more closely integrated with the local and central German state; and the professoriate developed almost Mandarin-like status in their role and influence in the new German Reich.[143] The main focus of applied scientific and technological research occurred in the *Technische Hochschule* which expanded greatly in the last decade or two of the nineteenth century, although Siemens interestingly considered that the work found there was rather too practical and too little concerned with fundamental principles.[144] However, by 1910 Germany had 25,000 students of science and technology, compared with just 3000 in Britain. By then the German state had developed a relatively effective nationally organized system of technical education: a fact clearly recognized in contemporary analyses such as J. C. Smail's 1914 report on *Trade and Technical Education in Germany and France*, and as important, a very strong and growing demand for such trained workers from private industry.[145]

Unlike the USA, however, as 'new' professions developed, particularly that of the engineer, they adopted the model of professionalization provided by the existing 'old' professions (clergyman, physician, lawyer and academic professor). This involved a process much more tied into the state than was the case in the USA. McClelland summarizes:[146]

> The connection of the prestige of a learned profession with the officially prescribed initial steps in a career (culminating in higher education, state examinations and apprenticeships) indicates that association with public authority (the churches or the state) rather than with the 'professional' organizations tended in 1860 to establish the identity of a profession.

As the new occupations began to organize they necessarily remained well-integrated with the state; indeed they did not campaign for dissolving their ties with the state but rather for their rearrangement. Many occupations vigorously campaigned for greater state recognition and regulation of their professional status.[147] This was particularly the case because of the very recent unification of the Reich in 1871, which meant that much of this state regulation was organized on a local or regional level and that the professions had much difficulty in organizing nationally (compared with both Britain and the USA). The separate German states discouraged the formation of independent professional organizations and they were often able to effect this policy since many 'professionals' were in fact public employees.

Therefore, in contrast with France or Britain, there was a massive expansion in the numbers and influence of engineering and technical workers, particularly after the turn of the century when the *Technische Hochschule* attained formal equal status with the classical university through the right to confer doctorates. Furthermore, a very much higher proportion of such trained engineers worked in industry as compared with France, where, for example, less than 10 per cent of graduates from the *École Polytechnique* worked in private industry between 1870 and 1914.[148] However, compared with the USA these developments had less significant effects on the rest of society: partly because such engineers in private industry took their model of professionalization from the state-regulated older professions; partly because many engineers thought of themselves as *Privatbeamte* (private civil servants) – this resulted from the high esteem attached to the civil service which was to be found in most German states since the late eighteenth century; and partly because engineers did not provide a model which could be emulated by other occupational groups which still needed state support, recognition and regulation.[149] Hence, although *within* private industry the effect of the growth of engineering was profound, resulting in, for example, high status for the engineer and high standing for industry as a whole, this did not activate the causal powers of the service class to the degree found in the USA. The powers of the German state (both local and national) remained centrally significant and have in a sense constrained the growth of the 'higher education–professions–private industry and foundations' nexus which has been so important in the making of the American service class. The importance of the Nazi period was, of course, central to this. To take just one indicator: the number of German students in higher education fell from a peak of 127,000 in 1930 to less than 50,000 in 1940 and the former figure was only reached again in the mid-1950s (in West Germany).[150]

Sweden

In Sweden in the middle of the nineteenth century it was not possible to distinguish between those with and those without a technical education. Apart from a very few specialized schools there was very little development of engineering as a qualified, theoretically-based, scientific training.[151] Generally the technician in industry was either an entrepreneur or a worker/apprentice. There were very few salaried posts for engineers. Similar to the case in Britain engineering was essentially transmitted through learning-by-doing on the shopfloor rather than through theoretical analysis in schoolrooms. Engineering work was mainly found in military, cartographic and mining contexts.

However, as this situation slowly changed towards the end of the century, the category of 'engineer' was gradually extended to the mechanical and industrial engineers. However, unlike the USA, the industrial engineer in Sweden did not develop an exclusive professionalization as such, but merely became part of the *general* category of engineer. Moreover, up at least until 1920 or so, recruitment of engineers to managerial positions was not especially dependent upon educational credentials.[152]

Overall, the development of managerial hierarchies resulting from new forms of management does not seem to have been particularly developed in Sweden during this period. For example, there was little or no development of the multidivisional company in Sweden until after the Second World War.[153] Also few substantial research and development departments developed in Swedish industries before the First World War and there seems to have been little possibility of engineers developing professional careers within industry.

Nevertheless, there were considerable efforts made in Sweden in the first decade of the twentieth century to encourage the rationalization of Swedish industry. In particular, in order to prevent widespread emigration, it was necessary to develop a 'forceful Swedish industrial policy'.[154] In terms somewhat similar to American progressivism there was a wide-ranging debate in Parliament, in professional associations, in the state bureaucracy, and in the trade unions, concerned with the perceived need to raise the very low 'efficiency' of Swedish industry. Particularly because of its dependence on exports it needed to be successful in the increasingly competitive world market and to do so it needed 'a harder work effort', a progressive industrial policy and a much greater commitment to practical work in industry. An important role in the encouragement of this was played by the Swedish Society of Engineers – a national society for higher engineers which advocated the ideal of the 'administrative engineer' (following the German *der Verwaltungsingeneur*) who would combine together knowledge of technology, business, administration, and organization.[155] This Society of Engineers also interestingly advocated the organization of everyone into corporate groups (guilds) which would represent their interests in a future 'corporatist' society. There was a strong emphasis in this Society on steering a middle way between capital and labour, even being able to act as a mediator or a bridge between social classes. Some distance from the immediate interests of capital was also to be found in the Swedish Industries Association (*Sveriger Industriforbund*) founded in 1910. It was argued that the notion of *laissez-faire* should be replaced with that of the responsible social order in which all groups would partly share in an expanding economy, albeit one that was most definitely organized on capitalist lines. Runeby refers to this as involving the advocacy of the 'liberal corporate social order'.[156]

Central to these proposals were some detailed recommendations on the reorganization of Swedish industry. It was widely believed that factories were badly laid out and that there was an inadequate division of labour. The fact that workers were required to do lots of different tasks encouraged them to be inefficient, to do sloppy work and even to sabotage the industrial process.[157] The introduction, however, of scientific management was fairly slow. But some of Taylor's ideas were certainly noted and various Swedish engineers engaged in correspondence with him and other 'scientific managers'.[158] One argument of some influence, however, was the claim that the principles of scientific management had somehow to be adapted to the particular conditions in Sweden, including the numerous strikes, the high rate of emigration, low earnings and relatively high cost of living.[159] Moreover, the *Principles of Scientific Management* were only translated in 1914 and so although Taylorism was certainly more enthusiastically regarded than in Britain, the rationalization of industry only began on any scale in the 1920s. The Swedish Industries Association was in contact with the F. W. Taylor Co-operators in Philadelphia in 1917 (Taylor died in 1915), while a year earlier Jakob Sederholm published the first book in Sweden on scientific management arguing *inter alia* for mechanization, specialization, standardization, concentration of capital, and mass production.[160] He continuously emphasized that scientific management was essentially 'practical' and indeed could be applied to all spheres of social life, including household management. In other words, it was believed that there was *one* scientific solution ('One Best Way' according to Gilbreth) to industrial, managerial and social problems. Runeby summarizes the way in which this represented a new structuring of social and political life in the first quarter of this century:[161]

> Sweden had entered a new industrial era and the outlines of a new society can be seen in the demands for industrial influence and 'specialist' representation, for a new type of cooperation between state and industry, for reorganization of the state bureaucracy, for rationalized production and for the promotion of export interests. . . Democracy could be seen as a question of efficiency, social politics could mean organization and increased productivity, and labour market settlements should be 'non-political' and based on rational, objective calculations.

Clearly, then, the conditions for the growth of the Swedish service class were laid by the 1920s. However, its development was fairly slow until after the Second World War. The ratio of administrative:production employees in Swedish industry rose from 6.6 per cent in 1915, to 9.9 per cent in 1930, to 13.7 per cent in 1940, and to a spectacular 21 per cent in 1950.[162] This was also reflected in higher education which hardly grew at all during the inter-war period. There were 9000 university students in 1920 and only 12,000 in 1939. The number then rose to 15,000 in 1949, 33,000 in 1959 and an extraordinary 115,000 in 1969.[163]

The growth in the powers of the Swedish service class occurred in the post-war period and stemmed from two partly independent causes: first, the growth in the Swedish economy in the later 1930s and during the war which involved a rapid diffusion of new materials, new products, new methods of working and enhanced demand for engineering workers; and second, the extensive growth of public investment in the social infrastructure and the provision of an extensive range of public services under the auspices of social democracy, this being very much directed by a group of 'rationalizing intellectuals. . . participants in a social process that would bring to intellectuals like themselves greater power and status'.[164]

France

At the turn of the century, scientific management found in France a ready-prepared ground for expansion because of the existence of a well-established group of highly qualified technicians and engineers. They owed their existence to the fact that institutionalized technical education had been developed in the eighteenth century under the sway of mercantilist policies of the period – the institutions of influence being the *École Polytechnique*, the *Écoles des Ponts et Chaussées*, the *Écoles des Mines*, and the *École Centrale des Arts et Manufactures*.[165] French engineers, particularly those based in Paris, were paramount during the first half of the nineteenth century, but the schools did not greatly expand their output as the century went on. The number of engineers in France only doubled in the last quarter to about 28,000, and relatively few French engineers were employed in industry since a military career remained more attractive for most.[166] This was in part connected with the low status that private business enjoyed in French society. This resulted from, first, the nobility's long-standing detestation of businessmen stemming from the French Revolution; second, the continuing high status of the traditional professions of law, medicine, the clergy and government; and third, the strong anti-business pressure of Parisian intellectual and artistic opinion.[167]

One effect of this was that although engineers were very important at the topmost levels of the advanced industrial sectors, relatively fewer were recruited into the lower and middle levels compared with the USA. Those that did enter private industry had a considerable innovative influence, being, for example, the first in Europe to study and implement Taylorist systems of management. Particularly important were Henry le Chatelier and Henri Fayol.[168] One area where such theories were applied was the rapidly expanding automobile industry, especially at Renault and Pankard.[169] Fayol was instrumental in developing the idea that parallel with already recognized functions of management there was also something he termed the 'administrative function' which covered forecasting, organization, direction, co-ordination and supervision. However, it would seem that the *overall* impact of scientific management was less marked than in Germany, and it is interesting to note that in 1918 Clemenceau was suggesting that it was necessary to establish Taylorite planning departments.[170]

From the end of the First World War until the mid-1930s scientific management did have some considerable influences on parts of the French economy: the encouragement of large-scale production units, partly because many engineers had spent some time running large public services, such as a canal, a port or a railroad division; the favouring of horizontal agreements and cartels to develop larger production facilities and to standardize components; and the spreading of the idea (if not the practice) that management should be organized into elaborate vertical structures, of separating staff and line, of encouraging long-term financial planning, and of decentralizing routine decision-making. However, these changes were confined to particular firms, and there was little reduction of the very high proportion of skilled workers in French industry (65 per cent at Peugeot in the 1920s). Moreover, the depression of 1931 onwards brought about fairly massive opposition to the further implementation of new forms of management.[171] This was partly because there had been no attempt in France to develop new forms of 'industrial participation' or 'human relations' managerial practices. Indeed, one reaction to the worsening depression was to try to implement even more unpopular management schemes than those of Taylor, including that of Bedaux. Particularly from 1933 pits and factories were closed, the workforce was redistributed, productivity was substantially increased – all at the cost of further embittering industrial relations. Indeed, many engineers themselves lost their jobs and for those that did not there was a considerable fall in the status of engineering. There was a general revulsion against American methods which had reduced the autonomy of the individual engineer and contacts with the skilled workforce. Levy-Leboyer concludes that:[172]

> engineers' professional journals and corporate reports in the 1930s testify that there were fewer employment opportunities and at the same time a decline in loyalty and a fall in work standards previously unheard of. Unemployment and demoralization were reinforcing each other.

It is generally reckoned that the French experience of the 1930s strengthened both the small innovative enterprise on the one hand (which did not displace skilled labour), and the very large corporation based on stable technologies, diversified products and a good research base, on the other. Many enterprises intermediately placed between these went out of business or suffered substantial decline during this period, and it was these which had to a considerable extent implemented new management schemes in the preceding period.[173]

Thus attempts to scientize management occurred rather falteringly in France, and this was reflected in the relatively slow growth of management education. Although scientifically trained graduates from the very prestigious *Écoles* had occupied some of the command posts in the advanced sectors of French industry, there was no really systematic education *for business* until the 1950s.[174] That this did then occur was as a result of conscious organization by the French Chambers of Commerce which sent groups of businessmen to the USA to study new business organization and management methods. Within a decade or so there was an extremely enthusiastic acceptance of the need to establish new educational institutions based on Harvard, Massachusetts Institute of Technology, Stanford, Wharton and so on. As Story and Parrott conclude:[175]

> In no European country has American management been embraced so enthusiastically as in France . . . The whole love affair with American business started in the 1950s when streams of French businessmen poured across the Atlantic . . . The French enthusiasm for US management techniques was the more surprising in that French employers had until then (the 1960s) been among the most conservative in all Europe.

This radical change in attitude towards management education resulted from, first, the greatly enhanced competition for the products of French industry after the Second World War, and second, the perceived need by traditional French *patronat* to confront the nationalization, strikes and planning of the post-war period. The second point is summarized in the following comment in *International Management Developments*:[176]

> In the immediate post-war period the *patronat français* considered that something immediate and quite radical had to be done to combat the rising tide of nationalization. One of the piles in this breakwater was to ensure that the managerial class not just made proper use of modern management techniques but considered, studied and acted in consequence about the meaning and nature of the *entreprise libre*.

After the Second World War a range of different private and public institutions developed as part of a massive expansion of French higher education (numbers increased from 130,000 in 1948 to 540,000 in 1968).[177] The French service class formed itself in the two decades after the end of the Second World War.

Conclusion

We have thus shown that the form taken by the service class varies considerably between different societies, depending on a number of factors, including the power of skilled labour to resist the appropriation of knowledge, the pre-existing professional and bureaucratic structures, the power of the state, the spatial centralization of professional groups, the general status of business as opposed to professional activity, and so on. Nevertheless, in the post-war period, *all* five societies have experienced a substantial enhancement of the powers of the service class and this has transformed their respective trajectories of social-political development. As a prelude to the remaining three chapters, we will note some of the effects of this:[178]

1 'Knowledge' has been significantly appropriated away from the working class and embodied within the institutions of science, the professions and education, the directors of which constitute a class which serves capital but increasingly does so on its own terms.
2 The causal powers of the working class have been progressively weakened as that class is subject to control and reproduction by the service class.
3 The power of the service class appears to be legitimate since their work is premised upon 'technical rationality'.
4 The preferred form of work in such a society has come to be that of a career, the point of entry to which being dependent upon appropriate educational credentials. Few can avoid seeking such credentials and people's relative attainment structures their location within the system of social stratification.

5   The service class does not necessarily have interests coincidental with those of 'capital'. Much contemporary politics is organized around divisions *within* the service class, or conflicts between sections of that class and capital. Labourist/social democratic politics are heavily influenced by these developments.

6   A major division within all such societies is that between the public and the private wings of this service class: the relative power of the former has a major effect on the character and strength of socialist and social democratic politics in each society.

7   Much labourist or social democratic struggle, whether of manual workers or deskilled white-collar workers, is directed against the 'service class' rather than the capitalist class itself; the latter is anyway becoming 'depersonalized' and less obviously a target for political contestation.

8   The potential oppositional groupings to 'capital' are nevertheless exceedingly large. Many sectors of the service class organize to protect their interests and they will struggle very hard to preserve gains made or to extend those gains. Such groupings will use a variety of organizational means – profession, trade union or voluntary association – and their struggles often involve opposition to capital and/or the state.

9   The state is subject to 'overloading' by the demands that are made of it by the very many interest groups which are often made up of, or led by, the service class; and at the same time the state is experienced as something to be struggled against since it is 'over-strong', unrepresentative, or overly bureaucratic.

10 The service class has been partly responsible for generating new 'social movements', not directly structured by the relations of production, and these have led to the redrawing of the boundaries of social division, political conflict, and cultural experience.

7

Industry, finance, politics: modes of disorganization

In this chapter we will summarize a number of interconnected developments which are disorganizing western capitalist societies. These developments will be analysed under three headings: industrial, financial and political.

We have already noted in chapters 4 and 5 the widespread growth of global corporations. However, although companies have developed with turnovers in excess of the national income of individual nation-states, there has not been a marked increase in the degree of concentration in the world economy as a whole. Dunning and Pearce concluded that over the period 1962–77, four major industries showed a persistent trend of declining concentration in the world economy (petroleum; chemicals and pharmaceuticals; motor vehicles; and metal manufacture and products); five showed a more ambiguous trend to reduced concentration (aerospace; electronics and electrical appliances; shipbuilding, railroad and transportation equipment; food processing; and paper and wood products); three showed a clear trend to higher concentration (industrial and farm equipment; building materials; beverages); and two showed a more ambiguous trend to increased concentration (office equipment and computers; tobacco).[1] At the level of the world economy, then, there has not been the same tendency to increased concentration that characterized the earlier period.

The development of the large corporation had been a response not only to the growth of mass-production technology, but also to the efforts to orchestrate and regulate a given national economy.[2] With the development of disorganized capitalism, these exceptionally powerful 'global corporations': (1) cannot control levels of mass demand for their products within the central western economies; (2) will be able to orchestrate levels of demand in individual Third World economies, but this will provide only a small fraction of the mass market for any given product; and (3) because of reduced world concentration levels and increased import penetration of each given national economy, will experience heightened competition in all markets. For example, between 1970 and 1980 imports of goods and services rose as a percentage of GNP in the USA from 6 to 12 per cent, in West Germany from 20 to 29 per cent, and in France from 15 to 21 per cent.[3]

Yet, at the same time, individual nation-states are unable to 'organize' a given national economy. The following extract from the FAST Report comments on the position facing any one of the central Western European states.

> It is, for instance, vital to control the information technologies, because they constitute the 'nervous system' of our societies, and it is therefore dangerous to leave to others the work of designing and conceiving them. But such control does not *automatically* confer, in an open economy, the acquisition of the jobs related to the use of the technology. The development in some regions of Europe of robot welders, assemblers, fitters, or painters, does not guarantee that the robotized production of automobiles will take place in that region. It will take place, like any other 'world' technology, wherever the future pattern of comparative advantages dictates that it takes place.[4]

A further reason for this lack of control or organization over the effects of the global corporations' policies results from the way in which such corporations have restructured the very patterns and forms of international trade. Crouch and Wheelright argue:

> Increasingly, *trade is between corporations and not nations*, and is being conducted on the basis of the comparative advantage created and manipulated by the very corporations that reap the benefits. The flows of trade, their direction, volume and pricing, are more and more at the discretion of global corporations, which make these administrative decisions internally for the purpose of maximising global profit.[5]

Between 35 and 45 per cent of world trade now takes place internally within the global corporations.[6] This greatly increases the vulnerability of single nation-states which are unable to regulate and direct such flows of international trade taking place under the visible hand of the global corporation. At the same time, the major economies are increasingly dependent on the earning of exports (whether or not they are internal to a corporation) in order to counteract enormously increased import penetration. Hannah and Kay, for example, note that imports of manufactures increased sevenfold between 1952 and 1979.[7] This dependence of the major economies on patterns of world trade that are substantially produced by the visible hand of the global corporation can be dramatically seen by considering the position of the most powerful and wealthy western power, the USA. Between 1980 and 1984 the US trade deficit rose form $26 billion to $123 billion, nearly a fivefold increase in money terms.[8] During that time the proportion of the deficit contributed by the Japanese rose from $12 billion to a massive $37 billion. Thus, even the most wealthy of capitalist nations have been unable to regulate and direct current flows of international trade.

There are a number of causes of these major developments: the breakup during the 1950s and 1960s of the old empires and 'spheres of influence' that were very much part of 'organized capitalism'; the development of computerized systems of information, storage and retrieval, and of satellite-based communications that have enabled different operations within global corporations to be located in different parts of the world;[9] the long-term fall in the rates of profit in manufacturing industry in the western economies, and the consequential necessity for restructuring;[10] the growth of new international money markets (particularly the Eurodollar and Eurobond markets), which enabled large companies to engage in financial speculation and indeed to become, in a sense, bankers as they took advantage of differential exchange and interest rates; the general acceleration in the movement of capital, which has become less government-regulated as new loci of economic and financial power developed towards the end of the post-war boom; and the reduced ability of states to control interest and exchange rates and hence the tendency for economies to be subjected to balance of payments crises.

We will explore the last points in the next section. For the present, though, there are some important changes in the organization of the market which need to be considered. First, the era of organized capitalism was one firmly based on the spread of mass markets, on interchangeable components and long production runs. For the USA this market was principally provided internally. As Piore and Sabel argue:[11]

> Until the 1970s...American industry was largely independent of foreign markets. Numerous prosperous family farms, the willingness of an immigrant population to experiment with machine-made products, the absence of sumptuary laws or class barriers restricting consumption, and unlimited natural resources – all of these factors produced a mass market large enough for American manufacturers to obtain critical economies of scale without depending on exports.

The construction of mass-production markets elsewhere involved much higher levels of state involvement both to protect and sponsor domestic interests and to ensure access to overseas markets, especially through the development of empires and other trading agreements.

Now, however, there has been a considerable breakup of mass markets for standardized products.[12] In West Germany, for example, there has been an exponential increase in the number of new types of products since the mid-1970s, while the average demand per product type has fallen considerably.

In the USA, in bread production, overall output of mass-produced white bread fell by 15 per cent between 1972 and 1977, while the production of specialty wheat varieties increased by 62 per cent. Mini-mills have grown rapidly in the production of high-quality alloy steels – in the USA from 3 to 18 per cent of the market between 1960 and 1982.[13] In chemicals, the fastest growing firms have been those producing specialty chemicals, while the mass-production companies like Du Pont and Dow have recently moved into the production of customized goods.[14] The resulting factories are distinctively different; as the director of Polaroid explains, a specialty chemicals plant is like a set of 'giant test tubes, arranged as in a huge laboratory to let you make whatever you want'.[15] Likewise one of the most successful textile areas in the modern world economy is that, in central Italy, of Prato, whose success was due to a long-term shift from standard to fashionable specialty fabrics and a reorganization of production from large integrated mills to technologically sophisticated small workshops.[16] The machine-tool industry has also been revolutionized. The Japanese in particular have pioneered the development of small numerically controlled equipment which can be used as general-purpose machines to meet in effect the craft needs of the rest of the metalworking industry. Contrary to expectations, such computer-controlled equipment has been deployed not merely in large mass-production plants but rather in thousands of small and medium-sized workshops that undertake much batch production in metalworking.[17]

Thus there seems to be a widespread development of firms in many of the advanced capitalist economies shifting to a strategy of producing non-mass production specialty products in smaller workplaces, often using 'state of the art' technology. Three causes of this development are:

1   Changes in technology as, for example, in the microelectronics and machine-tool industries.
2   Changes in taste, particularly through the widespread rejection of mass-consumption patterns and a heightened 'postmodernist' demand for individually distinct, often 'naturalistic' products.
3   Competition on grounds of product quality due to an inability to compete on price with Third World production facilities.

Hirschhorn summarizes: 'a manufacturer can no longer rely on a single, slowly changing product with guaranteed name recognition and market.'[18]

This pattern of development, of 'flexible specialization', also appears to provide considerable advantages to small and medium-sized independent firms as against large companies, and to substantially independent subsidiaries within larger firms. Specialization and flexible equipment weaken the impact of economies of scale; vertical integration limits required flexibility; and smaller companies are thought to be better at acquiring knowledge of and responding to detailed changes in micro-markets. These developments have been reflected in Britain with the development of what has been termed a 'postmodern' industrial strategy which over-emphasizes the opportunities provided to labour that result from the undoubted development of flexible specialization in a number of manufacturing sectors (especially clothing and furniture).[19]

This relates to a further phenomenon. Just as there is a growing divergence of products *within* any market, so there is an increasing convergence of products *across* different markets. Companies are much less distinguishable by their previous participation in a given market. A particular market is much less controllable by a given set of firms since wholesale invasions can be mounted. In recent years a clear example of this has been the extraordinarily rapid capture of the market for watches by digital watch companies. Hirschhorn comments: 'The information capital content of digital watches did not develop from watch-production technology per se, and thus traditional watchmakers could not anticipate the scope and strength of their unanticipated competitors.'[20] The distinction between 'communications companies' and 'information-processing companies' has likewise broken down, as the shift of the communications company, British Telecom, into the position of a world leader in information-processing demonstrates. This breakdown of clear-cut markets is associated with an increased flexibility of the capital stock. There is a much greater ability to modify such stock for use in new markets or to compete with new processes. Industries like machine assembly, chemical processing and plastic-forming demonstrate this generic flexibility, in that machinery increasingly does not have a fixed cycle of action. Workers and designers are able to modify the controls so that a machine is able to perform new functions. Hirschhorn summarizes:

> Cybernetic technology increases the generic flexibility of the capital stock; the information capital content of goods creates market uncertainty; and more exacting standards, combined with the wealth-creating potential of the new technologies, create market structures in which quality demands and standards are the most important determinant of profitability. These trends all reinforce one another. The flexibility of the capital stock (and of the labor pool attached to it) supports, and is supported by, the greater variety of market conditions.[21]

So far, then, we have seen how in relation to manufactured commodities there has been considerable disorganization of the previously dominant mass markets in which there were clear market leaders, with particular firms dominating the mass markets for clearly identifiable products. However, the development of the 'particularism' of markets is also greatly reinforced by the extensive shift away from manufacturing to service employment in all the western economies. We have noted this very clearly in each of the five societies. The following are the main causes of the substantial and apparently homogeneous expansion of service employment:[22]

1   'Engels' Law' changes whereby increasing wealth leads to the growth of
    demand for more varied service functions based much less on mass

provision and more on individual need; yet this necessitates some tendencies to socialize their provision.

2   Changes in the mode of provision of particular service functions to households – initially through increased service provision and, latterly, through increased self-servicing with household production goods in which individuals are much more *selective* in the services provided (e.g. video films).

3   'Intermediate subcontracting' changes in which activities once part of manufacturing production *per se* become separated off and take the form of specialized 'producer services', particularly as a result of economies of scale in service provision and necessities implied by the falling rate of profit within manufacturing industry.

4   The productivity gap (and hence price gap) between labour-intensive service industry and capital-intensive manufacturing industry.

5   Occupational tertiarization which leads to overall increases in service occupations and within this to a decreasing ratio of clerical workers within the total.

6   The consequence of rising real incomes which means that fewer people, particularly white males, are willing to 'service' others on a one-to-one basis.

7   Political pressures which generate an expanded state and hence formal service industry and service occupations, rather than informal, voluntary or household provision of such service functions.

8   The development of new technologies within manufacturing industry which can enable service industry sectors to be socialized.

9   The extension of commodity production to new product areas, such as computer software, where most of those employed are to be found within service occupations.

BANKS AND FINANCE

We will now consider some crucial changes in the role of banks and money in contemporary disorganized capitalism. It will be remembered that a crucial feature of the concept of organized capitalism was a strong and close articulation between productive industry and the banks, to the extent that they constituted a unified 'finance capitalism'. The societies under investigation in this book varied in the extent to which this unified finance capitalism was in fact found. Germany and the USA have been noticeably more organized in this respect; while Britain has been less organized, so much so that Ingham has recently characterized the British case as exemplifying 'Capitalism Divided'.[23] This characterization may seem unlikely given what we know of the extraordinary wealth and power of the City of London. Ingham notes that no other international commercial, banking and financial centre has ever enjoyed such a continuous period of operation (i.e. 250 years).[24] Similarly no other country has hosted a financial centre which has undertaken such a large share of the world economy's commercial, banking and financial operations. The importance of this to the British balance of payments has been crucial – not just in recent years, but even from before the First World War when a substantial trade deficit was more than counterbalanced by the City's invisible earnings. But even in that period Hilferding noted that the development of a specific 'finance capitalism' was slower in Britain than elsewhere; and that this has continued as the 'City' essentially represents a set of highly specialized *commercial* operations which have resulted from Britain's historic role as the *Makler* economy.[25] London's role in the world system thus developed as the specialization in, and near monopolization of, the *commercial* activities based on the existence of international economic exchanges. The kind of activities engaged in have included the financing of trade, foreign exchange dealing, brokerage for commodity purchases and sales, insuring commodities and transport, managing sterling as a world currency, and the organizing of the massive Eurodollar market. There came to be fixed in Britain the core institutional nexus of the City of London–Bank of England–Treasury, a nexus established partly in the face of British industrial capitalism and one which has provided a critically significant condition for the contemporary disorganizing of western capitalism through the dissolving in other countries of the close articulation between domestic banks and domestic industry.

We can begin here by noting that much recent literature on the internationalization of contemporary capitalist relations pays inadequate attention to the internationalization of banking.[26] This is partly because the changes do not on the face of it seem so impressive as the extraordinary global transformations of industrial enterprises in the post-war period. However, if we consider the magnitudes of capital involved, the speed of transformation, and most importantly the creation of truly *multi*national entities, then there are involved here changes of an exceptionally profound sort.[27] Developments here include:

1 The extension of international branch networks, particularly by American banks in Western Europe; and in retaliation in order not to lose business, by European banks in North America and elsewhere.
2 The formation of international banking groups, such as EBIC (founded 1970), Orton (1970), Abecor (1971), Europartners (1971), Inter-alpha (1972), of which, for example, all the major British banks are constituent members.
3 The establishment of international consortia banks to serve a particular area, or a certain kind of business, or a particular sort of industry: by the mid-1970s there were about 60 such banks with over half based in London serving the Euromoney market.[28]

The development of such internationalized banking forms stems from a number of causes: first, the growth of the international division of labour which necessitates extensive cross-investments between different parts of the same company operating in different countries; second, the need for financing the massive merger boom of the late 1960s; third, the partial industrialization of certain Third World economies and the resulting investment and recycling requirements; fourth, the financing of substantial trade with Eastern Europe, most of which has had to be orchestrated by western banks; fifth, the oil crisis which both necessitated enormous sums of finance (for the oil producer for infrastructure, for the oil consumer to pay for higher prices, and for the governments of consumer countries to pay for the resulting payments deficit) and which generated extraordinarily increased revenues deposited in London and in the other leading banking centres; sixth, the effects of interest rate variation, the freeing of exchange rates, and the general relaxing of exchange controls, which generated increases in short-term capital flows; and seventh, the derestriction and deregulation of banks from the 1960s onwards.[29]

Clearly one of the absolutely central features of these developments has been the growth of the Euromoney market.[30] In order to examine this it is necessary to consider very briefly the patterning of international finance since 1944. In that year at the Bretton Woods Conference the post-war international money system was established in which the leading role was to be played by the dollar. There were three main features of the system: the dollar was to act alongside gold ('as good as gold') and the US government would convert dollars into gold at $35 per ounce; the value of other currencies was fixed in terms of the dollar, at rates that were pegged but could be intermittently adjusted (as in the British devaluation of 1966); and the International Monetary Fund (IMF) was established to regulate the exchange-rate system and to provide short-term loans to countries in order to overcome balance of payments deficits.[31] This system, which roughly speaking lasted until the early 1970s, can be seen as the most systematic effort to manage, or 'organize' contemporary capitalism in a period in which international economic developments were becoming increasingly significant. The system was to be based on each national government being willing and able to intervene constantly in the foreign exchange markets in order to maintain the pegged level of exchange rates. The Western European countries were generally willing to enter into these arrangements because of the massive American investment via the Marshall Plan which was announced in June 1947. Bretton Woods, the Marshall Plan, and the General Agreement on Tariffs and Trade, allowed the formation of a new *Pax Americana* with what van der Pijl terms a new 'Atlantic ruling class'.[32]

Post-war governments, apart from those in the USA, were thus charged with managing their national economies within the limits imposed by the international monetary system (that is, through the balance of payments). In the USA, by contrast, such constraints did not operate in the same way because its national money was also the international currency. In other words, when companies in the USA wanted to purchase commodities on the world market they simply used dollars, that is, their own national currency. By contrast, if a British company wanted to make the same purchase it needed to buy dollars to do so; and there would only be sufficient dollars in the Bank of England if (1) enough other companies have earned dollars in the world market, and (2) they happen to have cashed them in exchange for sterling. Evans neatly summarizes the situation in the USA which was rather like having a free gold mine at the bottom of the garden:[33]

> Since the dollar was as good as gold, and dollars were created in the US, it was possible for the private and government enterprises that make up the US economy to acquire resources from the rest of the world without having to part with items of comparable value themselves. US enterprises were able, on balance, to spend more abroad than they earned, resulting in the payments deficits.

Althoug the USA ran a substantial *trade* surplus during the 1950s and most of the 1960s, this was offset by two other items: (1) aid and military expenditure concerned with strengthening the *Pax Americana*, particularly during the Kennedy offensive and the Vietnam War;[34] and (2) massive direct overseas investment by American companies (unlike European investment overseas which was much smaller and was mainly 'portfolio' investment). Much of this came to be organized outside regulation by national governments. Such American companies would borrow the money needed for investment from European banks but the amounts borrowed would be denominated in dollars. This meant that the loan and the banks making such loans were not subject to regulation by either the American or the European government where the European bank was located. This then constituted a substantial 'offshore' money market of the market for so-called Eurodollars, of lending by European institutions to American companies for amounts denominated in dollars.[35] The main centre for this rapidly growing financial market was the City of London which had significant advantages: it was very long-established with procedures thought to guarantee confidence; there was enormous expertise available, particularly in financing overseas investment (as in the old 'British Empire'); it was much *less* tied into national industry than were many other financial centres; and it was less regulated by governments.[36] As a result:

> The rise of the Euromarkets meant the beginning of an important shift from international financial relations being conducted through the official channels of the Bretton Woods system towards the private markets of the Eurodollar system.[37]

The scale of development of this private market for really extensive loans has been astonishing. The external claims of the Eurocurrency banks rose from $44 billion in 1969 to $810 billion by 1980.[38] It is estimated that the assets of these banks now exceed the annual value of *all* international trade throughout the world.[39] Even by 1980 it was calculated that the Eurodollar deposits were equivalent to three or four times the entire money stock of the USA.[40] By 1983 the IMF calculated that the gross debt in the Eurocurrency market was almost $3000 billion, the growth rate having been something like 20 per cent per annum throughout the 1970s.[41] It is also worth noting that there has been a major growth of the Eurobond market as well, that is, of new borrowing through longer-term marketable bonds.[42] One further point to note here is that only a rather small proportion of this financial dealing is related to direct commercial needs. It is calculated that something like $250 billion changes hands each day in the world financial markets. Hogan and Pearce calculate that this is 20 times the activity that *could* be attributed to the requirements of trade and investment.[43]

Although we have termed these deposits as 'Eurocurrencies', this is not strictly correct. They are basically debt rather than a form of money and the growth of this debt has and undoubtedly will lead to major problems of debt default. Even within the wealthiest countries there has been an extraordinary rise in public and private indebtedness.[44] One particular difficulty for most countries is that the debt is expressed either in dollars or in one of the other major currencies (sterling, francs, Swiss francs, marks etc.). Hence, for those countries in which such borrowing takes place, the debt is incurred in an overseas currency. That debt has then to be repaid in that currency and that will only be possible if the country in question can increase its exports, which in turn will only be feasible if it can gain some competitive advantage through having put the loan to useful investment purposes.[45] But not all countries can achieve this simultaneously and so further increased indebtedness is necessary in order to avoid a country defaulting.

This enormous expansion of the private market for money outside the organized structures of Bretton Woods and the IMF occurred in part because the USA gradually broke the rules or forced other countries to break them. The rule-breaking was necessary at each stage in order to save the international monetary system from an even greater crisis.[46] Thus, for example, in 1970 there was the dramatic collapse of the Penn Central Railroad Company in the USA.[47] The response of the Federal Reserve was to encourage the vigorous expansion of credit by the commercial banks. As interest rates fell, there was an unprecedented departure from short-term credit which effectively led to the devaluation of the dollar and this partly solved the problem through lowering the price of American exports. However, there was still the further problem of the enormous sums of dollars now held throughout the world, especially in Europe and which under the two-tier system established in 1968 could be presented for conversion into gold. On 15th August, 1971, the commitment of the US government to convert dollars into gold was simply ended. The final link between gold and money was broken and in effect the world was forced to accept an international money system based on the dollar. Two years later, after a further run on the dollar and the closure of the foreign exchange markets for two weeks, the Bretton Woods system of fixed exchange rates was replaced by floating exchange rates dependent upon market forces. The justification for such a change, namely that surpluses or deficits in the balance of payments would be automatically eliminated through exchange-rate adjustments, was not by then plausible because of the massive growth of these short-term debts, of short-term foreign lending by banks based in Europe.[48] Indeed, if anything, floating exchange rates heightened the flows of short-term money and this in turn exacerbated balance of payments difficulties and hence generated 'highly unstable gyrations in the value of exchange rates'.[49]

The repercussions of this were considerable and most dramatic in the years 1979–82. The dollar crisis in 1979 led the American government to raise interest rates in order to attract short-term money to the USA and hence to protect the dollar. The rate shot to over 20 per cent, and although this protected the dollar, it weakened American export earnings and it lowered the rates of domestic investment. Hence, even the USA had to pursue policies which were heavily influenced by the new international financial system. However, the effects on the rest of the world were even more disastrous. Short-term capital was attracted away from all those countries where interest rates were significantly lower. In France this led to the abandoning of its reflationary policies after 1983 in order to protect the franc. In Argentina, Brazil and Mexico it almost produced complete bankruptcy for two main reasons: first, the recession produced a sharp decline in demand and hence in prices for primary commodities; and second, as interest rates increased in the USA, so too did the cost of servicing the debt for the less developed countries.[50] The deepening crisis was in the end averted through 'rescheduling' the debt – a policy in which the IMF played an imortant role by pressurizing private banks to participate. Evans nevertheless notes that:[51]

> The position that the IMF had come to ocupy was now a far cry from that envisaged at Bretton Woods. The reserves of this official institution had become dwarfed by the huge growth of those associated with private international financial markets.

Moreover, the system that has been established by the growth of these very powerful financial institutions is highly unstable. There have been three important constraints placed on the operation of the monetary system, constraints designed to minimize disruptive consequences of a financial crisis. These constraints have been:

1   The establishment during the 1930s of a fairly high ratio between bank reserves and liabilities.[52]

2 Generally banks have been safeguarded from short-term fluctuations in deposits held with them because of the 'law of large numbers'.
3 The socio-political guarantee that the major western states would not allow major bankruptcies among their banks.

The new system, dating from the end of the 1960s, has undermined all three constraints.

1 The reserves:liabilities ratio which, in the nineteenth century, was 40 per cent has now fallen to a tiny figure, on average 4 per cent in 1981 and in some banks less than 1 per cent.[53]
2 Banks have both concentrated their lending to particular countries (70 per cent, for example, of Bank of America's loans were to Mexico in 1981)[54] and have acquired very large creditors, particularly resulting from the huge growth of earnings stemming from the OPEC price increase in 1973 – shifts in funds by a handful of very large depositors can now undermine the entire structure of borrowing and lending that a bank has established.
3 During the 1970s a number of major bank failures did in fact occur and national states were unable to prevent them, for example, London and County Securities in the UK, Herstatt Bank in Germany, Franklin National and Pennsylvania in the USA.[55]

Overall, there has been since the 1960s a considerable process of bank deregulation, a process by which banks were encouraged to insert their capital in the emerging Atlantic circuit based on the Eurocurrency market.[56] For example, in France in 1966, banks were freed from the rules which separated out different banking functions: commercial and deposit banks, on the one hand, and long-term and medium-term credit banks, on the other, were allowed to expand into each other's sphere of activity. Similarly in the USA, New Deal legislation which aimed at separating bank functions was removed in 1970. Banks were increasingly able to diversify their activities, to shift from a 'custodial' to a 'competitive' functioning. In the UK, too, British banks played a crucial role in forming and enlarging the Eurocurrency market. In September 1971 legislation was passed enabling banks to develop directly as capital-groups and hence to occupy a pivotal position in the emerging Atlantic circuit. Similar developments occurred in Germany.

There are a number of further points to note here. This freedom accorded to bank capital led to a separate circuit of money-capital rather than an integrated circuit of the 'finance capital' of organized capitalism. The latter had occurred within a nation-state and was based upon the dominance of banking groups stemming from a given *national* currency. As we have seen, banks and industry have become dislocated in part because although both circuits have been internationalized, these circuits of banking and industrial capital are separate and have different rhythms. Moreover, although within, say, Britain there are important interlocks between banks and industry, these are not of the sort found under 'finance capitalism'. Scott and Griff show that there are distinct cliques operating in the British economy (for example, Hill Samuel, with Beecham, Rolls Royce, British Leyland, Stone-Platt, BPB Industries, Alkan, Marchweil) but that such bank-centred groups greatly overlap with other groups both in Britain and elsewhere.[57] There are not the separate and rival empires all competing with each other within a given national economy (or typically found in organized capitalism). This is because just as banks have moved into a variety of 'non-banking' activities, so too have industrial concerns come to operate in part as banks, borrowing and lending and participating in the growth of the new forms of financial inter-mediation. This is in turn a more specific example of the general tendency for the distinctiveness of an enterprise's products to have considerably declined. This was even more marked in 1986 when the 'big bang' hit the City of London. All sorts of restrictions on what financial services can be provided by particular firms have been swept away. The following summarizes what is expected to happen to one of the largest insurance companies in Britain, the Prudential (the Pru):

> The truth is that the Pru no longer wants to be known as an insurance company. By the time the 'big bang' hits in the autumn, it would like to be regarded as a supplier of a whole range of financial services.[58]

This is also shown in Britain by the decrease in the number of interlocking directorships with other companies in the *same* industrial sector.[59] Finally, it should be noted that the effect of these various developments has been to shift the balance of profit away from 'industrial' to 'commercial and financial' sectors of the economy. In the USA, for example, the profit share of produc-tive capital and of circulating capital (financial, trade, ground-rent, petroleum and coal, transport, communication and services) were approximately the same in the mid-1960s, but by 1982 the former had fallen to less than one-quarter of its earlier share and the latter had risen by nearly 60 per cent. In Britain (using non-comparable statistics) the profits of financial corporations rose as a proportion of net corporate income from about 10 per cent in 1968 to nearly 60 per cent in 1980; in France the increase was from 10 per cent to about 25 per cent, and in Germany from 20 per cent to 50 per cent.[60]

In summary, then, these tremendous changes in the past 20 years provide very clear evidence of a dramatic disorganization of all the western capitalist economies. What had been central to organized capitalism was the nation-state with its nationally-based banks 'looking after' a national currency. Obviously they did not always succeed (Germany in the 1920s, for example). But what has happened now is that both 'industry' and 'finance' have been internationalized but with separate and unco-ordinated circuits. This has then massively weakened the individual nation-state which places its economy within one or other vicious circle and makes the state unable to regulate and orchestrate its national currency.[61] This is for a number of reasons:

1   Apart from a country's central bank there are no longer nationally-organized banks which will act in a custodial fashion.
2   Exchange rates are highly variable and subject to massive international fluctuation, particularly due to currency competition.
3   The huge growth of the Eurocurrency markets have produced an extraordinary instability of national money markets, an instability in no direct way connected to changes in 'real' economic variables; as Hogan and Pearce conclude: 'Our message is that the Eurodollar market is a destabilising institution. It is destabilising of itself as well as a product of the false money with which the world is currently struggling.'[62]
4   These money flows are highly susceptible to small interest-rate changes, so that national economic policy is continuously thwarted by 'irrelevant' changes in such rates.
5   Control by the nation-state is made even harder because of the way in which internationalization of banking and of industry reinforce and develop each other creating structures even further from state control, either of a national or of an international sort.[63]

There are a number of possible outcomes stemming from this extraordinary degree of international instability, a situation resulting from the self-organization of market relations at a time when official institutions have failed to promote an internationally organized system compatible with new developments in the organization of capital. Aglietta summarizes these developments and indeed elaborates a possible future scenario of 'Financial Collapse and Fragmentation of the World Economy':[64]

> a fully-fledged international credit system, deterritorialized and beyond regulation by any sovereign state... The three essential functions of money are neither unified under a supranational monetary body nor managed through inter-state cooperation based upon universally agreed principles. Indeed, the instability of the reserve function leads to rivalry among convertible currencies which destabilizes the complementary relations joining national regimes of growth.

POLITICAL CHANGES

We will begin by considering two recently influential general analyses of contemporary politics which are at first glance consistent with the thesis of disorganization. These are the analyses of André Gorz in France and Eric Hobsbawm in Britain.

Gorz asserts that the pattern of capitalist development has generated a working class which has become generally unable to take command of the means of production and whose interests are not consistent with a 'socialist rationality'.[65] The individuated wage-earners produced by capitalist development possess interests, capacities, and skills functional to the present productive forces and hence to the very development of capital. In particular, 'capital has succeeded in reducing workers' power in the productive process. It has been able to combine a gigantic increase in the power of the productive process with the destruction of workers' autonomy. It has been able to entrust ever more complex and powerful mechanized processes to the care of workers with even more limited capacities.[66] Hence, the unity of the proletariat and the nature of work as the source of its power now lie *outside* of the working class. We need to say, he maintains, *Farewell to the Working Class* because the collective worker has been rendered impotent, unable to realize its collective powers. The proletariat has become like a mere 'machine', controlled and dominated by large-scale productive units and the 'technical, social and regional division of labour they embody'.[67] As Byrne points out, for Gorz the war of position is over, capital has broken through into a war of movement *and won*.

There are two difficulties with Gorz's analysis as it relates to our thesis. First, he is insufficiently aware of the changes in, or *reverses* of, contemporary economic, political and geographical development. The extreme organized capitalism he talks of has begun to change and become partially disorganized. And it is these changes, towards a disorganization, which, in part at least, account for some of the socio-political developments he himself analyses. Second, he fails to consider the sociological conditions for the collective action of the working class and to reduce it purely to 'capital' – his is, as Byrne points out, a capital-logic formulation with a vengeance.[68]

It is this second point which is specifically examined by Hobsbawm, who maintains that a number of economic and social conditions have conspired to halt the 'Forward March' of labour and will preclude it restarting in anything like the same form. The main developments which Hobsbawm identifies in the UK are:[69]

1 The decline in the proportion of non-agricultural manual workers which in post-war Britian once constituted almost 70 per cent of the British population and now is barely one-half.
2 A decreased importance of the skills possessed by these manual workers, both as a result of technical changes especially associated with new ways of producing energy, and as a consequence of the growth of white-collar workers (often female) organizing and administering manual work.
3 The decline in the significance of capitalist competition and capitalist crisis in determining political events, both because of the growth of large international monopolies and because of the development of a large public sector, now accounting for about one-third of all employment.

4   The decline in the significance of a distinctively *proletarian* pattern of life from the 1950s onwards, a pattern focused on trade unionism, the Labour Party, the co-operative, particular forms of holiday, recreation, cultural practice, and so on. These have been undermined by relative affluence, the growth of sectional conflicts between groups of workers, and the homogenizing effects of mass education and the mass media.

5   The failure of the proportion of workers within trade unions to increase (it has recently begun to fall) combined with the declining numbers voting Labour and the fall in the proportion of workers voting Labour.

There is little doubt that most of these developments have been found in all five societies under investigation. However, it does not follow that the *Forward March* has in fact been halted and Therborn has strongly argued that in terms of a wide number of criteria (especially connected with levels of welfare expenditure) it has not.[70] Furthermore, even if the *March* has at present halted (in Britain, USA and FRG, at least) it does not follow that this is permanent and that there is terminal decline. And even if it has in fact halted, it is not clear that the factors identified by Hobsbawm are the only or principal features involved in that process. In short, Hobsbawm has specified a research agenda which we shall examine in the following, concentrating on four aspects of contemporary politics which relate to his general claims. These aspects are: the nature of contemporary voting patterns and particularly the 'class dealignment' thesis; the development of 'new social movements' strongly related to the recent growth of a powerful service class; the changing character of working-class communities and localities; and the degree to which the welfare state remains of structural significance in contemporary western politics. Our comments will be selective and mainly illustrative, beginning with recent voting patterns.

We will deal here mostly with Britain and Sweden because these two countries have in the past enjoyed some of the highest levels of class voting and hence of support for parties of the left. Table 7.1 indicates the general level of left voting over the course of this century for all five societies.

Table 7.1   Left percentage of votes in five societies, 1900–1980

Society	Pre-war	Inter-war	1946–60	1961–80
France	13	32	43	41
FRG	31	40	34	41
USA	4	5	1	0
Sweden	13	46	52	51
UK	5	33	48	45

Source: W. Korpi, *The Democratic Class Struggle* (London, RKP, 1983), p. 38.

The traditional explanation of relatively high levels of left voting was that a considerable majority of the manual working class voted for the left, particularly those workers who were unionized. There is indeed some correlation between left voting figures and levels of unionization in each society, the level for the mid-1970s ranging from 71 per cent in Sweden, 44 per cent in the UK, 35 per cent in the FRG, down to 27 per cent in the USA and 25 per cent in France.[71] At the same time, among non-manual workers, there was an even more marked tendency to vote for parties of the right. One's occupational class provided a fairly good predictor of one's voting patterns. Britain and Sweden were two of the societies with the highest levels of class voting. In the period 1952–62, of the four countries analysed by Alford (Britain, Australia, USA, Canada), Britain had the highest rate of class voting at around 40, that is, the percentage of non-manual workers voting for left parties subtracted from the percentage of manual workers voting for left parties.[72] In Sweden, even in the 1970s, the index of class voting was 45, higher than all other OECD countries apart from Denmark and Finland.[73]

In Britain there has been a considerable process of class dealignment; in other words, the association between an individual's occupational class and party support has faded away.[74] This is shown in table 7.2. It should be noted that over the period 1959–83 there have been substantial changes in the occupational structure. In particular, there has been a most marked increase of non-manual employment, particularly of a deskilled sort within the public sector, and that in part explains the decline of class voting among non-manual workers.[75] At the same time, however, the declining proportion of manual workers in the employed population, together with the process of class dealignment, radically changes Labour's social base.[76]

There are a number of other social variables connected with occupational class which must be considered here. First, union membership makes some difference to Labour voting and this factor has slowed down the process of class dealignment. In 1983, for example, non-trade unionists were split 34:34.[77] Second, as Dunleavy has extensively shown, home ownership produces a considerable independent influence upon voting. In 1983 manual workers who were owner-occupiers voted only 36:33 in favour of Labour, while workers who were council tenants voted 54:23 in favour.[78] More generally, it has been argued that there are distinct consumption sectors in Britain which structure electoral preferences. Dunleavy's analysis of the February 1974 election showed that home-owners were 2.35 times more likely than council tenants to vote Conservative, while those in households with two cars were 1.87 times more likely to vote Conservative than those without a car.[79] He argues that housing and transport locations have to be viewed in terms of 'private-commodity' and 'public-collective' modes of consumption, and that this distinction can explain voting rates almost as well as the occupational structure. The increasing rates of home ownership and of private transport structurally favour the position of the Conservatives.[80] Third, it is

Table 7.2   Class voting patterns in Britain, 1959–1983

	1959	1964	1966	1970	(Feb) 1974	(Oct) 1974	1979	1983
Proportion of non-manuals voting Conservative	69	62	60	64	51	51	60	55
Proportion of manuals voting Labour	62	64	69	58	57	57	59	46
Non-manual Conservative plus manual Labour voters as % of all voters	65	63	66	60	55	54	55	n/a
Class index of labour voting	40	42	43	33	35	32	27	9

Source: B. Särlvik and I. Crewe, *Decade of Dealignment* (Cambridge, Cambridge University Press, 1983), p. 87, for 1959–1979; Dunleavy and Husbands, *British Democracy at the Crossroads*, p. 129, for 1983.

also necessary to investigate the patterning of social groups within local areas. Here we find that although class has declined as a predictor of an *individual*'s vote, the class composition of a constituency is a very good predictor of the election results across constituencies.[81] While Crewe and Särlvik have shown that much of the variance of the vote in England cannot be explained in terms of individually-held social variables, Miller has shown that class, when measured by the percentage of employers and managers among occupied and retired males, explained almost four-fifths of the variance in the two-party vote between constituencies.[82] This result derives from the so-called 'neighbourhood effect', that high local concentrations of employers and managers produces a kind of contagion, affecting other people in the constituency and shifting their voting away from what their occupational class would lead one to expect.[83] Miller maintains that as the individual class effect has declined in importance, so these area-based forms of political partisanship and action have become more important, especially during the 1970s; and these may take either a class effect or a class-less effect in terms of regional/local politics, and, we may add, of gender politics.[84] It is important to note that although class voting for individuals has declined, the voting for Labour has become increasingly dependent upon working-class votes, particularly those cast in northern cities and conurbations (where the Conservative vote has collapsed).[85] Crewe summarizes:[86]

The majority of the working class has ceased to vote Labour but most Labour MPs represent overwhelmingly working class areas. Both parties, as a result, may cease to be broad, national coalitions of interest.

Thus, in British organized capitalism, an individual's occupational class was the best predictor of voting (note, incidentally, how a woman's occupational class was generally presumed to be that of her husband), other local and non-functional determinants were thought to be of declining importance as the electorate was 'nationalized', and electoral results were determined by the industrial and occupational structure of different constituencies. In disorganized British capitalism, by contrast, an individual's occupational class becomes a relatively poor predictor of voting: there is increasing importance of determinants such as individual/collective modes of provision, as well as a heightened significance of locally specific processes in which core classes and other social groups 'distort' people's electoral choices, distorting each individual's determination of voting by occupation.

Alongside this process of 'class dealignment' there has also been a process of 'partisan dealignment',[87] that is, the growth of third party voting; changes in the issue bases of British politics; and an increase in electoral volatility.

There has been a substantial decline in the popular vote enjoyed by both Conservatives as well as by Labour.[88] In 1955 the two major parties took 96 per cent of all votes cast; in 1983 they took 70 per cent. Both parties have in a sense been in electoral decline. The Conservative Party used to gain around 50 per cent of the popular vote when winning and over 40 per cent when losing elections; the figures now are 43 per cent and 37 per cent respectively.[89] The Conservatives have lost votes in almost all areas of the country but especially in Scotland, the north and the north-west, and in the large cities. For example, between 1955 and 1983 the Tories' support in Glasgow fell from 48 per cent to 19 per cent; in Liverpool from 53 per cent to 29 per cent; in Edinburgh from 55 per cent to 35 per cent, and so on.[90] Labour Party support nationally has fallen from 48 per cent in 1950 and 1951 to under 30 per cent in 1983.[91] Figure 7.1 indicates the long-term pattern of Labour Party development. Liberal Party support, by contrast, which had fallen from a peak in 1860 with over 65 per cent of all votes cast to 3 per cent in 1951, was 25 per cent in 1983.[92] Governments now win elections with progressively lower proportions of the popular vote. In the apparently landslide election of 1983, only 30.8 per cent of the total electorate actually voted for the Conservatives.[93]

There have been important changes in the issue bases of modern politics away in part from those issues that simply divided Labour from Conservative. Particularly significant for Labour here has been the apparently declining support for further nationalization, extending the welfare state, and maintaining the close links of Labour with the trade union movement. Conservatives likewise have suffered because of their apparent association with many of the

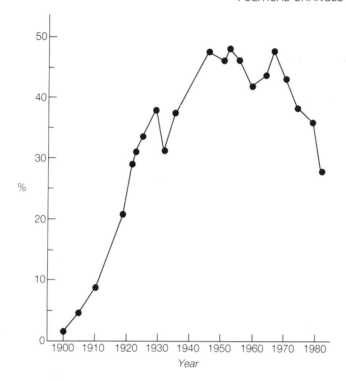

Figure 7.1   Labour Party percentage of the popular vote, 1900–1983
Source: J. Ross, *Thatcher and Friends* (Pluto Press, London, 1983), p. 16.

traditional 'establishment' features of British life, such as the monarchy, House of Lords, judges, the upper class social season, which are viewed increasingly cynically. Moreover, a variety of issues have come on to the mainstream political agenda, which cross-cut political divisions (e.g. the EEC), or to which the major parties have enormous difficulty in responding (ecology, feminism, regional autonomy), or about which the parties appear unable to do anything effective (nuclear warfare, unemployment).

The previous two factors have both increased electoral volatility, so that on average one in three voters now change their vote between elections, and between some elections two in five change.[94] There has been a really marked decline in the amount of *constant* support for either of the main parties, which has fallen from 51 per cent in 1959–64 to 42 per cent in 1974–79. Comparing the last two elections, only 80 per cent of those voting Conservative in 1979 voted the same way in 1983, while the Labour figure was an extraordinarily low 67 per cent.[95] Särlvik and Crewe suggest that each of the two main parties can count on the unswerving support of only about one-quarter of the electorate.[96] There has been an apparently marked decline in the proportion of the electorate strongly identifying with one or other of the major parties.

This fell from two-fifths to one-fifth between 1970 and 1979. Indeed, in the 1983 election it seems that a strong basis for voting was the dislike of the other party, and not a strong preference for one's own.[97]

In Sweden there have been some similar processes at work but they have developed rather more slowly. Sweden always enjoyed high levels of class voting – in 1956 it was 53 on the Alford index.[98] Over 80 per cent of the working class voted for left parties, and high proportions of the 'middle classes' voted for parties of the centre and the right.[99] These patterns were very well established and relatively unchanging. Sweden enjoyed very high levels of electoral stability and mass participation in which political landslides were unknown. From 1946 until the late 1960s fluctuations in popular support between the two major blocs averaged only 2 per cent in successive elections.[100] There was a high degree of party loyalty, attachment and organization. For example, in 1970 there were almost 1 million members of the Social Democratic Party.[101] There was a marked identification of the working class with that party, 58 per cent of workers strongly identifying in 1968, and this was particularly marked among members of the LO affiliated unions.[102] There has been a long-established regional patterning of Social Democratic support, although interestingly the percentage vote from different industrial sectors (agriculture/forestry, manufacturing, services) has not varied very much.[103]

In recent years there has been some decline in the degree of class voting in Sweden. On the Alford index there has been a fall from 53 in 1956 to 36 in 1976, rising to 43 in 1982.[104] Partly this has resulted from some decline in the attraction of the Social Democratic Party to manual workers and partly from increased 'left' voting by non-manuals, especially after the failure of the bourgeois parties to organize effective political rule in the late 1970s.[105] At the same time, there has been greater volatility of the Swedish electorate. This is reflected in very considerably increased swings between the major parties as reflected in the opinion polls.[106] And it is also reflected in the dramatic rise in the proportion of voters switching between parties between two consecutive elections – that proportion nearly doubled between the late 1950s and early 1980s.[107] Partly this has resulted from exchanges between the 'bourgeois' parties but also in part from exchanges *between* the two blocs of left and right. It also appears that voters make up their mind which way to vote rather later than they used to. The proportion reporting that their party choice had been decided 'for a long time' fell from over 80 per cent in the early 1960s to 70 per cent by the later 1970s. There has also been some decline in the levels of party identification.

In the USA – considering Democrats and Republicans here – there have of course been low levels of class voting. During the 1950s, while the rate of class voting in Britain was around 40, it was only about 15 or 20 in the USA (depending on the survey).[108] This resulted from a number of factors, including the enormous size of the country; its division into 50 states with real degrees of sovereignty; the considerable ethnic and religious diversity; the political weakness of American trade unionism; and the decentralization of the party system which reflected the federal and pluralist character of American society. Though in presidential elections the level of class voting reached a peak with the election of Truman in 1948, it is likely, as Alford notes, that there was no appreciable change in the level of class voting between the 1930s and 1950s. The major shift towards class alignment, of course, took place with the formation of the New Deal coalition in the 1930s.

Three significant developments in American voting patterns in the last couple of decades should, though, be noted. First, it had been argued that there was a steady nationalization of the American electorate with a resulting decline in the impact of constituency forces on congressional turnout and voting patterns.[109] However, recently this nationalization seems no longer to be operating and Mann argues that there is 'an increasing localization of political forces in congressional elections'.[110] Claggett, Flanigan and Zingale also note that:[111]

It remains surprising that 'the great contests for the presidency' appear to generate no more of a uniform response on the part of the electorate in the age of television than they did at the turn of the century.

That the mass media do not seem to generate a national response is because various nationalizing developments have the effect of producing highly *dissimilar* behaviour within diverse geographic units and hence distort these various national factors, such as that of occupational class.

Second, since 1964 party partisanship has been declining in importance in the USA since the period of relative stability between 1952 and 1964.[112] This decline in partisanship has affected all age groups, but especially those in their twenties. At the same time, issues appear to have become more prominent in shaping electoral outcomes. Or to put the argument more generally, the large national parties *were* the basic structuring form of American politics and there was a high degree of political partisanship which accounted for voting patterns. Now, however, ideology disputes around particular issues have in part replaced partisanship as the crucial determinant of electoral outcomes. This partly accounts, for example, for the fact that while the Democrats enjoy a higher level of partisan loyalty, they have in fact lost most of the recent presidential elections.

Third, there has been a secular decline in the proportion actually voting in presidential and congressional elections. The highest turnout was reached in 1960 when 63 per cent of the electorate voted. By 1980 it had fallen to a mere 53 per cent.[113] Abramson and Aldrich maintain that there are two factors explaining this: the weakening of party loyalties that we have just noted, which accounts for between 25 and 30 per cent of the decline in participation in presidential and congressional elections; and the reduction in the belief about government responsiveness and effectivity which also accounts for about 25 per cent of the decline in turnout.

Overall, then, we can see the same patterns of class and partisan dealignment noted in Britain, although clearly the USA started off from considerably lower levels of class voting. A similar pattern can also be found in West Germany. In 1953 the Alford index of class voting registered a score of 30; by 1983 that had fallen to 10, partly because of the considerable increases in SPD voting among non-manual workers. In 1976, for example, 44 per cent of 'lower and middle grade' white-collar workers voted SPD.[114] In 1956 four-fifths of those voting SPD were manual workers, but by 1976 this had fallen to 53 per cent. In 1976 half the membership of the SPD were 'white-collar' and only 42 per cent 'blue-collar'.[115] Furthermore, only just over one-third of all Germans in the mid-1970s classified themselves as 'working class' and most significantly two-fifths of SPD 'hard core' supporters thought of themselves as essentially middle class.[116]

At the same time there was a considerable decline in the influence of old third parties in the FRG up to 1976 (when 90 per cent voted for the Christian Democrats and the Social Democrats), but since then there has been a substantial increase in 'third party voting', most interestingly of course for the Greens. This party was founded in 1979, and within five years it possessed 27 deputies in the Bundestag, had seats in six out of the 11 *Land* parliaments, and gained 2.1 million votes in the 1983 election (5.6 per cent of the vote).[117] The Greens gained most support in the north, in Protestant and urban areas with high levels of service employment, and in university towns.[118] They did not do well in rural and Catholic areas nor in those centres of heavy industry such as the Saar and the Ruhr which have historically formed the backbone of SPD support.

In France the most significant event electorally has been the first election in the post-war period of a left-wing government committed in principle to a substantial change in the balance of class forces.[119] There are five points to note about the 1981 election. First, the share of the electorate voting for the left (for both the Socialists and Communists) was a mere 38.6 per cent.[120] Second, the Socialist vote among industrial workers rose significantly, compared with previous elections – in the second round of voting Mitterrand won 72 per cent of the workers' vote. Indeed, while de Gaulle had taken 45 per cent of the working-class vote in 1965, Giscard d'Estaing only managed 27 per cent in 1981.[121] Third, there has been a very limited process of class and partisan dealignment compared with the other countries being investigated here.[122] There was some fall in both these measures in 1981 – thus only 38 per cent of white-collar workers supported Giscard d'Estaing in the second ballot, compared with the 53 per cent vote for de Gaulle in 1965 – but these may well be temporary. Fourth, there has been a marked decline in the Communist vote and this was especially marked in Paris where between 1969 and 1981 the vote for the Communists fell from 18.6 per cent to 9.2 per cent. There was also a notable decline in such support from industrial workers, especially those in the previous Communist strongholds in the belt surrounding Paris.[123] Finally, the tendency for women to vote less enthusias-tically for left parties has been declining throughout the 1960s and 1970s.[124]

A number of other facts, though, attest to the decline in the class character of French political life. There has been a decline in the proletarian nature of the Socialist Party. The Socialists' share of the working-class vote fell sharply from the first elections after the Second World War. Working-class proportion of party membership declined from 44 per cent in 1951 to 19 per cent in 1973. Equally the proportion of Socialist mayors and councillors declined precipitously to a level of 2 per cent by 1972. In 1978 there was not a single working-class deputy among Socialist parliamentarians, and the proportion of even previously highly represented primary school teachers declined in favour of upper manage-ment and the higher education sector. Perhaps most important was the shift in official party ideology away from proletarian principles, consecrated by its rechristening at the end of the 1960s – as Mitterrand moved to take over leadership – of the old *Section française de l'Internationale ouvrière* (SFIO) as the *Parti socialiste* (PS).[125]

There are three important correlates of these processes of dealignment which, as we have seen, are to be found in all five societies, albeit to varying degrees. These correlates are, first, the growth of new forms of politics based around what are sometimes called the 'new social movements'; second, the changes in the organization of working-class communities; and third, the degree to which the new balance of social forces can and will protect the welfare state system which is quintessentially a feature of organized capitalism.

The first of these has been well documented and we will merely highlight some analytical issues involved here. Habermas has neatly summarized the shift in political forms by arguing that the 'new conflicts are not sparked by *problems of distribution*, but concern the *grammar of forms of life*'.[126] This new type of conflict is the product, he says, of the 'silent revolution' identified by various writers which note the thematic change from the 'old politics' of economic, social, domestic and military security, to 'new politics' based around questions of the quality of life, equality, individual self-realization, participation and human rights.[127] In the mid-1970s Hildebrandt and Dalton suggest that 11 per cent of the West German electorate adopted a 'post-materialist' New Politics orientation, and that this orientation was particularly marked among the better-educated, the young, the 'new middle class', and SPD voters.[128] This has had a major impact on reducing the level of class voting, as we saw above, particularly among these groups. As 'post-materialist concerns and values' become more prominent in politics and more salient to growing proportions of the German electorate, so it is argued that the division between bourgeoisie and worker becomes less important in structuring German politics, although obviously for many there will be a mix between the New and Old Politics.[129] Interestingly, Habermas distinguishes between feminism, on the one hand, and the enormous diversity of other social movements, on the other. It is only the former which, he claims, is strictly speaking an offensive movement, against 'patriarchal oppression', while the other movements are primarily defensive. Anti-nuclear and environmental campaigns, the peace movement, citizens' action, squatters, tax protest movements and so on all seek to *stem* or block the formal 'organized' spheres of activity, but they do not seek to conquer new territory. Feminism by contrast does.

At the same time, however, it is argued by Offe and Granow that the growth of a number of social and political developments have served to 'fragment' West German political culture.[130] They summarize:[131]

> Far from Bonn's atmosphere of professional power administration, a political culture based on communal households, nursery schools, street festivals, economic self-help and self-organization developed, all with a considerable range and radical democratic, ecological and socialist goals.

They suggest that developments of this sort enable us to speak of a 'left development' by the early 1980s, although this does not correspond to the traditional conception of the German left since there is little or no orientation toward obtaining political power in an established sense. Moreover, much of this alternative political culture has arisen out of opposition to the state, and particularly to the welfare state. Most of the social democratic parties have advocated and have helped to introduce or force other parties to introduce highly *statist* conceptions of welfarism. The alternative political culture is therefore partly caused by the existing forms of state-mediated reformist politics. Granow and Offe summarize:[132]

> Such statist correctives of power-relations in society, however, always have as the negative consequence of supporting what is exactly opposed to their intention, in that those compensated are not only *unburdened*, but are at the same time *deactivated*; i.e. they are themselves prevented from conceiving and autonomously realizing their own conceptions of what is necessary to improve their own lives. Citizens are reduced to objects of administrative care.

The problems of a one-sided 'statist' conception of reformism can be seen both in the success which the rightist critique of the state and bureaucracy appears to be currently enjoying, and the 'fundamental hostility with which the participants in "alternative" economies and culture confront Social-Democratic administrators of statist rationality'.[133] In the case of the Green Party this is even reflected in the organizational form which it has developed, that is, comprised of decentralized, manageable grass-roots units and based on the principle of rotation among those elected to the Bundestag.[134] There is, in other words, a further objective determination of social structure over and above that of social class, and that is the contradiction between the state and the people. Conceptualizing this further contradiction points out both that there may well be a relative continuity over time of popular traditions, and that popular forces and notions can be appropriated and reappropriated by *different* social classes and social forces. In Britain, Hall has noted how the contradiction between the state/the people has been neutralized by the 'New Right which is through Thatcherism apparently acting with and for the people against the state'.[135]

Offe and Granow suggest that the left is singularly unable to do much about such developments, certainly in the FRG, because of the '*total lack of any normative perspective* in the political culture of social democracy';[136] in other words, they say, the basic values canonized by the party, such as 'freedom', 'justice', 'solidarity', have not been translated into concrete conceptions of an enhanced quality of life in the workplace, in the family or in the city. The only normative element which attempts any kind of mobilization is that of 'modernization', but this does not succeed in providing the basis for a coherent socialist political culture. Partly this is because the old and the new politics are divided by 'modernization'. The 'new politics' generally opposes modernization, while the 'old politics' more readily embraces it, yet is itself rooted in a set of institutional practices from organized capitalism which are anything but modern. Granow and Offe conclude:[137]

> Traditional social-democracy is thus eroded, losing its 'oppositional' elements, without being able to integrate 'alternative' ones. This development has the appearance of tragedy, only because another kind of reformism based programmatically on *social* forces and struggles, open to alternative and oppositional cultures and thus regaining normative perspectives is quite conceivable.

Similar analyses have been developed about some of the other working-class supported political movements. In the USA, for example, Toffler and Toffler argue that the slogans of the Democratic Party increasingly fall on deaf ears even among the working class and the unemployed. This is because that party still thinks in terms of 'masses' and large deliverable voting blocs and yet according to Toffler and Toffler the emergence of 'post-industrialism' has demassified the old society, creating much greater diversity, a growing demand for individual treatment, and the generation of 'a fragmented electorate made up of thousands of tiny, transitory groupings rather than the large blocs manipulated by parties like the Democrats'.[138] The Tofflers maintain that the Democrats have not begun to come to terms with these changes, since the party is still stuck in the 'smokestack era'. At the same time, however, it has been argued that since the 1960s some of these new social movements have been of considerable influence in American politics. Vogel expresses this well:[139]

> A loose coalition of middle class based consumer and environmental, feminist and civil rights organizations, assisted on occasions by organized labour, aided by a sympathetic media and supported by much of the intelligentsia, were able to influence both the terms of public debate and the outcomes of government policy in a direction antithetical to the interests of business.

This can be seen in a variety of contexts. First, in terms of the control of the political agenda a wide variety of issues became matters of political debate in opposition to the interests of business. These issues included environmental protection, occupational health and safety, consumer protection, price controls on energy, affirmative action, product liability, expansion of the welfare state, tax reform, regulation of multinational corporations, 'corporate lawlessness', investment practices overseas, and so on. Second, there was also in this era a marked increase in legislation that was adopted in spite of corporate opposition: between 1965 and 1975, 25 major pieces of legislation were passed regulating corporations in terms of consumer and environmental protection, occupational health and safety, and personnel policy. There was a fivefold increase in federal staff to oversee such regulatory statutes. Third, there has been a marked increase in forms of corporate representation, especially in Washington. Particular attention came to be paid to the monitoring and managing of 'emerging issues', and to the development of greater cohesiveness between business leaders. The development of such a capitalist class consciousness from the later 1970s onwards is taken by Vogel as indicating a lack of effective intervention in the preceding decade or two.

Analyses similar to that of the Tofflers have appeared in Britain. From the Conservative Party, David Howell has argued that both the ideologies of 'state centralism' and of 'liberal market economies' are increasingly inappropriate to contemporary economic, social and political developments. On the former he argues that[140]

> The corporatists, who rested their thinking on big unionism, big government and big industry have seen their edifice collapse...because this degree of centralism has simply become outdated.

The growth of small cells and social groupings are becoming 'the more natural and stronger social pattern than the unnatural centralised systems and class organisations upon which Marxian analysis rested and round which our policies have been built'.[141] At the same time, however, he argues that the 'maps' used by the Conservatives, although functional in dismantling some of the centralized structures, are less helpful in charting future directions. Partly this is because central to Conservative economic policy has been the maintaining of tight control of the money supply, but this is itself a centralist and nationalist philosophy or technique. It in turn battered against one aspect of the new politics which is in favour of a greater 'localism'. More generally, Conservatives have not got used to the view that the relationship between work and leisure is one that is changing, and therefore that those currently unemployed are not to be viewed simply as 'scroungers'. Moreover, modern Conservatism fails to get to grips with the emergence of new social groupings and forms of social organization which are not simply generated by or related to developments in the market-place. To put it slightly differently, the combination of the strong state and the unregulated market excludes and alienates many contemporary social forces and sets of social relations.

Somewhat similar analyses have been produced on the left in Britain. Stuart Hall argues that the modern Labour Party is conspicuously unable at the national level to grasp the language and concerns of the new social movements which in part go beyond or are transforming the simplicity of the relationship of class versus class.[142] There are two remaining important areas of Labour support in Britain, the 'regional heartlands' and the 'inner areas' of some of the large cities, and it is in the latter, amongst what has been called the 'urban left', that the new alliances and social movements have become particularly influential.[143] That the Labour Party and the labour movement are unable to go 'beyond the fragments' can be seen by briefly considering the nuclear disarmament movement which, on the face of it, would appear to be the movement most embraced by that party.[144] The most distinctive feature of this movement is its highly decentralized and diverse forms of social support. There are literally thousands of different campaign groups which have an enormous variety of different objectives and preferred forms of action. John Keane suggests that its guiding maxim is 'Divided we stand, united we fall'.[145] Indeed, he suggests that the one thing that does unite it is a mobilization against the suppression of difference. The peace movement serves as a crucial reminder that social movements are not driven by some pre-given essence but rather are typically fragmented and divided internally. There are thus two characteristic features of the peace movement: it is highly pluralistic and it is anti-statist (even if many of its members are state employees)[146] since nuclear weapons are ultimately weapons of the state.[147] Keane goes on to argue that the decisive significance and political potential of the movement lies in its 'militant defense of a democratic civil society against the state'.[148] Defending civil society in this way involves restricting the power of the bureaucratic (and militaristic) state over civil society by way of social struggles that open up new non-state spheres of democratic accountability and social practice; it also involves restructuring state institutions such that they become more strictly accountable and protectors of the diverse social practices within civil society. Indeed, Keane suggests that the peace movement has in effect suggested that the development of nuclear weapons and the resulting new forms of administrative and military control and surveillance have violated the contract between civil society and the state to which citizens grant their loyalty in exchange for a guarantee of personal freedom and security. Much of the strength, then, of the peace movement stems from 'a resistance to intrusive forms of state power that are seen to restrict and overwhelm the plurality of independent public spheres that are the stuff of which civil society potentially exists'.[149] What, though, is not made clear by Keane is that these 'independent public spheres' are overwhelmingly *local*; they consist of *forming* real bonds and developing shared objectives and common programmes with those close by without setting up and running large hierarchically organized bureaucracies.[150] The strength of the peace movement and the formation of these *resistant* public spheres is primarily local. Indeed, the number of local groups in the Campaign for Nuclear Disarmament (CND) rose from 150 in 1979 to a staggering 1100 in 1984.[151]

Two of these features also characterize the women's movement in Britain. First, its strength now is primarily local through the formation of a multitude of locality-based campaigning and other social groups. And second, there is a similarly strong resistance to the central state which seems to have violated much of the trust placed in it (through, for example, failing to prevent wife-battering, rape etc.). The national state, which was once seen by women as necessary to ensure that, for example, local councils were forced to provide decent welfare facilities, is now very much viewed as the problem rather than the solution, and this has become more the case as 'the state, violence and sexuality' have become centrally salient issues in the contemporary movement.[152]

These beliefs are also embodied in the modern ecology movement, whose support in the last decade in Britain has risen from 600,000 to more than 3 million. The politics of ecology emphasize flexibility, co-operation, production for use, local production for local need, labour-intensive production, decentralization, direct democracy, non-hierarchy, and so on. At the same time, there has been an extensive growth of tenants' associations, local community groups, and more generally of what has been termed the 'urban left'. This has been analysed by Samuel Beer, who argues that in Britain there has been a particularly marked collapse of the previously dominant 'civic culture'.[153] In its place there has been the growth of a new populism which involves the exaggerated assertion of the values of radical democracy, individualism, participation, majoritarianism and egalitarianism. In Almond and Verba's classic study they found a deferential political culture in Britain in which citizens were willing to turn power over to political leaders. There was a widespread sense of trust in those leaders. By the 1970s this sense of trust had significantly declined. Kavanagh concluded that the evidence showed a much lower level of confidence in government and a 'general lack of trust in the country's leadership'.[154] This was particularly marked among young voters but there was pretty widespread dissatisfaction among all groups by this time. Kavanagh concluded that 'the traditional bonds of social class, party and common nationality are waning, and with them the old restraints of hierarchy and deference'.[155]

Beer goes on, though, to argue that this apparent dissatisfaction and lack of trust especially in the outputs of British governments is not simply negative but rather involves the assertion of partly different values and beliefs. As Marsh says, 'deference is no longer a force in British political culture . . . [it] has given way to a concern for influence in the decisions of the political community'.[156] According to Beer, the inspiration for this derives from a wide-ranging spiritual transformation, of a romantic revolt concerned with the challenging of vertical or horizontal solidarities, the re-emphasizing of subjectivity, and the celebrating of experience and the quality of life. The *May Day Manifesto 1968* was the clearest political statement of this programme for participation, decentralization and 'single issue campaigns'.[157] In chapter 9 we will consider some more obviously 'cultural' correlates of this new radical populism. We have already seen some of the industrial correlates of this in the increasing tendencies to sectionalism and the breakdown of some of the overarching national structures in the union movement. Beer puts this well:[158]

> Impelled by highly local pressures and certainly not set off by national leadership, the wage-strike explosion [late 1960s] reflected a radically new offensive stance on the part of trade unionists. It is indeed as if they had taken to heart the harsh populistic rejection of party, government, and trade union movement put forth in the May Day Manifesto of 1968.

Beer, however, points to a further profoundly important aspect of these developments and that is the growth of a 'new group politics'.[159] This occurred because, as the activities of the state expanded, it had to rely upon the co-operation of diverse categories of producers, unionists and consumers who were affected by various policy changes. The state thus in a sense constructed various categories of producer and user and the members of these categories, influenced by the 'new populism', became organized. There has been a spectacular growth in the number of resulting pressure groups in Britain. Of the 350 groups listed in the 1980 *Guardian Directory of Pressure Groups and Representative Associations* over half had been formed in the 1960s and 1970s, paralleling the sharp growth of professional, scientific and technical members of the civil service.[160] In fact, the number of groups of significance is very much larger than this number. Beer notes that in 1979 the Royal Commission on the Health Service (the Morrison Commission) took evidence from 1224 associations,[161] while Newton found that there were a staggering 4250 pressure groups operating to influence public policy in Birmingham in the 1970s.[162]

Brittan has generalized from the development of such group pressure to argue that representative democracy is seriously challenged in Britain because of (1) the generation of excessive expectations, and (2) the disruptive effects of the pursuit of group self-interest in the market-place.[163] He quotes Olson, who maintains that the distinction between privileged and latent groups 'damages the pluralistic view that any outrageous demands of one pressure group will be counterbalanced by the demands of other groups'.[164] Brittan argues in particular that small sectional groups of trade unionists are increasingly able to mobilize collectively and to alter the distribution of resources. This is because such groups are progressively locked into a competitive struggle. Rival coercive groups in pursuit of self-interest exclude other less organized groups, enlarge the state, and protect their own place in the national distribution of income and resources. They thus, through their agency, change the structure. He also argues that there is a noticeable lack of a budget constraint among voters so that people expect too much from government at too little cost. There are excessive expectations generated in which it makes a great deal of sense rationally for politicians to offer more than they can provide. Competition between parties encourages excessive expectations. Moreover, these 'economic contradictions of democracy' have become more significant because of the increasingly obvious lack of any widely shared belief in the legitimacy of the present order. As a consequence Brittan maintains that liberal representative democracy suffers from such internal contradictions that will increase with time.

In Sweden the development of social movements and other group politics has taken place much more in the context of social democracy. Particularly important have been the development of issues relating to the environment, the conservation of natural resources, the question of energy supply and the general virtues or vices of advanced technology and large-scale organization.[165] Korpi, though, shows that these issues have not come to equal in importance the left–right dimension in Swedish politics even at the time, for example, of the 1980 consultative referendum on nuclear energy. This is because 'the groups of voters for whom nuclear power and ecological questions are the decisive issues have remained relatively small.'[166] The position of women in Swedish society has made some difference to recent Swedish politics, although it does not seem to divide voters very substantially. For example, in the late 1970s it was found that an extraordinary 88 per cent of young people in Sweden *disagreed* with the statement that 'Men should go out to work while women stay at home and take care of the house'.[167] It was also found that there was widespread support for building more day-care centres, and this was true of both 'workers' and 'middle strata', and of men and women.[168] The only issue which did seem to divide male and female voters was the introduction of a sex quota to the Riksdag. Here over 50 per cent of women were in favour, while young 'middle strata' men especially were opposed.[169] One apparently important determinant of political preferences is whether the voter is employed in the private or in the 'reproductive' part of the public sector. By 1980 there were 20 per cent more workers in the public sector in Sweden than there were workers in manufacturing industry; and in 1979 12 per cent of that category supported the Communist Party, while only 5 per cent of industrial workers were Communist supporters.[170]

Finally, there have been a wide range of new social and political movements influential in France since 1968. These include democratizing communication media; regional pressure groups (as in Brittany); urban social movements (as in Paris or Dunkirk); an extensive women's movement (especially over abortion and contraception); and an important anti-nuclear energy movement (especially after 1977 and the beginning of the first fast breeder reactor).[171]

These multifarious movements had a major impact on the Socialist Party which, as Cohen argues, 'took up issues and themes first raised in May 1968 and articulated throughout the 70s by actors other than the industrial working class, serving, in part, as a voice of and for society and social movements'.[172] The Socialists became in effect the party of the active, and the 1981 government implemented certain of the activists' demands (such as a ministry for women's rights; decentralization to locally and regionally elected bodies; bargaining rights to unions at enterprise level; an agency for energy control; setting up of 'free' radio stations etc.).[173] However, the implementation of such demands was generally in the form of legislation from the centre and in terms which do not seriously challenge the predominant social relations of French society. The growth of the social movements has, though, changed the society: Lipietz talks of the 'men and women who have struggled since 1968. . . in all fields of social change, for justice, freedom, individual and collective emancipation, against stunting and alienating social relations, sometimes against the Socialist Party and usually without it. . . who danced at the Bastille in May, 1981, for the victory of a man who did not represent them but in whom they were ready to place their confidence.'[174]

Simultaneously with these developments have been massive changes in the organization of the industrial working class. We noted some of these transformations in chapters 4 and 5, particularly the spatial redistribution of both population and employment away from the industrial heartlands and especially from the older central areas of larger cities. This has led to the general breakdown of old-style 'occupational communities' which had been singularly important even in the USA. As Alt notes:[175]

> Industrial class struggle presupposed a social form of leisure which was grounded in class experiences and which provided the social bonds necessary for political organization and action.

Such occupational communities have also been dissolved because of the growth of mass consumption and consumerism which elevates the principle of individual competitiveness. As one of Seabrook's working-class respondents noted:[176]

> What we've got now, it's nothing to do with socialism. It's a mocking of all the things we fought for. . .I don't know what's happened to folk. They've all got greedy – grabbing, that's the trouble.

Another put more tersely: 'When we had nowt, we threatened the rich. Now we act like they did.'[177] Alt notes that through consumerism workers are able to shed their fetishized status as wage-labourers and to participate within, and partake some of, the private comforts and privileges of a Veblenesque leisure class. Thus, 'while consumerism represents a new mode of class hegemony and legitimation, it is popularly perceived as mobility and increased freedom', particularly from the enforced constraints of labour and the workplace.[178] Old-style occupational communities have been undermined by the atomization of the worker; by higher wages and consumerism; by reduced work time; by individual mobility and changed residence patterns; and by the increased availability of highly differentiated consumer goods. To argue thus, however, is not to mythologize traditional working class as in the 'embourgeoisement' literature of the 1960s, nor to suggest that these processes presage the end of industrial and political opposition in contemporary western societies.[179] Apart from the 'social movements', there are a number of enduring sources of social conflict: first, some persisting occupational communities which do sustain militant opposition and organization;[180] second, the fairly extensive character of shopfloor organization in Britain, Sweden and in parts of the French economy; third, the ubiquitousness and persistence of industrial conflict, particularly in France, Britain, and the USA;[181] fourth, the extension of unionization to white-collar workers, to public employees, and to large numbers of women workers; and fifth, the increased significance and salience of locally-based struggles particularly focused on protecting localities from the effects of international capital and the national state. However, Cronin well summarizes the position facing the British and most other labour movements apart from the Swedish:[182]

> Working class strength is overwhelmingly local in character, centred in the workplace or the community and best tapped by such forms of collective action as strikes or local elections. Projecting such loyalties into the arena of national politics does not come easily. The national power of unions helps, but in general the result is a very troubled relationship between the political party oriented to the capital and its local bases of support.

Organized capitalism was a historically specific period in which national organizations were contingently established and which in all the societies under investigation led to a significant expansion of welfare state expenditure. However, under disorganized capitalism, some at least of those national structures have begun to dissolve. As we have seen, that has not eliminated social conflict, but we will now examine what its effects are on welfare state expenditures, particularly in Britain and Sweden. We will approach this final issue through directly considering Therborn's recent claims, namely, that contemporary capitalism is still fundamentally and irreducibly organized; that class-versus-class relations are pre-eminent; that there is no significant decline either in overall levels of public spending or the proportion of social expenditure within this total; and that the rise of welfare state capitalism is an irreversible and historical conquest which *cannot* be democratically undone.[183] Therborn thus most effectively challenges the view that anti-socialist or anti-social democratic forces can simply and unproblematically dismantle social welfare provision; and they cannot do this, he argues, in part because of the strength of the working class in most major western countries.

Nevertheless, there are a number of problems in Therborn's salutary and suggestive analysis. First of all, part of the reason, of course, why public spending remains high is because of increased military expenditure and of 'inevitable' spending on benefits for the unemployed and the rising numbers of the elderly who are not any more healthy than before. Further, it is necessary to examine who *benefits* from such expenditure. In most countries it is the 'service class' which has most benefited, particularly because of the expansion of higher education from the late 1950s onwards.[184] Indeed, the principle of universalization first developed in Sweden and then enshrined through Beveridge in Britain is negatively redistributive, and this can be seen with respect to pensions, housing benefits, and health care. It is also necessary to consider alongside expenditure the distribution of social *rights*. Thus, although public expenditure did not significantly fall in Nazi Germany, fascist Italy or Vichy France, there was an obviously massive reduction in a wide variety of political and social rights. Likewise, the effect of Thatcherism has been to effect a substantial undermining of in particular workplace-based social rights. At the same time, in recent years where there have been extensions of such rights many of these were *not* directly won by or for the working class as traditionally conceived. Two examples of this are worth noting: the Great Society Legislation for various minorities in the Johnson administration, and the legislation supposedly guaranteeing equal rights for women in many western countries.[185]

We would argue that the period of class-specific and positively redistributive social insurance corresponds to the early stages of organized capitalism; while the development of universalism represents the later stages, that is, when class and nation are united. In disorganized capitalism the 'traditional' working class (that is, predominantly male, seeking a secure 'family wage') has been joined by a plethora of welfare-recipients (including the 'service class', 'women', ethnic minorities, single-parent families, old-age pensioners and so on) each constituted as 'groups-for-themselves', as well as by groups of public employees with a vested interest in maintaining previous levels of public employment.[186] It is this changed balance of social forces which accounts for the fact that social-democratic governments have not in fact been *noticeably* more successful in developing patterns of high social spending. Christian Democracy in West Germany has been the main architect of high levels of social spending.[187] France likewise under conservative administrations has enjoyed high levels of welfare provision. In 1977 nearly two-thirds of all French public expenditure was devoted to income maintenance, health and social care, and education. Finally, as Therborn himself notes, few, if any, social democratic administrations presided over greater increases in social spending than did the 'bourgeois' government in Sweden between 1976–1982. Thus, the causes of high levels of social expenditure have become more complex, or disorganized, and much less tied in directly to the power and effectivity of the 'traditional' working class.[188] Indeed, although the labour movements particularly during the Depression and after the Second World War played a major role in forcing substantial increases in welfare state expenditure in Britain, there have been a number of major consequences of that development which have in effect transformed the social structure. Dunleavy has gone so far as to say that 'the growth of the welfare state in a capitalist society is a politically self-stabilizing process'.[189] This suggestion, however, attributes to the growth of the welfare state too much significance and ignores the wide variety of other determinants of political organization and social policy outcomes analysed in this book. Nevertheless, what Dunleavy correctly notes is that the very growth of significant welfare state expenditure does transform the social structure and political contours of a given society in ways which will both preclude further substantial extensions of the welfare state, and prevent à la Therborn massive reductions at the same time.[190] The following are some significant consequences of welfare state growth: expansion of state employment and hence of both a more publicly-oriented service class and of deskilled white-collar workers; growth of more typically feminized forms of employment; changed composition of the labour movement, particularly of its leadership and of its typical issues; partial replacement of income with the 'social wage' as determining an individual's welfare; generation of new consumption-based divisions, that is, between beneficiaries of, and contributors to, through taxation, social welfare provision; new political mobilizations around protecting public expenditure versus those wishing to cut taxes; political conflicts between national and local levels of government, particularly where there are locally-based taxes and/or substantial provision of services locally; some effect in generating the 'second wave' of feminist politics through extensive female employment in education, health, care for children and the elderly, social work etc.;[191] levels of unionization higher than they would otherwise have been and a strong commitment of public sector workers to prevent reductions in the size or range of social welfare provision; strongly held beliefs that personal freedoms are being unduly restricted by the growth of an 'oppressive', 'bureaucratic' state; and the development of a division between the 'state' and the 'people' or the 'public' and the 'private' which now structures politics in disorganized capitalist western societies as much as does the division between capital and labour.

Clearly, how these developments will work themselves out will vary greatly in different societies, partly depending on relatively contingent factors such as the results of particular elections and the policies pursued by leading groups in the governing party. However, it is nevertheless clear that because of the points mentioned just above: 'welfare states' will not continue to appropriate a rising share of national income; to the extent that welfare states' can be protected this will depend upon a variety of social movements supporting and protecting state expenditures. And yet because of the salient division between the people and the state much potential support will be diverted into generating less bureaucratized, more decentralized and in cases more privatized forms as the welfare state of organized capitalism makes way for a much more varied and less centrally organized form of welfare provision in disorganized capitalism. Skocpol has described the American system as 'America's incomplete welfare state', noting that universal social solidarity was never the aim of the system.[192] What is now happening in some at least of the European countries is the development of a similar two-tiered arrangement, depending on the balance of characteristically disorganized capitalist social and political forces.

8

The changing structure of trade unionism: the end of neo-corporatism?

One of the central characteristics of organized capitalism in at least some societies has been the development of certain 'corporatist' or 'neo-corporatist' institutions. With the contemporary disorganizing of western capitalism, such institutions, we shall argue in this chapter, are in process of dissolution. A number of commentators have advanced 'cyclical' accounts of this, in which the breakup of corporatist arrangements is explained by economic recession.[1] The account proposed here is, in contradistinction, structural.

Corporatism we take to be a system in which:

1 There are organized interests in civil society, particularly of employers on the one hand, and workers on the other.
2 These interests are represented by some form of national organization, of employers and of national federation(s) of labour.
3 Considerable organizational and cultural resources are available within civil society by which such interests can be mobilized.
4 The state is one that is relatively modernized or rationalized; that is, there are a number of ministries having an extensive range of policy-making and implementing functions.
5 A *quid pro quo* is struck in which the organizations in civil society control their membership and accept reasonable settlements in a spirit of 'national unity', in exchange for which the national-level organizations are given considerable powers within the state apparatuses.
6 In some cases labour is included in the corporatist arrangements, as in Sweden or Britain, and sometimes it is excluded, as in Vichy or Gaullist France.[2]

Whether or not such a set of corporatist institutional arrangements develops depends on many factors. One necessary condition for such a development is the appearance of a nation-wide trade union movement which occurred in all five countries at the end of the nineteenth century. However, whether this provides the basis of a corporatist pattern is dependent on two particular historical conditions. The first is the form which a national union movement takes at the moment of initial recruitment of the unskilled. If craft unionism is hegemonic over industrial and territorial unionism at this point in time, then adequate organizational resources for the later development of corporatism will be largely absent. This was the case during the organization of the unskilled in the emergence of the 'New Unionism' in Britain in the 1880s. The craft principle of the American Federation of Labor also triumphed over the territorial and industrial principle of the Knights of Labor towards the end of the same decade. In France of the 1880s and 1890s territorial unionism (whose basis was the government-sponsored Bourses de Travail) coexisted with industrial unionism in the *Confédération Générale du Travail* in the 1890s, with the industrial principle finally winning the upper hand, especially over the craft unions. In Germany and Sweden the craft form of initial national organization was secondary.

The second condition concerns the relationship of initial national union federation, on the one hand, and the working-class political party on the other.[3] If union and party formation are synchronized and the party stands in a strong power position *vis-à-vis* the unions, then conditions are propitious for corporatism. If they are desynchronized and the unions only marginally accountable to the party of the left, then conditions are unpropitious. In Germany and Sweden, socialist parties contributed to the enrolment of the unskilled in unions. This enhanced their involvement in and subsequent authority over national union federations. In Britain, where the unions created the party, the legitimate authority of the latter over the former has been comparatively weak. In France, the fetishism of union independence and the early growth of much parliamentary socialism, largely apart from any organized working-class base, made any subsequent corporatism difficult to develop.[4] The fact that in the USA there was no socialist party at all meant that corporatist development would be particularly weak.

Whatever corporatist arrangements that had developed began one after the other to collapse or enter into crisis in the 1970s (Britain, West Germany) and the 1980s (France, Sweden). This collapse stemmed from a number of causes, all at least loosely connected with capitalist disorganization.

(1) Corporatism has been fundamentally a national project, a matter for compromise between social classes in very much a national context of resource distribution. However, as we have seen, there has been a heightened internationalization of the world economy since the 1960s. This has been so, both in the development of a new international division of labour, and of an

increasing import-penetration and hence of dependence on exports. These developments have dislocated the national economy and have made assessments of what are appropriate sacrifices in the national interest much more difficult to determine and to justify.[5]

(2) The decline in the relative importance of indigenous mass production industries to the national economy of each of the major western economies (because of shifts of production overseas, growth of the service sector etc.) means that the workers in those industries which had been at the heart of corporatism's centralized bargain, have become so unrepresentative of the national labour force that a corporatist solution will become increasingly unworkable.

(3) The decline in the collective identity of each national working class because of (a) the reduced plausibility of leadership by mass production workers; (b) increased division between private and public-sector workers as the latter have numerically expanded; (c) the increased feminization of the labour force which in part challenges the previous 'leadership' provided of the national union movement by mainly male workers in mass-production manufacturing industries; (d) as economies are progressively internationalized, a heightened conflict between the need to divert resources into the private export-oriented sector and to limit increases in the public sector resulting in heightened militancy among the latter and an enhanced hostility to 'public expenditure' among the former; (e) a reduced importance of the sphere of production and an increased importance of the sphere of consumption – as collective identities for working-class youth have increasingly been formed in relationship to the codes and discourses of modes of consumption, which are in part 'privatizing' and in part 'classless'.[6]

(4) The oil crises of 1973/4 and 1979/80 which curtailed the tendency for real incomes for most workers to continue to rise since 1945. As a consequence – partly because of their exacerbation of import penetration and deleterious effects of the 'national' character of western political economies – the corporatist solution in which at least all organized workers could be both bought off through the annual wages round and provided with an increasing 'social wage' through enhanced welfare state provision, became increasingly difficult to ensure.

The initial consequence of these developments was a substantial mobilization of workers in the late 1960s, especially young workers developing a radicalized popular-democratic consciousness stemming from a number of interrelated factors:

1 The breakup of the many well-established working-class neighbourhoods, as indicated in chapters 4 and 5.
2 The growing affluence of workers, and especially of young workers, and an increased diversity of consumer goods and fashions.

3 The 'birth' of adolescence in the 1950s, which in Britain at least, happened first in the working class and led to a significant challenging of trade union and social-democratic hierarchies.
4 Contagion from the student movement, most especially in France and Italy.
5 The growth of a relatively classless (relative to the previous 'class cultures' of the proletarian neighbourhood) popular culture.
6 Further expansion of the tertiary sector and hence of a service class, of higher education, and of deskilled white-collar positions which articulated a partial oppositional culture to capital and upon which workers could draw.[7]

This development had two significant consequences: to encourage governments especially in France and Britain, to attempt to regulate and control such militancy by renewing (neo-)corporatist tentatives in the 1970s; and to undermine working-class 'unity', and hence organization and cultural resources, which had been a necessary but not sufficient condition for corporatism in the post-war period. The consequence of these contradictory effects, combined with the other dissolving processes noted above, meant that whatever corporatist forms developed were short-lived. We shall show that in the four countries where some such developments were found they all had dissolved or were under great pressure by the mid-1980s. And we shall show that in each case an absolutely central role in that dissolution was played by the substantial growth of a militant public sector; that an internationalization of each economy, combined with growing crises of accumulation, meant that resources had in part to be squeezed out of the public sector through 'austerity' and into export industry; and that complex spatial, social and political changes in the class structure meant that there was virtually no unified 'working class' able to deliver a corporatist bargain to capital and the state.

Throughout the West this disorganizing process brought Keynesian stabilization under attack, both from labour and from capital. On the part of labour their attacks first took the form of the 'great mobilization', i.e. the resurgence of class conflict, of the late 1960s and early 1970s. This offensive, closely connected with the rise of the new social movements, gave birth to labour's changed strategies in face of crisis from the mid-1970s; to strategies of micro-economic public investment, industrial democracy, and reduced labour-time. For the part of capital, the disorganizing processes of labour-market fragmentation and internationalization laid open the possibility to pursue different, anti-Keynesian and anti-corporatist, strategies. The growth in public-sector employment and concomitant formation of powerful unions created a potential crucial division within the labour movement. Internationalization, and especially import-penetration, exacerbated this division. In 1965 in Britain exports of 'visibles' made up 13.9 per cent of GDP, and imports 16.2 per cent; in 1981 the corresponding figures were 20 and 21 per cent. In West Germany in 1965 such exports and imports comprised respectively 15.6 and 15.2 per cent of GDP; in 1981, 25.9 and 24.0 per cent. In France the proportion of GDP accounted for by trade of visibles increased from 13.3 per cent in 1965 to 23.1 per cent in 1981; in Sweden this proportion stood already at about 26 per cent in 1975. In the USA finally in 1965 exports and imports of goods stood respectively at 3.9 and 3.1 per cent; in 1981 at 7.8 and 8.9 per cent.[8] The relative diminution of industrial workers within western labour movements combined with import-penetration – which legitimated the shift of resources from the public sector to export-oriented industry – created a divisive 'dualism' in the working class. To this capital was able to respond with dualist strategies, including the encouragement of company unionism in the 'primary labour market', which helped to shatter already tenuous Keynesian and corporatist stabilization.[9]

We shall begin our analysis here with Sweden, the classic case of Keynesian and corporatist consensus, and then proceed to the consideration of Germany, France and Britain, which have undergone, with somewhat different consequences, surprisingly similar courses of disorganization.

SWEDEN: THE CRISIS OF CENTRAL BARGAINING

No country has come as close to approaching the corporatist ideal-type as Sweden. The Keynesian welfare state and neo-corporatist and social-democratic consensus which became common currency for many nations after the Second World War was on the ground in Sweden in the 1930s. Not only was Sweden the first neo-corporatist nation, it has been the most durable one. Yet capitalist disorganization has come seriously to threaten even the renowned 'Swedish Model', as centralized bargaining by trade union and employer confederations broke down for the first time in three decades in 1983 and 1984,[10] and though subsequently restored is still under threat in 1987.

The end of the Keynesian and neo-corporatist consensus, though it became manifest from 1983 and was catalysed by a shift to the right in the Swedish national politics of industrial relations, had in fact been on the cards from the late 1960s and especially the mid-1970s. It was the object of challenge from the left as well as the right. Two central phenomena of capitalist disorganization, a decentralized 'social movement' consciousness and the internationalization of commodity markets, played key roles here. The trade union left in Sweden responded to both by going beyond the Keynesian consensus.[11] The shopfloor mobilization of the late-1960s and early 1970s and the subsequent industrial democracy demands and legislation took place partially in response to the former. The response to internationalization and the corresponding investment crisis led to public investment policies, in the Swedish case to the proposal and subsequent legislation of public investment through wage-earners' funds.

These responses took place on a large scale from the middle 1970s. At the same time, internationalization was the condition for a different and contradictory challenge to the social-democratic consensus in general, and to centralized bargaining in particular. Its concomitant labour-market dualism provoked an aggressive response by the Swedish Employers Federation to uncouple the dynamic export-oriented sector in bargaining. And this was facilitated by the growing split between private-sector and public-sector wings[12] of the labour movement which was itself a manifestation of such dualism and of the relatively increased weight of public-sector employees in the labour market.

The early development of neo-corporatist institutions in Sweden was in large part due to the fact that, whereas in most nations there was a considerable hiatus between organization in the economy and organization in civil society, in Sweden these two phenomena were roughly contemporaneous. Arguably explicable through 'economic backwardness' Sweden had national, centralized and imperatively co-ordinated trade union and employer confederations on the ground at a time at which capital was only beginning significantly to accumulate.[13] Most important – and surely most unusual – was the extremely early beginnings of the Swedish Employers Federation, Svenske Arbatsgivareförenigen Federations, SAF, which was formed in 1902 in response to the general strike of that year. The SAF from the start recognized the legitimacy of trade unions; its central leadership was vested with considerable power (more than in the LO, the central trade-union confederation for manual workers) from the very beginning; and it used the lockout with extraordinary effect from the first decade of the twentieth century.

Given this state of affairs, three other elements were necessary for the establishment of durable centralized bargaining in Sweden. First, was 1928 legislation by a bourgeois coalition government which forbade wildcat strikes during the life of a collective agreement.[14] This legislation was in response to Swedish strike rates which ranked among the highest in Europe in the 1920s. The SAF and LO opposed it, but the latter was to recognize its importance in promoting trade union centralization in the subsequent decade. Second, was the rapid increase in SAF membership density from the late 1930s. And third was a change in LO statutes of 1941 which made the right to strike of individual unions contingent on approval from the LO secretariat.[15]

Centralized bargaining was in force, in the event, from the Saltsjöbaden Basic Agreement of 1938 and through the Second World War. During the brief post-war return of LO radicalism, agreements took place on a national union level with LO recommendations. In the face of 1950s inflation there was an exceptional central agreement in 1952 and then regular agreements from 1955 to 1982. The basics of Swedish Keynesianism – the fundamentals of what came to be known as the Swedish Model – were present in the Rehn Model adopted by the LO in the early 1950s and in all essentials extant until the middle 1970s. The Rehn Model was designed to combat both inflation and unemployment. Its aims were full employment, substantial levels of growth, low inflation and a technologically advanced and competitive export sector. The idea was to achieve full employment with a restrictive fiscal policy. The key to keeping aggregate demand at controllable levels was centralized bargaining itself. In as much as the claims of the Phillips Curve were at that time accepted, it was understood that such controls on aggregate demand would lead to unemployment which was to be combatted by labour market policy. In fact the funds available to the 1948-established labour market board were quadrupled from 1957 to 1960. Growth in the dynamic export-oriented sectors was to be based on the beginnings of a 'solidary wage policy' which provided for equal pay for equal work (the other main tenet of the solidary wage policy is the principle of declining pay differentials). What this meant was that less efficient firms would go to the wall – their redundant workers being the subject of the labour market policy – while dynamic, export-oriented firms would register reasonable profits. The Rehn Model assumed such a high level of wages, though, that even dynamic firms would have problems in the internal generation of capital for investment; thus a large-scale pension programme was envisaged to help buttress capital markets.[16]

We agree with Walter Korpi that the breakdown of the Swedish 'historic compromise' should be dated from the late 1970s, though it was fore-shadowed by a chain of events which began in the late 1960s. There have been four central elements to the breakdown of the compromise and latterly the disruptions of centralized bargaining. The first of these was the pervasion of a decentralizing, new social movements, ideology. This was partly the Swedish counterpart of what was happening elsewhere in the late 1960s, but exacerbated by reaction against Social Democratic policies which were seen to have destroyed regions, damaged the environment, centralized and rationalized the local state and trade unions, and favoured nuclear power. New social-movement ideology was particularly strong in the renovated Centre and Communist parties. The nuclear power issue was the primary cause of Social Democratic defeat by the bourgeois coalition in 1976 and the nuclear referendum dominated politics on the eve of the *Storkonflikte* (great strike) of 1980. Such a decentralizing consciousness was arguably central to the wave of wildcat strikes of 1969–70, in whose spirit the succession of industrial democracy laws, culminating in the Joint Consultation Law of 1976, were enacted.[17]

The second, and in our view the most important element has been the decoupling of private- and public-sector trade unions in the bargaining process. In 1980 55 per cent of employees in the main bargaining groups worked in *non*-private-sector enterprises. Moreover, as table 8.1 shows, only about 25 per cent of these employees were private-sector *industrial* workers – a figure representing the 'core' working class. The point here is that the Swedish Model and the solidary wage policy has always been based on the private-sector blue-collar unions being the wage setters for the whole labour market. If the public-sector unions are wage leaders in

Table 8.1   Employers' side bargaining units in Sweden, 1980

	Members	Manual workers	Other employees	Total employees
Largest SAF groupings				
Engineering employers	2,267	196,452	126,116	322,568
Commercial employers	11,323	42,715	163,564	206,279
General grouping[a]	1,645	66,701	62,291	128,992
Building employers	1,726	62,190	21,799	83,989
Iron-works employers	72	45,836	19,269	65,132
Food-processing employers	366	34,021	14,223	48,244
Vehicle transport	4,179	39,804	7,061	46,865
Wood industry	832	28,995	9,102	38,115
SAF totals	38,311	783,904	534,354	1,318,258
Public-sector employers				
Co-operatives	380	58,409	29,980	88,389
Co-op and public housing	4,422	25,320	6,157	31,447
State				547,000
State-owned industry	255	70,000	41,000	111,000
Communies	279	283,000	180,000	463,000
Counties	26	213,035	123,222	336,257
Other	26		20,122	0,122
Non-private totals[b]		649,746	401,327	1,602,561

[a] Bargain in chemicals, rubber, mining, laundries and other service branches.
[b] Excludes state workers, all of whom are civil servants and hence, counted as salaried employees.
Source: SAF, 'Arbetsgivarorganisationer i Sverige 1980', Stockholm, August, 1980.

bargaining rounds, then the whole primacy of the LO–SAF agreement, on which the Swedish Model is based, begins to look anachronistic. But this is precisely what has happened in conjunction with every bargaining round that has yielded significant wage rises since 1970. In the 1971–3 central agreement, the LO, which attempted to force the white-collar unions into simultaneous settlements, were frustrated by TCO–S, the state sector white-collar bargaining cartel which secured a prior agreement. This was for a very high wage rise, higher than the LO initially wanted, but which in the event became the target for the blue-collar central. In the 1975–6 wage explosion, in the aftermath of 1974 wildcat strikes, again the public-sector unions went first and LO was – because of the large pay rise of the former – able to secure contractual increases of 11 and 7.8 per cent respectively over the two years. The low pay rises of 1974, 1977–9, 1981–2 and 1985 were in situations in which a more or less centralized LO private sector was the wage leader. The large pay increases following the great strike of 1980 were also catalysed by the public sector going first.[18]

The reason why the public-sector unions have been leaders in high-settlement bargaining rounds is due to a conflict of interests between workers in dynamic private-sector firms and the rest of the labour force. This has centred around the issue of wage-drift. In the rounds of low settlements, wage-drift typically fully equals the negotiated central rise, and public-sector and white-collar workers become relatively worse off. They attempt then to restore parity with the private-sector blue-collar workers by negotiating high rises centrally in the subsequent round. In the 1980s the four largest public-sector groupings – the blue-collar municipal workers, the blue-collar state workers, the white-collar municipal workers and the white-collar state workers – have bargained together. These groupings together represent a membership which is at least 2–3 times larger than that of the LO members in dynamic private-sector firms. It is the inordinate increase of such sectors of the labour force, together with their grouping together in cohesive bargaining cartels in the 1970s which makes it unlikely that they should or will ever fall passively in line with the deal that LO can negotiate for their private-sector members.[19]

The same is partly true for the white-collar private-sector cartel, the *Privattjanstemannkartellen* (PTK), which was formed in 1973. It has tended to fall in line with the private-sector LO unions in the years of low centrally-negotiated wage rises and bargained apart from them in the years of high expected rises.

The third element which is integrally entwined with the second is the increasing role of the state in bargaining, which has violated one of the central tenets (i.e. that Swedish corporatism had uniquely little state intervention) of the Swedish Model. In settling first – or at least giving indications that it might settle first – with the public-sector unions, the state has already taken on a considerable role. To this has been added the state's practice of offering tax incentives for low wage settlements since the middle 1970s. Moreover, the state's role has been enhanced in so far as the role of mediation commissions has become an ever pervasive presence from the 1970s. All this is without mentioning that the industrial democracy legislation of 1971–6 and the wage-earner funds legislation of 1984 were – though originally LO proposals – the product of state enactments.[20]

The fourth element concerns the problem of investment, and the shift of political–economic debates from the demand side to the supply side from the late 1970s. This is, to quote Korpi, the 'question of how to finance the investments which are necessary for the renewal and expansion of export industries',[21] or, in other words, the struggle over whose model of capital accumulation will prevail, with both left and right proffering models which break with the Keynesian consensus. For the LO, the development of an industrial policy became an issue from 1966–7, when the old Keynesian mix proved insufficient to prevent the appearance of balance of payments deficits. LO proposals here included a state investment bank – which was rapidly created –; the establishment of indicative planning; the creation of a state enterprise board; a public research and development sector; and finally, legislation permitting pension funds to serve not only as loan but as equity capital. The most important of these initiatives of course has been the idea of public ownership through wage-earners' funds. The first OPEC price rise, coupled with very high wage settlements, came to affect Sweden only as late as 1977, at which point low profitability made the shortage of investment capital the key issue – and legitimating argument – for the wage-earner funds. In the original Meidner Plan proposals for collective wage-earner shareholding in industry of 1975–6 the main supporting arguments were that the funds would reinforce the solidary wage policy, that they would counteract the increasing power of monopoly interests in the economy and that they would strengthen the influence of wage-earners in industry. It was only in 1978, with growing awareness that Sweden was faced with *chronic* accumulation, balance of payments and investment difficulties, that the paucity of private investment capital itself became the prime argument for the creation of the wage-earner funds.[22]

The most notable change from the Meidner proposal to the 1981 final LO–SAF agreement on what should be legislated – leading to the Social Democratic legislation of January 1984 – has been the shift from a 'syndicalist' to a statist basis for the operation. Now no longer would the unit which held the funds be the individual firm; nor would the employees in a given firm be given the majority of representation at the firm's shareholders' meetings. Instead control over the funds was concentrated in 24 regional boards, whose electorate was comprised of all wage-earners in a region. When a regional board began to buy shares in a given company – and the boards were free to buy shares in firms throughout Sweden and expected to act like institutions on private capital markets – representation of the funds at shareholders meetings would be equally divided between the regional board and the firm's employees. Once the funds made up 20 per cent of all shareholders' representation in a given firm, any further growth in funds equity holding would result in increases in representation for regional boards only. Further moves away from a syndicalist model were in terms of the sources of the funds which now would no longer be made up of only 20 per cent of excess profits (the definition of 'excess profits' seems to remain rather elusive) but also from an increase of 1 per cent in the payroll tax. Finally, the mediating body for the holding of funds has become statized in the pension system. Thus both excess profits and the increment in payroll tax would be paid neither into a firm's wage-earner funds nor even into regional boards, but into the – now heavily depleted with increased outlays – state pension system which would allocate resources to the regional boards.[23]

An anti-Keynesian, supply side strategy has also emerged on the right. The 'bourgeois' coalition government of 1976–82 was able to restore profitability and investment at least for a while. With the depletion of the pensions funds, an increased share of private savings as proportion of total savings characterized capital institutions from the late 1970s. Moreover, bourgeois government relief from taxation on equity and employer-designed shareholding schemes for individual employees came to provide a significant flow of resources for industrial investment, undercutting the growth arguments of the left for the wage-earner funds.[24] All this is best understood in any event in the context of the Swedish Employers Federation (SAF) offensive against the Keynesian consensus which culminated in the 1983 breakdown of central bargaining and, worse, of the solidary wage policy.

The SAF-catalysed 1983 breakdown evolved quite directly out of what was sensed as a substantial employer defeat in the 1980 strike. The latter, as we shall see below, itself was in large part the culmination of the increased tension in Swedish industrial relations since the wildcat strikes of 1969–70.[25] Just a few months after the belated 1980 settlements, the Engineering Employers Association (VF) – far and away the most important and powerful SAF branch organization – voiced demands for the establishment of branch-by-branch negotiation. A number of employers' leaders felt that branch negotiations would be a stepping-stone to company-wide negotiations, which was what the large and dynamic export-oriented companies really wanted.[26] Eventually, in January 1981, the VF acceded to the conclusion of a central bargain on the condition of a low pay rise. In fact the LO seems to have accepted a low settlement – a two-year agreement with 3 per cent wage rises, price guarantees and wage-drift compensation – partly due to fear of the VF's threat. The writing was on the wall in the sweeping statute changes that the SAF carried out in 1982. Now no longer did SAF branch associations need the approval of the SAF board to conclude collective agreements. As important, now branch associations would have the right to declare lockouts without central organization approval.[27]

The VF took full advantage of these statutory alterations in the 1983 round, the chronology of which was: the LO made a very low pay bid of 2.1 per cent; the SAF did not immediately respond to this pay bid, but instead voiced demands for (decentralizing) procedural changes in bargaining; the VF announced it would bargain separately; the remainder of SAF presented a phoney offer of 0 per cent to the LO, which the latter rejected in February 1983 because it would ruin the solidary wage policy; the VF persisted with the Metalworkers Union and concluded a separate agreement in March for a 2.2 per cent rise, including bonus provisions for skilled workers and no wage-drift compensation; this was followed by the threat of selective strikes by the LO; after a day of these the SAF settled with the remainder of the private-sector LO unions; also in March the public-sector agreement was concluded; in June 1983 the private-sector white-collar bargaining cartel, the PTK, concluded a two-year deal with an 8.3 per cent rise (except for the largest PTK union, the SIF, whose membership is highly qualified, predominantly male and comprises middle and lower management, some clerks and technicians, but not foremen); two weeks later the SIF settled an 18-month deal with the VF for a 4.6 per cent rise with productivity provisions.[28] Although a Thatcher-type ideology has been spreading throughout the SAF from the mid- to late-1970s, there are two straightforward reasons to explain their volte-face. Basically their agreement to centralized bargaining meant sacrificing much employer power in (external and internal) labour markets. The pay-offs for such a sacrifice were industrial peace and a privileged position for dynamic export firms in the private sector. The industrial peace began to waver from the late 1960s and seemed to employers to be travestied by the 1980 conflict. And the increasing weight of public-sector unions and the state in the bargaining process nullified the privileged position of the big export firms.

We will turn now to brief consideration of the centrifugal and centripetal interests in accounting for the breakdown of bargaining and solidary wage policy of 1983/4, in the context of long-term trends in the fragmentation of Swedish labour markets. The main centrifugal interests which we will discuss are the Engineering Employers (VF), the Metalworkers Union, and the white-collar unions. The main centripetal interests are the Municipal Workers Union and the LO itself.

The Engineering Employers (VF) and metalworking union

The VF bargains with engineering workers, with steelworkers from privately-owned firms, and with workers in the electronics industry. The power of the VF stems from the fact that approximately one-half of total Swedish exports are produced in the metal industry and that about one-half of production from the metal industry is exported. It has been a traditional Swedish maxim accepted by the LO, the SAF, government and public opinion that the export industry is the dynamic centre of the Swedish economy. This has also been the primary argument put forward for the claim that private-sector bargaining between the LO and SAF should set the framework for public-sector bargaining. Thus 860,000 wage workers in the private sector were to set the frame for the approximately 3 million economically active in Sweden. In effect, the VF in some sort of association with the Metalworkers Union has pushed this argument to its logical conclusion. In what is arguably the latter's view, now the metal industry alone (including some 400,000 workers, themselves making up just a portion of the now only 25 per cent of employees who are private-sector industrial workers) should set the framework for the entire economy.[29]

The initiative was thus taken by the Metal Employers in early 1983 to bargain apart from the central SAF–LO agreement. In taking this decision to contravene a norm extant for a generation, the VF has responded to a dissatisfaction felt by employers in the metal industry since the middle 1970s. The dissatisfaction was mainly with the solidary wage policy that had been the foundation of LO–SAF agreement since the end of the 'fifties and whose governing principle brought about an accelerated wage convergence of higher and lower paid industrial manual workers from 1969 to the middle seventies'.[30] On the face of it, the metal employers would seem to have benefited from the agreement which has kept wage levels in the most dynamic firms at quite moderate levels. And in fact profits have been enormous in firms such as Volvo, which recorded unprecedented profit levels in 1984 with the upswing in demand from the United States and elsewhere in conjunction with the devaluation of the Swedish krona. Yet they have opposed the solidary wage policy on a number of grounds. First, they point to an increasing resentment of skilled versus unskilled workers within metallurgy plants. They argue that skilled labour is increasingly difficult to attract, not so much in 'external' labour markets, but in the internal labour market of metalworking and electronics firms, in which there is little incentive for workers to take training courses to move into more qualified positions. This lack of incentive is all the more negatively viewed in the dynamic metallurgy-sector firms the number of skilled jobs is increasing, while the number of unskilled jobs is diminishing. Such a state of affairs characterizes engineering and particularly electrical firms such as Ericsson, in which the shift from electro-technical to microelectronic products has accompanied the destruction of large numbers of assembly jobs. The dynamic metallurgy firms – which predominate on the board of directors and the national bargaining committee of the VF, and for whom the VF officers are employees – would prefer a system of decentralized bargaining with 'strong and responsible' local unions. They argue that the industry's interests would be best served by productivity deals, for which local unions would be held responsible; according to the SAF metal employers the (comparatively low) level of unofficial strikes is altogether too high and centralized bargaining has been more part of the problem here than part of the solution. Such 'local responsibility' would, of course, be incompatible with the LO's solidary wage policy.[31]

The Metalworkers Union, which has always been the driving centre of the Swedish labour movement, had a number of means at its disposal to force the Engineering Employers back to a central bargaining table. It is likely that the latter acted in 1983 under the hypothesis that the union would not oppose them. In the event, the metal union's bargaining committee did not think that their members would support a struggle over the grievance of bargaining structure.[32] This is not surprising. The 'Action Programme' adopted by the 1981 union congress had already shown dissatisfaction with diminishing industrial differentials. Here it was decided that 'the wage differences within the LO–collective have become so small that further evening-out will no longer lead to decreased income disparity in the whole of society. The equalization policy should continue, but it has to embrace all wage-earner groups.'[33]

Entirely fitting with this statement was the immediate explanation given by a national union representative, in his account of why Metall had not more strongly opposed the 1983 rift. 'We were losing too many members to SIF', was the response. Technological change in the industry had, while leading to the destruction of a number of unskilled jobs, created a number of highly qualified posts; posts which typically involved some work in the office and on the shopfloor, and that especially involved working with computers. These jobs were the object of intermittent raiding between SIF and Metall, with – even after the break with centralized bargaining, and the resulting large wage gains for the most highly-paid manual workers – the SIF gaining most of the successes.[34]

There is some dispute as to whether the metalworkers (Metall) came back into the LO fold at the beginning of 1984, and more generally whether the 1984 round(s) have been more centrally co-ordinated than those of 1983. After the metallurgy sector's separate peace in 1983, the rest of the LO private-sector unions struck a central bargain with the rump of the SAF. In 1984, on the other hand, each union concluded its own separate bargain. The most destructive (to centralized bargaining) aspect of this was that the agreements were made for inordinately different time periods, ranging from 12 months to two years, a temporal disparity which made a return to centralized bargaining more difficult. In 1984, the public sector went first and – with the encouragement of government – concluded a two-year agreement, in the hope that other unions would follow and a new central bargain would be possible at the beginning of 1986. The metalworkers, some thought deliberately (though the union's argument was for reasons of flexibility), then proceeded to conclude a 13-month contract.[35]

However, some steps seem to have been taken towards the re-establishment of centralization. First, in 1984 there was a general LO meeting, in which the metalworkers participated, on bargaining strategy. Here a general policy was decided on the issue of compensation for private-sector wage-drift in which lower wage-drift workers would receive in their contracts up to 1.2 kronor per hour to compensate for a predicted average industrial wage-drift. To Metall this seemed a victory against low differentials; they understood this as giving to low drift workers only about one-half compensation for a 3 per cent average industrial drift which was predicted before the 1984 round. But after the conclusion of the round, it was estimated by the LO's chief statistician that this 1.2 kronor payment would compensate for nearly all of average industrial drift, partly perhaps because 1984 contractual settlements were so high.[36] Also indicative of a step back towards centralized bargaining is the fact that the public-sector agreement included a guaranteed 100 per cent *Lohneglidningskompensation* (wage-drift compensation), and that reasonable settlements were won in declining and low-paid private-sector branches such as clothing and textiles, partly through the threats of supportive industrial action by Leif Blomberg, Metalworker Union's chairman.

Why the volte-face of the metalworkers? Sceptics from other unions point to the dissatisfaction of lower-paid engineering employees in the absence of wage-drift compensation in the 1983 agreement. And indeed the average metal wage is some 10–20 per cent lower than the average in the building industry and not a great deal above the mean industrial wage. There are great numbers of low-skilled, low-paid jobs in the specifically metalworking branch for example – in comparison to transport equipment and electrical engineering – and the female workforce in the engineering industry as a whole (15.4 per cent of the workforce in the mid-seventies and 17.8 per cent in the mid-eighties) is particularly poorly paid.[37]

Equally, it is true that Metall has largely got its way, and that it will increasingly set the agenda for the whole of the LO. Thus can be explained by the talk of LO leadership in 1984 of a 'third [between centralized bargaining and that year's relative anarchy] way'. The sacrifices of Metall in regard to *Lohneglidningskompensation* are not great. Indeed, it was the prediction of the chief LO statistician[38] that 1984 would see an increase in differentials. Also, such compensation is only for the *average* industrial drift, and does little towards compensating for the extremely high drift of groups of highly qualified engineering workers. Perhaps the most important explanation in regard to Metall's return to central bargaining is on the level of collective representations, and the fact that there are few symbols in Sweden that are more highly loaded with social and national meaning than the solidary wage policy.

The white-collar unions (TCO)

Two aspects of the fragmentation of Swedish labour markets which we have just discussed are the growing proportion of public employees and the privileged position of a part of the engineering workforce. A third aspect has been the extraordinary increase in the size of the white-collar workforce, and more important the increase in highly qualified positions and the relative decline of unskilled positions, within the white-collar sector. The TCO unions, like the public sector, have been expected to follow, and generally have followed, the framework set by the LO's private-sector unions with the SAF.[39] And this by 1984, when total TCO membership was at well over 75 per cent of the membership of the LO private-sector unions, has appeared, to say the least, a bit strange to white-collar union leaders. The crisis of centralized LO bargaining has meant a much greater deal of autonomy for the white-collar unions in the pursuit of their members' interests.

The TCO is an umbrella organization and does not itself bargain. During the 1970s, however, three 'cartels' were created among the TCO unions: in the private sector the PTK, whose membership in 1984 was about 500,000; in the municipal and county sector the KTK, whose membership in January 1984 stood at 275,386; and in the state sector the TCO–S, whose membership was closer to 100,000.[40]

According to PTK leaders, the 1973 establishment of the cartel created a new balance of forces between LO and white-collar workers. As well, the main bone of contention between the cartel and LO (i.e. the statistical measure by which wage rises should be calculated) remains. The LO wants to calculate wage rises by an increase in how much individuals are paid; the PTK, with their typical white-collar career trajectories, want to understand salaries as characteristics of jobs and not of individuals. A further indicator of PTK/LO divergence of interests is the changing skill composition of the former. The union in the cartel with the greatest workplace strength is the SIF, which boasts, for example, some 5000 members in Volvo alone. In SIF, according to union estimates, unskilled clerical jobs are disappearing through technical change at the rate of 2000 per year, thus enhancing the position of the higher paid within this 'vertical' union.[41]

Differences of interest between the TCO unions and the LO (also over tax policy) have had repercussions on the level of politics. The PTK and the PTK leaders, formerly publicly sympathetic with the Social Democrats, stress their political independence, and even distance themselves from the party. This was most evident in the demonstrations of white-collar unions outside of the TCO offices in 1983 *against* any possible confederation support of the proposed wage-earner funds legislation of January 1984. This is not true just in the private sector, but also in the public sector, for example in bargaining with local authorities. Here the main union groupings are the mammoth Municipal Workers Union, *Svenska kommunalarbetareförbundet* (SKAF), the PTK and the SACO–SR. According to KTK sources, the white-collar workers get a better deal to the extent that bargaining is decentralized. Public-sector bargaining, more than private-sector negotiations, resembles a zero-sum game. The more that SKAF receive, *ceteris paribus*, the less that the day-care teachers, nurses and administrative workers of the KTK earn. From the standpoint of the KTK, the SKAF has, *inter alia*, two cards at its disposal, the LO and the SAP (Social Democratic Party). The disruption of centralized bargaining effectively diminished LO support of the Municipal Workers to the benefit of KTK. On the other hand, the renewed (since 1982) predominance of Social Democrats on the county and municipal employers' bargaining side favours agreements which will enhance the position of the Municipal Workers against the higher paid KTK unions.[42]

We have thus noted three changes in the composition of labour markets which are indicative of progressive fragmentation:

1   The new salience of a highly paid, highly qualified section of the manual working class in export-oriented, high-profit private industry; this grouping is predominantly male and has a very visible shopfloor profile.
2   The massive growth in number of highly qualified and well-paid white-collar workers, many female.
3   The increasing proportion of the labour force comprised of public sector employees.

To each of these changes have been corresponding shifts in the objectives of interest groups, To the first corresponds shifts in the Metalworkers Union and their employer counterparts. To the second and third correspond the increasing independence and strength of the PTK, KTK, TCO–S and SACO–SR. It should be underlined that in each of these three cases the change in labour markets and the shifting orientation of interest organizations are in the same direction; that is, as the labour markets fragment, the interest organizations come to favour decentralization.

Feminization and the Municipal Workers

A further qualitative transformation of Swedish labour markets has been the great increase in the female component of the employed population. The most important union in regard to the representation of mainly female public-sector employees and the low paid – in fact, the key *new* actor on the stage of Swedish industrial relations in the late 1970s and especially in the 1980s – is the Municipal Workers Union (SKAF). In 1984, with over 600,000 members, this was Sweden's largest union. It is 80 per cent female, 50 per cent part-time,[43] yet recognized as highly effective. Only about 25,000 members are in the traditional 'men's jobs' – fire service workers, sewer workers, dustmen (garbage) – while 68 per cent of the membership are in the areas of care (*omsorg*) or nursing. In the latter group, this very young union (40 per cent of its members are under 30) includes the union's largest occupational group, the hospital employees; the day-care centre workers, who in a number of workplaces have considerable shopfloor strength; and the difficult-to-organize home-helps and child-minders, the latter who are paid by the municipalities. The union's very top national leadership is still male, drawn from the traditional 'male' municipal occupations, but women are increasingly moving into leadership positions on section and branch levels.[44]

It is important to note that the 1980 strike was catalysed by, and largely carried out by, public-sector workers. Action began, indeed, in the public sector among KTK nurses and SKAF hospital laundry staff. Strategic Stockholm underground workers were then pulled out by SKAF, effectively closing down the system, to which the municipality responded (in order that those not working though not on strike should be on the union and not municipal payroll) by a lockout. Settlement via mediation boards in both sectors were successful from the point of view of wage rises, but rather less successful from the point of view of union rights: as nurses found to their disappointment, they were effectively denied the right to strike because of disapproving public opinion. The point, however, is that such mobilization took place. Few now doubt that the predominantly female public-sector unions could bring their members out with considerable strategic effectiveness.[45]

The irony here is that the labour-market situation of mobilized public-sector workers has led to a greater *dis*-organization than would have been the case in the absence of such mobilization. The paradox is that the powerful Municipal Workers Union, partly because its members are low paid, endorsed a centripetal solution to the disruption of centralized bargaining; if anyone it is they who have acted as the main groups inside the LO to struggle for the resurrection of centralized negotiations. Their action, however, in its unanticipated consequences – because of SKAF's members' differential labour-market situation and because of the union's very power – has constituted an important centrifugal force.[46]

The LO

The student of Swedish politics and industrial relations must be struck by one central phenomenon: the extent to which the Swedish Model has been the work, not of the Social Democratic Party, but of the LO.[47] The LO has been above all a political force, exerting pressure on governments primarily directly, but also through the mediation of the party. The LO's considerable political power has been particularly based on the solidary wage policy, through which the LO itself has been arguably the most important instrument of Swedish economic policy. Although such policy was carried out by means of the LO–SAF central bargain in the private sector, the situation has been one in which the LO itself has been far and away the most important collective actor. First, the solidary wage policy is not an SAF, but an LO policy. Second, a lot of effective LO control over setting the rules for Swedish labour markets has come not just through the LO–SAF private-sector inaustrial worker bargain, but through LO control over its expanding public-sector unions, and ability to set the terms for the white-collar unions.[48]

Though central bargaining has now been restored, the LO is still in a bit of a double bind. Its political power is based on its control over the price of labour in Sweden and on the solidary wage policy. If the federation sticks to the principle of the wage policy, it may mean the renewed independence of the Metalworkers Union and hence loss of political clout through the inability to control labour markets. To the extent that it wins Metall back into the fold, it might mean sacrificing political power through the effective termination of the solidary wage policy. The main hope, for the LO, is that Metall continues to accept the principle of the solidary wage policy. Such an outcome is dependent on the metalworkers' instrumental interests being outweighed by the level of their collective identity. And one should not underestimate the collective identity of Swedish workers and especially metalworkers. Collective identity is constituted through a set of symbols and their multifarious meanings.[49] Symbolically-constituted identity is also a matter of social actors' attributing to themselves a positively valued status. This is why a 'proletarian' collective identity in the literal sense of the word 'proletarian', is a contradiction in terms. There is no incentive to establish a collective identity which attaches a negative valuation – as would a proletarian identity – to an individual or collective social actor. Representatives of the LO stress how much the LO, centralized bargaining and the 'folkhem' (people's home) welfare state notions are 'Swedish', in explanation and in defence of these institutions.[50] Such assertions are tantamount to making a statement about the creation of colective identity through meanings. The LO itself is thus an important symbol to metal workers and in particular to active unionists among them. The LO is a symbol whose polyvalent meanings are such stuff as the highly-developed welfare state; the solidary wage policy; national respectability and power; the initiators of progressive Swedish social policy; the most important hand controlling Swedish labour markets; the association with Social Democracy's universalistic and internationally esteemed foreign policy. Such meanings establish a positively valued identity for Swedish workers in two senses. First, as Swedes, in as much as these are the 'typically Swedish' characteristics that give Sweden a high status in the international context. Second, *as workers*, in as much as it is the LO and the SAP that have so much made Sweden what it is. And we must emphasize this capacity in its literal sense. It is hardly coincidental, especially in the context of collective-identity formation, that – unlike, for example, in West Germany and Italy – almost all of the important officials in any of the LO unions and in the LO central office itself are from shopfloor backgrounds.

It is surely this set of meaning-laden symbols that pushed the Metalworkers Union to reconsider its break with the blue-collar central. But even if Metall has fully come back to the embrace of the federation, there would still be the ever-growing centrifugal force of the three white-collar cartels and the SACO–SR. Equally Metall has not fully come back on the LO's terms. Most important is that LO has not asked Metall to come back on the LO's terms, but rather changed the LO's terms to accommodate Metall. Municipal Workers Union representatives interviewed seemed to consider that their union was increasingly coming to replace Metall at the heart of the LO. Metalworkers' officials, though more or less concerned with criticisms regarding their loyalty to the LO, seemed – partly becausse so much of collective identity lay in being *metal*workers rather than workers *tout court* – not to be very concerned whether they were or were not the union most central to the LO. On the other hand, LO representatives are of the opinion that metalworkers were indeed still the soul of the LO. Here LO leader Stig Malmstrom's talk of a 'third way' in between centralized and decentralized bargaining is not so far from Metall leader Leif Blomberg's advocacy of a rougher framework for centralized bargaining. Malmstrom's idea is for rather more general guidelines to be worked out centrally, but to give the individual national unions more flexibility to determine the distribution of wages within their industrial branch. This idea is also instantiated in the development by the LO's statistical office of a job evaluation scheme from 1978–84. This scheme, whose development was in response to demands of representatives of skilled workers, measures the difficulty of jobs. It could possibly become a new basis for the all-important LO calculation of differentials, which have previously – in the absence of an adequate job-evaluation scheme – been determined in terms of the average wage of each (of 125) bargaining groups. More important, it could provide a basis for the legitimation of increased differentials.[51]

Some LO officials have argued, on *prima facie* reasonable grounds, that the metalworkers are more concerned about the deterioration of their relative wages versus those highly-paid white-collar workers than about differentials between themselves and less favourably placed manual workers.[52] This, however, would not justify an LO policy of support for increasing differentials among manual workers. Moreover, the LO – with the relative expansion of the organized white-collar groupings – is in a position in which it is decreasingly able to do anything about differentials between white-collar and blue-collar workers.

Few of these tendencies were significantly reversed in the 1984–5 wages round. Although the LO has claimed that this round has seen a successful return to centralized bargaining, it appears on closer view to have been a (Social Democratic) government attempt to initiate a *de facto* wage policy, which was *then* 'centrally bargained'. Indeed the VF–metalworkers deal was only marginally affected by the central bargain; glaring splits remained between public and private sectors and within the public sector; and the state continued to increase its interventionist role. The inflation-conscious government, anxious to avoid the 1983 and 1984 free-for-alls, called the LO, SAF and all the union cartels together in April and then June 1984 for what became known as the Rosenbad Talks. Now Metall in principle and the private-sector white-collar cartel more concretely claimed to favour central negotiations, though the SAF resisted. The government – in parallel with a vigorous press campaign – insisted that the unions agree to a 5 per cent wage ceiling (including drift), in return for which they promised a rate of inflation of under 3 per cent and significant tax reductions for all employees. In early summer the SAF – motivated by the stick of government pressure and the carrot of low wage bills – reluctantly consented to a central bargain. But now the public-sector unions, especially the TCO-S and the Municipal Workers, demanded the two-year agreement they had concluded in 1984 – which had allowed for re-opening the contract in the event of private-sector wage rises – be rebargained. The two largest private-sector LO unions, Metall and the General

Factory Union, riposted with the threat that they would not centrally bargain if the public-sector contracts were rebargained.[53]

In any case, autumn negotiations – verbally downplayed by the SAF and overplayed by the LO – proceeded, culminating in a February 1985 agreement that all unions had to accept (but this was previously decreed by government) a 5 per cent pay ceiling. Worse for the LO than the too imprecise nature of this central bargain was the fact – admitted to by Stig Malmstrom – that the deal implied no relative wage increases for the low paid. The already thin central bargain seemed to vanish altogether a month later when the metalworkers concluded an agreement with the VF for *no* general wage rise at all. Instead the entire 1.40 kronor per hour which constituted the ceiling would be distributed through workplace bargaining – an event which can be taken as further evidence of a VF desire for bargaining to be decentralized beyond the branch level. Worse for the solidary wage policy, the engineering sector agreement recommended higher wages for those with an 'unfavourable wage development' (i.e. the already higher paid workers). A month later, however, towards the end of April, the individual engineering firms had not signed agreements, both sides dissatisfied with the 5 per cent roof. On 22 April the VF and the Metalworkers Union concluded a branch agreement, in response to which workers at the sector's largest firm, Volvo in Gothenburg, went out in wildcat strikes. In May 1985, public-sector division was confirmed by TCO–S strikes which were followed by a state lockout that paralysed some essential services. The TCO–S had come out in dissatisfaction with rebargaining of the public-sector contracts of 1984. They won significant rises here, from which – though TCO–S fought the battle alone – the other public-sector unions benefited.

Despite these tensions, most observers – whether academics, unionists or employers – at the time of writing in March 1987, seem to agree that 1984–5 did constitute a return to central bargaining. The 1985–86 round saw a much less ambivalently concluded central bargain. No matter what differentials were after wage-drift was taken into account, the centrally concluded bargain was seen as reconfirming the spirit of the solidary wage policy. At the 1986 LO annual congress, divergences between Metall and the Municipal Workers surfaced again; but a subsequently created LO wage-policy committee overrode these differences and succeeded once again in defending the principle of the solidary wage policy. In the 1986–7 round the Metal Employers once again have broken ranks (as they did not do in 1984–5 and 1985–6) with the rest of the employers' federation. They have been again attempting to force the Metalworkers Union to bargain separately from the LO. The union is doing its utmost to resist these attempts. If this turns out to be the only way in which the latter can conclude a bargain, it still seems almost certain that Metall will so co-ordinate this separate bargaining with the rest of the LO unions that there will be effectively central bargaining in the 1986–7 round.

WEST GERMANY: CO–DETERMINATION AND DISORGANIZATION

Organized capitalism, we have stressed, was centred around a certain salience of working-class capacities, which can take, as in Britain and Sweden, a class-with-class form, or, as in France and Italy, a 'class-versus-class' form. In Germany a class-versus-class configuration dominated, either with the effective exclusion of the working class from the polity before the First World War and in the Third Reich, or in the heightened class struggle of the aftermath of the First World War and the Weimar Republic. An externally-imposed democracy combined with a badly weakened working-class movement created the conditions for a class-with-class solution, an effective neo-corporatist framework which grew from the end of the 1940s until the mid-1970s. The two other key preconditions of Germany neo-corporatism were the growing centralization of the trade unions and the effects of co-determination legislation of the early 1950s. As elsewhere, German neo-corporatism (and German organized capitalism) was challenged from the right and the left. From the right in the ending of a neo-corporatist *quid pro quo* signalled by the Social Democratic state's restrictive fiscal policies from the early to middle 1970s. From the left, not only in the rise to centre-stage of the new social movements, but in the increasingly militant posture of the Social Democratic Party and the unions. This has led to the substantial extension of co-determination legislation in the 1970s and to the strikes for reduced working time of 1978–9 and 1984, whose upshot has partly been a greater fragmentation of collective bargaining and consequent threat to the power of the national industrial unions. We will deal, then, with the social forces that have contributed to first the organization and then the disorganization of the German politics of industrial relations.

The framework for German neo-corporatism was set by, on the one hand, a weakened and centralized post-war labour movement, and on the other, by a conservative yet pluralist Christian Democratic state. The Nazi regime had decimated the working-class movement in Germany. Although former activists were able quickly, after the war, to reconstitute the SPD and unions, ordinary workers seemed to have little interest in political or industrial militancy. First, the Nazi experience was wholly demoralizing; second, the organizational embodiments of the old class consciousness had let down wage-earners in their failure to combat effectively National Socialism; third, workers were disillusioned with the sectarian strife between communist and socialists and were largely fed up with politics after an overdose of politics in the Third Reich; fourth, the construction of new housing outside the often bombed-out old proletarian areas isolated workers from one another; fifth, the mass media, and especially television, kept workers away from the traditional political mass meetings, while post-war newspapers were largely 'apolitical', replacing the earlier socialist and explicitly bourgeois papers (which had had a wider circulation); and sixth, the creation of the Eastern bloc – which cut traditionally militant Berlin and Saxony off from the West German labour movement – reinforced by the violent repression of strikes in East Germany in 1953, helped foster an apolitical anti-communism among workers.[54]

Among the trade unions themselves, there were parallel processes of centralization and depoliticization. The key events here took place between 1949 and 1953. The year 1949 marked the founding of the German trade union confederation, the Deutsche Gewerkschaftsbund (DGB). It was comprised of 16 industrial unions which carried out bargaining on national and regional levels, with mutually exclusive spheres of influence. In the early 1950s, however, bargaining remained decentralized with little control by national unions over regional collective bargaining units and with large numbers of small-scale strikes. The effects of these on upwards wage pressure and inflation were nullified, though, by the unusually 'loose' labour markets given the influx of refugees from the East. In any event the *Einheitsgewerkschaft* (trade union unity) framework provided the necessary conditions for the centralization of bargaining. The first real 'wage round' took place in 1952. The Metalworkers Union (IG Metall), which came to be the wage round leader after the collapse of a hard-fought strike in Bavaria in 1954, decided to co-ordinate centrally regional bargaining, and signed their first central accord in 1956. Further steps towards centralization in the late 1950s and 1960s were the reassertion of DGB power *vis-à-vis* the individual national unions, first in 1958 and then, with the onset of 'Concerted Action' with the accesssion to power of the 'Great Coalition' government of Social Democrats and Christian Democrats, in 1966–7. In both cases it was the more conservative currents of the union movement which initiated such DGB hegemony. As regards the individual industrial unions, centralization proceeded in so far as bargaining competence and financial resources were shifted from regional to national levels; all of which was accompanied by a qualitative increase of middle-class influence in the number of professionals employed by the national federations.[55]

The shift to the right of the DGB occurred in three phases:

1 The defeat of communists and militants in the factory councils.
2 The replacement in the early 1950s of the old guard unionists by a new group led by IG Metall's Otto Brenner, which entailed substantial depoliticization as resources were shifted from the sphere of politics to collective bargaining and the individual member unions were strengthened against the central DGB.
3 The emergence of a new right-wing current in the confederation promoting 'responsible' wage policies, centralization of power to the DGB and the SPD's (Social Democrats) Keynesian Programme at the Bad Godesberg Conference of 1959.

Weakened by crushing fines in the Federal Labour Court in connection with the illegal IG Metall strikes of 1956–7, Brenner and what had become the left were overtaken by moderates at the DGB Congresses of 1959 and 1962. The upshot was the 1963 Dusseldorf Programme, in which nationalizations and planning were de-emphasized and the legitimacy of the Federal Republic as a *Rechtsstaat* (state based on the rule of law) was recognized.[56] During the next two years IG Metall itself was converted to wage moderation. These political shifts were crucial in the development of German neo-corporatism, in that it was necessary to the latter that West Germany's largest union, IG Metall, begin to develop more of a social control profile in order to moderate wage rises. This was surely a necessary condition of the establishment of Concerted Action in 1967. In addition, a non-political reading of co-determination had to become pervasive in order that such a consensual system of industrial relations could become established.

German co-determination consists of two interconnected, workplace and enterprise, levels. The workplace level legislation of 1952 (Works Constitution Act) contributed importantly to the establishment of German neo-corporatism and pushed German capitalism more generally to higher levels of organization.[57] The Act was a highly conservative piece of legislation, which constituted part of an employers' and Christian Democratic offensive against the resurgent post-war left and their basis in the Works Councils (*Betriebsräte*). Counterparts elsewhere of this legislation have been the Swedish 1928 law discussed above prohibiting breach of collective contracts, the American Taft-Hartley Law and Britain's Industrial Relations Act of 1971. The German law established the works councils. These were to be elected by all workers (and not just trade union members) in establishments with six or more employees, and they were to be the only legal representative of workers on the shopfloor. It defined the factory council's functions as contributing to the efficiency of the workplace. The law provided that the councils could neither engage in wage bargaining nor mobilize strike action. Related legislation of the first half-decade of the new-born Republic outlawed the closed and the union shop; legally obliged unions to maintain labour peace throughout the life of a contract; made unofficial strikes illegal; curtailed the rights of public employees to industrial action; and created a Federal Labour Court (*Bundesarbeitsgericht*) to ensure the strict application of much of the above. As in Sweden, the unions, who initially bitterly opposed the Works Constitution Act, came easily to live with it to the extent that it reinforced the power of the national unions over the shopfloor. In doing so it favoured the development of corporatism.[58]

The Christian Democratic polity of the 1950s was markedly neo-liberal. Their idea of the 'social market economy' was based on a set of mostly anti-Keynesian principles. The state, for example, was to set the framework for the economy and then to withdraw. It provided a large role for monetary stability; any counter-cyclical policy was to be not fiscal but monetary, the balanced budget was sacred and government even planned for budget surpluses;

it wanted to discourage industrial monopolies and the trade union closed shop; finally, it supported – against trade union protests – an export-led model of economic growth which depended on restricted domestic consumption. The only 'social' characteristic was the provision of an adequate social security programme. Neo-corporatist means of wage control were not necessary until the late 1950s in as much as surpluses of labour supply kept profits high and inflation low. The shift away from strict monetary policies of Christian Democracy from the late 1950s was not a conversion to a Keynesian primacy of fiscal policy, but only a movement in the direction of an incomes policy in order to control inflation.[59]

Christian Democracy (the CDU) nevertheless did initiate the first steps of policy which later was developed by Social Democratic Concerted Action into a fully-fledged neo-corporatism. The CDU reacted to the inflationary pressures brought about by a tight labour market from the middle 1950s. The year 1957 was the first to see large wage rises and from 1960 wages began to rise more quickly than productivity. In response to this the government from 1960 began to call publicly for wage restraint and in 1963 established the Council of Economic Experts. The Council suggested rises in annual wage rounds on predicted rises in productivity and inflation. In the 1963 wage round the conservative construction workers settled first in accordance with the new productivity formulae. From 1964 to 1965 IG Metall also began to comply and henceforth opened all wage rounds with attention to these inflation and productivity guidelines. It is difficult to explain this willingness of trade unions to co-operate with the CDU state in the absence of the type of *quid pro quo* they were subsequently to receive from governments from 1966 to 1975. It is likely, however, that workers were ready to exercise restraint after seven to eight years of unprecedented wage rises; that unions were flattered to be ,cast in a role of political responsibility; that the rank and file was at the time quite conservative; and finally that the CDU had provided to workers not inconsiderable welfare state benefits.[60]

The neo-corporatism which followed the accession of the Great Coalition to power in 1966 differed in three main ways from the state of affairs of the early 1960s: first, through the presence of qualitatively greater social spending; second, because economic policy was one not of deflation but of reflation; and third, because policy was thoroughly Keynesian, including the creation of a special investment budget, accelerated depreciation measures from new investment, legislation attributing new fiscal powers to central government, and a package of welfare-state spending measures. Concerted Action itself, beginning in February 1967, went beyond previous co-operation in the establishment of a tripartite body including representatives of labour, management and government to exchange information and discuss economic policy. The effectiveness of the body went further than its juridical status: it came to be an institution in which policy was negotiated; and in addition granted for the first time public recognition and status to trade unions.[61]

Disorganization

This Keynesian and neo-corporatist consensus came under attack in West Germany, as in Sweden and Britain, not just from the right, but from the left. Again, the new social-movements of the late 1960s seemed partly to provide an ideological context. The reappearance of *Mitbestimmung* (co-determination) demands from the DGB in 1968 – once again in a framework for economic democracy – was followed by a wave of wildcat strikes in 1969 and the highest strike rates yet recorded in the Bundesrepublik in 1971. Another qualitatively more substantial ripple of industrial disruption – this time with the participation of many women and foreign workers – followed in 1973. After the wage stabilization of the initial years of Concerted Action, and spurred by rank and file pressure and a tight labour market, wages shot ahead in the early 1970s; the result was higher inflation, reduced profits and investment and, in conjunction with higher social spending, balance of payments problems and burgeoning signs of fiscal crisis. The DGB's *Aktionsprogramme* of 1972 featured a larger role for *Mitbestimmung*, the creation of an economic and social council, the importance of the quality of work-life, and was uttered in an altogether more militant and assertive vernacular. The unions and the new left were able to work together on the need for investment programmes, in opposition to rearmament and against the Emergency Laws of May 1968.[62]

The irony is that the two main programmatic aims rising from this 'great mobilization' of the late 1960s and early 1970s – the extension of co-determination and the improvement of the quality of work-life – may have had the effect of fragmenting German industrial relations and undermining the power of the national unions. The extension of co-determination would lead in this direction because it has consolidated trade union power on an enterprise level which has been separate from, and often at odds with, national branch unions. Further, such company-union power had been primarily effective in the very large firms of the 'primacy labour market' and most of all in the *manpower policies* of these firms. Here they have erected important protections against redundancies which have helped create a safe and insulated labour market in the large dynamic firms. This would tend to promote, *ceteris paribus*, identification by workers with the firm at the expense of the national union.[63]

'Economic Democracy' has been a goal of German trade unions since the middle 1920s. The idea was that co-determination would be instituted at all levels: from workplace to enterprise to industrial branch; from local chambers of commerce to a national economic and social council. The initial co-determination legislation in the Federal Republic was the enabling (for unions) Coal and Steel Co-determination Law of 1951 which provided for full parity of workers' representatives on supervisory boards in the industries. The law also provided for a labour director on the management board in these sectors, over whose appointment worker representatives would have effective veto power. The main effect of this law has been to ensconce trade union power at an enterprise level. The labour directors have been generally either former works council chairmen or full-time trade union officials. They have been able thus to carry out recruitment policies which enforce a *de facto* closed shop in coal and steel and which have in turn ensured unusually high levels of trade-union dominance in the sector's *Betriebsräte* (works councils). The labour director is given statutory power in all manpower and personnel matters. He or she has worked closely with works councils and has encouraged more important contacts between management boards and works councils *prior* to supervisory board meetings, which has resulted in an enhanced place for manpower policy in the framework of company decisions. This has been important in protecting those already employed in these declining sectors against redundancies. It has resulted, however – as the report of a 1970 investigating commission showed – in an identification of the union with the efficiency of their company.[64]

The 1952 Works Constitution Act was constraining legislation, because the parity principle of worker representatives in coal and steel was discarded so that only one-third of supervisory board members in large firms in other sectors to be drawn from workers' representatives. But the trade unions, where they were strong, were able to use the works councils, also created in the legislation, to their advantage. First, councils became *de facto* union bodies in workplaces of high organizational density. Second, though bargaining and strikes were precluded as council functions, in fact important wage-drift occurred as a result of council pressure, and more restricted forms of industrial action were pursued in the workplace. Third, the councils gave the German unions – which like the French and Italian unions (and unlike Swedish, American and British unions) had previously been centred in local branches outside of the workplace – a shopfloor presence. Finally, councils (much more than co-determined supervisory boards) were the vehicle of a union role enhanced well beyond statutory provisions – which was especially important in manpower policy – in the 1950s and 1960s.[65]

The 1972 and 1976 co-determination legislation resulted from the 'great mobilization' of the late 1960s and early 1970s. Key here was not so much the 1976 Act extending worker rights on supervisory boards which has received so much attention from commentators, but the 1972 recasting of the Works Constitution Act. The 1976 legislation gave to large heavily-unionized firms in all sectors a similar profile to what we have just described was earlier established in coal and steel. Two central provisions of the 1972 Act contributed more fundamentally to the disorganization of German industrial relations. The first was the creation of central, *enterprise* works councils. This created a partner in enterprise co-management which could come to important decisions with the management board before supervisory board (and enterprise council chairmen often double as supervisory board vice-chairmen) meetings. The second was an extension of council (and especially enterprise council) competence in the area of manpower policy. Now councils had co-determination power on all matters of labour-time; on the engagement, grading and transfer of personnel; and they had the legal right to demand that internal candidates would be given priority consideration for vacancies. One result of this has paradoxically been an increase in management's 'right to manage', in as much (similarly to coal and steel) as union gains in a protected internal labour market have been traded for increased managerial flexibility in the use of that labour-power which has been protected. There has also been increased identification with company prosperity by leading enterprise council trade unionists. The latter have become independent powers in national branch union politics and are potentially in a position to outmanoeuvre their national branch colleagues who sit on company supervisory boards because of their already accumulated knowledge/power as works council chairpersons. All this has disorganizing potential for German capitalism, not just in the fragmentation of union power residing in the national branch and on the company level, but through the establishment of a relatively safe and protected primary labour market reinforcing tendencies towards labour-market dualism.[66]

The 1984 struggles over reduced labour-time (the 7-week strike led to the loss of 5.4 million workdays, more than the total for any previous *year* in the Federal Republic's history), which must be seen in the context of a decade-old DGB concern for the quality of work-life, have important implications for organizational fragmentation. Historical union struggles for the reduction of the working week had been legitimated through the benefits that individual strikers could receive in terms of reduced strains on the individual of the labour process. In contrast, the 1978 and 1984 metalworkers' action had as their ultimate aim a 'public good', i.e. the reduction of unemployment. In this, employed metalworkers were engaged in collective action for the benefit of a third party, the unemployed. The question was how could individual metalworkers, and their collective organization, IG Metall, avoid paying the costs, so not ending as 'suckers' in a game in which the unemployed figured as 'free riders'. For metalworkers any benefits that might be reaped through the tighter labour market that reduced hours could create were easily outweighed by costs of wage loss, the strike action itself, and intensification and compression of work. To motivate action the instrumentally rational calculus of costs and benefits had to be mitigated by normative legitimations of commitment to the unemployed and, later and more effectively, in the face of concerted employer attacks, of loyalty to the union.[67]

The settlement of the strike involved a trade-off in which normal weekly hours were set at 38.5 with full compensation for the 3.5 million workers in metallurgy; this was followed by a comparable contract in the printing industry. The employers for their part achieved gains, in that wage bargaining was precluded until 1986, but more importantly in the gaining of flexibility in work-time scheduling. While it is not clear that the reduction in work time will in fact have any effect on unemployment, it is apparent that the flexible scheduling will have a further disorganizing effect, in terms of reducing central (i.e. national branch union) power in the regulation of labour markets. Employers can now flexibly schedule work weeks from 37 to 40 hours with workers receiving no extra compensation for working more than 38.5 hours. Such flexible scheduling in the off-season will surely compromise the agreement's employment-creating effects. At worst, this is an increase of unilateral power of capital as a collective actor; at best, in large, strongly unionized firms, factory councils will share with employers in the regulation of work time. In both cases, the consequences would seem to be a loss of central regulative powers and increased fragmentation for IG Metall.[68]

The 1984 IG Metall action, in conjunction with the reflourishing of the social movements since the end of the 1970s, could be seen in terms of the beginnings of a restructured and resurgent political culture of the left. But in fact, from even the early 1970s up until the present, it has been the right which has been making most of the running in the disorganization of German capitalism. From the point of view of employers and the state, Concerted Action and its accompanying social-Keynesianism began to be increasingly seen as a mistake. In particular, the unions were not complying with their portion of the implicit *quid pro quo*. Nominal wage rises which had only exceeded 9 per cent in two of 20 years in the 1950s and 1960s were over 9 per cent for six years in *succession* from 1969 to 1974. Partly in consequence, inflation rose to a high of 7 per cent in 1974 and the current account surplus fell by 9 million marks from 1968 to 1972. Government response was marked by the exit of Concerted Action architect, Karl Schiller, as Economic Minister after the 1972 elections and the rise to prominence of Helmut Schmidt as Finance Minister. Schmidt – in agreement with business and academic circles which, disenchanted with Keynesianism, advocated policies of monetary manipulation, the freeing of exchange rates and a calculated deafness to incomes policies and unemployment – effected his first spending cuts in early 1973. These were paralleled by the much more strenuous efforts of the Bundesbank which, from the summer of 1974, began to set interest rates at quite high levels and fix restrictive annual targets for the increase in supply of central bank money. The trade union response was to moderate wage demands, and nominal wage rises have indeed been low from 1975 through 1984/85. Tight government fiscal policies have forced unions to shift action (hence additional drift away from the neo-corporatist framework) from politics to the labour market, whose 'looseness' in conjunction with employer aggression has resulted in a number of defeats. Unemployment did decrease marginally during the mild boom of 1976–9, but the second oil crisis, along with restrictive fiscal policy, by Social Democrats and Christian Democrats from 1982, and technological change, forced unemployment upwards from 3.8 per cent in 1980 to 8 per cent in summer 1985.[69]

Employers, for their part, began an offensive against 'labour-market rigidities' at least from 1976, whose effects have been eminently disorganizing. First, a series of offensive lockouts were initiated, as capital's labour-market position improved; the upshot was June 1980 legislation against such tactics. Simultaneously the employers' association launched a lawsuit questioning the constitutionality of the 1976 Co-determination Law. Employers argued that workers had achieved *de facto* parity of decision-making power in the 1972 Works Constitution Act and that the extension of workers' rights promised by the 1976 Law ran counter to what they interpreted as Federal Republic constitutional provisions guaranteeing the rights of private property. The Federal Constitutional Court ruled that the 1976 legislation was indeed in keeping with the constitution. The employers' lawsuit, however, provoked a DGB walkout from Concerted Action talks, which never have been reconvened, and whose end, there is reason to believe, was applauded by employers. A final employers' initiative to override the neo-corporatist regulation of firms has been the encouragement of employee equity participation schemes. Spurred partly by a 20-year decline in the availability of equity capital in capital markets, the employers' federation – with support from the white-collar *Deutsche Angestellten Gewerkschaft* (DAG) and the textile union – have put not insubstantial resources into making such schemes attractive. For a number of reasons there was little take-up of employee share ownership until 1984. At this point the CDU–Free Democrat coalition government passed legislation providing that employees would pay no income tax on 50 per cent of securities held in their employers' firm and that employers would be granted tax deductions for loans to employees to buy securities.[70]

Despite this myriad of pressures promoting fragmentation, the German trade union movement had managed, it seemed clear by the end of 1986, to preserve a remarkable degree of strength and unity. The similarities with Sweden are striking to the observer. While most advanced capitalist countries have experienced recent significant dips in union density, Swedish union density has held constant, and German density has in fact increased. West Germany has equally not felt the painful division of interests between male, skilled, private-sector, 'primary labour market' workers and a largely feminine and unskilled public sector, as have a number of other western countries, including Sweden and especially Britain. In autumn 1986, Franz Steinkuhler, probably the most clear-sighted and modernizing left-wing union leader in Western Europe, acceded to the leadership of IG Metall, the world's largest union. Despite a parallel process of polarization now taking place on West Germany's increasingly energetic right, the trade union movement seems to be well placed as a force to be reckoned with in West Germany's particular brand of disorganizing capitalism. The 1984 strike for reduced labour-time – which propelled its Stuttgart based leader, Steinkuhler into national prominence – seems to have been of a scope of significance not incomparable to the British miners' strike of 1984–5. In the German case the trade union movement has come out strengthened and unified, in the British case, weakened and splintered. The point is that in Germany as in Sweden, primary labour market workers (IG Metall, Swedish Metall) were willing to sacrifice sectional interests for a much more general interest. Only where this is possible can labour survive and thrive as an effective collective actor in the era of disorganized capitalism.

FRANCE: LABOUR EXCLUDED

Organization of the French state arrived later than in other nations. It came on to the political agenda in the 1930s, but it was implemented only under the German occupation during the Vichy regime. The political form here was a mixture of 'statism' and corporatism which excluded labour. Following the war, after a brief flirtation with tripartite corporatism (state, capital and labour), the earlier 'state corporatism', was reasserted from 1947 until the end of the 1960s. At this point French capitalism began to disorganize at the bottom and the top, in civil society and the state, virtually simultaneously. At the bottom, the social movements entered upon the scene, and the labour movement became more genuinely pluralist with the birth and thriving of the *Confédération française démocratique du travail* (CFDT), whose decentralizing and classless ideology presented the union federation as one among several social movements. At the top, planning became de-emphasized in favour of an export-oriented meso-economic sector, the result of whose dualism and national economic dislocation led to the advent of the crisis of France's Keynesian welfare state beginning with the Barre government's austerity measures in the latter half of the 1970s. The socialist accession to power in 1981 yielded the possibility of a gradualist transition to socialism via a quasi-corporatist bargain with the main trade unions. However, the pre-eminently cross-class, hence eminently disorganized capitalist, basis of Mitterrand's support made such a solution untenable.

During the Second World War the basic groundwork for French post-war planning was laid. In particular, August 1940 legislation created the framework of the Vichy industrial structure, which was a mixture of (foreign) statism, with up to 50 per cent of total manufacturing output of the occupied zone delivered to Germany, combined with a corporatism which systematically excluded labour. The basic corporate unit was the *Comité d'Organisation* which replaced pre-existing employers' groups. These proposed price schedules for different industries, regulated competition and set wages. Other Vichy 'innovations' involved the tightening of state control over the banks and substantial increases in the ratio of investment to national income.[71]

After the war the planning ideal was particularly developed by Jean Monnet, who envisaged a corporatist structure involving the state, capital and labour. The nationalizations of 1946 (electric power and gas in March, and insurance and coal in April) were carried out in a framework advocating tripartite control. Monnet's Plan of 1946 provided for 18 sectoral 'Modernization Commissions', with labour representation. In addition, the national Planning Council had substantial labour representation. Indeed, all interest groups on the latter, including the *Confédération Générale du Travail* (CGT), approved of the plan, which was submitted to the Council in November, 1946. However, in the end, the spectre of Marshall Aid from the Americans, and rank and file demands for wage rises, led the Communists to leave government and the CGT to terminate tripartism in 1947.[72]

The first plan, effective from 1946 to 1952, was situated in the general framework of the Vichy-initiated organized capitalist political economy. Its main departures from Vichy's institutional arrangements were that capital's corporate bodies, the Modernization Commissions, took on more genuinely intermediating functions; the innovation of targets for six sectors, namely, coal, steel, electricity, transport, cement, farm machinery; its strategic use of the nationalized industries; and the fact that the *Commissariat Général du Plan* was a body separate from government ministries and hence more dependent on persuasion through argument than on imperative co-ordination. Although it is arguable that the second plan (1954–7) represented an increase in organization – in as much as now targets were cited for 17 sectors – it was a type of organization in which the role of capital, in comparison to the state and labour, was strongly enhanced. The vestiges of labour participation were eliminated, as in the early 1950s the tripartite boards of nationalized industries gave day-to-day operations over to management. The very emphasis on targets for an expanded number of sectors meant a less central place for the nationalized industries; so did the new focus on consumer goods production, international competitiveness, and the shifting of iron and coal to a place under the supranational authority of the Jean Monnet-headed European Coal and Iron Community. Finally, subsidies from the French state and aid from foreign states played a qualitatively diminished role.[73]

Thus the French polity from 1948 until the late 1960s was characterized by a mixture of statism and corporatism, whose operating rules effectively excluded labour from the 'national consensus'. The end of the 1960s signalled a crisis of French organized capitalism which transformed the right and the left of the French polity. On the one hand, there were a series of changes in which the right became much less the representative of national interests and instead became more visibly the representative of sectional and class interests. This was first a question of parliamentary and electoral politics. Whereas de Gaulle as President was cast in the role of leader of the French people, his successor Georges Pompidou presided just as much over the organization of the conservative parliamentary majority. At the same time, this majority's electoral basis shifted from the cross-class, and urban as well as rural, appeal of Gaullism to a more rural and pronouncedly middle-class basis. This political/sociological change was paralleled in the decline of the 'national' quality of economic policy.[74] French planning, with its emphasis on the interarticulation of domestic industrial sectors, assumed and promoted an integrated *national* economy. From the end of the 1960s, due to increased import-penetration and largely through the agency of an increasingly 'monetarist' Finance Ministry, French planning went into decline. Focus in plans was now no longer on interarticulation of domestic industry, but on the promotion of rapid modernization of export-oriented sectors. Thus more selective and conjunctural policies came to replace the importance of targets, input–output projections and the role of nationalized industries.

While the right was becoming somehow less national and more class based, the left in the latter half of the 1960s was undergoing an opposite process, becoming more national and less class based. This is the great paradox of the French left, a logic which was misread by the French Communist Party and brilliantly read by François Mitterrand. What we mean is that, in order to once again become a national political force, the left had partly to separate itself from the working class. Disorganization on the left was happening so fast during the heady days of the late 1960s that few – exceptions were Alain Touraine and Serge Mallet – had any idea of how to chart or analyse political developments. The following events are not just indicators of 'pluralism' or 'militancy' but also of disorganization:

1 The very sudden rise of the new social movements.
2 The fact that the general strike of 1968 started as a grass-roots affair and was touched off by a non-class issue, the *lutte étudiante* (students' struggle).
3 The rise of the union federation, the CFDT, especially from 1968 as a formidable force on the industrial left alongside the CGT; an organization with a decentralizing *autogestion* (workers' control) ideology; a movement with a self-conception which paralleled the non-proletarian social movements and a 'new working-class' ideology.
4 The transmogrification of French socialism, which was at the same time (a) a shift to the left: whereby a party whose identity was formed around the discourse of national consensus *against* an excluded (largely communist) left was replaced by a party which joined forces with this excluded left and simultaneously transformed it, turned it into a national force and came to dominate it; and (b) a shift away from the former working-class base: reflected in the declining proportion of working-class vote among the party's electorate; the declining proportion of parliamentary deputies, local councillors and party militants who were manual workers; and the change in party doctrine at the end of the 1960s (marked by the ascendancy of Mitterrand, a figure never identified with the working-class left) and symbolized by the rechristening of the old *Section française de l'Internationale ouvrière* (SFIO) as *Parti socialiste* in 1969.[75]

In retrospect, perhaps the most distinctive characteristic of the great working-class mobilization in France of the late 1960s was its very brevity. In Britain, this mobilization spanned the mid-1960s to the mid-1970s; in Italy it spanned the hot summer of 1969 to the mid-1970s. In both Britain and Italy, it involved a significant devolution of trade union power to shopfloor organization and resulted in the largest percentage increases in the West in union density. In France, the mobilization by some accounts could be reckoned in weeks; decentralization remained as not much more than ideology (though this alone is significant); and increases in membership were comparatively negligible. Both the CGT and CFDT remained confederations virtually unparalleled in the West for their centralization of decision-making power, and the 'autogestion' which spread from the latter to the former was not an immediate demand, but a vague programme for implementation under conditions of socialism.[76] It was the very centralization of the two confederations upon which the 1968 *Accords de Grenelle* were contingent. The CGT here was the main interlocutor for labour. What was won at Grenelle included both organizational gains for the CGT (and CFDT) unions and a substantive shift of resources towards labour. The main organizational gains were in the extension, or more accurately the initial *de jure* establishment, of union rights in the factory, and more important, a move towards providing left-wing unions with the same level of state subsidy as conservative unions; by the mid-1970s, the CGT indeed drew 20 per cent of its income from state subsidies. Gains for workers included a raising of the minimum wage, a shortened working week, wage concessions and a solidifying of social legislation. Most of these concessions were won not from the state, but from the employers' federation (CNPF), to which the state attributed power to make concessions which were forbidden by their confederational statutes. The *quid pro quo* here, which may have played no small role in laying a basis for rapid French economic growth from 1969 to 1974, included the establishment of a moderate profile by the CGT and the tacit concession of the 'right to modernize' to employers.[77]

If 1968–73 were years of offensive for an increasingly nationalized union movement, then 1974–8 were years of defensive centralization. CGT strategy in the former half-decade was to wring concessions from the CNPF and the state on a national level. During 1974–8 the renewed 'unity of action' of the CGT and CFDT was similarly on a national scale, and entailed the mobilization of union resources for a series of 'days of action' whose ultimate goal was political mobilization for a left victory in the legislative elections of 1978. The accession to office of the West's first avowedly monetarist head of government, Raymond Barre, in 1976 did result in the withdrawal of subsidies from declining sectors. The still relatively formidable and unified union movement was able to keep membership losses minimal and put rather strict limits on Barre's attempts at austerity in social spending.

The left's defeat at the polls in 1978 changed all this. Employers, who had for a decade at least visibly encouraged responsible bargaining, did not seem to want to bargain at all and launched an offensive against the unions. Membership dropped precipitously: by one account the CGT lost 20–25 per cent and the CFDT 12–15 per cent of their members from 1977 to 1981.[78] Social spending cuts were substantial in more than one area.[79] The split in the political left from 1977, which played a considerable role in the electoral defeat, was replicated in different and more complex terms in the labour movement. The unity of action for four years, which like the first confederational alliance of 1964–8 was more beneficial to the CGT than the CFDT, was effectively ended by the latter's 'recentrage' policy enunciated in January 1978. What recentrage meant was a shift away from the close identification with political parties of past years. It was instead an attempt to build union power on the shopfloor and to 'mobilize the base'; a move towards establishing localized collective bargaining frameworks; and more generally a model in which the confederation would rely more on 'economic' than 'ideological' incentives to attract membership and commitment. Though there was a left, socialist and autogestionnaire interpretation of recentrage with which CFDT leader, Edmond Maire, was initially identified, the more conservative reading of the policy, as a contractualism which harked back to the days prior to the confederation's 1966 conversion to principled opposition to capitalism, came to predominate by the end of the decade. The problem was that by 1978 employers were not in the slightest interested in 'contractualism' with the CFDT, preferring to bargain with the much more straighforwardly conservative *Force ouvrière* (FO), or better with no one at all.[80]

At the same time, changes were taking place within the CGT. An important section of the confederation at the November 1978 Congress, which became identified as 'proposition force', also advocated a shift towards economic incentives, and a new focus on labour-market struggles. These struggles would be not just for wages but also for objectives regarding firm and sector investment policies. In the face of an expected continuation of right-wing rule, the plea was for an interventionist unionism with objectives of broader social reform and the shaping of state investment plans. The proposition force group led a quite successful mobilization at the beginning of 1979 around their alternative plan for the restructuring of the steel industry. But the orthodox Communist 'opposition force' tendency took over control of the confederation's March 1979 march on Paris, over-politicized the action and destroyed the steel-workers' bargaining position which had been based on the realistic proposition force plan. By 1980 it was clear that the orthodox and maximalist opposition force grouping had gained the upper hand.[81]

We are not, like many who think that the inevitable future is monetarist, necessarily pessimistic about the medium and long-term prospects for progressive social change in disorganized capitalism. We think, however, that socialist governments will rule in less close connection with trade union movements than in the past and will need more consciously to aggregate the interests of the social movements and the public-sector middle class. They will also need to produce policies which are less centralist and homogenizing than previously and be more attuned to the differences of particular constituencies and to individual, local and group autonomy more generally. In this context, the French experience, especially of 1981–3, is of especial importance. In particular it seems that whatever French 'transition' to socialism took place in 1981–3 proceeded via a rather small level of corporatist and trade union mediation, and that unions played a less important role as a corporate body, especially in their social control functions, than was the case in the years immediately after the Second World War.

Those who believe that the unions have played a central role in regard to the Socialist government have pointed out that CFDT leaders have been given prominent positions in more than one government department and that labour leaders' access to information and to civil servants increased from 1982.[82] They also have pointed to the new workplace legislation brought in by Jean Auroux, Minister of Labour. Yet this interpretation,especially one emphasizing the importance of a corporatist bias, is at best problematic. First, Mitterrand quite rightly saw the CGT as a more important actor in regard to social control problems than the CFDT; this was the crucial incentive for including Communist ministers in government. Any promotion of the organizational interests of the CFDT would not have been for 'corporatist' social-control reasons, but with the objective of mobilization of larger sectors of wage workers. Strike rates were indeed uncharacteristically low from 1981 to 1983, but so they were in 1980 under right-wing rule.[83]

Equally, for corporatism to be effective, there has to be willingness on the side of union leaders; yet the results of a 1982 survey showed that union leaders did not want 'to claim frequent contacts with government officials because of fears of accusations of collaboration with government'.[84]

Even the Avroux reforms are not the unmitigated blessing to trade union organization that they, *prima facie*, seem to be. The August 1982 legislation was clearly set in the context of, and legitimated by, its facilitation of techno-logical change. Positive gains included legal protection and extended paid hours to carry out union business for trade union delegates; access for the latter to company information; obligatory annual negotiations for companies on wages, and work conditions; and the formation of *groupes d'expression* (GE) for work units. On the negative side of the balance the obligatory negotia-tions and establishment of *groups d'expression* – whose competence extended to all matters relating to shop operation, including the possible consequences of firm investment on the organization and conditions of work – were only incumbent on companies of 200 or more employees. Moreover, there was no prescription that the annual negotiations should end in a collective agreement. Most important was that there was no provision for union representation on the *groupes d'expression*. Whether the representative of a GE would be a trade unionist or a supervisor depended on the balance of shopfloor power.

Management had the cards stacked in their favour here. They had previous experience in the employers' offensive begun at the end of 1977 with the paternalist strategy of substituting supervisors for union delegates in grievance procedures, and straight away were successful in enrolling FO supervisors as representatives to preclude the possibility of leadership from CGT or CFDT. In the latter two centrals there was little grass-roots pressure for shopfloor democracy, and with numbers of CFDT militants seduced into devoting their time to Socialist politics, little encouragement from confederation headquarters and militants to struggle over representation in the GE.[85] Even where the Auroux laws might lead to more pervasive union participation, the outcome could well be the development of company identification among workers and of 'company unionism'. By the end of 1986, studies had shown only partial success (for workers) in the operation of *groupes d'expression*; even in some strongly unionized plants, workers have been suspicious of management co-optation of the groups. In a similar vein to West Germany, central agreements and legislation on reduced work time of the early 1980s seem to have had the effect of strengthening the employers' hands in the determination of 'more flexible' hours of work in individual enterprises.

Not only, though, was corporatism impossible, but more important for the left, national economic integration (one of corporatism's key preconditions) also seemed excluded from the agenda. The Socialists were self-consciously swimming against the international economic tide when, upon their accession to power, they decided to pursue Keynesian budgetary and national economic integration policies. This was the logic which contextualized the nationalizations, the raising of the minimum wage, the creation of public-sector jobs and the increases in social spending (especially on family allowances) that marked the first months of Socialist power. However, balance of payments difficulties, despite successive devaluations of the franc and the opposition of the employers' federation, whom the Socialists at first attempted to isolate and then found they could not work without, were causing unbearable strains. Before the end of 1981, Finance Minister Jacques Delors and left-wing Socialist Research and Industry Minister, Jean-Pierre Chevènement, were calling for a pause in reforms. The summer of 1982 was marked by a four-month wage and price freeze and the replacement of big spending social services minister, Nicole Questiaux. Chevènement's replacement in 1983 by budget-conscious Laurent Fabius (later to become prime minister), and the departure of the Communists from government marked the definitive end of the national integration option.[86]

The problem precluding further transition towards socialism was not, however, simply that of international economic dislocation. Also important were the situation of working-class and social-movement grass roots on which any such transition depends: certain social movements, obviously that of the students, had entered into decline, while the trade union grass roots were becoming demobilized. The split in the left and reStalinization of the

Communist Party of 1977–8 meant the exit from both Communist and Socialist ranks of large numbers of public-sector service class militants and the political disillusionment of working-class activitists. The service class, with their important ideological role *vis-à-vis* the public sector, seemed to have deserted both Marxism and the left.[87]

Because of the systematic exclusion of labour from the polity; because of the ideological cast of trade unions; because of a long-standing history of plural unionism at unusually low levels of union density – France diverged widely from the type of neo-corporatism experienced in Sweden and Germany. Yet the same basic disorganizing process of the politics of industrial relations that has taken place elsewhere has also taken place in France – only with somewhat different effects. In France, as elsewhere, the rise of the new social movements paralleled the great mobilization of the late 1960s and early 1970s. Internationalization and the economic crisis beginning in the mid-1970s have hampered the national solutions of a trade union movement – solutions which have not been dissimilar to elsewhere, except that low union density and plural unionism made things even with the potentially very favourable Mitterrand administration even more difficult than elsewhere. The polarization of industrial workers against white-collar workers has been repeated in France, with the mainly white-collar and conservative *Force ouvrière* reinforcing its position in the face of the decline of the two mainly manual-worker confederations – the membership loss of the CFDT and especially of the CGT. Finally, trade union and left responses to the crisis, i.e. industrial democracy and reduced labour time, may have, as in Germany, reinforced the disorganization process. That is, they may be leading potentially to the promotion of company unionism, and further attenuating the power of national-level unions.

BRITAIN: CAPITALISM'S WEAKEST LINK

The politics of British industrial relations has disorganized sooner, more abruptly and more profoundly than in other European nations. Britain's characteristically *organized* capitalist system of industrial relations, based on bargaining at the national-union, or 'industry', level came under heavy fire as the loci of industrial relations shifted, first to the shopfloor; then, in response to this and balance of payments crises, to the more centralized level of the state and the Trade Union Congress (TUC); and finally to the level of the individual enterprise. The British peculiarity lay in the fact that the corporatism entailed by the transfer of power to the state and the TUC was not as elsewhere a normal state of affairs for organized capitalism, but was an attempted solution to an already profoundly disorganizing patterning of British capitalism. That British neo-corporatism has been such a failure is largely due to its attempted introduction at a time when its preconditions (especially the existence of an importantly 'national' economy and of centralized trade unions) were clearly being undermined. With the breakup of the old 'mode of regulation', two accumulation strategies joined combat. Spurred by the 'second shop stewards movement' and the wave of middle-class radicalism, the trade union and Labour Party left turned, as elsewhere, to micro-economic strategies to stem the investment crisis. The right, especially with the rise of Thatcherism, pursued strategies which exacerbated the growth of dualism in the labour market and the labour movement and thus the breakup of organized capitalism. An important irony here is that the left mobilization of the 1960s indirectly, yet effectively led to an extension of company bargaining in the private sector whose result has been in part to undermine class solidarity and the unity of the trade union movement.

Undermining the organized capitalist consensus: from unofficial strikes to public-sector militancy

The traditional organized capitalist system of national branch bargaining began in the inter-war period in Britain. This was made possible with the defeat of the first shop stewards movement from the early 1920 through a combination of state repression, national union and TUC incorporation, and unfavourable labour markets. A series of unofficial strikes hit the mining industry in the 1950s leading to the elimination of piece-work and the effective centralization of bargaining in mining from 1958. Yet industry-level bargaining, which had been encouraged by government during the Second World War, continued to dominate much of the best of UK manufacturing through to the middle 1960s. Strike rates outside mining remained relatively low, and failures to reach agreements normally led to mediation and conciliation, often through the Ministry of Labour.

From the middle 1960s, however, the situation was rapidly transformed. Between 1963 and 1970 strike rates in most sectors outside of mining and shipbuilding more than doubled, the majority of these recorded as unofficial strikes. The key sectors were transport equipment and engineering more generally, the wildcat strikes becoming larger and longer and affecting previously peaceful sectors as the decade progressed. Concomitantly the number of shop stewards multiplied – from an estimated 90,000 in 1961 to over 250,000 in 1978.[88]

The initiatives of the Labour government between 1964 and 1970 were brought about by characteristically disorganizing processes, the decentralization and intensification of industrial conflict and economic internationalization reinforcing the comparative weakness of Britain's economy, and exacerbating recurrent balance of payments deficits. Government voluntary and then statutory incomes policies followed by attempted industrial relations legislation were an attempt to remedy these, as well as an attempt to shore up the competitiveness of British exports through indicatively-planned modernization. Internationalization and fragmented industrial conflict were responsible for the breakdown of the 1960s initiatives. Balance of payments problems in the summer of 1965 led to Labour's deflationary policies which undermined any possibilities of planned and modernized growth. The trade union movement, deprived of the growth and social-spending sweeteners made impossible by such restrictive fiscal policy, had little incentive to enforce incomes policies. In the event, the 1968–9 wave of unofficial strikes ended any chances of corporatist success.[89]

As in Sweden and Germany, the organized capitalist consensus was challenged from the left, not just through decentralized militancy, but through trade union initiatives in micro-economic planning. Although the TUC was thrust into a political role during the 1960s on incomes policies and reiterated attempts in tripartite planning for growth and modernization, they did not begin to take the *initiative* in such a role until the very end of the decade. This was partly in response to a transformed self-conception due to the role that political parties and the state had cast them in; and partly due to the coercive, statist and anti-union direction that seemed to unfold from the logic of such policies, namely, restrictive industrial relations legislation. What the Labour Party had promised in *In Place of Strife* in 1969, mainly the placing of legal restrictions on unofficial strikes, the Conservatives delivered in 1971. To the supremely decentralized British trade union movement – though not at all dissimilar legislation has been passed in Sweden in 1928, the USA in 1947 and West Germany in 1952 – such legal regulation appeared draconian. Thus the TUC acted to nullify its introduction by the Conservatives in 1971, and attempted to ensure, through amplification of its political role, that Labour could not again act in such independence of its trade union wing.[90]

The TUC had begun publishing the annual *Economic Review* in 1968, and in the Reviews of 1972 and 1973 they called for the creation of a new public investment board. The February 1973 document published by the Liaison Committee of the TUC and the Labour Party's left-dominated National Executive Committee was probably the definitive step in the direction of what was to be the 'social contract' of the TUC with the Labour government that came to power in 1974. The document proposed an extension of nationalizations; the alleviation of regional disparities; union participation in economic planning on all levels; and industrial democracy, with worker representatives on their boards, in firms. The 'corporatism' that the social contract promised was corporatism indeed with a difference. First, it was initiated – unlike previous British corporatisms – not by the government, but by the TUC. Second, it promised as a *quid pro quo* not just the characteristically corporatist substantive gains for the labour movement, but a particularly enhanced *procedural* role for the unions. Thus the term social contract itself evokes an imagery, and partly a reality, in which the Labour Party was bound in advance by the unions. Third, the social contract's *original* 'contract' entailed hardly a *quid pro quo*, at least on the union side, at all; the issue of a voluntary incomes policy only came to the fore in 1975, a year after the contract was in operation.[91]

The TUC, perhaps as much from a sense of responsibility to the nation in the face of unprecedented inflation as anything else, did indeed carry out an incomes policy. The government, as is well known, with the exception of enabling industrial relations legislation, violated the contract in its other essential components. Partly in response to this, by 1977 the majority of active opinion inside the TUC came to accept the 'alternative economic strategy', which rejected incomes policies, and proposed price controls, a wealth tax, and reduced defence spending as alternative anti-inflationary fiscal policies. The importance of public investment through the National Enterprise Board was again thematized in conjunction with compulsory planning agreements and import controls. The only innovation added to this policy mix by the TUC in the first half of the 1980s (staggered and disoriented by unemployment and a series of resounding setbacks in industrial conflicts) were some proposals on reductions of labour-time. Now the TUC has come to terms with the unlikelihood of reducing unemployment through increased advanced-technology investment. Equally, the position on voluntary incomes policies, given a future Labour government, had, at the time of writing partly through the very paucity of recent discussion been left rather ambiguous.[92]

In the 1960s corporatism was formulated as a response to shopfloor militancy; it was undermined by governments who were unable to deliver their half of the entailed *quid pro quo* because of import-penetration and trade unions who were unable to deliver their side of the bargain because of continued unofficial industrial action. Corporatism in the 1970s, on the other hand, was formulated as a response to the activity of newly mobilized public-sector unions; it was undermined on the government side in response to further internationalization, on the union side by the activity of these same public-sector unions. The 1960s and 1970s saw the creation at an accelerated rate of massive numbers of public-sector employees who especially in the seventies and eighties have created their own specific and powerful interest organizations. At the same time, the rise of the 'export imperative' has led governments to launch attacks on this public sector in conjunction with their equally well-organized colleagues in the declining industrial branches. Thus in Britain from the 1970s, as in Sweden of the 1980s, public-sector unions came to assume centre stage. Though most of the public-sector unions had been established from the 1950s, membership multiplied during the 1960s and 1970s. Most important here was the growth of the two large local government unions; the National Union of Public Employees (NUPE) (mostly non-skilled manual workers) from 200,000 in 1960 to 699,000 in 1980; and the National and Local Government Officers Association (NALGO) (white collar) from 274,000 in 1960 to 782,000 in 1980. The other big public-sector growth area was in the health services, where union membership increased from 370,000 in 1968 to 1,318,000 in 1979; here – unlike local government – change was accounted for not just by increased employment, but by large increments in union density from 38 per cent in 1968 to 74 per cent in 1979.[93]

The Labour government in the latter half of the 1960s, linking wage claims of the expanded public sector with inflation and balance of trade problems, led an attack on the principle of 'comparability' in the determination of public-sector wages. Public-sector pay had already fallen relative to the private sector from the beginning of the decade due to wage-drift resulting from the decentralization of bargaining in the private sector, and the Labour government's policies furthered this trend. The Conservative government from 1970 reinforced such strategies, which along with the Industrial Relations Act, were conceived as part of the neo-*liberal* renaissance among Tories which began in the middle 1960s. The idea was to extend the neo-liberal, anti-corporatist productivity–bargaining ethos of the Donovan Report (see below) to the public sector. Such were the recommendations of a series of government White Papers and reports of the National Board for Prices and Incomes from the late 1960s. These were influential in the sweeping 'rationalization' reforms of local government, the civil service and the health service of the late 1960s and early 1970s. The Heath government (1970–4) went further to make a virtue of 'taking on' the public-sector unions, propounding an 'n–1' pay formula which provided that each succeeding public-sector pay settlement should be lower than the previous one. The reaction was two waves of official public-sector strikes; the first from autumn 1970 to early 1972 involved local government workers and postal employees and culminated in a miners' strike (centralized bargaining had hurt their relative wages) which led to power cuts and a three-day working week. This strike convinced Prime Minister Heath of the necessity to institute a statutory incomes policy, whose decreed pay standstill led to another wage of public-sector strikes, in the gas industry, the National Health Service and among civil servants, again culminating in a miners' strike which this time led Heath to call a general election.[94]

Though 'comparability', as opposed to efficiency and 'productivity', principles had been putatively re-established during the years of the social contract, the voluntary incomes policies of 1975–8 did not prevent wage-drift from once again establishing marked disparities between private- and public-sector pay. Thus, after the firemen's strike at the end of 1978, early 1979 saw mass action in all four of the main public-sector non-manufacturing areas of employment – in local government, the civil service, the health service and by teachers. This was paralleled by public-sector political action, and especially NUPE, in 1975–8 on the National Steering Committee against public expenditure cuts. Though 'cash limits' enforced in regard to expenditure on local authorities, the National Health Service (NHS), the civil service and nationalized industries have been in effect since 1975, substantial real cuts in public-sector employment came only with the Thatcher administration in 1979. Once again, comparability confirmed in the 1982 Megaw Report was discredited as a concept. These 'cuts' were not just in planned growth and capital spending, but became absolute cuts; there was, for example, a 14 per cent decline in manual workers' jobs in the public sector between September 1979 and September 1981. Further, successful attacks on public-sector manufacturing jobs came in steel, where in 1980 alone 50,000 jobs disappeared, and throughout the period in mining.[95]

Central to post-1979 Conservative strategy have been the Employment Acts of 1980, 1982 and 1984. These were rather unusual in comparison with industrial relations legislation in the other countries being discussed here in that they did *not* attempt to control the shopfloor through the extension of national union power with respect to the workplace. Instead national unions and the labour movement in general were the object of attack.[96] The legislation was characteristically disorganized capitalist. The provisions on secondary picketing in the 1980 Act would tend to decentralize conflicts to the plant level, although this legislation was used in a rather different (and devious) way by Rupert Murdoch against the print unions in January 1987. The balloting provisions of 1984 were intended to have a similar atomizing function.

Towards company unionism?

The specific mode of operation of dualism in Britain has been the promotion of plant and company unionism at the expense of working-class power both on the very localized work-group level *and* on the very centralized and aggregating level of the national branch union and union confederation. The shift to plant and company-level bargaining is 'dualist' in so far as it is a result of, and in turn reinforces, the schism between dynamic private-sector export-oriented firms which bargain on a plant or company level, and the public sector, on the one hand, and most declining sector firms, on the other, which bargain on a national level. This dualism is characterized in the primary sector by identification with the firm instead of the wider labour movement; by the separation of the safe internal labour markets of such firms; by bonus schemes and wage-drift more generally which produces divergent interests between primary-sector workers and others; and by workers enjoying workplace trade union protection that is not enjoyed by other workers.

Multi-employer bargaining had begun in Britain at the beginning of organized capitalism; it arose in the compromise of employers with craft unions after the struggles in engineering in the 1890s. This system of multi-employer bargaining grew over the succeeding decades. Yet a large amount of pay determination was still decided at the immediate point of production. Nationally-negotiated contracts were not legally enforcable and were complemented by workplace bargaining – which took place in plant departments, work groups or, very often, for individual workers – that was carried out with foremen, line managers or rate-fixers.[97]

In the 1950s with tight labour markets a shop steward *movement* developed, unofficial strike rates began to soar and the extent of fragmented workplace bargaining, management sensed, was getting out of hand. From the end of the 1950s, then, *companies* began to take an interest in the industrial relations of their establishments, and began to appoint industrial relations specialists, whose objective was the centralization of the bargaining function at the *company* or at least the plant level. The preponderant existence of this second, informal and fragmented system of bargaining, was the central finding of the Donovan Commission, convened in 1963, which proposed not that bargaining be recentralized on a multi-employer level, but that workplace bargaining should become formalized. We should stress here that the Donovan proposals were anything but corporatist. Both the formalization of workplace bargaining, which was subsequently instituted, and the recommended introduction of productivity bargaining, which was not, would tend to relocate bargaining at the company or plant level. The logic of this is to undermine power in national unions and the TUC, and to further segment labour markets.[98]

Since the 1968 Donovan Report, formalization and centralization of workplace bargaining has indeed come about, primarily through procedural formalization and management's introduction of a new type of payment system. Procedural formalization in plants has increased by enormous proportions. A 1972 survey showed that some 50 per cent of establishments sampled had written workplace procedures, a figure that increased to about 80 per cent according to the 1978 Warwick study. Such formalization has been encouraged by the Trade Union and Labour Relations Act of 1975, in which it has often been a matter of an exchange of union acceptance of formal rules for managerial acceptance of the closed shop. Some formalized procedures have thus been the result of a workplace agreement between management and stewards; others – for example, regarding dismissals and health and safety regulations – have been largely set by 1970s legislation itself; still others have been unilaterally introduced by management. In each of these cases, though, rule formalization removes an area of norm determination from the sphere of workplace bargaining. Shop stewards are often cast into the roles of implementing procedures rather than bargaining. In this they have been aided by Labour's mid-1970s legislation which has provided for more working time-off as well as paid study-leave for stewards. The result was a four-fold increase in the number of full-time stewards from 1968 to 1978. Management has often aided them with the provision of offices, secretaries, photocopiers and so on.[99]

The restructuring of payment systems had had a similar effect. There has been an increase in payments by productivity, which has been carried out through moving away from the old practices of piece-work, 'measured daywork' and productivity bargaining. The last of these was abandoned by the middle 1970s, as it developed into little more than a method to get round government incomes policies. Piece-work, the old system, was the supremely fragmented system of wage payment in that wages were often set with worker, rate-fixer and steward on the spot at the level of the individual worker. The change has been to performance schemes in which standards are set not by piece but by time; to schemes in which traditional rate-fixing as well as the 'time–motion' men are replaced by rationalized work-study techniques: bonuses are then linked to specific levels of productivity and often profitability of a work group or department. More important, and in tandem with the pervasion of work-study, has been the adoption of job evaluation methods. It was estimated that in 1977 some 55 per cent of manual and 56 per cent of non-manuals in manufacturing establishments of 50 or more employees were covered by job evaluation schemes, and that the number of workplaces using such methods had increased by half since 1972. The point here is that by definition such schemes must cover, not the work group or department, but the entire bargaining unit; they were indeed found to be much less common in establishments which principally engaged in multi-employer bargaining. Job evaluation techniques, moreover, reduce the number of pay grades, facilitate the move of workers from one task to another without pay loss and have thus the general effect of shifting bargaining to the company or plant level.[100]

One of the most striking of the 1980 Workplace Survey findings was the existence of two *different* industrial relations systems in Britain. The survey found that more than half of British establishments (including non-manufacturing and the public sector) of more than 25 employees which engaged in collective bargaining did so principally at the national or regional levels. What this survey has done is point to the existence of a massive public sector engaged in national or regional bargaining existing side by side with a sector of smaller companies engaging in multi-employer bargaining. By contrast, there is a large enterprise export-oriented sector engaged in plant- or company-level bargaining and roughly coinciding with what we have been speaking of as the 'primary labour market'. A branch-by-branch breakdown of the 1980 data showed that national/regional (i.e. multi-employer) bargaining outside the public sector was predominant in branches – such as construction, textiles, printing, paper – with many small firms of low capital requirements. Company-level bargaining dominated in non-manufacturing and in industries such as chemicals, and automobiles, in which the shift at, for example, Leyland from plant to enterprise bargaining in 1981–2 functioned to roll back the shop steward movement with integrated production units. Plant bargaining predominated – and size of plant was an important variable here – in metal manufacture, mechanical and electrical engineering, shipbuilding, other vehicle manufacture and metal goods.[101] The 1984 Workplace Survey, published in 1986, showed a rather similar profile, though indicated a further trend towards company-level bargaining.

This importance of plant bargaining in primary labour-market firms in Britain underlines a differing logic of collective action for capital than for labour. In effect, what is taking place in these firms is that labour is bargaining at a plant level, while capital is engaging at an enterprise level. There are a number of advantages to capital to keep it this way. Capital can carry out company policy largely independent of union influence. Wages can be reduced by capital's argument that individual plants must be profitable and by adducing comparability – in poorer regions – with local labour markets. Plant bargaining, as opposed to company agreements, facilitates performance-related payment schemes. More important, the 1980 Workplace Survey showed that where enterprise bargaining was the most important level, plant management was less often consulted than enterprise management was where plant bargaining was the most important level. [102]

It seems, then, in the primary labour market Britain is moving closer to a model of more centralized single employer bargaining. It is likely that the shift to company bargaining will still further increase, because it is becoming the dominant form in Britain for private-sector non-manual workers who are rapidly expanding as a category relative to plant-bargaining manual workers. The single union, single status, strike-free deals promoted by employers in the newspaper industry, by Japanese and American firms in Britain in other sectors and by the electricians' union (EEPTU) are perhaps the most vivid manifestations of the movement in this direction.

The shift towards dualism, we have seen, in the 1970s took place through the formalization of plant-level (and company-level) industrial relations and concomitant decline in salience of the national branch and of class identification in primary labour markets. If anything, the further trend against corporatism in the 1980s has been a matter of trying to bypass negotiations with unions altogether. Thus, along with the replacement of 'corporatist' Campbell Adamson by 'monetarist' John Methven at the Confederation of British Industry (CBI) in 1981, the 1980s have seen a burgeoning of joint consultation schemes. The CBI response to the Bullock Report, which would have brought about the compulsory recognition of enterprise shop steward combine committees, was to encourage the growth of industrial democracy 'organically' at the plant level in the form of Joint Representative Committees. The idea here is to promote union identification with the company, to legitimate – and consultation is, note, the operative term, not negotiation – company policies and to remove areas of norm regulation from collective bargaining. Among other strategies has been the encouragement of employee equity-ownership schemes: as of 1980 only 11 per cent of manufacturing companies had such schemes; but nearly one-third of these had been introduced since 1977, encouraged by tax advantages as a result of the 1978 Finance Act. Also, subcontracting has been taken advantage of by primary-sector firms to stabilize their own employment while leaving additional employees at the mercy of the fluctuating status and often non-union framework of the subcontractors. Finally, some very aggressive employers – and British Leyland in the early 1980s and the National Coal Board in the aftermath of the 1984–5 strike are two examples here – have attempted to bypass stewards altogether with ballots, referenda and simple unilateral decision-making. The upshot of this has been a recent new diminution in the centrality of the industrial relations function for British firms. [103]

Thus we have seen how, in disorganizing capitalist Britain, dualism has come to pervade union–management relations. Labour, we have seen, has reacted with the adoption of a number of appropriate policies. The issue is that given what seems to be a secular trend (in the absence of reduced working-time schemes) in labour-market development in conjunction with the diminution of the core working class, the union movement is not possessed with sufficient *resources* to carry out its strategies. The miners' strike of 1984–5 – the largest-scale industrial action in British history – exemplifies both of these developments. It seems probable that a transformed and reduced mining industry was an integral part of the strategy of the Thatcher government. The main objectives were to deal a heavy blow to the union, to close 'uneconomic pits', and to privatize the very profitable pits. Conservative MP, Nicholas Ridley, formed contingency plans for an expected prolonged strike as early as May 1978. The National Coal Board (NCB) under Labour rule prepared one of the conditions for this strategy by a departure from centralized branch bargaining through the introduction of an incentive bonus scheme in 1977/8. It was clear to the government that massive pit closures would lead to a prolonged strike; that the strike would set miners from less profitable pits off against those from highly profitable ones was something that the government must have taken into consideration, but hoped for rather than counted on. The logic of the government's strategy of privatization – especially if it were to be several companies to buy a number of pits each – would be a company unionism which could do little to aid the unity of the National Union of Mineworkers (NUM). Several Midlands mining constituencies had fallen to the Conservatives in the 1979 and 1983 elections. Miners from other areas putting up secondary pickets in Nottinghamshire and other Midlands areas of non-strikers noted how 'middle-class' it all seemed: the pits were newer; incentive bonuses were big; miners lived in semi-detached houses in the countryside. In the event, the strike was much more solid in areas threatened by pit closures than in prosperous areas. A Welsh miners' leader in April 1985 argued that the miners, in going back to work without a negotiated settlement, risked fragmentation, and forecast that the inevitable separate negotiations by area coal boards with area unions would pave the way for eventual privatization, and this might come if the Conservatives secure a majority at the 1987 general election. Yet the Nottinghamshire miners have in part broken away to form a rival union, which miners' leaders have estimated could attract some one-third of original NUM membership. Part at least of the strength of this breakaway has been a populist groundswell against the centralist tendencies of Arthur Scargill and current NUM leadership which seems at odds in the decentralized and participatory trends of disorganized capitalism.[104]

The miners' strike also has, in the context of a diminished core working class, important implications for the formation of alliances with sections of the service class, deskilled white-collar workers, and new social movements which are necessary for left strategy in disorganized capitalism. It is clear that the miners could not, as they had done in 1972 and 1974, win a large-scale struggle on their own in 1984/5. Total support of all pits was necessary, as well as a large commitment of solidarity in industrial action from key areas of the trade union movement and support from large areas of non-working-class public opinion. It has been maintained in this context that such support may have been won had the NUM held a national ballot and hence responded to contemporary 'radical individualism' and concern for the languages of rights and a pluralist commitment to autonomy;[105] if the NUM had relied more on the media and mass meetings to convince rather than on the secondary picketing of non-striking pits and steelworks; and if they had roundly condemned violence on all sides. We do not want to engage in counterfactual argument here, but want instead to note the *successes* in moulding key alliances for the left that arose from the strike. There was considerable support during the strike from churches, embattled local authorities, the CND, political branches of the Labour Party; mobilized women from the mining villages have engaged in joint discussions and action with Greenham Common women and other feminist groupings, which have, for example, led to the creation of women's community co-operatives. A left-alliance new social-movements type of consciousness spread to the mining communities themselves. The NUM championed, for instance, the demands of women, blacks and gays at the 1984 Labour Party Conference. There was unprecedented activity of mining-village women in miners' support groups – even men in some villages, it is reported, began to use the term 'chair-person' at meetings – which would have been unthinkable in the absence of the influence over a number of years of feminist ideas nationally.[106] The aftermath the strike may be more significant. Key here may be the effects upon young people, and in particular youth outside of the core working class. A July 1985 poll showed that Labour's strongest gains were among the 18–24 group; some constituency Labour Parties have reported an influx of young members; the previously apathetic rock music scene – to the consternation of many, though canny Labour television political broadcasts have been taking advantage of it – seemed in 1985–6 to have undergone overnight mass politicization.[107]

Conclusions

At the outset of organized capitalism economically generated groupings began to form interest groups on a national scale in civil society. As these organizations consolidated, they came, at an accelerated pace during periods of national crisis, particularly during the First World War and the depression of the 1930s and the aftermath of the Second World War, also to organize on the level of the state. Where governance takes place partly through the mediation of such interest associations which in return exercise a certain imperative control over their constituents, it is possible to speak of corporatism. Given especially a labour movement with suitable ideological and organizational resources, class compromises have been concluded which have made possible the existence of fully-fledged tripartite neo-corporatist politics. In the absence of such conditions (and ideology is as important as organization) class compromise has proved impossible and a corporatism, or statist-corporatism, which has excluded labour, has been the upshot, as in Italy from the 1920s, Germany during the Third Reich, and Gaullist France. The point that we have wanted to stress here, however, is that *either* sort of corporatist arrangement is only possible in organized capitalism; or alternatively, as capitalism disorganizes, corporatism wanes. Corporatism begins tendentially to wither, we have argued, largely because of the disorganized capitalist decline in size, resources and homogeneity of the working class. One major factor in the decline of such homogeneity has been the growth of public-sector unionism, whose development has been contingent, paradoxically, on more unified working-class struggles in organized capitalism itself. Corporatism assumes the existence of three *national* and coherent corporate bodies: capital, labour and the state. Disorganized capitalist internationalization – with its new prominence of the export of means of production, of finance capital and most importantly of commodities – has been crucial in the undoing of neo-corporatism.

With internationalization, capital above all ceases to be a national class, the state loses control over important economic processes, and the heterogeneity of working-class interest groups is severely aggravated. Most important here has been the creation of a dualism which has separated those employed in export-oriented industry from the rest of the organized (and unorganized) potential labour force, especially from much of the well-organized public sector. Perhaps most debilitating to class unity has been the promotion in all countries of company unionism in the protected labour markets of the dynamic export-oriented firms. This dualism has been most apparent in countries with strongly-organized public sectors, such as Sweden and Britain. In both countries the sectionalism of electrical and engineering workers in the 'primary labour market' has threatened labour unity. In Germany and France, with more weakly-organized public sectors and (perhaps partly as a result of this) engineering unions with more universalist aspirations, labour-movement resources have still been too weak to resist some public spending cuts, and industrial democracy and reduced labour-time objectives of left union groups may have paradoxically reinforced any pre-existing tendencies towards company unionism and in some cases increased the area of managerial discretion.

Because of space limitations and its very 'exceptionalism' we have not included a lengthy section on the United States in this chapter. It should be noted, though, that in many of its essentials, American developments were a rather thinner version of their European counterparts. A limited development of quasi-corporatism came in the years leading up to the First World War with the collaborative initiatives of the American Federation of Labor and the National Civic Federation and the (limited amounts of) dialogue between labour and the state which took place during the First World War, the New Deal era and even later into the Nixon and Carter administrations. The relative paucity of any type of corporatist developments in the USA has been because, as we have suggested in previous chapters, the United States effected a transition from liberal to *dis*organized capitalist polity and civil society virtually without, or with at best, the most rudimentary development of an organized capitalist interim. Thus the main political party opposition to big business has come from parties first with a primary basis in small property owners and later one in which the 'new middle classes' played a predominant role, but never in an essentially working-class party. Thus the main initial burst of public spending – in the New Deal – was less than elsewhere the initiative of working-class organizations, or even of government in response to the *threat* of working-class struggle. And the second such burst in the 1960s was mainly in reaction to the black and student movements. It may be accurate to date the existence of an organized capitalist polity in the USA from the 1933–5 New Deal legislation enabling trade union organization to the draconian Taft-Hartley Act, passed under a Democratic administration, in 1947. Succeeding Democratic governments elected with active trade union organizational support were unable or unwilling to produce substantially mitigating industrial relations legislation. Moreover, certain aspects of trade union political activity itself came under legal prohibition. Two key factors disorganizing American capitalism *avant la lettre* were, as we noted in chapter 6, the premature appearance of a large and well-organized service class (and more broadly new middle classes) in the inter-war period, and the fact that the American working class was 'dualist' – largely because of ethnic schisms – before the advent of internationalization. Thus can be interpreted the split between the craft workers of the AFL and the belatedly organized mass-production workers of the CIO from the 1930s, and the schism between 'primary labour market' workers and the largely non-union remainder of the labour force as the American Federation of Labor and Congress of Industrial Organizations, under the hegemony of the former, merged in the middle 1950s (AFL-CIO). In any event, during the 1970s and 1980s, American industrial relations have pursued their disorganizing process marked by inordinate loss of membership (well before general western membership decline set in from the end of the 1970s) and the pervasive development of employee equity schemes since the middle 1970s.[108]

At the outset of this book we introduced two theses in terms of the disorganization process of contemporary capitalism. The first was a 'descriptive' thesis, which stated that certain disorganizing processes were taking place in advanced capitalism and detailed what these phenomena were. The second was a 'comparative' thesis, stating that the more fully a country had been historically organized, the less fully it would be characterized by disorganization under the conditions of the present restructuration. The comparative thesis was also concerned with how particular countries have organized and disorganized. Some countries, like the USA and Japan, have been particularly strongly organized at 'the top', and hence capital has been the key collective actor in the organization process; other nations, such as Sweden, have become especially strongly organized at the bottom and labour (although capital has continued to accumulate) has been the salient collective actor in the process of organization.

What is important in this context in terms of the comparative thesis is that the *collective actor in a given country which most clearly puts its mark on the organization process will be also well placed to exercise considerable influence over the process of disorganization*. Thus in Japan and the US it has been capital which has virtually unilaterally begun to institute characteristically disorganized capitalist industrial relations, with the initiation of 'flexibility' and 'quality circles'. In France, where the state has been the key collective actor in promoting characteristically organized-capitalist forms of collective bargaining, it is also the state which has begun to engineer disorganization in the form of the 1984 and 1986 flexibility legislation. In West Germany and Sweden by contrast labour has been able to play a key role in the new restructuration. Whereas, at the end of 1986, British, American and French union density had seemed to enter into secular decline, West German density was on the increase and Swedish figures had held constant. Britain seems to be increasingly threatened by labour movement dualism, and the USA and Japan seem increasingly characterized by the juxtaposition of a unionized primary labour market and a non-unionized secondary labour market, but West Germany and Sweden have struggled to maintain a still impressive degree of trade union movement unity.

Thus, all things being equal, when labour is an important collective actor in organized capitalism it will also be an important collective actor in disorganized capitalism. But all things are *not* equal. Strategies also count. In Britian, labour was indeed an important collective actor in the age of organized capitalism, yet capital seems to be making all the running in determining the shape of the new structure. Britain was surely, as we have argued through this book, strongly organized at the bottom. Unionization of the non-skilled on a substantial scale took place in this country before the end of the nineteenth century. By the second decade of this century Britain was a leader in social spending. In Britain the historic proportion that the core working class made up of the economically active was unmatched by any other country, and not even nearly approached by any other country discussed at length in this book. Britain's level of union density even at the time of writing in March 1987 is only matched by Italy among medium and large-sized capitalist countries.

Thus Britain's working class as a collective actor ought to bear more similarities with the German and Swedish cases than with the American and Japanese cases – that is, it ought to continue to wield considerable resources in the era of a disorganizing capitalism. Yet if we look in 1987 at membership levels, results of industrial conflicts, a number of indices of shopfloor power and the content of flexibility agreements, British labour seems only to have taken a beating, and capital (with of course enormous doses of aid from the state – consider the miners' strike of 1984–5 and Wapping, for example) has almost solely determined the course of the new restructuration.

How can this British labour weakness – particularly in comparison with German and Swedish labour strength – in disorganized capitalism be accounted for? Three factors can be isolated, two of which have received some attention above:

(1) *Work organization*. The move from Taylorism and Fordism to flexibilization is an integral part of the disorganization of contemporary capitalist societies: it is in particular a key component in the decentralization of contemporary industrial relations. German and Swedish trade unions have taken a role in the initiation of flexibility in the workplace, in the promoting of job enrichment through the broadening of job classifications. They have in part been able to make flexibility work for labour. British unions in their blanket rejection of such change have let employers initiate flexibility in a way that has been very damaging to the interests of workers and unions.

(2) *Worker participation*. Any substantial discussion of flexibility or 'quality circles' is beyond the scope of this book. A few remarks must suffice. Quality circles, often introduced in tandem with flexibility, are just one characteristically disorganized capitalist form of worker participation. The others take place on other decentralized levels of industrial relations – for example, worker representatives on boards of directors at a company level, or German *Betriebsräte* or Swedish *Medbestämming* on a plant level. Now worker participation institutions on either a company or plant level can be made to work either for capital or for labour. To make them benefit working people, trade unions must take a hand in initiating and shaping such institutions, as they have done with varying amounts of success in Germany and Sweden. If such institutions are rejected outright or ignored, as seems to be the case in Britain, then only capital can determine their context, to the detriment of both workers and unions. Quality circles are institutions of worker participation on a department or workgroup level. Other types of such institution are the groups of direct expression, created through left-wing legislation in France in the early 1980s. These most highly localized institutions can also function as organs of worker democracy or as convenient ways to help capital carry out demanning. Again, if they are ignored, as seems mostly to be the case in Britain, only employers will be making use of them.

(3) *Collective identity in the primary labour market*. Labour-market dualism in disorganized capitalism does not have to lead to labour *movement* dualism.

If primary labour-market workers (the prototypical male, white, skilled, private and export sector workers) can sustain a high enough level of collective identity, as seems to be the case in Sweden and Germany, they will forgo certain advantages of sectionalism that can lead to split labour movements, and in particular splits between primary labour-market unions and public sector unions. In Britain at the moment, sectionalism and labour movement dualism seem to be on the cards.

9

Postmodern culture and disorganized capitalism: some conclusions

The first part of this chapter is devoted to making some connections between the processes of capitalist disorganization and cultural changes, in particular the development of a post modernist culture. The second part is devoted to drawing together themes that we have stressed over this entire volume and giving a synthetic account of our conception of capitalist disorganization.

THE SOCIAL BASES OF THE POSTMODERNIST SENSIBILITY

In the last chapter we traced the disorganization of contemporary industrial relations, first to the decentralized shopfloor radicalism of the late 1960s and early 1970s, and then the shift from national bargaining to enterprise-level bargaining in recent years that has accompanied the demise of neo-corporatism. What such transformations assume, we suggested, is a fragmentation of working-class collective identity. But collective identity is also in part a *cultural* matter. Similarly in chapters 4 and 5 we traced a whole series of spatial transformations that are integral to the disorganization of capitalist societies. The significance of such spatial changes however is partly a question of how they are socially perceived. And such social perceptions are dependent on *representations* of space and thus on *culture*. In chapter 6 we spoke of the rise of the service class in part as a cause of capitalist disorganization. But the rise of this class is impossible without some dependence upon a range of *cultural* resources. Indeed it might well be true, as we shall suggest below, that the fractions of the service class are crucial in establishing a transformed cultural hegemony in disorganized capitalism.

We think thus in a book that has largely been a 'political economy' of capitalist disorganization that each thematic social factor we have stressed is inevitably embedded in a *cultural* substrate. We think further that the contemporary cultural substrate bears certain features that can best be understood under the rubric of 'postmodernism'. We want then in what follows very briefly to address postmodernist culture, and draw some of the connections between it and the disorganization of contemporary western societies.

Let us underscore, however, that we are not arguing that there is any one-to-one, reductionist state of affairs in which postmodernist culture is somehow a reflection of the phase of disorganized capitalism. We are moreover not arguing that all or even the major part of contemporary culture is postmodernist. We do, though believe that postmodernism is an increasingly important feature of contemporary culture, and we intend to try in a preliminary fashion to show how it articulates with some features of disorganized capitalism. We thus intend – in considerations of postmodern culture sometimes as cause but mostly as effect of disorganization – to make some preliminary inroads into the 'political economy' of postmodernism.

We will address this issue by asking what the *social* conditions of postmodernism are. Or more specifically, what social conditions specific to an era of disorganizing capitalism are conducive to the creation of an audience which is predisposed towards the reception of postmodernist culture? Before we outline these conditions, we will briefly delineate what we mean by postmodernist culture.

Postmodernist culture may be distinguished from, on the one hand, 'classic realist' and, on the other, 'modernist' cultural forms. Classic realism on this account is grounded in the Quattrocento perspective in Renaissance painting in which a three-dimensional object is painted onto a two-dimensional canvas as if the latter were literally a window on the former; and in the narrative assumptions of the nineteenth-century novel. The birth of modernist culture which breaks with these assumptions takes place around the turn of the twentieth century. Modernist culture (Adorno's exemplars here were Picasso and Schönberg) is 'auratic' in Walter Benjamin's sense of the term. 'Aura' according to Benjamin assumed the radical separation of the cultural forms from the social: aura entails that a cultural object proclaim its own originality, uniqueness and singularity; it assumed finally that the cultural object is based in a discourse of formal organic unity and artistic creativity. Modernism is thus confined to high culture, while classic realism – in the popular novel, popular urban theatres, in cinema – comes also to pervade popular culture in the early twentieth century.[1]

Postmodernist culture, for its part, like modernism departs from the visual and narrative assumptions of classic realism. But at the same time it, unlike modernism, is emphatically *anti*-auratic. Postmodernism signals the demise of aesthetic 'aura' in a number of ways.

1 It proclaims not its uniqueness but is positioned in a context of mechanical, if not electronic, reproduction.
2 It denies the high-modernist separation of the aesthetic from the social and any other hierarchical dualisms; and in particular it disputes the contention that art is of a different order from life.
3 It disputes the high-modernist valuation of such unity through pastiche, collage, allegory and so on.
4 Whereas high-modernist cultural forms are received by audiences in what Benjamin called a state of 'contemplation', postmodernist forms are typically consumed in a state of distraction.
5 Whereas high-modernist art is to be appreciated for the coherent use and the formal properties of the aesthetic material, postmodernist culture affects the audience via its immediate impact, via an 'economy of pleasure'.
6 Postmodernism in its challenge to aesthetic aura does not assume a high-modernist diremption of high and popular culture.

Given this definition, the first flourishings of post modern culture appeared in the historical avant-garde of the 1920s, in the critique of high modernism launched by, among others, the dada and surrealist movements. One major reason why the postmodern 1920s avant-gardes did not penetrate into popular culture was because a sufficient audience with the relevant predispositions was not present.[2] In recent decades such a popular-culture audience has however begun to take shape. Thus there has been the pervasion of postmodern forms in popular cinema, in which in the largest moneyspinning films postmodern 'impact' and 'spectacle' has progressively displaced the privacy of classic-realist narratives. Likewise in advertising and video, pictoral realism has been progressively replaced by dadaist and surrealist techniques of collage and montage. And also, there is to be found an intentional dissonance and shock value in punk and performance art.[3]

Let us turn now to the social conditions for the creation of an audience for each cultural forms. We will analyse these social conditions under three headings:

The semiotics of everyday life Postmodern cultural forms, we just noted, refuse the distinction between art and life, between the cultural and the real. We shall argue that an audience is sensitized to the reception of such cultural objects, because of a 'semiotics of everyday life' in which the boundary between the cultural and life, between the image and the real, is more than ever transgressed. Or because of a semiotics in which already cultural images, that is, what are already representations in television, advertisements, billboards, pop music, video, home computers and so on, themselves constitute a significant and increasingly growing portion of the 'natural' social reality that surrounds people.

New class fractions In this section we assume, with Pierre Bourdieu, that goods are consumed for their symbolic power to establish invidious distinctions between one social class, or class fraction, and another. We then argue that sections of the service class use postmodern cultural goods to challenge traditionalist culture. That is, that postmodern cultural goods are in the 'ideal interests' of these 'new middle classes', who, in their rise, will benefit from the extent to which the whole of society comes to share their valuations of such cultural forms.

The decentring of identity   We argue that the reception of postmodernist culture is enhanced by the decentring of subjectivity. We consider in this context several processes integral to the disorganizing process of contemporary societies, which foster such decentred identities and collective identities. These are (1) changes in the class structure, in particular the fragmentation of working-class community and the occupationally-structured experience of sections of the service class; (2) the influence of the electronic mass media; and (3) disruptions in our perception of time and of space in everyday life.

The semiotics of everyday life

Jean Baudrillard is perhaps the foremost figure to discuss the relation of post-industrialism to the sphere of culture. He gives an account of the transition from 'industrial capitalism', to 'consumer capitalism' and consumer capitalism is for him very much as disorganized capitalism is for us.[4] Baudrillard analyses how this transition brings about what might be called a transformed 'semiotics of everyday life' which predisposes audience reception of post-modernist culture. Baudrillard uses the conventional semiotic 'triangle', where the signifier is an image, a sound, a word, or an utterance; the signified is a meaning, usually a thought or a concept; and the referent is the object in the real world to which both signifier and signified point. In industrial capitalism in this context, domination is effected through the referent which for Baudrillard is capital, both as means of production and as the commodities produced. In industrial capitalism then the 'social bond' is through the exchange of exchange-values; and the centrality of exchange-value itself is legitimated through use-value, or a set of arguments based around the maximization of utility.

What is then most important for Baudrillard about contemporary *consumer* capitalism is that we consume, no longer products, but signs: that we consume the signs of advertisements, of television; and that objects of consumption themselves have value for us as signs. It is the image, then, in contemporary capitalism, that is consumed, the image in which we have libidinal investment. The exchange-value of commodities thus has been transformed into a 'sign-value'. Signs – which comprise both signifier and signified – 'float free from the referent' or product, and domination and the 'social bond' are no longer through the referent but the sign.[5] Moreover, our identities are constructed through the exchange of sign-values, and the means of legitimation of the signifier (or the image) is the signified. Baudrillard's consumer capitalism has become a fully-fledged 'political economy of the sign'.

Domination through the sign takes place through the arbitrary assignments by established power of signifieds, or meanings, to signifiers. The type of signifieds in which Baudrillard is interested are not ordinary denotations or connotations, but fundamental ideologies or ultimate values.[6] Domination through the sign or at least through discourse would characterize not just consumption but the sphere of production in today's service and information-based economies in which employer–employee relations are no longer so often mediated by means of production.[7] Domination here is through the assignment of a single and univocal meaning or signified to the signifiers.

Resistance, by contrast, contends Baudrillard, takes place through the refusal of the 'masses' in contemporary consumer society to accept this connection of signifier to signified. Baudrillard's argument is that the masses reject the signifieds attached to media images, both by established power, as well as the signifieds which the left has promoted (such as 'the people', the proletariat). Instead, he contends, the masses accept *all* images in the spirit of *spectacle*; that is, they refuse to attach meaning to images which have been intended to carry meaning. Baudrillardian spectacle is no longer a universe of referent, signified or even signifiers, but of the 'model', of 'simulation' and of 'hyperreality'. What television broadcasts for example is not reality, but – through choice of subject matter, editing and so on – a *model*. The masses of viewers, he observes, are no more taken in by the putative reality of television images than they are by its meanings. They *know* that it is a simulation; they are cognizant of the hyperreality of the image; and they thrive on its 'fascination'. In their turn the masses simulate the models of media images, and in their conformity to media 'hyperreality', the masses become models themselves. Everyday life and reality itself then become 'imploded' into the hyperreality of the spectacle.[8] Baudrillard's world of spectacle is a world of 'simulacra', that is, where there is no original and everything is a copy. The masses simulate the media which in turn hypersimulate the masses. It is a depthless world of networks of information and communication in which 'the sender' (TV, computers) is the receiver,[9] and in which the subject like the media is a 'control screen', a 'switching centre'. It is a universe of communication networks in which information is purely instrumental in that it 'has no end purpose in meaning'.[10]

We agree with much in Baudrillard's analysis: with the importance of the sphere of consumption for the constitution of individual and collective identity; with the idea of post-industrial domination through communications in the sphere of production; with the idea that in contemporary capitalism what is largely produced – in the media, a large part of the service sector, in parts of the public sector – consists of communications and information. We agree also with his contention – and this is of course a hallowed idea whose lineage stretches from Veblen to Bourdieu – that images rather than products have become the central objects of consumption. This point is borne out in research carried out by William Leiss on changes in advertising practices. Leiss examined national (as distinct from specialist) product advertising in two Canadian general circulation magazines from 1911 to 1980.[11] He found over this period and in particular after the Second World War a decline in printed text and a concomitant rise in visual imagery. He also found a decline in 'propositional content', that is of (often specious) arguments regarding the utility of the product to an 'almost purely iconic representation' of images put into juxtaposition with the product. In the early decades of Leiss's sample advertisements were intended to convince consumers to purchase manufactured products. With this aim they contained detailed descriptions of products, focusing on values of efficiency, durability, reliability and cleanliness. Women were cast in functional, if traditional roles, as they were instructed how to use the products in the household. In recent decades utility and functionality are increasingly dispensed with. Appeal is no longer to practical rationality, as a Watsonian behaviourist (or Freudian) conception of an irrationalist human nature is assumed. Instead of being cast in functional roles, women become sex objects and images which are helter-skelter attached to products like adjectives. Instead of being told how to use products, women are directed to use the product in order to be like the sex object associated with it; men to use the product in order to *have* her.[12]

The main problem however with Baudrillard's argument is that what he understands as the principle of cultural resistance in contemporary consumer society is in fact more often than not its principle of *domination*. That is, that domination in the semiotics of contemporary everyday life is not through the attachment of signifieds, of meanings to images by culture producers, but by the particular strategies of dominant social groups to *refuse* to attach any meanings to such images. That is, the implosion of meaning, subjectivity and the real world or the social is not primarily a way for Baudrillard's 'silent majorities' to resist domination, but instead a way that 'masses' are indeed dominated. It is plausible that the overload of sounds and images that we experience in everyday life, over the television, radio, walkman, billboards and bright lights, has helped create a sensibility to post-modern cultural objects in which meaning is devalued. But surely cultural producers, in for example today's cinema of the spectacle are aware of this change in the audience and produce films that cater to it. So our first point against Baudrillard is that dominant culture often operates itself through the delinkage of meaning from images. Our second point is that there is not anything necessarily disruptive, much less subversive, about masses who implode meaning and their subjectivities into flat hyperreality. In explanations of social movements, resistance is conditional upon coherent forms of identity, or more precisely collective identity. And by most accounts collective identities are constituted around ultimate sets of meanings. Finally, if subjectivity is imploded into the unfortunately too lifelike Baudrillardian networks of communication and information, there is little place left from which to launch any type of substantive critique.

Simon Frith's recent work on popular music gives an excellent illustration of how cultural products which feature the primacy of image and spectacle can at one moment be disruptive of the conditions of consumer capitalism and at another moment function to reproduce just such conditions. Frith distinguishes 'rock' from 'pop' critiques of consumer society.[13] The 'rock' critique, dominant until the 1970s, is an effectively 'modernist' critique of consumer capitalism in its preference for an auratic culture of authenticity, the natural, and live performance.[14] The 'pop' critique by contrast is effectively post-modernist and grew out of the late 1970s and especially from punk.

Punk challenged the modernist and auratic dispositions of rock in a number of ways. It mocked the rock cult of the LP (long-playing record), whose original and auratic pretentions bore careful listening the first time through. Punk instead foregrounded the single; instead of originality, repetition was thematized, and to listen to a punk recording for the first time was like already having listened to it before.[15] Whereas rock was essentially to be listened to, and thus consistent with modernist aurality, punk was a matter of the visual, the image; it was to be seen.[16] Whereas rock propounded the modernist thematic of the creative artist, punk only entailed the learning of a few chords (and at that, badly), and at least some kids on any block were capable of that. While rock featured a modernist aesthetics of beauty, punk foregrounded an anti-aesthetic of discordant and intentionally nerve-jangling cacophony. Where rock promoted, especially in the LP, at least some notion of the (modernist) integral work of art, pop's avant-garde critique promotes the heterogeneous, in pastiches such as Malcolm McClaren's *Duck Rock*, which mixes together a number of previously recorded sound sequences.[17] Whereas (typically American) rock artists had or seemed to have genuine connections with the popular communities from which they sprung, the (typically British) pop artist was from an art school background, and self-consciously differentiated him or herself from the masses in the audience. Thus a number of pop performers promoted an avant-garde and 'camp' (in Sontag's sense) consciousness of the image, sang in detached and ironic tones, and laid open sexual (and also racial) ambiguity. They expressed contempt for the mass audience they intended to shock, and self-referentially mocked their own popularity.[18]

The pop (and post-modern) critique of consumer capitalism through spectacle was, as Frith observes, but a short step from the celebration of music's commodity status. This has taken place via a pop music, quite disconnected with avant-gardes, whose rise to fame has been most of all dependent on the video. The replacement of the critical avant-garde by video-pop is partly explicable in terms of the late 1970s slump in record sales, itself explicable by the rise in youth unemployment but also by the new competition for youth leisure time via home computers and video recorders. The record companies' response to this, notes Frith, was swift: they shifted to a younger market and promoted singles at the expense of LPs; they built on what had always been a visual orientation of this early-teens market and thus focused on promoting stars; and these now became 'multi-media performers' with heavy record company investment in videos.[19] The reponse, though inconclusive, has been an increase in sales in the mid-1980s. But the new video-based music has meant 'the incorporation of pop into the aesthetics (and we would add, the politics) of advertising'.[20]

We have then, partly via a critical analysis of Baudrillard's work, given an account of how the semiotics of everyday life in consumer (disorganized) capitalism predisposes an audience to the reception of post-modern cultural forms. The most important features of such a semiotics which bear affinities with characteristics of post-modern culture that we outlined are: the consumption of images instead of products; the new importance of spectacle at the expense of meaning; and a situation in which the boundaries between the realm of culture and everyday life itself are continually transgressed and blurred. Here the 'masses' not only 'simulate' the media, but popular culture, the media and pop music are themselves inseparable from the semiotics of everyday life, a phenomenon emphasized by Andy Warhol's photorealism in which paintings are not windows out onto the world but windows out onto the media, the advert, the image.[21] It is an everyday experience of a reality which itself – through the walkman, video, television, adverts, styles – is already cultural and hence a hyperreality that creates an audience attuned to the anti-auratic and figural or spectacular nature of post-modernist culture.

New class fractions

Our central claims in this section will be that it is the developing service class which is the consumer *par excellence* of post-modern cultural products; that there is a certain 'hegemonizing mission' of the post-modern tastes and lifestyle of significant sections of this new middle class;[22] and that there are certain structural conditions of the service class that produce a decentred identity which fosters the reception of such post-modern cultural goods. The best way to address these points is via Pierre Bourdieu's notion of the 'habitus'.

Bourdieu speaks of various classes and class factions as having a habitus. A class's habitus most importantly consists of a set of classificatory schemes. These are basically cognitive structures which themselves structure the 'orienting practices' and activities of agents. These schemes underpin, and are more fundamental than, consciousness and language. All social class habituses are grounded in two principles. The first is a principle of classification based on adjectives such as noble versus low which are themselves grounded in the opposition in the social order of elite and mass. The second principle is based on the opposition of light versus heavy; it is exemplified by the distinction within elites of warriors versus clerics in pre-modern societies and bourgeois versus intellectuals in modernity.[23] Given this general framework shared by all social classes, Bourdieu's vision of class, taste and habitus is marked by the following features.

(1) Each class and class fraction has its own variants of the habitus, whose classificatory schemes are at the same time systems of ultimate values. The latter, Bourdieu insists, are dispositions of the body, 'visceral tastes and distastes in which the groups' most vital interests are embedded.[24]

(2) Groups struggle to 'impose taxonomies most favourable to their own characteristics' on other groups and the whole of society; the dominant classes are usually most successful in this.[25]

(3) There is a key role in these struggles for the institutions of culture, the educational system and intellectuals more generally.

(4) These 'classificatory struggles' are also struggles which determine the shifting boundaries, and even the existence, of the groups themselves. Groups mobilize their 'economic and social capital', Bourdieu claims, in order to exist, and to legitimate their own existence in the occupational structure.[26] Our arguments in chapter 6 about the service class's struggles to create space for itself in the occupational and industrial structure bear witness to this claim. We would like to extend this aspect of Bourdieu's framework and note that the new middle classes are characterized not just by different classificatory structures and perceived boundaries than other and traditional social strata, but by a looser, more fluid, in effect destructured and decentred 'group' and 'grid'.[27] It is both of these characteristics, we shall see below, which sensitizes these classes as an audience for postmodern culture.

(5) Bourdieu's classificatory struggles leave open the possibility for entire classes to experience mobility *vis-à-vis* other classes.

(6) These struggles have for stakes not of course only the shape of the habitus, but also 'material and cultural goods'. Bourdieu's central claim that we consume not products but symbols with the intention of establishing distinctions between ourselves and other social strata is in line with Fred Hirsch's arguments about 'positional' consumption, and the general debate about social limits to growth.[28] In the latter the distinction is made between traditional societies, in which most consumption is for subsistence and only elites engage in competitive consumption and advanced capitalism's democratization of competitive consumption. In this framework the postmodern cultural hypostatization of the image and spectacle has a contradictory role and unanticipated consequences. If in organized capitalism underconsumption, or an 'underload' of demands created the conditions for advertising and the consumption of and hegemony of the image, then in disorganized capitalism this now fetishized image is at least partly responsible for positional consumption and demand *over*loads. In this sense postmodern culture also had had *dis*organizing effects on western economies.

(7) The consumption of postmodern culture is not only contingent on given classificatory schema and a destructured habitus, but also on what Bourdieu calls the 'cultural capital' that a group possesses. Cultural capital is not just a matter of abstract theoretical knowledge but the symbolic competence necessary to appreciate certain works of art. Without the 1960s expansion of Western European higher education it is unlikely that groupings would possess the cultural capital necessary for the appreciation of postmodern high or even 'middlebrow' culture; in Britain, for example, such cultural magazines such as *The Face* and *New Musical Express* assume a rudimentary knowledge of aesthetic avant-gardes.

These comments made, we will consider the connections between the service class and postmodernism which can be drawn from Bourdieu's work on class taste patterns and lifestyles in France. The main divide that Bourdieu draws within the 'dominant class' is between 'intellectuals' (in his survey mainly higher education teachers and artists) and the 'bourgeoisie'. The former are high on cultural capital but possess little economic capital, while the latter are weaker on cultural capital and strong on economic capital. The primary classificatory schema of the habitus mentioned above which distinguished between elite and mass is at the same time to be understood as a distinction between culture (elite) and nature (mass). The second principle of classification which counterposes intellectuals and the bourgeoisie repeats this culture/nature opposition, with the bourgeoisie (nature) 'their material, base, this-worldly satisfactions' dependent for signs of distinction on the intellectuals (culture).[29] Thus Bourdieu contrasts the 'aesthetic-asceticism' of intellectuals' tastes for a spare functionalism/modernism in design with the sumptuous interiors of the bourgeois, and the intellectuals' liking for the spare sets of Parisian left-bank theatre with the bourgeois tastes for the baroque and indulgent sets of boulevard theatre.[30] Bourdieu interprets this as a symbolic subversion (by intellectuals) of the rituals of bourgeois order by 'ostentatious poverty'. This symbolic reversal of nature and culture takes place also in sport with the intellectuals' preference for mountaineering, hiking, walking, representing their taste for 'natural, wild nature', as opposed to the bourgeois' 'organized, cultivated nature'.[31]

Bourdieu elaborates a further grouping, the 'new bourgeoisie' which possesses considerable quantities of cultural as well as economic capital. It is comprised largely of private-sector executives, especially those active in the production of non-material products, in areas such as finance, or design. It is populated by individuals, unlike the bourgeois fraction of commercial and industrial employers, who are rarely from popular backgrounds. The new bourgeois, if in industry, is not in research and development but in finance; not in engineering but in marketing; not in production but in purchasing. He or she is part of an international class, is not only Francophone, but speaks English and reads the *Financial Times* or the *Wall Street Journal*; he or she partakes in an 'international symbol market, and eschews champagne for whisky, and apparently indulges in 'California sports' such as hang-gliding, jogging and windsurfing.[32] This new bourgeois according to Jameson imparts his ethos to post modern films like *Diva*.[33] According to Bourdieu, he or she has a good chance of setting the taste patterns for the dominant class in France.

Also highly important for postmodern cultural consumption is what Bourdieu calls the 'new petit bourgeois' (for us a member of the lower echelons of the service class). Bourdieu's new petite bourgeoisie includes 'all occupations involving presentation and representation' and occupations in all institutions providing symbolic goods and services. Much of this entails the 'symbolic work of producing needs' in advertising and sales, but also in public-sector jobs which involve the production of needs for public services as well as the provision of those services in for example day-care centres, drug abuse centres and in race relations.[34] This new 'cultural' petite bourgeoisie thus includes those active in medical and social assistance (marriage guidance, sex therapists, dieticians, vocational guidance) and those involved in direct 'cultural production and organization' (youth leaders, tutors and monitors, radio and TV producers and presenters, magazine journalists). The new petite bourgeoisie typically contains individuals whose quantity and quality of cultural capital does not tally well with other of their social characteristics, and especially individuals whose educational qualifications are lower than their social capital and social origins, and those who occupy 'positions which hold out the highest profits for non-certified cultural capital'.[35] This status-inconsistent new petit bourgeois can follow several career trajectories and strategies to success and often to membership of the new bourgeoisie. They, for example, often struggle to *create* jobs suited to their ambitions, even in the public sector in which semi-voluntary jobs have gained public-service status and local government finance. They can succeed through professionalization strategies, through struggles to legitimate new licences and certifications, partly through the promotion of a 'therapeutic morality' as legitimating ideology, in the case of for example, sexologists and marriage guidance counsellors.[36] They can, Bourdieu holds, finally succeed 'by the symbolic violence needed to create and sell new products' and/or through social capital which, in areas such as television, journalism and cinema, brings people into jobs, and the social capital of new contacts which once in jobs helps them to stay there.[37] That is, partly in compensation and as a means to overcome inadequate or inappropriate accumulation of cultural capital, a number of new petits bourgeois succeed through the promotion of needs for and the actual creation of post-modern cultural goods.

In promoting themselves, this new cultural petite bourgeoisie also encourages 'symbolic rehabilitation projects'; that is, they give (often postmodern) cultural objects new status as part of rehabilitation strategies for their own careers. In their work in the media, in advertising, in design, as 'cultural intermediaries' they are taste-creators. Their own tastes, Bourdieu's survey shows, tends to be in not quite legitimate culture such as jazz and cinema. Their taste in painting is in the avant-garde (Dali, Kandinsky, Braque).[38] The new petits bourgeois, often downwardly mobile in terms of their original social capital and not accepted by the cultural-capital establishment, applies the 'cultivated disposition to not-yet-legitimate culture'.[39] Among intellectuals, they can find allies in newcomers to cultural-capital institutions; among left academics, in the new institutions of higher education which became pervasive from the 1960s, into whose classrooms the new petit bourgeois was finally admitted.[40] In the new institutions of higher education this newcomer *bas-clergé*, partly through a self-legitimation strategy *vis-à-vis* the established academy, has often played a radicalizing and democratizing role, either as Marxist or some variety of 'postmodernist'. The *mainstream*, however, of this postmodern petite bourgeoisie of cultural intermediaries perhaps as Bourdieu argues plays an objectively reactionary role. In possible alliance with the new bourgeoisie – whose international, anti-traditional and leisure tastes they share – the new petit bourgeois produces images that 'legitimate the lifestyle' of the new-bourgeois 'ethical avant-garde of the dominant class'.[41]

The decentring of identity

But this new petit bourgeois not only has a habitus which predisposes him or her to the reception and production of postmodern cultural objects, but, we recall, a pre-eminently *de*structured and decentred habitus. Thus he or she is low on 'grid' (i.e. classificatory structures) and lives for the moment 'untrammelled by constraints and brakes imposed by collective memories and expectations'. He or she is also low on 'group' (the strength of boundary between 'us' and 'them'), particularly, Bourdieu observes, in a refusal to be a petit bourgeois. This is at the same time a 'refusal to be pinned down in [any] particular site in social space.' These new cultural intermediaries would rather view themselves as 'excluded' or 'marginal'.[42] The point in this context is that if this new petite bourgeoisie and new bourgeoisie – and they are particularly well placed to do so given their increasing numbers and strategic location as taste makers – are able hegemonically to imprint their postmodern cultural ethos on the habitus of other social classes. Thus Bernice Martin speaks of an effectively destructured habitus developing among the British working-class young with the 'birth' of adolescence from the late 1950s, and among middle-class youth more generally in the youth culture and rise of higher education from the 1960s. This she attributes to a 'liminality' which ensues with the decline of parental control in a period created when one is neither a child nor adult. She argues that a particularly extended period of liminality develops in the new middle classes in that they have a destructured habitus not only in youth but, due to the nature of their occupations as for example cultural intermediaries, in adulthood too.[43]

Collective identities are structured through 'grid', that is classificatory schemata and 'group' – the boundaries set up to distinguish what is external to and what is internal to a collectivity. This decentring of identity in the working class and in the middle classes as well as in other collectivities is furthered by the effects of the electronic media. Collective identity, both group and grid, are based, as Meyrowitz notes, on 'shared but special information systems'.[44] Such information systems would be specific not just to social classes, but to gender, age, ethnic and regional groups. What especially television does is to minimize the importance of these separate and distinct information systems both through exposing individuals of all groupings to the general information system and through giving each age, gender, class grouping a chance to see the intimate spaces of the lives of other groupings, a chance which otherwise would not have been available.[45] In addition of course, isolation in one's living room will have a negative effect on the solidification of collective identity.

There are two rather contradictory outcomes of this. On the one hand, there is the facilitation of a postmodernist sensibility in that this decline in the boundaries of group and grid corresponds with the transgression of boundaries (between life and art, high and popular culture and so on) which are constitutive of postmodernist cultural forms themselves. This boundary is reinforced by television's own proclivity to break down the barriers between the 'frontstage' and 'backstage' regions of fictional and non-fictional figures. Moreover, as we noted, television is part and parcel of the Baudrillardian society of the spectacle, in which meaning is devalued at the expense of impact. On the other hand, this dissolution of collective identity which television fosters can lead to the development of more universalist identities of communicative rationality and the creation of public spheres in Habermas's sense of these terms.[46] There are several processes working in this direction. First, television offers individuals of a given age, class, gender or ethnic grouping a less selective diet of information than was previously available.[47] Second, television can offer increased public access to information which can augment the power of the public relative to authority.[48] For example, consider interviews with hostile foreign heads of state like Fidel Castro in the USA, or with Irish Republican Army (IRA) members in Britain, or above all the scenes from the war in Viet Nam which, entering American living rooms, contributed so considerably to the undermining of political authority. Third, new forms of universalism are encouraged. Television may well have sexist content, yet girls are, for example, able to observe a variety of both male and female patterns of behaviour with which they may identify or model themselves on, in a way that was impossible in a much more restricted pre-television culture.[49] Finally, the breakdown of particularist identities – both in the fostering of weaker group boundaries and the development of more generalist and universalist (grid) classificatory structures – would also entail that particularist legitimacy arguments would suffer losses in validity. Hence the pervasion of universalist arguments based on the notion of human rights,[50] which in the USA for example grew in the Civil Rights movement of the 1960s, spread to the student movements and antiwar movements later in the decade, became a basis of feminism in the 1970s, and now, in the 1980s, is quite common in conservative political discourse.

The spread of television culture has been crucial in its spatial implications. But a set of *temporal* phenomena have been equally important in the decentring of identity and the development of the audience for postmodernist cultural forms. Here the temporal disruptions, incoherencies and inconsistencies involved in postmodernism's break with narrative realism is mirrored in the experienced temporality of everyday life. Thus Jean-François Lyotard, for example, celebrates the disappearance of 'metanarratives' in the postmodern era,[51] whereas Frederic Jameson descries the loss of these *grand récits*.[52] Jameson's position is particularly fruitful on this matter. He distinguishes postmodern 'pastiche' from modern 'parody'. Parody stands in a relationship to a 'linguistic norm' in real historical time; in pastiche however there is the disappearance of the original and real historical referent at the expense of a 'fragmentary group of ideolects'. This leads for example to a postmodern architecture without any knowledge of original meanings, that is, without any historical sense. The same, Jameson continues to argue, is true of our postmodern interest in nostalgic, as distinct from historical, films and in *la mode retro*, in which 'we are condemned to seek the historical past through our own pop images and stereotypes about the past which remain forever out of reach.' Pastiche then, for Jameson, fragments time into a 'series of perpetual presents'.[53] Jameson's more encompassing view is that our identities are constituted via a 'political unconscious', which itself is structured, not by Lacanian discourse, but through the temporality of *narratives*, and in particular through narratives studded with national political and class figurations. He argues for Marxism as the most valid of all these narratives, the most encompassing of the metanarratives. His despair is with a postmodernity in which narratives are displaced by spectacle and the unconscious suppressed through its flattening into a largely schizophrenic reality. The result is that history itself is suppressed and our identities and especially political and collective identities rendered incoherent.[54]

Cultural conservatives such as Christopher Lasch and Daniel Bell develop a not wholly dissimilar argument. Not only has our sense of history been lost, they contend, but the narrative temporality of our immediate experience has disappeared. We no longer live our lives through identities imbued with the consciousness that I am the son of my father, who was the son of his father and so on. Our intragenerational narratives are equally forgotten. Fascination with immediate gratification in consumer society means that lifelong narrative projects like marriage dwindle into a succession of disconnected love affairs or a succession of marriages. With the putative demise of the work ethic, we no longer live our careers as lifelong projects with a continuous temporality of causes and effects. Instead life becomes a succession of discontinuous events.[55]

While this line of argument for a postmodern decentred subjectivity through the destruction of narrative temporality has considerable plausibility, we think that it has only partial application. Temporality in modernity is not only a narrative temporality, but a new experience of abstract and homogeneous time. This was the experience of the worker entering the factory who had such a time sense imposed on him or her by employers who imposed a similar temporality on themselves. It is less, much less likely that we have broken with this eminently modern and rationalist structuring of time. In fact it has probably increased in the move towards 'flexible specialization' in office and factory work which demands the self-imposed rationalization of abstract, homogeneous time, as well as in the sphere of consumption in which we increasingly parcel our leisure time and holidays into homogeneous blocks, in which we calculatingly plan sporting activities and exercise in order to enhance the image of our bodies. These last points are particularly telling in regard to the postmodern experience of time. Its individual blocks are increasingly abstract, calculated and rational, but its overall narrative perspective is less rational and has come to resemble a succession of disconnected events. Our temporality is in part then a 'calculating hedonism' in which these 'mini-rationalities' are packed into a larger and overarching irrationality.[56]

A crucial effect then of the electronic media and spatio-temporal changes in our disorganizing capitalist societies has been the decentring of identities and the loosening or destructuration of group and grid. The result has been, on the one hand, the creation of a sensibility conducive to the reception of postmodernist cultural objects, and on the other, the opening of possibilities for a more universalist and rational subjectivity. Note that we do not view postmodernism as at all necessarily reactionary in implication. Indeed the 'carnival' associated with Dionysian cultural forms has often been integral to political protest.[57] And we are at the same time well aware that the rejection of the possibly negative and totalizing consequences of communicative rationality will tend to have appeal in the context of the breakdown of the older, organized capitalist forms of identity and especially of collective identity.[58]

In any event, if these arguments about the hegemonizing mission of this new petit bourgeois postmodern culture and the destructuration of group and grid across social classes are true, the political implications may be vast. Postmodern ideology, on its negative side, its new-bourgeois side, is pre-eminently consistent with Thatcherism, Reaganism and, among the masses, with what Stuart Hall has called 'authoritarian populism'.[59] On its positive side it is antihierarchical and consistent with principles of radical democracy. It may have played a significant role in fostering the shopfloor revolts in Britain and elsewhere of the late 1960s and early 1970s, whose decentralized ethos was radical-democratic rather than simply class-ideological.[60]

A radical-democratic ethos is shared by the various new social movements and would it seems to have to be a binding force to aggregate interests in any contemporary left counter-hegemonic political culture.[61] In terms of cultural objects, cultural stakes and cultural needs, it would seem that strategies for a reconstituted left political culture, in an age of disorganizing capitalist societies, will have to take, if not take on, postmodernism very seriously indeed.

CAPITALIST DISORGANIZATION AND POLITICS

Having set out some of the recent transformations of culture which characterize certain advanced western societies we will in this second section of the chapter try to draw together the main themes of the book overall. We have analysed in detail five major western societies: the two most economically forward and relatively large western countries, Britain and France; the most 'organized', Germany; the most powerful and successful western nation, the United States; and that where social democracy has had most impact, Sweden. We have shown that the routes that each of these have followed have been different, but despite such variations organized capitalism has been established in each, at both the top and bottom of the society.

However, we have gone on to show that in the recent period there have been major transformations in the structuring of these western societies, transformations that have resulted from the operation of three parallel processes. First, individual national societies have been subject to a variety of 'internationalizing' processes from *above*. Among these are the development of new forms of economic organization – including global corporations with an international division of labour and high levels of vertical disintegration; the declining distinctiveness of companies producing fixed products for a given (generally) national market (whether financial or industrial); and the growth of new circuits of money and banking separate from those of industry and which are literally out of the control of individual national economic policies. Also important have been the development of new international state structures, and of modes of entertainment and culture which transcend individual national societies. Second, a variety of 'decentralizing' processes have in a sense undermined such national societies from *below* rather than from above. Many of the central structures and processes of key industries, classes and cities, which had produced a particular spatial fix of each national society have been dislocated. Processes involved here include the decentralization of population and industry; the declining attractiveness of mass organizations; the increased emphasis upon the 'local'; the pursuit of sectional interests; the declining salience of class; and the transgression of fixed boundaries by a set of new cultural forms. And third, the growth in the size and effectiveness of the service class has transformed such societies in a sense from *within*. Such a class has realized considerable powers in each of the societies and this has led to a heightened significance of a stratification system based upon individual achievement, upon 'service' class issues in politics, on professionalization strategies, and on new cross-cutting forms of social division and cultural conflict. Our overall claim has been that each of these processes have been proceeding in each of the five societies under investigation. Existing analyses have at best tended to focus on only one process. We have also tried to develop a comparative argument: that each society can only be understood in terms of the particular way in which these three processes have historically intersected. In particular we have tried to trace the differernt paths along which these nations became organized capitalist societies; and given this pattern, attempted to explain to what degree, and in what forms, such societies have begun to 'disorganize'.

We were forced to work through this reconstructed periodization of western societies because of the inability of existing attempts to establish a satisfactory chronology. In the non-Marxist literature the main periods identified have been those of 'pre-industrial' and 'industrial' society. It is often further claimed that there is a process of *convergence* of industrial societies, particularly because of the mobilizing power of advanced technology. The main critiques of this have been either to emphasize the diversity of industrial capitalist societies and the resulting process of divergence, or to maintain that contemporary capitalism in at least some societies has moved into a new 'post-industrial' or 'de-industrial' period. In the Marxist literature the main periods identified have been those of 'competitive capitalism', 'monopoly capitalism', and 'late' or 'state monopoly' capitalism. Each of these periodizations suffer from a number of deficiencies. Firstly, they are reductionist in that the crucial determinant of each period is held to be the economy (whether in the form of technology or in terms of the monopolistic control of markets) and other social institutions and practices are presumed to take their characteristics from it. Secondly, such accounts do not take sufficient notice of the fact that capitalist social relations are necessarily embedded within individual nation-states, so that what may be true at the level of the world economy (increasing concentration in a sector) is not true at the level of each nation-state (where there might be increased competition). Thirdly, they do not consider the changing nature of class politics in such societies, and especially with the capacities and resources of such classes and indeed of other social groupings. Fourthly, they do not consider the spatial scale of such politics and especially whether it is locally, regionally or nationally organized. And finally, they neglect the changing nature of the state and its role in the structuring of the society and particularly of the forms of politics.

In this book by contrast we have employed a threefold periodization. We have argued that *each* western society has moved through three periods or stages: liberal, organized and disorganized. Such a chronology is based on a rejection of economism, on a concentration on the individual nation-state, and on analysing the complex and diverse structuring of societies. We have tried to show that although each society proceeds through these three stages, they take very different forms. We have attempted to account for these differences. In particular, chapters 2 and 3 analysed the comparative trajectories by which five of the major western societies became organized, beginning with the case of Germany, which was the organized capitalist society *par excellence*. Heavy industry, particularly iron and steel, was centrally important in the economy from a very early period; industry was highly bureaucratized, concentrated, and cartelized; there was an early development of the joint-stock company; there was a pervasive interarticulation of banks and industry; the state was interventionist and welfarist; and there was extensive growth of employers' organizations, bureaucratized trade unions and mass political parties. Germany rapidly acquired leadership in the crucially important industries, in iron and steel, chemicals and the electrical sector. The state played a considerable role in creating German organized capitalism, through protectionism, the promoting of cartels; the strengthening of demand in certain sectors; the expansion of public expenditure; a general intertwining of the bureaucracy with the interests of big business; the introduction of a welfare state from above; the development of some degree of corporatism during Weimar; and the growth of an authoritarian organized capitalism under Nazism. Organized capitalism was introduced from above partly in response to the perceived strength of the rapidly growing urbanized, unionized and politicized working class.

In Sweden, by contrast, organization at the bottom has been of unsurpassed strength and has given a particular cast to that nation's social structure. This was however only the case in the second moment of Swedish organized capitalism. In the first moment finance capital played the central role. Especially important economic developments in the late nineteenth/early twentieth century involved substantial increases in the export of grain; the enormous expansion of the railway network; the importance of timber, paper and pulp; the still considerable export of iron and steel; the development of the home market as a motor for industrial growth; and the early and extensive growth of mechnical and electrical engineering industries. Centrally important in this development were the financial institutions, whose influence really began on a major scale in the 1890s. There had been a relatively early development of commercial banks whose loans had been predominantly made to agriculture in the form of long-term mortgages. This then became the major initial form of credit extended to industry. By the last quarter of the nineteenth century a central bank had developed which began to function as the 'bankers' bank'. Prior to the First World War industry remained relatively unconcentrated; this soon changed after the First World War as Sweden began to engage in head-to-head competition with the large firms in the other capitalist nations.

By the 1950s Sweden boasted the highest levels of concentration of any major western country. A central role in this process of concentration was played by the Swedish banks who had rapidly become major shareholders in leading industrial companies.

Other crucially important aspects of Swedish development were the attachment of the Swedish bourgeoisie to parliamentarism, and the constitutional establishment in 1809 of the *dual* power and countervailing forces of parliament and king; the possession of the basis of a comparatively modern civil service from the middle seventeenth century; a long-standing commitment to free-trade policies; and the fact that the first party to establish itself as an electoral organization was the SAP, the Social Democrats. They came to power in 1932 and figured crucially in orchestrating the second moment of Swedish organized capitalism. Important features of Swedish social democracy were the pursuit of Keynesian deficit-spending policies; the birth of Swedish corporatism in 1938; the ideological notion of the *folkshemspolitik* ('people's home'): and the support for welfare measures to prop up the declining birth rate. But it is important to note the relative lateness of the Swedish welfare state compared with the rest of Scandinavia. In the end though, the Social Democrats were able to force through a remarkably universalistic welfare policy, this was made possible because of the exceptional levels of organization at the bottom of the society: the high levels of union density; the early establishment of national bargaining; the power of unions on the shop-floor; and high levels of 'class voting'.

Britain by contrast organized fairly early on at the bottom but rather late at the top. This was not so much the consequence of the destructive role of the financial sector and particularly of the Bank of England, but reflected the more general character of the *Makler* or 'middleman' British economy, a feature which stemmed from its premature industrialization. Britain failed to organize at the top in the decades before the First World War. While the strength of its economy lay in food and drink, insurance and banking, commerce and services – it failed in both heavy industry and in the new industries. Industry was less concentrated than that in Germany or the USA during this period and even where mergers did occur resulting firms remained as loose federations rather than undergoing 'real' concentration through integration. It was only in the inter-war period that Britain *began* to organize at the top: with the growth of new industries, the development of functionally-departmentalized firms and 'managerial enterprises', and the growth of the 'rationalization', movement including some development of a 'corporate bias'. But overall such initiatives were relatively limited. Because Britain was the first industrial nation, an extensive and systematic set of market mechanisms existed, the 'invisible hand', which made it 'unnecessary' for a systematic 'visible hand', to be developed. Especially important were the commercial services provided by the City of London, services which the City effectively monopolized from a very early stage in the development of the world economy.

Again it was only in the inter-war period that there was much borrowing in the City by domestic industry rather than by government or overseas enterprises.

In terms of organization at the bottom, the 1880s were a crucial decade in Britain as general unions began to develop, wage differentials declined, collectivist ideologies became more widespread, and social classes were coming to replace the individual as the policial unit of society. This power of labour at the bottom, or at least of unionized male labour, was reflected in the pre-war origins of the welfare state. However, early organization at the bottom also reflected the strong influence of 'organicist' conservatism of a pre-industrial sort, and of a social-liberal bourgeoisie concerned in part to mobilize, human resources for the benefit of the nation as a whole.

The development of France in part parallels that of Britain in that it too suffered from premature industrialization. Indeed in terms of a number of criteria France can be said to have suffered from 'economic forwardness', even more so than Britain. This can be seen in an early high emphasis upon secondary production; a labour force top-heavy with highly-skilled workers; the early shift into the production of semi-finished goods; industrialization at quite low levels of concentration; highly localized product markets; a marked lack of integration of banks and industry during the initial decades of organized capitalism (bank policy inhibited lending to industry); an orientation to foreign markets for both commodities and labour (the Industrial Revolution passed *through* France). Development was therefore remarkably dislocated with an almost Third World lack of national economic or social integration. Some exceptionally successful companies did develop and these were run by a highly rationalizing corps of engineers. One marked peculiarity of French development was the relative absence of population growth which was significantly connected to the strength of French smallholder agriculture and the 'rational' limitation of progeny.

Capital was therefore relatively less organized at the top compared with both Germany and Sweden. By contrast the state in the later decades of French organized capitalism developed considerable powers of planning, expenditure and regulation. Some development occurred of corporatism which in the main excluded labour particularly because of the weakness of organization at the bottom of French society (low union membership and trade union instability). By the mid-1950s an extraordinary growth had occurred in welfare spending under the direction of non-socialist governments. A particular feature has been the central importance of family allowances which have been struggled for in Catholic countries separately from the labour movement's efforts to gain other welfare benefits. Overall, while the state in France has been well organized from the 1940s onwards, civil society has remained remarkably weakly organized.

Finally, in the USA in the early decades of this century there was an exceptional fusion of banks and industry. The state really did appear as the instrument of the economically dominant class. This was combined with relatively weak organization at the bottom, and that was only to be found during the 1930s and 1940s. The investment banks played a major role in the merger movements in the 1880s and before the First World War, which resulted in a remarkable role in the control of American industry and finance by Morgan and Rockefeller. There were several stages here: (1) horizontal integration in the 1880s; (2) vertical integration under the sway of the banks between the 1890s and 1920s; (3) the creation of multidivisional enterprises from the 1920s onwards as the influence of the banks began to wane somewhat; and (4) the 1960s formation of giant conglomerates in which industrial capital takes on the role of finance capital.

Central to understanding the trajectory of American politics was the phenomenon of progressivism which dated from the turn of the century. Particularly important in the Progressive era was the Sherman Anti-trust Act which seems to have encouraged capital to establish its own regulatory agencies. In general though the state very much operated as the instrument of the economically dominant class during the Progressive heyday of the first two decades of this century. However, progressivist ideology undoubtedly contributed to the manner in which the state developed a degree of autonomy during the 1930s New Deal; and it contributed more generally to the development of the American 'welfare state'. There are a number of other features of welfare legislation: in the USA it developed more slowly and less extensively than in Europe; a greater emphasis was placed on social assistance rather than social insurance; the working class played a weak, and the service class a major, role in its development; and early expansion of 'educational opportunity' was a sort of functional replacement for tardily developing social insurance coverage. Somewhat like France, the state played an active role in promoting the organization of American capitalism at the bottom particularly in creating conditions for the growth of union density before and during the Second World War. But at the same time the war saw an enhanced role for capital interior to the state apparatus itself in return for business support for the war effort – a role from which labour was effectively excluded. Unlike any of the other societies under investigation it is only in the organized capitalist USA that such a large measure of the challenge to capital and the creation of some degree of the relative autonomy of the state derives not from labour but from the service class.

In chapters 4–9 we examined a wide range of processes which are 'disorganizing' these western societies. In order to show this however we had to reconsider aspects of the history of those countries: of spatial/geographical changes (chapters 4 and 5); of managerial/educational developments (chapter 6); of industrial/financial changes (chapter 7); of political developments (chapter 7); and of transformation of labour organizations and industrial relations systems (chapter 8).

We argued that there are specific 'spatial' patterns associated with each phase of the development of capitalist societies. Particular attention is devoted to elucidating the diverse forms taken by the spatial division of labour and to the dimensions of the spatial structuring of civil society. In the genesis of disorganized capitalism a central role has been played by the emergence of giant corporations within certain industrial sectors, corporations whose attachment to any national territory is limited and who are able to subdivide their operations so taking advantage of variations in operating conditions across the globe. Major spatial and industrial changes of a disorganizing kind occurred in Britain from the 1960s onwards: these include the collapse of spatially concentrated manufacturing employment; the increase in service employment which is more spatially dispersed; the decline in population in the cities and the extensive process of 'counter-urbanization'; the shifting of industry away from the major urban centres especially in the north and west of Britain; the reduced significance of 'regions' as any sort of organizational entity and the central importance of *local* variation; increases in the number of smaller plants, enterprises, home-workers and the self-employed; the 'unbundling' and development of specialized producer services firms; the flattening out of trade unionism between different areas; and the declining significance of the 'city' for oppositional activity. A similar set of developments was to be found in the USA, although many of them occurred considerably earlier than in Britain. Decentralization of industrial plants appears to have commenced from the First World War onwards and to have been explicitly linked to the need to avoid the 'contagion' of labour disputes. More recent changes have been linked to the increasing capital-intensity of enterprises and the resulting need for large amounts of land away from the city centres. These has been an exceptionally widespread process of suburbanization especially after the Second World War onwards. Likewise, the development of the Sunbelt has been an integral part of the very process of capitalist disorganization in the USA.

Socio-spatial development in France has been characterized by a peculiar combination of very modern' and very 'backward' aspects. This pattern of unevenness was fixed in the post-Napoleonic period, particularly through the transformation of the French peasantry into a peasant freeholding class which failed to generate a capital surplus, taxation revenue, or landless labourers to stimulate French industry. The latter was itself highly uneven with *industries de pointe* in an otherwise unchanging pattern of traditional industry. Centrally important though within France has been the extraordinary dominance of Paris, not least because of the concentrated market it provided for luxury goods. This dominance was reinforced by the 'Haussmannization' of Paris during the Second Empire. Apart from the highly sophisticated international capital city, France remained up to the Second World War a series of relatively localized and separate economies which made regional or national alliances of workers hard to establish and sustain. Spatially, France rapidly organized in the period between the 1930s and the 1960s. By the 1970s clear indicators of spatial disorganization began to show, and in that process considerable social conflict was generated, partly because of the relatively recent establishment of French organized capitalism.

By marked contrast with the French case Germany experienced very rapid urbanization in the late nineteenth century, particularly in the western areas of the country as well as in Berlin. This was linked to an exceptionally rapid transformation of the industrial structure which in turn was facilitated by a very considerable increase in agricultural productivity. Before the development of the Ruhr, German industry had been far more dispersed and this militated against concentrations of political power by the industrial bourgeoisie. German industry became much more geographically concentrated in the years around the First World War and this provided the context for major labour unrest. There were very clear regional economies established which remained of importance during the Nazi period. Attempts at the end of the Second World War at disaggregation were only partly successful. By the late 1970s considerable decentralization of population had begun, particularly as the dominance of the Ruhr declined and oil became a much more important energy source. There was a considerable urban–rural shift both within West Germany and throughout the world economy.

Although Sweden also industrialized extremely rapidly, urbanization was a rather slower process. One reason for this was that the industrial sectors in Sweden were fairly decentralized; iron and steel, for example, was organized with small self-contained 'bruks'. Industrial unions nevertheless developed from a fairly early period. As urbanization developed in the inter-war period particular emphasis came to be placed on developing the neighbourhood unit which in part at least reinforced the role of the 'housewife' in Sweden in the 1940s and 1950s. Recent changes have suggested at least a modest disorganization: the population of the major cities has begun to fall; the places with the largest population increases are very small settlements; there have been marked reductions in industrial employment in highly urbanized centres even where these areas enjoyed a favourable industrial structure; there has been a substantial process of de-industrialization of the employment structure, and the industrial working class has markedly declined in size.

Overall then it is shown that during the period of organized capitalism a particular 'spatial fix' got established between the dominant manufacturing/extractive industries, major industrial cities, particular regions dominated by such industries, and labour and capital 'organized' in a given structural pattern. The spatial fix varied between the five societies but overall it appeared that there were a set of interconnecting processes, of growing towns and cities, dominant industries, increasing size of workplaces, well-organized regional economies, which would serve to reinforce a structuring of social classes of capital versus labour. We have seen though that this spatial fix has begun to dissolve in all five countries, although this is most developed in the USA and Britain.

We then addressed the issue of how each society has begun to be disorganized in a sense from *within*, as a result of the development of what we term the 'service class'. The growth of this class occurred first on any scale in the USA. Its development was by no means inevitable. Although it has arisen in the context of a given labour–capital relationship, its emergence has depended in part on such a class being in a sense able to 'form itself'. Crucially important in that process was the growth of 'modern management' and indeed there was in effect a class struggle between it and existing capital. In the USA, but not in the Britain or France, capital, so to speak, lost and complex managerial hierarchies developed. That in turn helped to produce an extensive growth of white-collar employment, which itself helped to generate an interlocking complex of new institutional developments: of colleges and universities; of private foundations; of professionalizing occupations in both the private and public sector; and of large corporate and state bureaucracies. These institutions developed and extended themselves between labour and capital within American organized capitalism, constituting themselves as a kind of wedge or third force. As the service class then formed itself it transformed the society, strengthening American capital, weakening labour, and expanding the growth of an educationally-based stratification system. Although a service class has now developed in all the European countries under investigation, its development has in each case been later and taken a rather different form. Its consequences have therefore been less marked and its disorganizing effects rather more mediated than in the US. In Britain for example, it was something that was much more state-sponsored and occurred during a particularly progressive period. In West Germany, although scientific management was implemented on a much wider scale than in Britain, the new occupations adopted the model of professionalization provided by the older professions and hence were much more tied into the state. Engineers did not therefore provide a model of independent professionalization which was so influental in the USA. In Sweden, although there was some development of scientific management in the early decades of this century, the main growth of a service class occurred during the post-war period. This stemmed from two causes: rapid economic acceleration from the late 1930s onwards, a growth involving new materials, new products and new ways of working; and the extensive increases in public investment particularly in a large range of social services. In France, there had always been highly qualified engineers from the eighteenth century onwards. However, their numbers did not increase much during the late nineteenth and early twentieth centuries and many of them refused to consider a career in private industry. The depression years reinforced this reluctance. There was also little development of systematic education for business until after the Second World War when there was an exceptionally fast and wide-ranging development of the French service class.

There are a variety of political developments which are connected with these structural changes. There has been a marked decline in the levels of class voting especially in Britain and West Germany. There has also been a related process of 'partisan dealignment' in Britain, that is, the growth of third-party voting as both the Conservatives and Labour have been in electoral decline; changes in the issue bases of politics; and a noticeable increase in electoral volatility. In the USA there has been an increasing localization of politics, a declining degree of party partisanship, and a secular decline in voter participation in national elections. In Germany the development of the Green Party has provided the most striking example of third party development. In France, while class voting to a certain extent re-appeared in the 1981 election, there has been a pronounced bourgeoisification of the Socialist Party. These voting patterns in all five societies have in turn been associated with a number of other changes. There appears to have been a growth in a set of values associated with so-called 'new politics' and this partly involves an extensive critique of the state and of its reformist potential. Such a critique also extends to the form of organization itself: Green parties, feminist groupings, anti-nuclear organizations, all tend to be decentralized and opposed to co-ordination from the centre. Social democracy which is typically committed to what are often statist notions of 'modernization' has had considerable difficulty in dealing with such development on the left. Conservative forces similarly have had considerable trouble in responding. In Britain, for example, the Conservative ethos of the strong national state and the unregulated market excludes and alienates many of these new social groupings. The development of these has however been less marked in Sweden, where the Social Democratic Party still provides the substantial framework for left-of-centre politics.

Simultaneously with these developments has been the general breakdown of working-class 'occupational communities', partly because of various spatial changes but also because of the growth of less class-specific mass consumption and leisure patterns. This does not suggest though that social conflict will disappear. On the contrary there are many enduring sites of opposition and struggle, but many of these are irreducibly local and whether they can in any sense take on a wider dimensions is at the moment rather doubtful. It is even questionable whether the labour movement will be able to defend the welfare state successfully from a variety of attacks. Support for welfare policies now derives from a more complex set of social forces, much more fragmented than previously, and it is a much more contingent matter as to whether a centralized welfare state system can be defended.

One reason why this is a particularly significant question is because national economies are increasingly out of control. This is partly because of the development of global corporations and the resulting fragmentation of the production process for particular commodities within any given national territory. It is also because of the way in which they have restructured the very patterns and forms of international trade, so that all the major economies are now particularly dependent upon the patterns of world trade. And it is because there has been an extensive growth of internationalized banking forms, of the so-called Eurodollar and Eurobond markets which are essentially privatized and outside of the control of either national governments or of international regulatory bodies like the IMF. Indeed there has been an extensive process of bank deregulation from the 1960s onwards in all these countries. As a result there has grown up a circuit of privatized money-capital now effectively separate from industrial capital. Both money-capital and industrial capital are consequently internationalized but have separate and unco-ordinated circuits. Under organized capitalism mainly nationally based banks looked after a national currency; under disorganized capitalism such structures have proven ephemeral as an extensive deterritorialization of the international money and banking system has taken place.

The effects of such internationalization can be particularly seen in the steady erosion of corporatist or neo-corporatist institutions which have been most marked in Sweden, but have also been found to varying degrees in France, Germany (FRG), and Britain. The structural decline in such arrangements is part of the very process of disorganization. Corporatism was fundamentally a national project, a matter of compromise within a national context of resource distribution. Internationalization and the greatly enhanced openness of western societies dislocates that set of arrangements and makes assessments of what would be appropriate sacrifices in the national interest difficult to determine and justify. The statistical decline in the number and proportion of indigenous manual workers in mass production means that those workers who have been at the centre of the corporatist bargain have become unrepresentative. The oil and other crises have made it increasingly difficult to ensure that organized workers could be bought off through rising real and social wages. Internationalization has also meant an increased disarticulation between capitals located with a national territory, so that it becomes more difficult to strike a national bargain. In particular, it becomes more and more necessary to divert resources into the mainly private exporting sector and to limit increases in the expanding and more feminized public sector. This sets up particular strains which make it harder to sustain the collective identity of each national working class. Such a process is further reinforced by the increased importance of the sphere of consumption generated in part by and through international forms of cultural production and transmission. Such cultural forms are in part 'privatizing' and in part 'classless' and make allegiance to class collective modes of social organization and control through centralized trade unions increasingly implausible.

Let us restate this last argument. At the beginning of chapter 4 we set out a number of minimal conditions that would have to be met for a 'working class' in a major western country to enter into and sustain enduring forms of class actions, whether of a revolutionary or reformist character. Central to these conditions were aspects of the spatial structuring of such societies. Overall it once appeared that a whole set of economic, spatial and social developments in organized capitalism were propelling the working class forwards: it was on the side of history; it represented the 'modern'; it was interconnected with the forces which would reorganize society so as to realize some at least of this class's potential causal powers. These developments did not of course necessarily occur, and even when they did the results were often deeply disappointing. However, what our claim amounts to is that such a possibility has in a number of specific western societies disappeared. Time cannot be set in reverse, the moment has passed. The power of a mass industrial working class to shape society in its own image are for the foreseeable future profoundly weakened. This can be summarized by returning to the conditions referred to in chapter 4. The working class in any of these five western societies has enormous difficulties in sustaining national-level collective action for the following reasons.

(1) The radical restructuring of modern industry and policies of residential relocation have undermined some of the conditions which historically facilitated 'dialogue' both within class-homogeneous communities, and between such communities.

(2) It is now the case that local civil societies are less simply structured by divisions based on the conflict of labour and capital – the division between the 'people' and the 'state' being an equally important underlying social relation. Moreover, the growth of 'low cost' home ownership has broken down many of the class-based patterns of residential differentiation; at the same time the internationalization of capital has reduced the degree to which there are locally resident bourgeoisies which are spatially differentiated and yet sufficiently adjacent for them to provide targets for oppositional struggle.

(3) There has been an extensive expansion both in the number and range of voluntary associations and socio-political groupings and in the significance and impact of the means of mass (rather than class) communication. Both developments mean that civil society is structured on a progressively 'horizontal' rather than 'vertical' basis.

(4) Class relations between labour and capital do not appear to *cause* the entire patterning of social inequalities, particularly because of the 'apparently' increased importance of the division between the state and the people, gender divisions, age differences, and the relations between ethnic groups. All these may generate forms of non-class collective action which can provide bases for achieving gains and benefits.

(5) Many social groupings have now concluded that collective action can be successful and is worth pursuing. Many groups in the 'service class' pursue their goals through collective action. This development stems from the increased horizontal fragmentation of civil society, some breakdown in patterns of deference, the growth of a political and cultural pluralism which has created conditions for a marked 'decentring' of individual and collective identity.

But cross-national differences are vast. And the working class as a collective actor is in some nations better able to cope with the enormous centrifugal pressures of capitalist disorganization than in others. Where the working class as a collective actor was able to play an important part in determining the form of a national organized capitalism, it should also be able to play a prominent role in the shape of things to come. Thus disorganized capitalist political culture in a country like Sweden is and will be vastly different from that in, for example, the USA. Where trade unions, as we outlined in the conclusion to chapter 8, will take on an important role in initiating forms of work organization and worker participation in the new restructuration – as they have done in Germany and Sweden, though not in Britain or the USA – labour-movement strength can survive and potentially thrive. Where broader forms of collective identity are strong among male, while, skilled, export-sector, primary labour market workers (as has been the case in Germany and Sweden) then labour-movement dualism can be avoided.

Left political culture in every country in disorganized capitalism is now necessarily a pluralist political culture in which new social movements and class forces, depending on the nation, play greater or smaller roles. Primary labour market workers may be able to pursue their interests in disorganized capitalism apart from the political left, but it is unlikely, on an industrial or political level, that the left will be able to get very far without the support and participation of primary labour market workers. The reconstruction of a viable left political culture cannot proceed via the condescension of the 'new' social forces to class forces, but must proceed through genuine dialogue.

Yet transformations are occurring in the very structuring of western societies. As the working class, as conventionally conceived, appears to be more and more old-fashioned, rooted in a previous spatial and cultural fix, so newer forms of politics, which can provide also for the possibility of a reconstituted class politics, and newer forms of cultural experience have come to the fore. The introduction of post-modernism within popular culture – in advertisements, television, video, pop music, and everyday experience of the social in which representations multiply and telescope to the point at which they intermix and become largely indistinguishable from the real – breaks for a final time the mould of organized capitalist certainty centred around a set of more stable cultural forms. Contemporary culture, operating through a combination of often figural, anti-auratic, electronic and spectacular symbols has had the effect of disintegrating older modes of individual and collective identity and, at times, reconstituting new ones and leading, it seems, ineluctably to a twenty-first-century experience in which a social structure based on massive industrial core working classes, huge industrial cities, the capital–labour relationship structuring society, a minor and insignificant service class, have all been left far behind. The world of a 'disorganized capitalism' is one in which the 'fixed, fast-frozen relations' of organized capitalist relations have been swept away. Societies are being transformed from above, from below, and from within. All that is solid about organized capitalism, class, industry, cities, collectivity, nation-state, even the word, melts into air.

Notes

1 INTRODUCTION

1 K. Marx and F. Engels, *Manifesto of the Communist Party* (Foreign Languages Press, London, 1888), pp. 53–4.
2 Ibid., p. 65.
3 M. Berman, *All that is Solid Melts into Air. The Experience of Modernity* (Verso, London, 1983). Also see S. Kern, *The Culture of Time and Space, 1880–1918* (Weidenfeld & Nicolson, London, 1983).
4 *Organiserter Kapitalismus*, ed. H. Winckler (Vandenhoeck & Ruprecht, Gottingen, 1974).
5 See J. Kocka, 'Organisierter Kapitalismus oder Staatsmonopolistischer Kapitalismus? Begriffliche Vorbemerkungen', ibid., pp. 20–4. For a related formulation, see R. Torstendahl, 'Technology in the development of society 1850–1980: four phases of industrial capitalism in Western Europe', *History and Technology* 1 (1984), pp. 157–74.
6 A. Gorz, *Farewell to the Working Class* (Pluto, London, 1982); E. Hobsbawm, *The Forward March of Labour Halted?* (Verso, London, 1981); C. Offe, *Disorganized Capitalism* (Polity Press, Cambridge, 1985).
7 See G. Therborn, 'The prospects of labour and the transformation of advanced capitalism', *New Left Review* 145 (1984), pp. 5–38.
8 See P. Anderson, *Lineages of the Absolutist State* (New Left Books, London, 1974).
9 See S. Lash and J. Urry, 'The new Marxism of collective action: a critical analysis', *Sociology* (1984), pp. 33–50.
10 See S. Beer, *Britain against Itself* (Faber, London, 1982).
11 D. Gallie's *In Search of the New Working Class* (Cambridge University Press, Cambridge, 1978) puts well the case *for* French working-class radicalism.
12 See D. Bell, *The Cultural Contradictions of Capitalism* (Heinemann, London, 1976).
13 F. Jameson, 'Post-modernism, or the cultural logic of late capitalism', *New Left Review* 146 (1984), pp. 53–92.
14 J. F. Lyotard, *Discours, figure* (Klincksieck, Paris, 1971).
15 See B. Ehrenreich, *The Hearts of Men* (Pluto Press, London, 1983).

16 M. Poster, *Foucault, Marxism and History* (Polity Press, Cambridge, 1984).

17 B. Martin, *A Sociology of Contemporary Popular Culture* (Basil Blackwell, Oxford, 1981).

18 There are obvious parallels between our views and those of Claus Offe, as in *Disorganized Capitalism* (Polity, Cambridge, 1985). For a sympathetic critique of our position which focuses on the 'economic' level, see P. Cooke, 'Spatial development processes: organized or disorganized?', *Nordplan Seminar*, Cambridge, December 1985. On presence-availability, see A. Giddens, *A Contemporary Critique of Historical Materialism* (Macmillan, London, 1981) among many other works.

19 See B. Anderson, *Imagined Communities* (Verso, London, 1983) on liberal capitalism and the growth of print-capitalism; P. Bairoch, 'The main trends in national economic development', in *Disparities in Economic Development since the Industrial Revolution*, ed. P. Bairoch and M. Levy-Leboyer (Macmillan, London, 1981), pp.3-17, on the main economic changes involved; J. de Vries, *European Urbanization 1500-1800* (Methuen, London, 1984) on urban development; and Giddens, *Contemporary Critique*.

2 THE DEVELOPMENT OF ORGANIZED CAPITALISM (1)

1 See P. Milward and S. Saul, *The Development of the Economies of Continental Europe 1850-1914* (Allen & Unwin, London, 1977), pp. 20-4.

2 See here D. Landes, *The Unbound Prometheus* (Cambridge University Press, Cambridge, 1969), pp. 319ff.

3 Ibid., pp. 353-3; W. G. Hoffmann, *Das Wachstum der deutschen Wirtschaft seit der Mitte des 19. Jahrhunderts* (Springer Verlag, Berlin, 1965), pp. 340, 352-3; W. Feldenkirchen, *Die Eisen- und Stahlindustrie des Ruhrgebiets 1879-1914* (Steiner, Wiesbaden, 1982), pp. 321-3; Milward and Saul, *Continental Europe*, p. 25; J. Kocka and H. Siegrist, 'Die hundert grösten deutschen Industrieunternehmen im späten 19. und frühen 20. Jahrhundert', in *Recht und Entwicklung im 19. und frühen 20. Jahrhundert* (Vandenhoeck & Ruprecht, Göttingen, 1979), pp. 72, 86-8.

4 See Milward and Saul, *Continental Europe*, pp. 26f., and Feldenkirchen, *Stahlindustrie*, p. 322.

5 See A. Chandler and H. Daems, 'Administrative coordination, allocation and monitoring: concepts and comparisons', in *Recht und Entwicklung*, pp. 46-7.

6 Feldenkirchen, *Stahlindustrie*, pp. 114ff.

7 See Kocka and Siegrist, 'Industrieunternehmen', pp. 69-72; Milward and Saul, *Continental Europe*, p. 29; E. G. Spencer, 'Rulers of the Ruhr: Leadership and authority in German big business before 1914', *Business History Review* 53 (1979), p. 53.

8 It was not only the new industries, as we shall see below, that developed modern managerial structures early on, but heavy industry as well. Between 1896 and 1914 it has been estimated that 75 per cent of the Ruhr's most powerful industrialists were managers without significant holdings in their companies. Of the 25 largest coal mines in 1914 which had been established in the nineteenth century, only three (but these include Krupp and Thyssen) were led at their beginnings by

owner–entrepreneurs who devoted most of their energies to their particular concern. In Ruhr heavy industry only a few especially prominent firms – Krupp, Thyssen, Haniel – were able to maintain entrepreneurial as distinct from modern managerial structures, because they were able to avoid the large-scale issue of shares. In other enterprises managers had, by 1900, become able to achieve a large degree of autonomy from boards of directors because the amount of stock capital required for viability was so great that no single investor (not even the Berlin banks and powerful individual figures like Hugo Stinnes) could maintain control. The position of managing directors became extraordinarily secure: most routinely serving until retirement, and some even choosing their own successors. Managing directors' philosophy often dictated giving large amounts of autonomous power to other top managers. This was especially true for the mining directors in backward integrating steel concerns. After mergers, at least initially, the old management structure of the acquired enterprise was left intact, and the leading managers were put on the executive boards and/or boards of directors of the acquiring firm. See Spencer op. cit., pp. 42, 52–5; J. Kocka, 'The rise of the modern industrial enterprise in Germany', in *Managerial Hierarchies*, ed. A. D. Chandler and H. Daems (Harvard University Press, Cambridge, Mass., 1980), pp. 77–116. See also T. Pierenkemper, 'Entrepreneurs in heavy industry: upper Silesia and the Westphalian Ruhr region, 1852 to 1913', *Business History Review* 53 (1979), pp. 69–70, 73–4.

9 On the German chemical industry see Kocka and Siegrist, 'Industrieunternehmen', pp. 74–7; and J. Kocka, 'Grossunternehmen und der Aufsteig des Manager-Kapitalismus im späten 19. und frühen 20. Jahrhundert: Deutschland im internationalen Vergleich', *Historische Zeitschrift* 232 (1981), pp. 46–7; J. Borkin, *The Crime and Punishment of I. G. Farben* (Free Press, NY, 1978).

10 The ratio of salaried employees:total employees for the two largest firms in chemicals for which figures are available are 10.8% and 19.7%, in iron and steel they are 9.0% and 3.9%; see Kocka and Siegrist, 'Industrieunternehmen', p. 111.

11 See ibid., pp. 107–10.

12 The growth of Siemens, depicted in Jürgen Kocka's magisterial *Unternehmensverwaltung und Angestelltenschaft am Beispiel Siemens 1847–1914* (Klett, Stuttgart, 1969) probably best epitomizes the growth of organized capitalism in Germany.

13 See Chandler and Daems, 'Administrative Coordination'; F. Blaich, 'Ausschliesslichkeitsbindungen als Wege zur industriellen Konzentration in der deutschen Wirtschaft bis 1914', in *Recht und Entwicklung*, pp. 319–20.

14 See Kocka, 'Capitalism and bureaucracy in German industrialization before 1914', *Economic History Review* 34 (1981), pp. 453–68.

15 For details here see W. Feldenkirchen, *Stahlindustrie*, pp. 110–14.

16 Ibid., pp. 118–20.

17 See ibid., pp. 121ff., and E. Maschke, 'Outline of the history of German cartels from 1873 to 1914', in *Essays in European Economic History, 1709–1914*, ed. F. Crouzet (Edward Arnold, London, 1969).

18 See, for example, R. Hilferding, 'Probleme der Zeit', *Die Gesellschaft* (1924), pp. 1–17; and Hilferding, 'Die Aufgaben der Sozialdemokratie in der Republik', *Sozialdemokratischer Parteitag, Kiel 1927* (Protokoll, Berlin, 1927).

19 See H. Böhme, 'Bankenkonzentration und Schwerindustrie 1873–1896', in *Sozialgeschichte Heute, Festschrift für Hans Rosenberg zum 70. Geburtstag,*

ed. H-U. Wehler (Vandenhoeck und Ruprecht, Göttingen, 1974), pp. 441, 443.

20 See Milward and Saul, *Continental Europe*, p. 48.

21 Ibid., p. 48. For the inter-war period see T. Balderston, 'The beginning of the depression in Germany, 1927–1930: investment and the capital market', *Economic History Review* 36 (1983), pp. 396–415.

22 See K. J. Hopt, 'Zur Function des Aufsichtsrat im Verhältnis von Industrie und Bankensystem', in *Recht und Entwicklung der Grossunternehmen im 19. u. frühen 20. Jahrhundert*, ed. N. Horn and J. Kocka (Vandenhoeck und Ruprecht, Göttingen, 1979), pp. 227–42.

23 D. Abraham, *The Collapse of the Weimar Republic* (Princeton University Press, Princeton, 1981) pp. 180ff.; H. P. Ullmann, 'Staatliche Exportförderung und private Exportinitiative, Probleme des staatsinterventionismus im Deutschen Kaiserreich am Beispiel der staatlichen Aussenhandelsförderung (1880–1919)', *Vierteljahrschrift für Sozial – und Wirtschaftsgeschichte* 65 (1978), pp. 157–216.

24 See G. Feldman, 'The collapse of the Steel Works Association, 1912–1919: a case study in the operation of German "collectivist capitalism"', in *Sozialgeschichte Heute*, ed. H-U. Wehler (Vandenhoeck & Ruprecht, Göttingen, 1974), pp. 575–93; K. H. Pohl, 'Die "Stresemannsche Aussenpolitik" und das westeuropaische Eisenkartell 1926, "Europäische Politik" oder nationales Interesse?', *Vierteljahrschrift für Sozial – und Wirtschaftsgeschichte* 65 (1978), pp. 511–34.

25 We should like to note here that there was an increase in public expenditure as a proportion of net domestic product from about 1870 onwards. Before then in peacetime years the proportion averaged about 5–6 per cent; from 1870 to 1890 during slower-growth organized capitalism the proportion averaged between 7 and 9 per cent; from 1890 to 1913 in quickly-expanding organized capitalism it was between 9 and 11 per cent; and during the Weimar Republic it averaged 13 to 16 per cent. See Hoffmann, *Wachstum*, pp. 148–9, 825–8. The very high proportions during the Third Reich (21–29%) are mostly accounted for by very great military expenditure which takes up over half of state expenditure during that period.

For more general treatment of the German state in this period, see V. Hentschel, *Wirtschaft und Wirtschaftspolitik im Wilhelminischen Deutschland. Organiserter Kapitalismus und Interventionsstaat* (Klett-Kotta, Stuttgart, 1978); D. Baudis and H. Nussbaum, *Wirtschaft und Staat in Deutschland vom Ende des 19. Jahrhunderts bis 1918/19* (Akademie-Verlag, Berlin, 1978); and P. C. Witt, 'Finanzpolitik und sozialer Wandel, Wachstum und Funktionswandel der Staatsausgaben in Deutschland, 1871–1933', in *Sozialgeschichte Heute*, ed. H-U. Wehler, pp. 565–74.

26 See Spencer, 'Rulers of the Ruhr', pp. 47–8; Pierenkemper, 'Entrepreneurs in heavy industry', p. 68.

27 See Pierenkemper, ibid., p. 70.

28 See E. G. Spencer, 'Business, bureaucrats and social control in the Ruhr, 1896–1914', in *Sozialgeschichte Heute*, ed. H-U. Wehler, pp. 453–6.

29 On the former, see J. Caplan, '"The imaginary universality of particular interests": the "tradition" of the civil service in German history', *Social History* 4 (1979), pp. 299–317; on the latter see R. Bendix, *Kings and People* (University of California, Berkeley, 1978), ch. 11. Also note in this period the virtual exclusion of

Catholics, Jews and, of course, women from higher offices in both Prussia and the Reich. See J. C. G. Rohl, 'Beamtenpolitik in Wilhelmischen Deutschland', in *Das Kaiserliche Deutschland, Politik und Gesellschaft 1879–1918*, ed. M. Stürmer (Droste, Düsseldorf, 1970), pp. 287–311, 290–1; K. H. Jarausch, 'Liberal education as illiberal socialization: the case of students in imperial Germany', *Journal of Modern History* 50 (1978), pp. 609–30.

30 See P. Flora, 'Solution or source of crisis? The welfare state in historical perspective', in *The Emergence of the Welfare State in Britain and Germany, 1850–1950*, ed. M. Mommsen (Croom Helm, London, 1981). The Flora index consists of a weighted average of the per cent of the economically active population covered in four types of social insurance. Old age insurance receives a loading of 1.5, health and unemployment insurance both 1.0, and accident insurance 0.5. In the case of subsidized voluntary insurance the corresponding averages are halved. Note that education and housing are not included, and that the index relates to the percentage of the population covered and does not relate to the amount of coverage for given sections of the population. We are considering 'take-off' to be when a country's Flora index surpasses that of Germany in 1890; in each case this coincides with a qualitative leap in the index.

31 See J. Tampke, 'Bismarck's social legislation: a genuine breakthrough', ibid., pp. 71–83.

32 See H-P. Ullman, 'German industry and Bismarck's social security system', ibid., pp. 133–49, 138–40.

33 See W. Conze, 'Die politische Entscheidungen in Deutschland 1929–33', in *Die Staats- und Wirtschaftskrise des Deutschen Reichs 1929/33*, ed. W. Conze and H. Raupach (Klett, Stuttgart, 1967); and are more recently W. Conze, 'Zum Scheitern der Weimarer Republik', *Vierteljahrschrift für Sozial- und Wirtschaftsgeschichte* 70 (1983), pp. 215–21. Also see H. James, 'Gab er einer Alternative zur Wirtschaftspolitik Brünings?' *Vierteljahrschrift für Sozial- und Wirtschaftsgeschichte* 70 (1983), pp. 523–41.

34 See B. Weisbrod, 'The crisis of German unemployment insurance', in *Emergence of the Welfare State*, ed. W. Mommsen, pp. 188–204.

35 Maier, for example, argues that fundamental was its corporatism and points to a budding tripartism and relative social peace. Feldman argues that it was industry and in particular heavy industry that reorganized Germany after the war and that tripartite arrangements were unimportant. Borchardt, Erdmann and Abraham, from differing perspectives, maintain that it was grass-roots trade unionism and a powerful 'instrumental collectivism' which undermined business profitability and presaged the authoritarian response. See C. Maier, *Recasting Bourgeois Europe* (Princeton University Press, Princeton, NJ, 1975); G. Feldman, 'Das deutsche organisierter Kapitalismus während der Krieg und Inflationsjahre 1914–23', in *Organisierter Kapitalismus*, ed. H. Winkler, pp. 150–71, pp. 155, 158; G. Feldman, *Army, Industry and Labor in Germany* (Princeton University Press, Princeton, NJ, 1966), pp. 301–7, 316–21; C. Maier, 'Intervention in Bericht und Diskussion to H. Mommsen, "Abschlussetzung: Methodologische Ansätze und Ergebnisse"', in *Industrielles System*, ed. H. Mommsen et al., pp. 955–6; P. Wulf, 'Schwerindustrie und Seeschiffahrt nach dem 1. Weltkrieg: Hugo Stinnes und die HAPAG', *Vierteljahrschrift für Sozial- und Wirtschaftsgeschichte* 67 (1980), pp. 1–21; B. Weisbrod, 'Zur Form schwerindustrieller Interessenvertretung in der zweiten

Hälfte der Weimarer Republik', in *Industrielles System*, ed. H. Mommsen et al., pp. 675–89; U. Nocken, 'Inter-industry conflicts and alliances as exemplified by the AVI-agreement', ibid., pp. 315–39; G. Feldman, *Iron and Steel in the German Inflation, 1916–1923* (Princeton University Press, Princeton, NJ, 1977), pp. 455ff.; B. Weisbrod, *Schwerindustrie*, pp. 143–86; K. Borchardt, 'Wirtschaftliche Ursachen des Schieterns der Weimarer Republik', in *Weimar, Selbstpreisgabe einer Demokratie, Eine Bilanz Heute*, ed. K. D. Erdmann and H. Schulze, (Droste, Düsseldorf, 1980), pp. 211–50; K. Erdmann, 'Versuch einer Schlussbilanz', ibid., pp. 345–58; and D. Abraham, *The Collapse of the Weimar Republic* (Princeton University Press, Princeton, 1982).

36 See Feldman, *Iron and Steel*, pp. 82–3, 98–109; and 'Das deutsche organisierter Kapitalismus', pp. 158–61.

37 See Weisbrod, *Schwerindustrie*, pp. 299f.

38 See G. Feldman, 'Das deutsche organiserter Kapitalismus', p. 163.

39 See L. Jorberg, 'The industrial revolution in the Nordic countries', in *The Fontana Economic History of Europe: the Emergence of Industrial Societies – 2* (Fontana/Collins, London, 1973), p. 438. This section has benefited greatly from the comments of Göran Therborn on an earlier draft.

40 See Jorberg, ibid., p. 441.

41 See Jorberg, ibid., p. 448; Milward and Saul, *Continental Europe*, pp. 486–7.

42 See Karl-Gustaf Hildebrand, *Banking in a Growing Economy: Svenska Handelsbanken since 1871* (Esselte Tryck, Stockholm, 1971).

43 See Milward and Saul, *Continental Europe*, pp. 484–5; E. Söderlund, *Swedish Timber Exports 1850–1950* (Swedish Wood Exporters Association, Stockholm, 1952); L. Jorberg, 'Structural change and economic growth: Sweden in the 19th century', *Economy and History* 8 (1965), pp. 3–46, p. 21.

44 On the Swedish iron and steel industry see Milward and Saul, *Continental Europe*, pp. 471–2, 496; S. Pollard, *Peaceful Conquest: the Industrialization of Europe 1760–1970* (Oxford University Press, Oxford, 1981), p. 235; M. Flinn, 'Scandinavian iron ore mining and the British steel industry', *Scandinavian Economic History Review* 2 (1954); and M. Fritz, *Svenskjärnmalnsexport 1883–1913* (Gothenberg University Ekonomiskhistoriska institutionen, Gothenberg, 1967).

45 Jorberg, 'Den Svenska ekonomiska utvecklingen 1861–1983', *Meddelands från Ekonomisk-historiska institutionen Lunds universitet* 33, Lunds universitet, 1984, p. 16.

46 Ibid., p. 16.

47 See Milward and Saul, *Continental Europe*, pp. 448–9; Jorberg, 'Structural change', pp. 441–3; and A. Montgomery, *The Rise of Modern Industry in Sweden* (P. S. King, London, 1939).

48 See C-A. Nilsson, 'Business incorporations in Sweden: a study of enterprise 1846–1896', *Economy and History* 2 (1959), pp. 38–96, p. 62; L. Jorberg, *Growth and Fluctuations of Swedish Industry 1869–1912* (Almqvist & Wiksell, Stockholm, 1961).

49 For further details see I. Nygren, 'Transformation of bank structures in the industrial period. The case of Sweden 1820–1913', *The Journal of European Economic History* 12 (1983), pp. 29–68, pp. 30–1; K. Samuelsson, 'The banks and the financing of industry in Sweden, c.1900–1927', *Scandinavian Economic History Review* 6 (1958), pp. 176–90.

50 See ibid., pp. 37–8, 48–56; and Nygren, 'Kreditformer och Kreditinstitut i Sverige 1840–1910', in *Utviklingen av kreditt og Kredittinstitusjoner i de norkiske Land ca. 1850–1914*, ed. G. A. Blom (Tapir, Trondheim, Norway, 1978), pp. 1–8. See also L. Sandberg, 'Banking and economic growth in Sweden before World War I', *Journal of Economic History* 38 (1978), pp. 650–80; O. Gårslander, *History of Stockholm's Enskilda Bank to 1914* (Enskilda Bank, Stockholm, 1962).

51 See K. Samuelsson, 'The banks and the financing of industry in Sweden c.1900–1927', *The Scandinavian Economic History Review* 6 (1958), pp. 176–90, pp. 180–4; Nygren, 'Transformation', pp. 61–2; and E. Söderlund, *Skandinaviska banken i det svenska bankvasendets historia 1864–1914* (Skandinaviska Banken, Göteborg, 1964).

52 See K-G. Hildebrand, *Banking in a Growing Economy Svenska Handelsbanken since 1871* (Esselte Tryck, Stockholm, 1971), pp. 1–21; and T. Gårdland, *Svensk industrifinansiering, 1830–1913* (Svenska Bankföreningen, Stockholm, 1947).

53 See J. S. Bain, *International Differences in Industrial Structure, Eight Nations in the 1950s* (Yale University Press, New Haven, Conn., 1966).

54 See U. Himmelstrand, G. Ahrne, L. Lundberg and L. Lundberg, *Beyond Welfare Capitalism* (Heinemann, London, 1981), pp. 55–6.

55 For general discussion here, see K. Samuelsson, 'Banks and financing', pp. 185–9; and Söderlund, 'Skandinaviska banken'.

56 Samuelsson, 'Banks and financing', pp. 177–8; Hildebrand, *Banking in a Growing Economy*, pp. 38–52; and E. Cohn, *Den svenska cellulosaindustins utveckling och nationalekonomiska betydelse* (Stockholm, 1967).

57 See P. Anderson, *Lineages of the Absolutist State* (New Left Books, London, 1974), pp. 544ff. The civil service was developed by Gustavas Adolphus II by 1643, although at first it was structured along regional rather than 'functional–departmental' lines.

58 See D. G. Verney, *Parliamentary Reform in Sweden, 1866–1921* (Clarendon Press, Oxford, 1957); and H. Heclo, *Modern Social Politics in Britain and Sweden, from Relief to Income Maintenance* (Yale University Press, New Haven, 1974).

59 See D. Rushton, 'Scandinavia: working multiparty systems', in *Modern Political Parties*, ed. S. Newman (University of Chicago Press, Chicago, 1956), pp. 169–193.

60 See K. Samuelsson, *From Great Power to Welfare State* (Allen & Unwin, London, 1968), pp. 226–32. For further details see ibid., pp. 242–50.

61 E. F. Heckscher, *An Economic History of Sweden* (Harvard University Press, Cambridge, Mass., 1963), pp. 272–6.

62 G. Therborn, 'The working class and the welfare state. A historical–analytical overview and a little Swedish monograph', *5th Nordic Congress of Research in the History of the Labour Movement* (Murikka, Finland, August 1983), p. 20.

63 See A. and G. Myrdal, *Kris i befolkningsfrågen* (A. Bonnier, Stockholm, 1934).

64 See I. Schobbie, *Sweden* (Benn, London, 1972), p. 119; and P. Råberg, *Functionalistisk genombrott* (Norstedts, Stockholm, 1972).

65 See W. Korpi, *The Working Class in Welfare Capitalism: Work, Unions and Politics in Sweden* (Routledge & Kegan Paul, London, 1978), pp. 74–5.

66 See the comprehensive analysis in A. Kjellberg, *Facklig organisiering i tolv länder* (Arkiv förlag, Lund, 1983), pp. 57–66, 75–9.

67 See ibid., p. 223; and D. J. Blake, 'Swedish trade unions and the Social Democratic

Party: the formative years', *The Scandinavian Economic History Review* 8 (1960), pp. 25–6, 33.

68 See Mancur Olson, *The Rise and Decline of Nations* (Yale University Press, New Haven, Conn., 1982), pp. 90–1; S. Lash and J. Urry, 'The new Marxism of collective action: a critical analysis', *Sociology* 18 (1984) pp. 33–50.

69 See Blake, 'Swedish trade unions', pp. 19–23.

70 See S. Kuhle, 'The growth of social insurance programs in Scandinavia: outside influences and internal forces', in *The Development of Welfare States in Europe and America*, ed. P. Flora and A. Heidenheimer (Transaction Books, New Brunswick, NJ, 1981), pp. 26, 40; and K. J. Hojer, *Den svenska socialpolitiken* (Norstedt & Soner, Stockholm, 1965).

71 See Heclo, *Modern Social Politics*, pp. 46–7, 62; K. Joher, *Svensk social-politisk historia* (Norstedt, Stockholm, 1952).

72 See Heclo, *Modern Social Politics*, pp. 181f.; E. Liedstrand, 'Social insurance in Sweden', *International Labour Review* 9 (1924), pp. 177–95.

73 Cited in Therborn, 'The working class', p. 23.

74 P. Flora and J. Alber, 'Modernization, democratization and the development of welfare states in Western Europe', in *Development of Welfare States*, ed. Flora and Heidenheimer, pp. 37–80, p. 49.

75 See e.g. A. V. Dicey, *Law and Public Opinion in England during the 19th Century* (Macmillan, London, 1905), pp. 212–37; S. Beer, *Modern British Politics* (Faber, London, 1969), pp. 262–3, 297ff.; K. Middlemas, *Politics in Industrial Society* (Andre Deutsch, London, 1979), pp. 140–1, 188–90, 200–13; see also articles by M. Rose, E. Hennock and R. Hay in *The Emergence of the Welfare State in Britain and Germany*, ed. W. Mommsen; and D. Fraser, *The Evolution of the British Welfare State* (Macmillan, London, 1973) pp. 15–27.

76 See B. Supple, 'A framework for British business history', in *Essays in British Business History*, ed. B. Supple (Clarendon Press, Oxford, 1977), p. 10.

77 See H. Medick, 'Anfänge und Veraussetzungen des Organiserten Kapitalismus in Gross Britannien, 1873–1914', in *Organisierter Kapitalismus, Voraussetzungen und Anfänge*, ed. H. A. Winckler (Vandenhoeck und Ruprecht, Göttingen, 1974), p. 61.

78 See A. D. Chandler, *Strategy and Structures: Chapters in the History of the Industrial Enterprise* (MIT Press, Cambridge, Mass., 1962), pp. 19–50.

79 P. L. Payne, 'The emergence of the large-scale company in Great Britain, 1870–1914', *Economic History Review* 20 (1967), pp. 519–42.

80 See A. D. Chandler, 'The development of modern management structures in the US and UK', in *Management Strategy and Business Development: an Historical and Comparative Study*, ed. L. Hannah (Macmillan, London, 1976). pp. 37–42.

81 Chandler, *Strategy and Structures*, p. 28.

82 See here B. Supple, 'A framework for British business history', pp. 21–2.

83 See L. Hannah, 'Mergers in British manufacturing industry, 1880–1918', *Oxford Economic Papers*, new series, 26 (1974), pp. 2, 8–11. Firm 'disappearances' is commonly taken as an indicator of merger activity.

84 Ibid., p. 15.

85 See ibid., pp. 10–12 and D. F. Channon, *The Strategy and Structure of British Enterprise* (Harvard University Graduate School of Business Administration, Boston, 1973).

86 Hannah, 'Mergers, pp. 10–11.
87 See Supple, 'A framework for British business history', pp. 14–15, on these various
    points here.
       The importance of the sectoral balance of the British economy in this period
    can also be seen by considering in detail the British engineering industry. Saul
    convincingly shows that the latter was by no means technologically and commer-
    cially backward prior to the First World War. Indeed, it was advanced, but in
    terms of producing commodities such as steam machinery, locomotives, textile
    machinery, and so on – commodities which are more characteristic of liberal rather
    than organized capitalism. In almost all of the consumer and capital goods markets
    characteristic of organized capitalism (electrical engineering, automobiles,
    agricultural machinery, office equipment, and machine tools), British engineering
    simply did not, and could not, compete. Key was the machine tool industry, not
    only because it supplied machinery to the other engineering sectors, but because
    it was in machine tools that the new techniques were acquired and diffused. Britain
    was a pioneer in the development of milling machines and lathes, whose ultimate
    destination was the heavy engineering industry. The USA, however, was con-
    siderably stronger in machine tools oriented to the medium engineering market.
    Moreover, in no area could Britain compete with the US economies of scale. Britain
    neither developed the large firms and plant size characteristic of the USA, nor
    could they specialize as could the Americans in the production of grinding machines
    or turret lathes. The problem was mostly a matter of markets; of insufficient
    demand for the long-runs necessary for increased investment in machine-tool pro-
    duction. Many British engineering firms made their own machine tools; many
    others still did not use the grinding and milling machines because of the low price
    and large supply of skilled labour. See S. B. Saul, 'The engineering industries',
    in *The Development of British Industry and Foreign Competition*, ed. D. H.
    Aldcroft (Allen & Unwin, London, 1968), pp. 40–4, and *passim*; and 'The
    mechanical engineering industries in Britain, 1860–1914', in B. Supple, *Essays
    in British Business History*, pp. 31–49.
88 See, for example, Supple, 'Framework', pp. 20–5.
89 See here L. Hannah, *The Rise of the Corporate Economy* (Methuen, London,
    1976), pp. 30–43.
90 The experience of Lever Brothers (later Unilever) is illuminating in this context.
    William Lever began in the soap trade in the 1880s. His fast-growing firm
    succeeded in smashing the Soap Makers Association, a *de facto* cartel which had
    divided the UK into a set of monopolized geographical areas, partly to overcome
    some of the violent fluctuations in raw material prices. At about the time of the
    First World War, when Lever diversified into margarine production to compete
    on the British market with Dutch producers, he had developed soap enterprises
    in a dozen countries, including the United States, and through acquisitions
    accounted for 60 per cent of British soap output. Backwards integration into African
    investment, which would secure raw materials at low prices in conjunction with
    the collapse of these raw material prices in the early twenties, landed the company
    in financial difficulties. At this point, D'Arcy Cooper, an accountant and very
    much a 'rationalizer', was brought in to bail out Lever, who was basically still
    a Victorian radical. From 1921 Cooper was consulted on all matters of policy;
    from 1923 he joined the board of directors. Cooper immediately raised an £8 million

loan from Barclays which was itself contingent on the issue of debentures amounting to the same sum, and reformed the incompetent management of the African-based suppliers. He then put together a number of committees to look into various areas of company affairs and rationalized the main Merseyside soap production site. After Lever's death in 1926, Cooper became managing director and immediately proceeded to sell off the firm's surplus property, creating a company research programme, setting up an *ad hoc* committee for the expansion of advertising and encouraging greater coordination between salespeople. By 1929 profits had increased enormously. The only losses were in margarine production, so in September of that year Unilever was created from a merger with Dutch Margarine Unie. The rationalization of sales proceeded apace. Previously too many brands of soap had been produced in too small factories for too many regional markets. Up until 1931 Lever soap had 49 manufacturing companies and 48 separate sales organizations. Through the rapid rationalization of production and sales, at the same time as diversification and a new focus on the much in demand flakes and powders lines, Unilever was by the mid-1930s able to compete with German or American competitors. See C. Wilson, 'Management policy in large-scale enterprise: Lever Brothers and Unilever, 1918–38', in B. Supple, *Essays in British Business History*, pp. 124–40, pp. 124–7, 130–6; and C. Wilson, *History of Unilever*, 2 vols (Cassell, London, 1954).

91 See S. J. Prais, *The Evolution of Giant Firms in Britain: a Study of the Growth of Manufacturing Industry, 1909–1970* (Cambridge University Press, Cambridge, 1976), p. 4; and L. Hannah, 'Visible and invisible hands in Great Britain', *Managerial Hierarchies*, ed. A. D. Chandler and H. Daems (Harvard University Press, Cambridge, Mass., 1980), pp. 43–71, p. 50.

92 L. Hannah, 'Visible and invisible hands', p. 46.

93 Ibid., p. 48.

94 See ibid., pp. 53–8; and A. D. Chandler, 'The development of modern management structures', p. 44.

The UK tobacco industry usefully illustrates some of these points. Imperial Tobacco Company was formed in 1901 from a merger of 13 firms to which four more were added the following year. The head office's powers were limited: selling, costing, advertising, pricing and finance remaining under individual branch control. In the inter-war years Player began to match Wills as the company's strongest branch, the former providing the up-market brands for which there was increasing consumer demand and the latter less expensive cigarettes. In the late twenties and early thirties, companies like Phillips began to challenge Imperial's market domination, a challenge to which Imperial responded by acquiring its major competitors. Imperial Tobacco continued to control 79 per cent of the market as late as 1955. Up until 1939 ITC was basically a holding company, though taking on a number of multidivisional characteristics. There was, for example, much duplication of function, especially in marketing. Prior to the Second World War the Wills branch refused to recruit externally for management, and it was only during the war that a new generation of Imperial executives could begin to operate with freedom from Wills family control. See B. W. E. Alford, 'Strategy and structure in the UK tobacco industry', in L. Hannah ed., *Management Strategy*, pp. 73–84, and *W. D. and H. O. Wills and the Development of the UK Tobacco Industry, 1786–1965* (Methuen, London, 1973).

98 A very clear and well-informed account of this is F. Longstreth, *State Economic Planning in a Capitalist Society: the Political Sociology of Economic Policy in Britain 1940–1979* (PhD, London, 1982); and see F. Longstreth, 'The city, industry and the state', in *State and Economy in Contemporary Capitalism*, ed. C. Crouch (Croom Helm, London, 1979), pp. 157–90; and S. Aronovitch and R. Smith, *The Political Economy of British Capitalism: a Marxist Analysis* (McGraw-Hill, Maidenhead, 1981).

96 See on the latter L. E. Davis, 'The capital markets and industrial concentration: the US and UK, a comparative study', *Purdue Faculty Papers in Economic History, 1956–1966* (Homewood, Ill., 1967), pp. 663–82.

97 A. Gerschenkron, *Economic Backwardness in Historical Perspective* (Harvard University Press, Cambridge, Mass., 1962), p. 14.

98 G. Ingham, *Capitalism Divided. The City and Industry in British Social Development* (Macmillan, London, 1984), p. 5.

99 M. Weber, *Economy and Society*, vol. 1 (University of California Press, Berkeley, 1978), p. 164; and see Ingham, *Capitalism Divided*, p. 12.

100 Ibid., p. 36.

101 Ibid., p. 35.

102 Ibid., p. 94; and see p. 78.

103 See W. P. Kennedy, 'Institutional response to economic growth: capital markets in Britain to 1914', in L. Hannah (ed.), *Management Strategy*, pp. 151–83, pp. 155–6; J. Mossin, *Theory of Financial Markets* (Prentice-Hall, Englewood Cliffs, 1973).

104 See Kennedy, 'Institutional response', pp. 159–61; and P. L. Cottrell, *Industrial Finance 1830–1914: the Finance and Organization of British Manufacturing Industry* (Methuen, London, 1980).

105 See Kennedy, 'Institutional response', pp. 165, 169–71; Cottrell, *Industrial Finance*, pp. 188–9, 232–3.

106 See Kennedy, 'Institutional response', p. 173; Cottrell, *Industrial Finance*, pp. 174–6.

107 See W. A. Thomas, *The Finance of British Industry 1918–1976* (Methuen, London, 1978), pp. 24f.; J. Aitken, 'Official regulation of overseas investment 1914–1931', *Economic History Review* 23 (1970), pp. 24–35.

108 See Thomas, 'Finance', pp. 62–8; T. Balogh, *Studies in Financial Organization* (Cambridge University Press, Cambridge, 1950).

109 See, for example, M. Weber, *Wirtschaft and Gesellschaft* (Mohr, Tubingen, 1972), pp. 409–15.

110 See on these various points J. Tomlinson, *Problems of British Economic Policy, 1870–1945* (Methuen, London, 1981) pp. 26–42; and R. S. Sayers, *The Bank of England, 1891–1944*, vol. 1 (Cambridge University Press, Cambridge, 1976).

111 See on the following, Tomlinson, *Problems*, pp. 45, 60, 108–18; S. B. Saul, 'The economic significance of "constructive imperialism"', *Journal of Economic History* 17 (1957), pp. 173–92.

112 See, for example, L. Hannah, 'A pioneer of public enterprise: the Central Electricity Board and the National Grid, 1927–1940', in Supple, *Essays in British Business History*, pp. 107–26. Given the shell shortage of the First World War, the seemingly imminent collapse of British Dyestuffs, and the threats to the British market of I. G. Farben, a government contact proposed to Harry McGowan,

managing director of Nobel Industries Ltd, that he take over British Dyestuffs. McGowan's counterproposal was a wider merger with Brunner, Mond and United Alkali, to which the government was agreeable. This was only one of what were to be a host of links between the state and ICI. Alfred Mond of Brunner, Mond, first joint managing director of ICI, was an MP, a former minister of health, and became Lord Melchett. Lord Ashfield, the first chairman of the London Passenger Transport Board, and Lord Weir, who was connected with the Central Electricity Board, sat on the ICI board of directors. Government help was forthcoming to ICI in the Coal Mines Act of 1930. When ICI had invested heavily in the production of coal-based petrol, the government was persuaded to provide protectionist legislation in the Hydrocarbon Oils Production Act of 1934. But the relationship was a *quid pro quo*. The government was highly dependent on the company for war-related production dating from 1935; ICI even operated government-owned factories during the war. And ICI was eventually crucial in the development of the atomic bomb. See W. J. Reader, 'Imperial chemical industries and the state, 1926–1945', in Supple, *Essays in British Business History*, pp. 227–45; and L. F. Haber, *The Chemical Industry, 1900–30* (Clarendon Press, Oxford, 1971).

113 See E. Hobsbawm, 'General Labour Unions in Britain', in *idem.*, *Labouring Men* (Weidenfeld & Nicolson, London, 1968), pp. 185–95.

114 E. P. Hennock, 'The origins of British National Insurance and the German precedent', in *The Emergence of the Welfare State in Britain and Germany 1850–1950*, ed. W. Mommsen (Croom Helm, London, 1981), pp. 84–106, pp. 86–8; R. Hay, 'The British business community: social insurance and the German example', in Mommsen ed., pp. 107–32; M. E. Rose. 'The crisis of poor relief in England 1860–1890', in Mommsen ed., pp. 50–70.

115 See M. Foucault, *Surveillir et punir, Naissance de la prison* (Éditions Gallimard, Paris, 1975), pp. 180–5; English translation, Alan Sheridan, *Discipline and Punish* (Penguin, Harmondsworth, 1979).

3 THE DEVELOPMENT OF ORGANIZED CAPITALISM (2)

1 See J. H. Clapham, *Economic Development of France and Germany* (Cambridge University Press, Cambridge, 1936), and the discussion in C. Trebilock, *The Industrialization of the Continental Powers, 1780–1914* (Longman, London, 1981). For more detailed analyses, see J. J. Carré, P. Dubois and E. Malinvaud, *French Economic Growth* (Stanford University Press, Stanford, Calif., 1976), pp. 23–4; P. O'Brien and C. Keyder, *Economic Growth in Britain and France: Two Paths to the Twentieth Century* (Allen & Unwin, London, 1978), pp. 22, 194f.; and O'Brien and Keyder, 'Les voies de passage vers la société industrielle en Grande-Bretagne et en France (1780–1914)', *Annales ESC* 34 (1979), pp. 1284–1302, p. 1287.

2 See A. Gerschenkron, *Economic Backwardness in Historical Perspective* (Belknap, Cambridge, Mass., 1962), pp. 7–14.

3 See R. Roehl, 'L'Industrialisation française: une remise en cause', *Revue d'Histoire Economique et Sociale* 54 (1976), pp. 406–27; Trebilcock, *Industrialization*, pp. 112–14; Carré et al., *French Economic Growth*, p. 10; O'Brien and Keyder, *Economic Growth in Britain and France*, pp. 162, 194.

4 Ibid., pp. 150, 157–8.

5 See ibid. pp. 170, 192–3; Carré et al., *French Economic Growth*, pp. 14–15.

6 J. Bouvier and F. Caron, 'Guerre, Crise, Guerre', in Bouvier et al., *Histoire Economique et Sociale de la France*, Tome IV, *L'ère industrielle et la société d'aujourd'hui (siècle 1880–1980)*, 2nd vol., *Le temps des guerres mondiales et de la grande crise* (Presses Universitaires Françaises, Paris, 1980), p. 647; Trebilcock, *Industrialization*, p. 141; O'Brien and Keyder, *Economic Growth in Britain and France*, p. 161.

7 F. Caron, 'La stratégie des investissements en France aux XIXe et XXe siecles', *Revue d'Histoire Economique et Sociale* 54, (1976), p. 116.

8 C. Kindleberger, *Economic Growth in France and Britain, 1851–1950* (Harvard University Press, Cambridge, Mass., 1964), pp. 261–2.

9 See F. Caron, 'Investment Strategy in France', in *The Rise of Managerial Capitalism*, ed. H. Daems and H. Van Der Wee (University Press, Louvain, 1974), pp. 96–144, pp. 129–30, 261–2.

10 See O'Brien and Keyder, *Economic Growth in Britain and France*, pp. 162, 166–7; and chapter 5 below.

11 See Trebilcock, *Industrialization*, pp. 184–91; D. Barjot, 'L'analyse comptable: un instrument pour l'histoire des entreprises. La Société Générale d'Entreprises (1908–1945)', *Histoire, Economie et Société* 1 (1982), pp. 145–67.

12 See M. Levy-Leboyer, 'Capital investment and economic growth in France 1820–1930', *The Cambridge Economic History of Europe*, vol. VII, Part I (Cambridge University Press, Cambridge, 1978), pp. 231–95, p. 232; and Trebilcock, *Industrialization*, p. 198.

13 See C. Béaud, 'Une multinationale française au lendemain de la première guerre mondiale: Schneider et L'Union Européene Industrielle et Financière', *Histoire, Economie et Société* 2 (1983), pp. 625–46; and Barjot, 'L'analyse comptable', pp. 149–51.

14 See Carré, *Economic Growth*, p. 14; Caron, 'Investment strategy in France', p. 100.

15 See M. Levy-Leboyer, 'Le patronat français, 1912–1973', in *Le patronat de la seconde industrialisation*, ed. Levy-Leboyer (Éditions ouvrières, Paris, 1979), pp. 137–85, pp. 152–5; M. Levy-Leboyer, 'Hierarchische Struktur und Leistungsanreize in einen Grossunternehmen: frühe Management-Erfahrangen bei Saint-Gobain 1872–1912', in *Recht und Entwicklung im. 19. und frühen 20. Jahrhundert*, ed. Horn and J. Kocka (Vandenhoeck & Ruprecht, Göttingen, 1979), pp. 451–75, pp. 452–3, 457–60; and G. Lefranc, *Les organisations patronales en France* (Payot, Paris, 1976).

16 See Kindleberger, *Economic Growth*, p. 165.

17 J. Houssaix, *Le pouvoir de monopole* (Sirey, Paris, 1954).

18 F. Caron and J. Bouvier, 'Structure des firmes, emprise de l'Etat', in *Les Temps des Guerres*, ed. J. Bouvier, pp. 780–4.

19 F. Caron, 'Investment strategy', p. 130.

20 See Carré, *Economic Growth*, p. 91.

21 See A. Milward and R. Saul, *The Development of the Economies of Continental Europe 1850–1914* (Allen & Unwin, 1977), pp. 79, 83.

22 See Carré, *Economic Growth*, p. 97.

23 See Caron and Bouvier, 'Structure des firmes', pp. 784–5; C. Kindleberger, 'The

postwar resurgence of the French economy', in *France: Change and Tradition*, ed. S. Hoffman et al. (Victor Gollancz, London, 1963), pp. 118–58, pp. 130–1.

24 See Milward and Saul, *Development*, pp. 97–100; P. Fridenson, *Histoire des Usines Renault: 1. Naissance de la Grande Entreprise 1898/1939* (Éditions du Seuil, Paris, 1972), pp. 15, 54–76; and Fridenson, 'Unternehmenspolitik, Rationalisierung und Arbeiterschaft: französische Erfahrurgen im internationalen vergleich, 1900 bis 1929', in *Recht und Entwicklung*, ed. Horn and Kocka, pp. 428–50.

25 See P. Lauthier, 'Les dirigeants des grandes entreprises électriques en France, 1911–1983', in *Le patronat*, ed. Levy-Leboyer, pp. 101–36, pp. 107, 118–23.

26 Generally here see J. Bouvier, *Histoire économique et histoire sociale* (Droz, Geneva, 1968), especially pp. 173–4.

27 See J. Bouvier, *Un siècle de banque française* (Hachette, Paris, 1973), pp. 67–8, 200–7.

28 This is discussed in detail in chapter 5 below. See ibid., pp. 164–6, 196–7; Milward and Saul, *Development*, p. 116; Kindleberger, *Economic Growth*, pp. 42, 49.

29 On these various points, see Bouvier, *Un siècle*, pp. 39–40; Milward and Saul, ibid., pp. 117–18; J. Bouvier, *Le Crédit Lyonnais de 1863 à 1882, Les Années de formation d'une banque de dépôts* (Seupen, Paris, 1961); and J. Bouvier, *Le Krach de l'Union Générale* (Presses Universitaires de France, Paris, 1960).

30 M. Levy-Leboyer, 'La capacité financière de la France au début du XXe siècle', in *La position internationale de la France. Aspects économiques et financières XIXe–XXe siècles* (Éditions de l'École des Hautes Etudes en Sciences Sociales, Paris, 1977), pp. 7–36, p. 15.

31 See Milward and Saul, *Development*, pp. 133–4 for details.

32 See J. Bouvier, 'Monnaie et banque d'une après-guerre à l'autre, 1919–1945', in *Le temps des guerres*, ed. Bouvier, pp. 687–728, pp. 697–703.

33 Ibid., pp. 707–11; Bouvier, *Un Siècle*, p. 73; G. Bertin, 'La transformation du financement international et ses causes: l'exemple français, 1900–1970', in *La position international*, ed. Levy-Leboyer, pp. 453–69, p. 467; H. Bouin, 'Les banques ont-elles sauvé Citroën? (1933–1935)', *Histoire, Economie et Société* 3 (1984), pp. 453–72.

34 See R. F. Kuisel, *Capitalism and the State in Modern France: Renovation and Economic Management in the Twentieth Century* (Cambridge University Press, Cambridge, 1981), p. 208; Bouvier, 'Monnaie et banque', pp. 725–6; H. Koch, *Histoire de la Banque de France et de la Monnaie sous la IVe République* (Dunod, Paris, 1983), pp. 79f.

35 J-P. Patat, *Monnaie, institutions financières et politique monetaire* (Economica, Paris, 1982), p. 214.

36 See A. Shonfield, *Modern Capitalism, the Changing Balance of Public and Private Power* (Oxford University Press, Oxford, 1965), pp. 121–43.

37 See B. Brizay, *Le patronat* (Éditions du Seuil, Paris, 1975).

38 See Kuisel, *Capitalism and the State*, pp. 41–7; G. Hardbach, 'Französische Rüstungspolitik 1914–1918', in *Organisierter Kapitalismus* (Vandenhoeck & Ruprecht, Göttingen, 1974), pp. 103, 106–10. More generally on the formation of industrial ententes see H. Morzel, 'Contribution a l'histoire des ententes industrielles', *Revue d'Histoire Economique et Sociale* 54 (1976), pp. 118–29.

39 See C. S. Maier, *Recasting Bourgeois Europe* (Princeton University Press,

Princeton, NJ, 1975), pp. 403, 413, 400–8, 508–10; F. Goguel, *La politique des partis sous la 3ᵉ République* (Éditions du Seuil, Paris, 1957).

40 See Kuisel, *Capitalism and the State*, pp. 109–20; G. Lefranc, *Le mouvement syndicale sous la Troisième République* (Payot, Paris, 1967).

41 See Kuisel, *Capitalism and the State*, pp. 131–56; S. Hoffman, *France: Change and Tradition* (Victor Gollancz, London, 1963), pp. 74–5; S. Hoffmann, *Decline or Renewal? France since the 1930s* (Viking, New York, 1974); A. S. Milward, *The New Order and the French Economy* (Clarendon, Oxford, 1970), pp. 276–7.

42 Kuisel, *Capitalism and the State*, pp. 159–95; M. Burrage, 'Culture and British economic growth', *British Journal of Sociology* 20 (1969), pp. 117–33.

43 For analyses of state spending in France, see R. Delorme and C. André, *L'Etat et l'Economie. Un essai d'explication de l'évolution des dépenses publiques en France (1870–1980)* (Éditions du Seuil, Paris, 1983), pp. 34–55, 209–261. For a detailed competing account of the development of state spending in France, based on an application of Paul Boccara's overaccumulation and devalorization thesis, complete with detailed accounts of Kondratieff (Simiand) waves, see Louis Fontvieille, 'L'Evolution et croissance de l'Etat Français: 1815–1869', *Economies et Sociétés* 10 (1976). Boccara's work (see especially *Études sur le capitalisme monopoliste d'État* (ed. sociales, Paris, 1974)), formed the basis for the analysis of the French Communist Party during its liberal, 'class alliance' period, from the middle 1960s to the late 1970s and – it is less well known – for some of Ernest Mandel's analyses. For briefer explications, see L. Fontvieille, 'Dépenses publiques et problematique de la devalorisation du capital', *Annales, Economies, Sociétés, Civilisations* 33 (1978), pp. 240–54; C. André and R. Delorme, 'L'Evolution séculaire des dépenses publiques en France', *Annales, ESC* 33 (1978), pp. 255–78. For a related and interesting debate see Jean-Pierre Allinne and Michel Lescure, 'Pour une étude des appareils économiques d'Etat en France au XIXᵉ siècle', *Annales, ESC* 36 (1981), pp. 280–93; and Moreau, 'Les appareils économiques d'État en France au XIXᵉ siecle: question à J-P. Allinne et M. Lescure', *Annales, ESC*, 36 (1981), pp. 1166–69.

44 P. Flora and Alber, 'Modernization and democratization', in *The Development of Welfare States in Europe and America*, ed. P. Flora and A. Heidenheimer (Transaction Books, New Brunswick, NJ, 1981), p. 55; and Kohl, 'Trends and problems', in ibid., p. 339.

45 Kohl, ibid., p. 339, and more generally see B. Guy Peters, 'Economic and political effects on the development of social expenditures in France, Sweden and the United Kingdom', *Midwest Journal of Political Science* 16 (1972), pp. 225–38.

46 Kohl, 'Trends and problems', p. 341.

47 M. Foucault, *The History of Sexuality* (Pantheon, New York, 1978), pp. 103–5.

48 See Delorme and André, *État et l'Economie*, pp. 198–402; S. Grevisse, *Succès et faiblesses de l'effort social français* (Armand Colin, Paris, 1961), pp. 23–25.

49 See Delorme and André, *État et l'Economie*, pp. 450–2; and Kohl, 'Trends and problems', p. 341. On the weak development of pension legislation in France, see pp. 394–5 in the former, p. 340 in the latter. On health provision, see Delorme and André, pp. 416–25. This increased dramatically in the inter-war period as well as after the 1945 ordonnance.

50 See, for example, V. Carosso, *Investment Banking in America: a history* (Harvard University Press, Cambridge, Mass., 1970); D. M. Kötz, *Bank Control of Large*

Corporations in the United States (University of California Press, Berkeley, 1978), pp. 21–9; and G. Kolko, *Railroads and Regulation, 1877–1916* (Princeton University Press, Princeton, 1965), pp. 61–7.

51 R. L. Nelson, *Merger Movements in American Industry 1895–1956* (Princeton University Press, Princeton, NJ, 1959), pp. 34–5.

52 See ibid.; Kötz, *Bank Control*, p. 32; G. Kolko, *The Triumph of Conservatism. A Reinterpretation of American History, 1900–1916* (Free Press, Glencoe, Ill., 1963), pp. 30–9, 45–50.

53 See Kötz, *Bank Control*, pp. 35–9.

54 See Kolko, *Triumph*, p. 19; and Nelson, *Merger Movements*, pp. 36, 43–5.

55 On these various points see Kolko, *Triumph*, pp. 22–7; Kolko, *Railroads*, pp. 65–6; and L. Corey, *The House of Morgan* (G. H. Watt, New York, 1930).

56 On these points see Kötz, *Bank Control*, pp. 45–50; R. Goldsmith, *Financial Institutions* (Random House, New York, 1968); N. White, *Regulation and Reform of the American Banking System* (Princeton University Press, Princeton, NJ, 1983), pp. 82–9.

57 See P. G. Porter, 'Types of investment strategy in the United States', in *The Rise of Managerial Capitalism*, ed. H. Daems and H. Van Der Wee (Leuven University Press, Louvain, 1974), pp. 54–5, 65.

58 See on the following A. F. Chandler, *The Visible Hand: the Managerial Revolution in American Business* (Harvard University Press, Cambridge, Mass., 1977), pp. 320–4; R. W. Hidy and M. E. Hidy, *Pioneering in Big Business* (Harper, New York, 1955).

59 See H. F. Williamson and A. R. Daum, *The American Petroleum Industry* (Northwestern University Press, Evanston, Ill., 1959).

60 See A. D. Chandler, *Strategy and Structure, Chapters in the History of the Industrial Enterprise* (MIT Press, Cambridge, Mass., 1963), pp. 25–6.

61 A. Chandler, 'Structure of American industry in the twentieth century: a historical overview', *Business History Review* 43 (1969), pp. 255–98.

62 See L. Jörberg, *Svenska ekonomiska utvecklingen* (Ekonomisk-historiska institutionen, Lund, 1984), p. 33.

63 See Chandler, *Strategy and Structure*, pp. 207–22.

64 See ibid., pp. 55–76, 80–111; and A. Chandler and S. Salsbury, *Pierre S. du Pont and the Making of the Modern Corporation* (Harper & Row, New York, 1971), pp. 47–54, 227–46, 359–88.

65 See Chandler, *Visible Hand*, pp. 457–63; Chandler, *Strategy and Structure*, pp. 116–17; Chandler and Salsbury, *Pierre du Pont*, pp. 500f.; A. Pound, *The Turning Wheel* (Doubleday, Garden City, New York, 1934).

66 See R. Hofstadter, *The Progressive Movement* (Prentice-Hall, New York, 1963).

67 Kolko, *Triumph*, pp. 68, 73, 84, 118; and J. Weinstein, *The Corporate Ideal in the Liberal State, 1900–1918* (Beacon, Boston, 1968), pp. 62–4, 68–9.

68 See Kolko, *Triumph*, p. 66; Weinstein, *Corporate Ideal*, pp. 62, 67; and P. Foner, *History of the Labor Movement in the United States*, vol. 3. *The Policies and Practices of the AFL, 1900–1909* (International Publishers, New York, 1964).

69 See Kolko, *Triumph*, pp. 72–5, 81–2, 118; and Weinstein, *Corporate Ideal*, pp. 78–87.

70 See ibid., pp. 91–112.

71 Ibid., p. 115; and see J. Weinstein, *The Decline of Socialism in America,*

1912–1925 (Monthly Review Press, New York, 1967), and J. D. Greenstone, *Labor in American Politics* (University of Chicago Press, Chicago, 1977).

72 See Weinstein, *Corporate Ideal*, pp. 139–66; R. Hofstadter, *The Age of Reform* (Vintage, New York, 1955); L. Goodwyn, *Democratic Promise* (Oxford University Press, New York, 1976); S. Lash, *Militant Worker* (Heinemann, London, 1984), pp. 180–5.

73 E. Hawley, *The New Deal and the Problem of Monopoly* (Princeton University Press, Princeton, NJ, 1966).

74 Ibid., pp. 280–3, 288.

75 See E. Hawley, 'The New Deal and business', in *The New Deal*, vol. 1, *The National Level*, ed. J. Braeman, R. Bremner and D. Brody (Ohio State University Press, Columbus, Ohio, 1975), pp. 50–3.

76 See J. Buchanan, 'The economic constitution of the New Deal: lessons for late learners', in *Regulatory Change in an Atmosphere of Crisis*, ed. G. Walton (Academic Press, New York, 1979), pp. 13–25; B. J. Bernstein, 'The New Deal: the conservative achievement of liberal reform', in *Towards a New Past*, ed. B. J. Bernstein (Chatto & Windus, London, 1970), pp. 263–88, p. 267; and O. Graham, *Towards a Planned Society: from Roosevelt to Nixon* (Oxford University Press, New York, 1976), pp. 14–15.

77 See Hawley, 'Business', pp. 55–7; and Graham, *Planned Society*, pp. 3–5, on the following points.

78 See T. Skocpol, 'Political response to capitalist crisis: neo-Marxist theories of the state and the case of the New Deal', *Politics and Society* 10 (1980), pp. 155–201.

79 Hawley, 'Business', pp. 60–1; Hawley, *The New Deal*, pp. 53, 417; Skocpol, 'Political response', pp. 170–6; A. M. Schlesinger, *The Coming of the New Deal* (Houghton-Mifflin, Boston, 1958), pp. 146, 385–420.

80 Hawley, *The New Deal*, p. 132, and see pp. 140–4, 480–1.

81 See on this and the following points, J. Holt, 'The New Deal and the American anti-statist tradition', in *The New Deal*, vol. 1, ed. J. Braeman et al., pp. 26–45.

82 Some further support for a post NRA growth of the 'relative autonomy' of the American state can be seen in the various Roosevelt presidential elections. There was a marked increase in the class alignment of US voters between 1932, 1936 and 1940, and with a significant de-alignment in 1944 due in part to Roosevelt's abandonment of an anti-business rhetoric. See C. D. Hadley, *Transformation of the American Party System* (Norton, New York, 1975), pp. 71–3, 123.

83 Hawley, *The New Deal*, pp. 272–8.

84 Ibid., pp. 309, 342; Hawley, 'Business', p. 72; Bernstein, 'Conservative achievement', pp. 271–6.

85 See D. Brody, 'The New Deal and World War II', in *New Deal*, ed. J. Braemann et al., pp. 271–300, pp. 276–8; and see J. Hughes, 'Roots of regulation: the New Deal', in *Regulatory Change in an Atmosphere of Crisis*, ed. G. Walton (Academic Press, New York, 1979).

86 Brody, 'The New Deal', pp. 283–94.

87 See A. J. Heidenheimer, H. Heclo and C. T. Adams, *Comparative Public Policy. The Politics of Social Choice in Europe and America* (Macmillan, London, 1976), p. 191.

88 R. T. Kudrle and T. R. Marmor, 'The development of the welfare state in North

America', in *Development of Welfare States in Europe and North America*, ed. P. Flora and A. Heidenheimer (Transaction Books, New Brunswick, NJ, 1981), pp. 81–121; and M. Harrington, *The New American Poverty* (Holt, Rinehart and Winston, New York, 1984).

89 A. J. Heidenheimer, 'Education and social security entitlement in Europe and America', in *Development*, ed. Flora and Heidenheimer, pp. 269–304, p. 277.

90 See M. Janowitz, *Social Control of the Welfare State* (Elsevier, New York, 1976), pp. 34–5.

91 It is also important to consider the effects of the distribution of welfare resources within industry itself. Partly in reaction to the industrial struggles of the late 1880s, a number of businessmen developed private welfare schemes. A quantum expansion of such schemes took place along with the rapid rise of the National Civic Foundation, to whose Welfare Department many of these 'social–paternalist' firms belonged. It has been estimated that in 1908 some 1.5 million workers were covered by company welfare plans or plant safety programmes, and some 100 firms were represented in the NCH's Welfare Department; 'innovating' companies here included Proctor and Gamble, Eastman Kodak, General Electric, US Steel and International Harvester. Six years later 500 firms were represented in the Welfare Department and the NCF claimed to have evidence confirming the existence of at least some welfare policy in 2500 enterprises. The service class, or at least those of service class training and ideology, played an important role here. Engineers trained at MIT in the waning years of the nineteenth century, such as Alfred Sloan of General Motors, I. du Pont, Paul W. Litchfield of Goodyear, and NRA business leader, Gerard Swope of General Electric led the way. The welfare efforts were seen, not as philanthropy, but as 'social engineering', as the application of the principles of scientific management to human relations; and companies like General Electric established life insurance, retirement and disability programmes and began to toy with the idea of unemployment insurance. This 'welfare Taylorism' was reflected in the growth of numbers of personnel specialists among company executives, who administered employment and welfare policies. By 1935, 80% of firms with more than 5000 employees had personnel managers. Development of private welfare policies proceeded apace. Between 1910 and 1925 some 180 companies set up retirement plans; in a 1929 inquiry, 70% of companies surveyed boasted group insurance schemes.

See E. Berkowitz and K. McQuaid, *Creating the Welfare State. The Political Economy of Twentieth-Century Reform* (Praeger, New York, 1980), pp. 19–21, 52–6; I. Bernstein, *The Lean Years, A History of the American Worker (1920–1937)* (Houghton-Mifflin, Boston, 1960), pp. 144–64. Note incidentally that the importance of this private welfare apparatus should not be exaggerated: such schemes were often associated with company or yellow unionism; they were often voluntary and could be suspended at will (as in the 1930s), and they only covered at most 20% of employees in 1929.

92 More generally on the role of the middle classes, and especially of social workers themselves, in the development of the US welfare state, see W. I. Trattner, *From Poor Law to Welfare State: a History of Social Welfare in America* (Free Press, New York, 1979), pp. 6–12, 42–53, 160–1; R. Lubove, *The Struggle for Social Security* (Harvard University Press, Cambridge, Mass., 1968), pp. 97–102; and R. Bremner, 'Poverty in Perspective', in *Change and Continuity in Twentieth*

Century America (Ohio State University Press, Columbus, Ohio, 1964), pp. 269–77.

93 For some useful discussion of recent state economic policy, especially in contrast with that of France, see the chapters in *Industrial Policy: Business and Politics in the United States and France*, ed. S. Zukin (Praeger, New York, 1985).

4 ECONOMIC CHANGE AND SPATIAL RESTRUCTURING (1)

1 This issue is examined in detail in many of the chapters in *Social Relations and Spatial Structures*, ed. D. Gregory and J. Urry (Macmillan, London, 1985). Other recent examinations include N. Smith, *Uneven Development* (Basil Blackwell, Oxford, 1984); D. Massey, *Spatial Divisions of Labour* (Macmillan, London, 1984); N. Thrift, 'On the determination of social action in society and space', *Society and Space* 1 (1983), pp. 23–57.

2 This is discussed further in L. Murgatroyd, D. Shapiro, J. Urry, S. Walby and A. Warde, *Localities, Class and Gender* (Pion, London, 1985), ch. 21.

3 Marx, *Grundrisse* (Penguin, London, 1973), p. 539.

4 D. Harvey, 'The geopolitics of capitalism', in *Social Relations*, ed. Gregory and Urry, pp. 128–63, p. 145.

5 See M. Berman, *All that is Solid Melts into Air* (Verso, London, 1983); especially see Berman's chapter, on the massive changes produced in Parisian social life brought about by the building of its famous boulevards by Baron Haussmann in the Second Empire. On changes in the spatial distribution of knowledge, N. Thrift, 'Files and germs: a geography of knowledge', in *Social Relations*, ed. Gregory and Urry, pp. 366–403.

6 See Smith, *Uneven Development*, p. 152.

7 See J. Urry, 'Localities, regions and social class', in *International Journal of Urban and Regional Research* 5 (1981), pp. 455–74.

8 See M. Storper and R. Walker, 'Capital and industrial location', 5 (1981), pp. 473–529.

9 A. Sayer, 'Industry and space: a sympathetic critique of radical research', *Society and Space* 3 (1985), pp. 3–29.

10 On the interconnections of the social and the spatial with nature, see the discussion in Smith, *Uneven Development*, ch. 3; on some comments of the connections with time, see Urry, 'Space, time'.

11 See A. Sayer, 'Explanation in human geography: abstraction versus generalisation', *Progress in Human Geography* 6 (1982), pp. 68–88; and Urry, 'Space, time', pp. 36–8.

12 D. Massey, 'Regionalism: some current issues', *Capital and Class* 6 (1978), pp. 106–25, p. 116.

13 See most usefully here Massey, *Spatial Divisions of Labour*. The argument here is found in Urry, 'Space, time'. Also see D. Massey and R. Meegan, *The Anatomy of Job Loss* (Methuen, London, 1982).

14 A. Sayer, 'Explanation in human geography', p. 80.

15 See M. Taylor and N. Thrift, 'Models of corporate development and the multinational corporation', in *The Geography of Multinationals*, ed. Taylor and Thrift, (Croom Helm, London, 1982), pp. 14–32; F. Fröbel, J. Heinrichs and O. Kreye,

The New International Division of Labour (Cambridge University Press, Cambridge, 1980); and A. J. Scott, 'Industrialization and urbanization', *Annals of the Association of American Geographers* 76 (1986), pp. 25–37.

16 See R. Vernon, 'The product cycle hypothesis in a new international environment', *Oxford Bulletin of Economics and Statistics* 41 (1979), pp. 255–6, 258.

17 See H. Watts, 'The inter-regional distribution of West German multinationals in the United Kingdom', in Taylor and Thrift, *The Geography of Multinationals*, pp. 61–89, p. 61.

18 See I. Clarke, 'The changing international division of labour within ICI', in Taylor and Thrift, *The Geography of Multinationals*, pp. 90–116; and 'The imperial initiative', *The Guardian*, Feb. 19th, 1985, p. 24.

19 See Fröbel, Heinrichs and Kreye, *The New International Division of Labour*.

20 M. Taylor and N. Thrift, Introduction, in *The Geography of Multinationals*, pp. 1–13, p. 7.

21 See J. Dunning and R. Pearce, *The World's Largest Industrial Enterprises* (Gower, Farnborough, 1981), p. 115; and A. Lipietz, 'How monetarism choked Third World industrialization', *New Left Review* 145 (1984), pp. 71–87. See also I. D. Clarke, *The Spatial Organisation of Multinational Corporations* (Croom Helm, London, 1985), Table 1.1 which sets out the percentage changes in employment 1973–81 for all the leading UK multinationals.

22 Clarke, *Spatial Organisation*, p. 86.

23 See D. Harvey, *Social Justice and the City* (Edward Arnold, London, 1973); R. Walker, 'A theory of suburbanisation: capitalism and the construction of urban space in the United States', in *Urbanisation and Urban Planning in Capitalist Society*, ed. M. Dear and A. Scott (Methuen, London, 1981), pp. 383–430.

24 See J. A. Agnew, 'Homeownership and the capitalist social order', ibid., pp. 457–80.

25 See M. Aglietta, *A Theory of Capitalist Regulation* (New Left Books, London, 1979). More generally see K. Cox, 'Capitalism and conflict around the communal living space', in Dear and Scott, *Urbanisation*, pp. 431–56; P. Joyce, *Work, Society and Politics: the Culture of the Factory in Later Victorian England* (Harvester, Brighton, 1980), chs 3 and 4; and R. Hall, D. Thorns and W. E. Willmott, 'Community, class and kinship', *Society and Space* 2 (1984).

26 J. Seabrook, *What Went Wrong?* (Gollancz, London, 1978), pp. 174–5; and see Cox 'Capitalism and conflict', p. 435.

27 M. Paci, 'Class structure in Italian society', in *Contemporary Italian Society*, ed. D. Pinto (Cambridge University Press, Cambridge, 1981), pp. 206–22.

28 See J. Urry, 'Some themes in the analysis of the anatomy of contemporary capitalist societies', *Acta Sociologica* 25 (1982), pp. 405–18.

29 See C. Offe and H. Wiesenthal, 'Two logics of collective action: theoretical notes on social class and organizational form', *Political Power and Social Theory* 1 (1980), pp. 67–115; and the discussion in S. Lash and J. Urry, 'The new Marxism of collective action: a critical analysis', *Sociology* 18 (1984), pp. 33–50.

30 P. Bairoch, 'The main trends in national economic disparities since the industrial revolution', in *Disparities in Economic Development since the Industrial Revolution*, ed. P. Bairoch and M. Levy-Leboyer (Macmillan, London, 1981), pp. 3–17, p. 5.

31 See de Vries, *European Urbanization*, pp. 258–9, who points out the corresponding

334 NOTES TO CHAPTER 4

reduction of large-city growth to approximate proportionality with total population growth after 1750.

32 Ibid., p. 259.
33 See C. Tilly, 'Flows of capital and forms of industry in Europe, 1500–1900', *Theory and Society* 13 (1983), pp. 123–42, pp. 125–7.
34 Ibid., p. 131. Tilly's argument is particularly directed at John Merrington's analysis of how the territorial division of labour is redefined, enormously accentuating regional irregularities: 'far from overcoming rural backwardness...capitalist urbanisation merely reproduces it'; see Merrington, 'Town and country in the transition to capitalism', *New Left Review* 93 (1975), pp. 71–91.
35 Tilly, 'Flows of capital', p. 136.
36 See G. Ingham, *Capitalism Divided* (Macmillan, London, 1984), p. 226 and P. J. Perry, *A Geography of Nineteenth-Century Britain* (Batsford, London, 1975), ch. 2.
37 See F. Engels, *The Condition of the Working Class in England* (Panther, London, 1969); and the discussion in L. Mumford, *The City in History: its Origins, its Transformations and its Prospects* (Secker & Warburg, London, 1961), pp. 458f.
38 See *The Economist*, 20th June, 1857, p. 669 (italics in original). Also see Mumford, *City in History*, ch. 15, and D. Smith, *Conflict and Compromise: Class Formation in English Society 1830–1914* (Routledge and Kegan Paul, London, 1982), p. 15.
39 Smith, *Conflict and Compromise*, p. 72.
40 Ibid., pp. 69, 71.
41 See C. Pooley, 'Choice and constraint in the nineteenth century city: a basis for residential differentiation', in *The Structure of Nineteenth Century Cities*, ed. J. Johnson and C. Pooley (Croom Helm, London, 1982), pp. 199–234; D. Cannadine, 'Residential differentiation in nineteenth century towns', in Johnson and Pooley, *The Structure*, pp. 235–52; and R. Harris, 'Residential segregation and class formation in the capitalist city', *Progress in Human Geography* 8 (1984), pp. 26–49.
42 C. Calhoun, *The Question of Class Struggle* (Basil Blackwell, Oxford, 1982), p. 174. On the development of working-class 'leisure' in this period as segregated, specialized and institutionalized see J. Clarke and C. Critcher, *The Devil Makes Work* (Macmillan, London, 1985), ch. 3.
43 See Smith, *Conflict and Compromise*, pp. 7–8; and N. Thrift, 'On the determination of social action in space and time', *Society and Space* (1983), pp. 23–58, p. 26.
44 See Smith, *Conflict and Compromise*, p. 55; and Calhoun, *The Question*, p. 175.
45 Calhoun, *The Question*, ch. 7.
46 Smith, *Conflict and Compromise*, p. 64.
47 Ibid., p. 243.
48 See L. Hannah, 'Visible and invisible hands in Great Britain', in *Managerial Hierarchies*, ed. A. Chandler and H. Daems (Harvard University Press, Cambridge, Mass., 1980), pp. 41–76, for a convenient summary; as well as ch. 3 above.
49 See B. Robson, *Urban Growth* (Methuen, London, 1973).
50 See C. Law, *British Regional Development Since World War I* (Methuen, London, 1981), pp. 69–71.
51 See P. Cooke, 'Class practices as regional markers: a contribution to labour geography', in Gregory and Urry, *Social Relations*, pp. 213–41; and S. MacIntyre,

Little Moscows: Communism and Working Class Militancy in inter-war Britain (Croom Helm, London, 1980).
52 J. A. Hobson, 'The general election: a sociological interpretation', *Sociological Review* 7 (1910), pp. 105–17, p. 107.
53 Ibid., pp. 109, 113–14.
54 See on the following Law, *British Regional Development*; and M. Dunford and D. Perrons, *The Arena of Capital* (Macmillan, London, 1983).
55 See Smith, *Conflict and Compromise*, pp. 13, 16.
56 *Employment Gazette*, July, 1984, p. 511.
57 *Economic Trends*, June, 1984, p. 26.
58 *Employment Gazette*, July, 1984, p. 511.
59 *Employment Gazette*, table 1.4. various years.
60 S. Robert and W. G. Randolph, 'Beyond decentralization: the evolution of population distribution in England and Wales, 1961–1981', *Geoforum* 55 (1983), pp. 75–102, p. 79.
61 *Census of Population* (OPCS, London, 1981); and see A. G. Champion, 'Population trends in the 1970s', in *The Urban and Regional Transformation of Britain*, ed. J. B. Goddard and A. G. Champion (Methuen, London, 1983), pp. 187–214.
62 See Robert and Randolph, 'Beyond decentralization'.
63 S. Fothergill and G. Gudgin, *Unequal Growth: Employment Change in British Cities and Regions* (Heinemann, London, 1982), p. 59.
64 See also R. Leigh, D. North, J. Gough and K. Sweet-Escott, *Monitoring Manufacturing Employment Change in London*, vol. 1, *The Implications for Local Economic Policy* (Middlesex Polytechnic, 1983), on the decline in manufacturing employment in London in various industrial sectors.
65 See D. Keeble, P. L. Owens and C. Thompson, 'The urban–rural manufacturing shift in the European Community', *Urban Studies* 20 (1983), pp. 405–18, pp. 412–13.
66 Ibid., p. 415.
67 See J. Urry, *The Anatomy of Capitalist Societies* (Macmillan, London, 1981), on this distinction between economy/state/civil society. See also D. Massey, *Spatial Divisions of Labour* (Macmillan, London, 1984), which elaborates on many of the points made here, although there are useful correctives in A. Sayer, 'Industry and space: a sympathetic critique of radical research', *Society and Space* 3 (1985), pp. 3–30.
68 As Sir Frederic J. Osborn, editor of *Town and Country Planning*, argues about the central areas of cities, there is 'the lack of sufficient space inside cities for good family dwellings with private yards or gardens, for recreation, for industrial efficiency, and for the vegetative surroundings and the quiet and simple beauty man needs and desires for the fullness of life.' Cited in Y. Willber, *The Withering Away of the City* (Indiana University Press, Bloomington, 1964), p. 11.
69 A. J. Scott, *The Urban Land Nexus and the State* (Pion, London, 1981), p. 109.
70 See A. Townshend and C. Taylor, 'Regional culture and identity in industrialized societies: the case of north-east England', *Regional Studies* 9 (1975), pp. 379–93.
71 See Law, *British Regional Development*, p. 72; A. Lipietz, 'The structuration of space, the problem of land and spatial policy', in *Regions in Crisis*, ed. J. Carney, R. Hudson and J. Lewis (Croom Helm, London, 1980), pp. 60–92; D. Massey and R. Meegan, *The Anatomy of Job Loss* (Methuen, London, 1982).

72 S. Fothergill and G. Gudgin, 'Regional employment change: a subregional explanation', *Progress in Planning* 12 (1979), pp. 155–220, p. 157.
73 This is shown in detail in L. Murgatroyd and J. Urry, 'The restructuring of a local economy. The case of Lancaster', in *Redundant Spaces in Cities and Regions?*, ed. J. Anderson, S. Duncan and R. Hudson (Academic Press, London, 1983), pp. 67–98.
74 S. Kennett, 'Migration between British local labour markets and some speculation on policy options for influencing population distributions', *British Society for Population Studies Occasional Paper 28* (Conference on Population Change and Regional Labour Markets, OPCS, 1982), pp. 35–54, p. 40.
75 Law, *British Regional Development*, p. 132. And see J. Marquand, *The Role of the Tertiary Sector in Regional Policy* (Regional Policy Series, No. 19, Brussels, 1980), p. 69, on the location quotients of $\frac{\text{tertiary employment}}{\text{total employment}}$ for all the UK regions in 1971.
76 See D. Keeble, 'De-industrialisation means unemployment', *Geographical Magazine* 53 (1981), pp. 458–64, p. 460; and see B. Badcock, *Unfairly Structured Cities* (Basil Blackwell, Oxford, 1984), p. 156; and M. Dunford, M. Geddes and D. Perrons, 'Regional policy and the crisis in the UK: a long-run perspective', *International Journal of Urban and Regional Research* 5 (1980), pp. 377–411. More recently some 'regional' indicators are now showing increasing divergence.
77 S. J. Prais, *The Evolution of Giant Firms in Britain* (Cambridge University Press, Cambridge, 1976), table 4.1.
78 Ibid., table 4.1.
79 J. Boswell, *The Rise and Decline of Small Firms* (Allen & Unwin, London, 1973), p. 20.
80 See Fothergill and Gudgin, *Unequal Growth*; D. Storey, *Entrepreneurship and the New Firm* (Croom Helm, London, 1982); and A. Gould and D. Keeble, 'New firms and rural industrialization in East Anglia', *Regional Studies* 18 (1984), pp. 189–201, p. 189. Note incidentally the high 'death' rate for such new small firms.
81 See P. Ganguly, 'Life-span analysis of business in the UK, 1973–82', *British Business*, Aug. 12–18, 1983, pp. 838–45, p. 838. See also J. Curran, 'The sociology of the small enterprise', *Reviewing Sociology* 3 (1984), pp. 3–14, p. 4, who notes the 25% increase in the number of small manufacturing firms between 1963 and 1980.
82 See G. Gudgin and S. Fothergill, 'Geographical variation in the rate of formation of new manufacturing firms', *Regional Studies* 18 (1984), pp. 203–6; and P. Lloyd and C. Mason, 'Spatial variations in new firm formation in the United Kingdom: comparative evidence from Merseyside, Greater Manchester and South Hampshire', *Regional Studies* 18 (1984), pp. 207–20.
83 See S. Creigh, C. Roberts, A. Gorman and P. Sawyer, 'Self-employment in Britain', *Employment Gazette*, June, 1986, pp. 183–94.
84 See the discussion in J. Gershuny, *After Industrial Society* (Macmillan, London, 1978).
85 See T. Lloyd, *Dinosaur and Co. Studies in Corporate Evolution* (Routledge & Kegan Paul, London, 1984), p. 13; and see M. Binks and J. Coyne, 'The birth of enterprise', *Hobart Paper* 98 (Institute of Economic Affairs, London, 1983), ch. 4.

86 *Eurofutures: the Challenges of Innovation* (The Fast Report, Butterworth, Commission of European Communities with Futures, London, 1984), p. 133.

87 See C. Hakim, 'Homeworking: some new evidence', *Employment Gazette* 88 (1980), pp. 1105–9; and see C. Evans and P. Cooke, 'Women homeworkers and the defeminisation of industry', *Fifth Urban Change and Conflict Conference*, Brighton, April, 1985.

90 J. Rubery and F. Wilkinson, 'Outwork and Segmented Labour Markets', in *The Dynamics of Labour Market Segmentation*, ed. F. Wilkinson (Academic Press, London, 1981), pp. 115–32.

89 Ibid., p. 126.

90 See for a general argument on the re-emergence of craft rather than mass-production technologies, M. Piore and C. Sabel, *The Second Industrial Divide* (Basic Books, New York, 1984). For further discussion, see ch. 7 below.

91 See A. F. Rainnie, 'Combined and uneven development in the clothing industry: the effects of competition on accumulation', *Capital and Class* 22 (1984), pp. 141–56, p. 149; in the case of Marks and Spencer there are about 800 clothing subcontractors.

92 See R. Febvre, 'Contract work in the recession', *Annual Conference of the British Sociological Association*, Bradford, 1984; D. Roos and A. Altshuler, *The Future of the Automobile. The Report of MIT's International Automobile Programme* (Allen & Unwin, London, 1984), p. 73 and ch. 7; R. Moore, 'Aspects of segmentation in the United Kingdom building industry labour market', in Wilkinson, *Labour Market Segmentation*, pp. 151–66.

93 See A. Cadbury in *The Guardian*, Dec. 9th, 1981; and see J. Atkinson, 'Flexible firm takes shape', *The Guardian*, April 18th, 1984, p. 19.

94 See T. Lane, 'The unions: caught on an ebb tide', *Marxism Today*, September (1982), pp. 6–13.

95 D. Massey and N. Miles, 'Mapping out the unions', *Marxism Today*, May (1984), pp. 19–22.

96 Ibid., p. 19. On the overall fall in union membership see 'Membership of trade unions', *Employment Gazette*, (Jan. 1986), pp. 16–18.

97 Massey and Miles 'Mapping', p. 20.

98 Ibid., figure 4.

99 Ibid., p. 22.

100 Lane, 'The unions', p. 8.

101 Ibid., pp. 8–9.

102 See W. Daniel and N. Millward, *Workplace Industrial Relations in Britain* (Heinemann Educational Books, London, 1983), p. 218.

103 Lane, 'The unions', p. 11.

104 *Regional Trends* (HMSO, London, 1982), p. 117.

105 J. A. Cronin, 'Politics, class structure, and the enduring weakness of British social democracy', *Journal of Social History* 16 (1983), pp. 123–42, p. 133. See ch. 9 below for further discussion.

106 Lane, 'The unions', p. 13.

107 See J. A. Cronin, *Labour and Society in Britain 1918–1979* (Batsford, London, 1984), pp. 241–3.

108 D. Gordon, 'Class struggle and the stages of American urban development',

in *The Rise of the Sunbelt Cities*, ed. D. Perry and A. Watkins (Sage, Beverly Hills, 1977), pp. 55–82, p. 63.

109 Ibid., p. 64.

110 See A. Pred, *The Spatial Dynamics of US Urban-Industrial Growth* (MIT Press, Massachusetts, 1966), ch. 4 on 'The American mercantile city'.

111 See Gordon, 'Class struggle', p. 66.

112 See J. Long, *Population Deconcentration in the United States* (Bureau of the Census, Washington DC, 1982), p. 89.

113 US Bureau of the Census, *Historical Census of the United States: Colonial Times to 1957* (US Dept. of Commerce, Washington, 1960), pp. 14, 427, 429.

114 Pred, *Spatial Dynamics*, p. 18.

115 Gordon, 'Class struggle', pp. 71–2.

116 Ibid., p. 71.

117 See J. Alt, 'Beyond class: the decline of industrial labor and leisure', *Telos* 28 (1971), pp. 61–2.

118 See R. Lynd and H. Lynd, *Middletown* (Harcourt, New York, 1929), on Muncie, Indiana.

119 See Alt, 'Beyond class', pp. 63–4; and M. Byington, *Homestead: the Households of a Mill Town* (The Pittsburgh Survey, New York, 1911).

120 See L. Schnore and P. Knights, 'Residence and social structure: Boston in the ante-bellum period', in *Nineteenth Century Cities: Essays in the New Urban History*, ed. S. Thernstrom and R. Sennett (Yale University Press, New Haven, 1969), pp. 247–57, p. 255.

121 See P. Knights, 'Population turnover, persistence, and residential mobility in Boston, 1830–60', ibid., pp. 257–74, p. 264, who shows that the turnover in mid-nineteenth-century Boston was over a single decade several times the city's total population. Also see C. Griffen, 'Workers divided: the effect of craft and ethnic differences in Poughkeepsie, New York, 1850–1880', ibid., pp. 49–97.

122 See Alt, 'Beyond class', pp. 64–5; and S. Aronowitz, *False Promises* (McGraw-Hill, New York, 1973), p. 411.

123 See H. Gutman, 'The workers' search for power: labor in the Gilded Age', in *The Gilded Age, 1869–1878: a Reappraisal*, ed. H. W. Morgan (Syracuse University Press, New York, 1963), pp. 38–68.

124 The strike-rate increased threefold between 1881–5 and 1901–5; see P. K. Edwards, *Strikes in the United States, 1881–1974* (Basil Blackwell, Oxford, 1981), p. 15.

125 J. Cumbler, *Working Class Community in Industrial America* (Greenwood Press, Westport, Connecticut, 1979), p. 59.

126 See Gordon, 'Class struggle', p. 73; and see P. Foner, *History of the Labor Movement in the United States*, vol. 2 (International Publishers, New York, 1955).

127 See Gutman, 'The workers' search for power'; and S. Lash, *The Militant Worker* (Heinemann, London, 1984), pp. 174–5.

128 R. Warren, *The Community in America* (Rand McNally, Chicago, 1963), p. 5.

129 Lash, *The Militant Worker*, p. 185.

130 Y. Sabolo, *The Service Industries* (International Labour Office, Geneva, 1975), p. 9.

131 See ch. 3 above; and A. Chandler, 'The United States: seedbed of managerial

capitalism', in *Managerial Hierarchies*, ed. A. Chandler and H. Daems (Harvard University Press, Cambridge, Mass., 1980), pp. 9–40, pp. 26–9.

132 See C. Sabel, *Work and Politics* (Cambridge University Press, Cambridge, 1982), p. 33.

133 See Gordon, 'Class struggle', p. 74.

134 Cited ibid., p. 74.

135 Cited ibid., p. 75.

136 Cited ibid., p. 75.

137 Cited ibid., p. 75.

138 Cited ibid., p. 76.

139 See ibid., p. 76.

140 Ibid., p. 77.

141 See R. Fogelson, *The Fragmented Metropolis* (Harvard University Press, Cambridge, Mass., 1967).

142 A. Scott, *The Urban Land Nexus and the State* (Pion, London, 1981), p. 97; and see C. Leven, 'Economic maturity and the metropolis' evolving physical form', in *The Changing Structure of the City*, ed. G. Tobin (Sage, Beverly Hills, 1979), pp. 21–44, pp. 38–41.

143 See R. Walker, 'A theory of suburbanization: capitalism and the construction of urban space in the United States', in Dear and Scott, *Urbanization and Urban Planning*, pp. 383–430, p. 396.

144 Ibid., p. 397; and see J. L. Arnold, *The New Deal in the Suburbs* (Ohio State University Press, Ohio, 1971).

145 See B. Bluestone and B. Harrison, *The Deindustrialization of America* (Basic Books, New York, 1982), p. 112.

146 See ch. 8 below; as well as ibid., ch. 5.

147 See ibid., pp. 112–15.

148 Ibid., p. 120.

149 Ibid., p. 125.

150 See *Statistical Abstract of the United States 1984* (US Dept. of Commerce, US Bureau of the Census, Washington DC, 1983), table 1467.

151 See R. McDonald, 'The "underground economy" and BLS statistical data', *Monthly Labor Review* 107 (1984), pp. 4–18, p. 16.

152 Bluestone and Harrison, *Deindustrialization*, p. 114.

153 Ibid., pp. 114–117.

154 Scott, *Urban Land Nexus*, p. 101.

155 Willbern, *Withering Away*, p. 21.

156 A. Downs, *Opening Up the Suburbs* (Yale University Press, New Haven, 1973), p. 19.

157 Ibid., table 2.

158 M. Reinsberg, *Growth and Change in Metropolitan Areas and their Relation to Metropolitan Transportation: a Research Summary* (Northwestern University, Evanston, Ill., 1964), p. 23; and see Leven, 'Economic maturity', pp. 27–8.

159 Willbern, 'Withering away', p. 20, and see pp. 16–17; as well as P. Ashton, 'The political economy of suburban development', in *Marxism and the Metropolis*, ed. W. Tabb and L. Sawers (Oxford University Press, New York, 1978), pp. 64–89, p. 74.

160 Long, *Population Deconcentration*, p. 65.

161 Lash, *Militant Worker*, p. 177.
162 Downs, *Opening Up the Suburbs*, pp. 5–9.
163 See Scott, *Urban Land Nexus*, pp. 212–17.
164 Long, *Population Deconcentration*, p. 68.
165 See W. Kornblum, *Blue Collar Community* (University of Chicago Press, Chicago, 1974); as well as Lash, *Militant Worker*, p. 177.
166 Long, *Population Deconcentration*, p. 20.
167 Ibid., p. 81.
168 See R. Walker, 'A theory of suburbanization'.
169 See Sabolo, *Service Industries*; and Bluestone and Harrison, *Deindustrialization*, more generally.
170 See T. Noyelle, 'The implications of industry restructuring for spatial organization in the United States', in *Regional Analysis and the New International Division of Labor*, ed. F. F. Mouleert and P. W. Salinas (Kluwer, Boston, 1983), pp. 113–33.
171 See Noyelle, 'The implications of industry restructuring', p. 123.
172 P. K. Edwards, *Strikes in the United States*, p. 192.
173 Ibid., p. 193.
174 Ibid., p. 16.
175 See D. Perry and A. Watkins eds., *The Rise of the Sunbelt Cities* (Sage, Beverly Hills, 1977) amongst many sources.
176 Watkins and Perry, 'Regional change and the impact of uneven urban development', ibid., pp. 19–54, p. 42.
177 Leven, 'Economic maturity', p. 28.
178 See R. Estall, 'The decentralization of manufacturing industry: recent American experience in perspective', *Geoforum* 55 (1983), pp. 133–48.
179 Quoted K. Sale, *Power Shift: the Rise of the Southern Rim and its Challenge to the Eastern Establishment* (Vintage Press, New York, 1976), p. 4.
180 Ibid., p. 4. Between 1869 and 1945, for example, only two presidents were born outside the north-east.
181 See ibid., ch. 1. Sale notes that even in 1970 the gross national product of the southern rim (the area of the USA below the 37th parallel) was greater than that of the UK, Italy, Sweden and Norway combined.
182 Ibid., ch. 4. In 1964 the Republicans nominated Barry Goldwater, the Senator from Arizona, as presidential candidate.

5 ECONOMIC CHANGE AND SPATIAL RESTRUCTURING (2)

1 See C. Tilly, 'Flows of capital and forms of industry in Europe, 1500–1900', *Theory and Society* 12 (1983), pp. 123–42, p. 139.
2 B. R. Mitchell, *European Historical Statistics, 1750–1970* (Macmillan, London, 1975), p. 155.
3 See B. R. Palmer, *The Age of the Democratic Revolution*, 2 vols (Princeton University Press, Princeton, NJ, 1964); and C. Trebilcock, *The Industrialization of the Continental Powers* (Longman, London, 1981), pp. 135–9.
4 See D. Landes, *The Unbound Prometheus* (Cambridge University Press, Cambridge, 1969), p. 143.

5 See F. Crouzet, 'Les conséquences économiques de la Révolution: à propos d'un inédit de Sir Francis d'Invernois', *Annales historiques de la Revolution française* 34 (1962), pp. 182–217; and see Landes, *Unbound Prometheus*, p. 147, and Trebilcock, *Industrialization*, pp. 135–43.

6 See A. Milward and S. Saul, *The Economic Development of Continental Europe* (Allen & Unwin, London, 1979), pp. 262–5; and Trebilcock, *Industrialization*, pp. 133–5.

7 See G. Lefebvre, *Les Paysans du Nord* (Laterza, Lille, 1924), pp. 498–504.

8 See Trebilcock, *Industrialization*, p. 434.

9 See Milward and Saul, *Economic Development*, p. 353.

10 Trebilcock, *Industrialization*, p. 140.

11 See ibid., p. 145.

12 F. Crouzet, 'Western Europe and Great Britain; "catching up" in the first half of the nineteenth century', in *Economic Development in the Long Run*, ed. A. J. Youngson (Allen & Unwin, London, 1972), pp. 98–125, p. 108. Also, however, see P. Stearns, *Paths to Authority* (University of Illinois Press, Chicago, 1978), who warns against treating all entrepreneurs as in any way identical in either their beliefs or behaviour.

13 This is clearly shown in Landes, *Unbound Prometheus*, p. 159.

14 Trebilcock, *Industrialization*, p. 450.

15 See C. Kindleberger, *Economic Growth in France and Britain, 1851–1950* (Harvard University Press, Cambridge, Mass., 1964), p. 255.

16 See H. Clout, *The Geography of Post War France: a Social and Economic Approach* (Pergamon Press, Oxford, 1977), p. 502.

17 This is well shown in L. Chevalier, *Laboring Classes and Dangerous Classes: Paris in the first half of the Nineteenth Century* (Routledge, London, 1973).

18 See Clout, *Post War France*, and M. Berman, *All that is Solid Melts into Air* (Verso, London, 1983).

19 Berman, *All that is Solid*, p. 151.

20 Cited Clout, *Post War France*, p. 514.

21 Cited Berman, *All that is Solid*, p. 159.

22 See Clout, *Post War France*, p. 519.

23 See Berman, *All that is Solid*, more generally here.

24 See R. Aminzade, *Class, Politics, and Early Industrial Capitalism* (State University of New York Press, New York, 1981), p. 279 and *passim*; and R. Aminzade, 'Capitalist industrialization and patterns of industrial protest: a comparative urban study of nineteenth century France', *American Sociological Review* 49 (1984), pp. 437–53.

25 Aminzade, *Class, Politics*, p. 280.

26 See D. Geary, *European Labour Protest 1848–1939* (Croom Helm, London, 1981), pp. 61, 125. He also notes the crucial role of the repressive apparatus of the state in accounting for variations in the timing of French militancy.

27 See T. Judt, *Socialism in Provence 1871–1914* (Cambridge University Press, Cambridge, 1979).

28 See ibid., pp. 143–4; and see P. Cooke, 'Region, class and gender: a European comparison', *Progress in Planning* 22 (1984), pp. 89–146.

29 See W. Brustein, 'A regional mode-of-production analysis of political behaviour: the case of western and Mediterranean France', *Politics and Society* 10 (1981),

pp. 355–98, p. 386. More generally here see D. Gallie, *Social Inequality and Class Radicalism in France and Britain* (Cambridge University Press, Cambridge, 1983), ch. 11.

30 N. Hansen, *French Regional Planning* (Edinburgh University Press, Edinburgh, 1968), p. 27.

31 Ibid., pp. 27–8.

32 Ibid., p. 28.

33 Kindleberger, *Economic Growth*, p. 179.

34 Trebilcock, *Industrialization*, p. 198.

35 Ibid., p. 198.

36 B. Clout, *The Geography of Post War France* (Pergamon, Oxford, 1972), p. 1.

37 Ibid., p. 21.

38 See L. Franko, *The European Multinationals* (Harper & Row, London, 1976), p. 102.

39 See R. Gilpin, *France in the Age of the Scientific State* (Princeton University Press, Princeton, NJ, 1968).

40 See Franko, *European Multinationals*, pp. 102–3.

41 P. Aydalot, 'France', in *Industrial Mobility and Migration in the European Community*, ed. L. H. Klaassen and W. T. M. Molle (Gower, Aldershot, 1983), pp. 35–93, p. 37.

42 P. Aydalot, 'Questions for regional economy', *Tydschrift voor Econ. en Soc. Geografie* 75 (1984), pp. 4–14, p. 6.

43 Commission of the European Communities, *The Regions of Europe* (European Commission, Luxemburg, 1981), p. 20.

44 Clout, *Geography of Post-war France*, ch. 3.

45 F. Damette and E. P!oncet, 'Global crisis and regional crises', in *Regions in Crisis*, ed. J. Carney, R. Hudson and J. Lewis (Croom Helm, London, 1980), pp. 93–116, pp. 95–6.

46 European Commission, *Regions of Europe*, p. 138.

47 Aydalot, 'Questions for regional economy', p. 5.

48 Clout, *Geography of Post War France*, ch. 4.

49 Ibid., pp. 76–7.

50 Aydalot, 'Questions for regional economy', p. 6.

51 European Commission, *Regions of Europe*, p. 64.

52 Aydalot, 'France', p. 37.

53 European Commission, *Regions of Europe*, pp. 63–4.

54 On the following see Aydalot, 'France'; Aydalot, 'Questions for regional economy'.

55 Aydalot, 'France', p. 50; Aydalot, 'Questions for regional economy', p. 6.

56 Aydalot, 'France', p. 55.

57 Ibid., p. 57.

58 Ibid., p. 81, especially graph 3.1; and Aydalot, 'Questions for regional economy', p. 7.

59 See J. Marquand, *The Role of the Tertiary Sector in Regional Policy* (Commission of the European Communities, Brussels, 1980), pp. 28–9; and *Eurostat Review* (Statistical Office of the European Communities, Luxemburg, 1984), p. 121.

60 See Marquand, *Role of the Tertiary Sector*, pp. 67, 78.

61 *Eurostat Review*, p. 121.

62 Aydalot, 'Questions for regional economy', p. 9.
63 Landes, *Unbound Prometheus*, p. 336.
64 See D. Gallie, *Social Inequality*, p. 258.
65 See E. Shorter and C. Tilly, *Strikes in France, 1830–1968* (Cambridge University Press, Cambridge, 1974), p. 147.
66 See Mitchell, *European Historical Statistics*, p. 179.
67 Shorter and Tilly, *Strikes in France*, ch. 10.
68 Ibid., p. 231.
69 Ibid., pp. 140–2.
70 See the maps in D. Burtenshaw, *Economic Geography of West Germany* (Macmillan, London, 1974), p. 4.
71 See W. J. Mommsen, *Max Weber und die deutsche Politik* (Mohr, Tübingen, 1959).
72 See R. Dahrendorf, *Society and Democracy in Germany* (Anchor Books, Garden City, New Yori, 1967), p. 58.
73 W. Kollmann, 'The process of urbanization in Germany at the height of the industrialization period', in *The Urbanization of European Society in the Nineteenth Century*, ed. A. and L. Lees (D. C. Heath, Lexington, Mass., 1976), pp. 28–46, p. 30.
74 Ibid., p. 30.
75 F. Tipton, *Regional Variations in the Economic Development of Germany During the Nineteenth Century* (Wesleyan University Press, Connecticut, 1976), p. 95.
76 Kollmann, 'Process of urbanization', p. 32–3.
77 Ibid., p. 31.
77 Ibid., p. 32.
79 D. Geary, *European Labour Protest, 1848–1939* (Methuen, London, 1981), p. 32.
80 Kollmann, 'Process of urbanization', pp. 32–6; Tipton, *Regional Variations*, ch. 6.
81 Tipton, *Regional Variations*, ch. 6.
82 See ibid., ch. 6; and H. Matzerath, 'Berlin, 1890–1940', in *Metropolis 1890–1940*, ed. A. Sutcliffe (Mansell, London, 1984), pp. 289–318.
83 See Matzerath, 'Berlin', pp. 292–3; and see P. Schöller, 'The settlement system of the Federal Republic of Germany', in *Urbanization and Settlement Systems*, ed. L. Bourne, R. Sinclair and K. Dziewonski (Oxford University Press, Oxford, 1984), pp. 178–99, p. 181.
84 Tipton, *Regional Variations*, p. 82.
85 See ibid., p. 82; Y. Sabolo, *The Service Industries* (International Labour Organization, Geneva, 1975), p. 12; and J. Marquand, *Role of the Tertiary Sector*, p. 29.
86 See A. Gerschenkron, *Bread and Democracy in Germany* (Howard Fertig, New York, 1966), pp. 22–3.
87 Ibid., p. 23.
88 See ibid.
89 See ibid., pp. 56–7.
90 M. Weber, *Gesammelte politische Schriften* (Mohr, Tübingen, 1958), p. 109.
91 Dahrendorf, *Society and Germany*, p. 49. On recent debates in German historiography, see R. J. Evans, 'The myth of Germany's missing revolution', *New Left Review* 149 (1985), pp. 67–94.
92 See W. O. Henderson, *The Rise of German Industrial Power 1834–1914* (Temple Smith, London, 1975), ch. 17.

93 Landes, *Unbound Prometheus*, pp. 188–90.
94 Tipton, *Regional Variations*, pp. 45–8.
95 Ibid., pp. 122–5; and see B. Moore, *Injustice. The Social Basis of Obedience and Revolt* (Macmillan, London, 1978), table 6, p. 229.
96 Tipton, *Regional Variations*, p. 124.
97 Ibid., p. 128.
98 Ibid., p. 128.
99 See Moore, *Injustice*, pp. 233–5.
100 Although this should not be exaggerated – see ibid., pp. 238–9, on the system of inside contracting based on the *Maneradschaften*.
101 See ibid., pp. 242–4.
102 See D. Crew, *Town in the Ruhr: a Social History of Bochum 1860–1914* (Columbia University Press, New York, 1979), pp. 71–2.
103 See Tipton, *Regional Variations*, pp. 128–30 generally here.
104 See Crew, *Town in the Ruhr*, pp. 109–10.
105 See ibid., ch. 4 on Bochum.
106 Crew, ibid., p. 145.
107 See Geary, *European Labour Protest*, p. 105; and see Mitchell, *European Labour Statistics*, p. 174 on strike statistics.
108 Geary, *European Labour Protest*, p. 17.
109 Ibid., p. 17.
110 Moore, *Injustice*, p. 261; and see p. 265 on the separation of work tasks and hence of different categories of worker. See also Crew, *Town in the Ruhr*; and Geary, *European Labour Protest*, pp. 18, 78.
111 Geary, *European Labour Protest*, p. 57.
112 Ibid., pp. 62, 67.
113 Ibid., pp. 68–9.
114 Ibid., p. 75.
115 Ibid., pp. 92, 113.
116 Ibid., p. 99.
117 Ibid., p. 57.
118 Moore, *Injustice*, pp. 179–80.
119 See ibid., pp. 330–5 generally here.
120 Ibid., p. 332; see J. Tampke, *The Ruhr and Revolution* (Croom Helm, London, 1979), ch. 3.
121 Ibid., p. 35.
122 L. Franko, *The European Multinationals* (Harper and Row, London, 1976), pp. 19, 99.
123 Ibid., p. 34.
124 See ibid., pp. 33–5.
125 Dahrendorf, *Society and Democracy*, p. 110.
126 D. Petzina, W. Abelhauser and A. Faust, *Sozialgeschichliches Arbeitsbuch III* (C. H. Beck, München, 1978), p. 64; see also C. Hull, 'Federal Republic of Germany', in *The Small Firm*, ed. D. J. Storey (Croom Helm, London, 1983), pp. 153–78, p. 155.
127 Overall see Burtenshaw, *Economic Geography*.
128 See A. Shonfield, *Modern Capitalism* (Oxford University Press, London, 1965), pp. 241–2.

129 See ibid., pp. 242-3.
130 See ibid., p. 243, especially fn. 10.
131 A. Marshall, *Industry and Trade* (Macmillan, London, 1919), p. 567; and see Shonfield, *Modern Capitalism*, pp. 247, 253.
132 See ibid., p. 259.
133 See ibid., pp. 282, 296.
134 G. Krumme, 'Regional policies in West Germany', in *Public Policy and Regional Economic Development: the experience of Nine Western Countries* (Ballinger, Cambridge, Mass., 1974), pp. 103-36, p. 108; Burtenshaw, *Economic Geography*, ch. 2.
135 M. Blacksell, 'West Germany', in *Regional Development in Western Europe* (John Wiley, London, 1975), pp. 163-90, p. 168.
136 Ibid., pp. 168-9.
137 Ibid., p. 169.
138 See Fielding, 'Counterurbanisation', pp. 50-2.
139 See Scholler, 'The settlement system', pp. 194-5.
140 See Blacksell, 'West Germany', p. 174.
141 Ibid., p. 175.
142 See Burtenshaw, *Economic Geography*.
143 See Blackwell, 'West Germany', p. 176.
144 See D. Keeble, P. Owens and C. Thompson, *Centrality, Peripherality and EEC Regional Development* (Commission of the European Communities, HMSO, London, 1982), pp. 19-20.
145 See Blacksell, 'West Germany', p. 178; Shonfield, *Modern Capitalism*, pp. 240-1.
146 See Blacksell, 'West Germany', pp. 178-9.
147 See ibid., p. 179.
148 See ibid., p. 179.
149 F-J. Bade, 'Large corporations and regional development', *Regional Studies* 17 (1983), pp. 315-26, p. 317.
150 See ibid., p. 318; and Marquand, *Role of the Tertiary Sector*, p. 79.
151 Bade, 'Large corporations', pp. 322-3.
152 Ibid., p. 323; and see F-J. Bade, 'Federal Republic of Germany', in *Industrial Mobility*, ed. Klaassen and Molle, pp. 94-145, p. 101.
153 See Krumme, 'Regional policies', p. 105; Keeble, Owens and Thompson, *Centrality, Peripherality*, p. 19.
154 Ibid., pp. 20-1, and 'The Urban–Rural manufacturing shift in the European Community', *Urban Studies* 20 (1983), pp. 405-18, p. 412.
155 See the maps and diagrams in Bade, 'Federal Republic', pp. 116-20, p. 133.
157 Hull, 'Federal Republic of Germany', p. 159; and see Commission of the European Communities, *The Regions of Europe* (Brussels, 1980), p. 157.
158 W. Friedrich and E. Spitznagel, 'Wachstum, Beschäftigung und Investitions-tätigkeit im Verarbeiten Gewerbe', in *Mitteilungen aus der Arbeitsmarktund Berufsforschung* 13 (1980), pp. 514-20.
159 Infratest, *Begleitforschung zum Arbeitsmarktpolitischen Programm der Bundesregierung für Regionen mit besonderen Beschäftigungsproblemen*, Band 4 (Betriebserhebung, Munich, 1980).

160 *Eurostat Review* (Statistical Office of the European Communities, Brussels, 1984), p. 125.
161 Ibid., p. 124.
162 See Marquand, *Role of the Tertiary Sector*, pp. 64, 70.
163 Ibid., p. 79; see also the map on p. 187 in Scholler, 'The settlement system'.
164 See Franko, *European Multinationals*, p. 18.
165 On German companies in the UK, see H. D. Watts, 'The inter-regional distribution of West German multinationals in the United Kingdom', in *The Geography of Multinationals*, ed. M. Taylor and N. Thrift (Croom Helm, London, 1982), pp. 61–89.
166 F. Fröbel, J. Heinrichs and O. Kreye, *The New International Division of Labour* (Cambridge University Press, Cambridge, 1980), p. 9.
167 Ibid., pp. 19, 79.
168 Ibid., pp. 196–201.
169 See ibid., pp. 87, 108–10.
170 Ibid., p. 121.
171 See Stephens, *From Capitalism*, pp. 115–16.
172 L. Jorberg, *The Industrial Revolution in Scandinavia 1850–1914* (Fontana, London, 1970), p. 6.
173 See K. Samuelsson, *From Great Power to Welfare State* (Allen & Unwin, London, 1968), ch. 1.
174 See S. S. Duncan, *Class Relations and Historical Geography: the Creation of the Rural and Urban Questions in Sweden*, University of Sussex Research papers in Geography, No. 12 (1984), pp. 18–30.
175 See I. T. Berend and G. Ránki, *The European periphery and industrialization 1780–1914* (Cambridge University Press, Cambridge, 1982), p. 46.
176 Mitchell, *European Historical Statistics*, p. 162.
177 See Samuelsson, *From Great Power*, pp. 161–2.
178 See here ibid., p. 186; Jorberg, *Industrial Revolution*, p. 16; and R. Scase, *Social Democracy in Capitalist Society* (Croom Helm, London, 1977), p. 23.
179 Samuelsson, *From Great Power*, p. 74, and see p. 149. On the effects of such enclosures, see A. Pred, 'The social becomes the spatial, the spatial becomes the social: enclosures, social change and the becoming of places in the Swedish province of Skône', in *Social Relations and Spatial Structures*, ed. D. Gregory and J. Urry (Macmillan, London, 1985), pp. 337–65.
180 See Duncan, *Class Relations*, pp. 25–7.
181 Ibid., pp. 75, 145; and see W. Moberg's novels translated as *The Emigrants*, *Unto a Good Land*, and *The Last Letter Home*.
182 Samuelsson, *From Great Power*, p. 180.
183 Ibid., p. 182.
184 See Scase, *Social Democracy*, pp. 18–19, on these various points. On proto-industrialization in Sweden, see L. Schön, 'Proto-industrialisation and factories: textiles in Sweden in the mid-nineteenth century', *Scandinavian Economic History Review* 30 (1982), pp. 57–71.
185 See Samuelsson, *From Great Power*, pp. 182–3; and S. S. Duncan, *Class Relations and Historical Geography: the Transition to Capitalism in Sweden*, Graduate School of Geography Discussion Papers, London School of Economics, (1982), p. 41.

186 Duncan, *Class Relations and Historical Geography: the Transition*, p. 42.
187 Samuelsson, *From Great Power*, pp. 182–3.
188 Berend and Ránki, *European Periphery*, p. 146.
189 Ibid., p. 158; and see Jorberg, *Industrial Revolution*, pp. 122–3.
190 S. S. Duncan, *Class Relations and Historical Geography*, p. 45.
191 Samuelsson, *From Great Power*, p. 183.
192 Scase, *Social Democracy*, p. 23.
193 W. Korpi and M. Shalev, 'Strikes, industrial relations and class conflict in industrial societies', *British Journal of Sociology* 30 (1979), pp. 164–87, p. 175.
194 Samuelsson, *From Great Power*, p. 185; and see G. Heckscher, *Staten och organisationerna (Land of Organization)* (KF, Stockholm, 1951).
195 See M. Hancock, *Sweden, The Politics of Postindustrial Change* (Dryden Press, Hinsdale, Ill., 1972), pp. 37. He quotes the former Swedish Prime Minister Olof Palme on the Swedish 'character': 'We're probably shy and reserved, and you once said the humor of hell would have the humor of Sweden. We are distant and perhaps rather dull.'
196 See O. Wärneryd, 'The Swedish national settlement system', in *Urbanization and Settlement Systems*, ed. L. Bourne, R. Sinclair and K. Dziewonski (Oxford University Press, Oxford, 1984), pp. 92–112, p. 95, on these various points.
197 Ibid., p. 99.
198 See H. Berglind and B. Rundblad, *Arbetsmarknaden i Sverige* (Esselte Studium, Stockholm, 1983), pp. 133.
199 Franzen, ibid., p. 14.
200 Korpi, *Working Class*, p. 58; and see R. Scase ed., *Readings in the Swedish Class Structure* (Pergamon, London, 1976).
201 Ibid., p. 102; and Statistisk Årsbok för Sverige, 1984 (Statisticka Centraltyran, Stockholm, 1984), p. 21.
202 Wärneryd, 'Swedish national settlement system', p. 101; note that journeys-to-work are no longer offset against tax.
203 L. Berntson, 'Post-war Swedish capitalism', in *Limits of the Welfare State*, ed. J. Fry (Saxon House, Farnborough, Hants, 1979), pp. 60–89, p. 64.
204 Wärneryd, 'Swedish national settlement system', p. 109.
205 Ibid., p. 102.
206 See *Industrin i Sverige-va finns den?* (Sveriges Industriforbund, Stockholm, 1982), p. 16.
207 See the maps in ibid., pp. 19, 21.
208 See *Swedish Regional Policy 1982* (Ministry of Industry, Stockholm, 1983), p. 7; and L. Ohlsson, 'Structural adaptability of regions during Swedish industrial adjustment, 1965–1975', in *Spatial Analysis: Industry and the Industrial Environment*, vol. 3, *Regional Economics and Industrial Systems*, ed. F. E. I. Hamilton and G. J. R. Linge (Wiley, New York, 1983), pp. 299–335.
209 *Swedish Regional Policy*, p. 8.
210 Berntson, 'Post-war Swedish capitalism', p. 73.
211 L. Håkanson and L. Danielsson, 'Structural adjustment in a stagnating economy: regional manufacturing employment in Sweden, 1975–1980', *Regional Studies* 19 (1985), pp. 329–42, p. 331.
212 Ibid., p. 334.
213 Ibid., p. 34, and *Statiskisk Årsbok*, p. 189.

214 *Statisk Årsbok*, p. 189.
215 *Arbetsmarknadsstatistisk Årsbok 1982–3* (Statistiska Centralbyran, Stockholm, 1983), p. 51; and see *Industrin i Sverige*, pp. 22–3.
216 *Arbetsmarknadsstatistisk Årsbok*, p. 53.
217 See L. Lindmark, 'Sweden', in *Small Firms: an International Survey* (Croom Helm, London, 1983), pp. 187–90.
218 Ibid., p. 189.
219 Ibid., p. 190; and *Arbetsmarknadsstatistisk Årsbok*, p. 52.
220 Lindmark, 'Sweden', pp. 190–1.
221 Ibid., p. 194.
222 Ibid., pp. 194–5.
223 U. Himmelstrand, G. Ahrne and L. Lundberg, *Beyond Welfare Capitalism* (Heinemann, London, 1981), p. 155.
224 Ibid., pp. 155–6.

6 THE SERVICE CLASS

1 See N. Abercrombie and J. Urry, *Capital, Labour and the Middle Classes* (Allen & Unwin, London, 1983), especially part 1; and R. Carter, *Capitalism, Class Conflict and the New Middle Class* (Routledge & Kegan Paul, London, 1985).
2 On the notion of a service class see K. Renner, 'The service class', repr. in *Austro-Marxism*, ed. T. Bottomore and P. Goode (Clarendon Press, Oxford, 1978), pp. 249–52; J. H. Goldthorpe, 'On the service class, its formation and future', in *Social Class and the Divisions of Labour*, ed. A. Giddens and G. Mackenzie (Cambridge University Press, Cambridge, 1982), pp. 162–85; Abercrombie and Urry, *Capital, Labour*, part 2; J. Urry, 'Capitalist production, scientific management', and the service class', in *Production, Work, Territory*, ed. A. Scott and M. Storper (Allen & Unwin, London, 1986).
3 See A. Touraine, *The Post-industrial Society* (Wildwood, London, 1974), and the critique in J. Gershuny, *After Industrial Society?* (Macmillan, London, 1978).
4 See E. P. Thompson, 'Time, work-discipline, and industrial capitalism', *Past and Present* 38 (1967), pp. 56–97.
5 D. Nelson, *Managers and Workers. Origins of the New Factory System in the United States, 1880–1920* (University of Wisconsin Press, Madison, Wis., 1975), p. 4; and see H. Braverman, *Labor and Monopoly Capital* (Monthly Review Press, New York, 1974), and D. Montgomery, *Workers' Control in America* (Cambridge University Press, Cambridge, 1979).
6 See Nelson, *Managers and Workers*, ch. 3 on the 'Foreman's Empire'.
7 See C. Littler, 'Understanding Taylorism', *British Journal of Sociology* 29 (1978), pp. 185–202; M. S. Larson, 'Proletarianization and educated labour', *Theory and Society* 9 (1980), pp. 131–75; D. Stark, 'Class struggle and the transformation of the labour process', *Theory and Society* 9 (1980), pp. 89–130; and C. Littler, *The Development of the Labour Process in Capitalist Society* (Heinemann, London, 1982), ch. 11.
8 See Littler, *Development*, pp. 165–71; and see J. Buttrick, 'The inside contract system', *Journal of Economic History* 12 (1952), pp. 205–21; B. Scoffer, 'A theory of trade union development: the role of the ''autonomous'' workman',

Labour History 1 (1960), pp. 141–63, and D. Clawson, *Bureaucracy and the Labor Process* (Monthly Review Press, New York, 1980).

9 Clawson, *Bureaucracy*, p. 73; and see K. Stone, 'The origin of job structures in the steel industry', *Review of Radical Political Economy* 6 (1974), pp. 113–73; and Montgomery, *Workers' Control*, on how this constituted a form of 'workers' control.

10 See F. W. Taylor, *The Principles of Scientific Management* (Harper and Row, New York, 1947).

11 This is well discussed in H. Person, *Scientific Management in American Industry: the Taylor Society* (Harper and Row, New York, 1929), p. 9.

12 See Taylor, *Principles*, p. 36.

13 Ibid., p. 38.

14 See Person, *Scientific Management*, pp. 9–11.

15 See F. B. Copley, *Frederick W. Taylor*, 2 vols (Harper & Row, New York, 1923); L. Urwick, *The Meaning of Rationalisation* (Nisbet, London, 1929), on the nature of rationalization; Taylor, *Principles*; Littler, *Development*; J. Merkle, *Management and Ideology* (University of California Press, Berkeley, 1980); as well as the *Engineering Magazine* and *Transactions of the American Society of Engineers*.

16 See B. Palmer, 'Class, conception and conflict: the thrust for efficiency. Managerial views of labour and the working class rebellion 1903–22', *Review of Radical Political Economy* 7 (1975), pp. 31–49; as well as M. J. Nadworny, *Scientific Management and the Unions, 1900–1932* (Harvard University Press, Cambridge, Mass., 1955); and Nelson, *Managers and Workers*.

17 Merkle, *Management*, p. 62. See also Montgomery, *Workers' Control*, ch. 5; and Littler, *Development*, pp. 179–83.

18 On these points see S. Hill, *Competition and Control at Work* (Heinemann, London, 1982); and A. Chandler, 'The United States. Seedbed of managerial capitalism', in *Managerial Hierarchies*, ed. A. Chandler and H. Dames (Harvard University Press, Cambridge, Mass., 1980), pp. 9–40.

19 See chapter 4 above; see also Person, *Scientific Management*, pp. 24–5; Chandler, 'The United States', pp. 23–9; E. S. Herman, *Corporate Control, Corporate Power* (Cambridge University Press, Cambridge, 1981); Littler, *Development*, ch. 11.

20 See Herman, *Corporate Control*, p. 388; Littler, *Development*, pp. 162–3.

21 See Nelson, *Managers and Workers*, ch. 5; D. Noble, *America by Design* (Oxford University Press, Oxford, 1979); Montgomery, *Workers' Control*, ch. 2.

22 Nelson, *Managers and Workers*, p. 80.

23 S. H. Slichter, *The Turnover of Factory Labor* (D. Appleton, New York, 1919), p. 16; and see Littler, *Development*, p. 164.

24 See Nelson, *Managers and Workers*, pp. 81–2; Noble, *America*, pp. 57–8; and Littler, *Development*, p. 163.

25 See B. Ramirez, *When Workers Fight* (Greenwood, Westpoint, Conn., 1978), p. 133. As Noble, *America*, p. 58, says:

> Living in terms of their own cultural heritage, which they sustained and which sustained them in a strange and hostile environment, the new immigrants defied ready absorption into the industrial process.

26 See J. Bodnar, *Immigrants and Industrialization. Ethnicity in an American Mill Town, 1870–1940* (Pittsburgh University Press, Pittsburgh, 1977); and Littler, *Development*, p. 164.

27 See the discussion in P. Foner, *History of the Labour Movement in the United States*, vol. 2 (International Publishers, New York, 1955), pp. 16–19.
28 See Montgomery, *Workers' Control*, p. 34, and more generally on many of these points.
29 G. Adams, *Age of Industrial Violence, 1910–15* (Columbia University Press, New York, 1966), p. 228; and see Foner, *History*; Montgomery, *Workers' Control*, pp. 56–7; M. Dubofsky, 'Workers' movement in North America, 1873–1970. A preliminary analysis', in *Labor in the World Social Structure*, ed. I. Wallerstein (Sage, Beverly Hills, 1983), pp. 22–43.
30 See D. Brody, *Workers in Industrial America* (Oxford University Press, Oxford, 1980), ch. 1; Dubofsky, 'Workers' movement'.
31 See R. Bendix, *Work and Authority in Industry* (John Wiley, London, 1956), pp. 284–5; S. Haber, *Efficiency and Uplift* (University of Chicago, Chicago, 1964), ch. 7; and Stark, 'Class struggle'.
32 See Noble, *America*, pp. 38–41; and see E. Layton, *The Revolt of the Engineers* (Press of Case Western Reserve University, Cleveland, 1971), more generally on American engineers.
33 Noble, *America*, p. 43.
34 See, among many sources, G. Kolko, *The Triumph of Conservatism* (Free Press, New York, 1963); Haber, *Efficiency*; Palmer, 'Class, conception and conflict'; Ramirez, *When Workers Fight*, part 3.
35 See J. Litterer, 'Systematic management: design for organizational recoupling in American manufacturing firms', *Business History Review* 37 (1963), pp. 369–91, pp. 360–8; Haber, *Efficiency*; Palmer, 'Class, conception and conflict', p. 35; Littler, *Development*, pp. 174–5, for further details.
36 Haber, *Efficiency*, p. xi.
37 See Copley, *Frederick W. Taylor*; and Palmer, 'Class, conception and conflict', pp. 34–5.
38 See Nadworny, *Scientific Management*, ch. 4.
39 See ch. 3.
40 Stark, 'Class struggle', p. 101.
41 See Nadworny, *Scientific Management*, ch. 4; and M. Burawoy, 'Towards a Marxist theory of the labour process: Braverman and beyond', *Politics and Society* 3–4 (1978), pp. 247–312, p. 277.
42 Quoted Nadworny, *Scientific Management*, p. 53.
43 Ibid., ch. 6.
44 See Palmer, 'Class, conception and conflict', p. 42.
45 As in the coal and garment-making industries in this period; see H. Benenson, 'The reorganization of US manufacturing industry and workers' experience, 1880–1920: a review of "Bureaucracy and the Labour Process" by Dan Clawson', *Insurgent Sociologist* 11 (1982), pp. 65–81.
46 Palmer, 'Class, conception, and conflict', p. 41.
47 Person, *Scientific Management*, p. 20.
48 C. B. Thompson, *The Theory and Practice of Scientific Management* (Houghton Mifflin, Boston, 1917), p. 269.
49 Brody, *Workers in Industrial America*, pp. 44–6.
50 Burawoy, 'Towards a Marxist theory', p. 284.
51 See Haber, *Efficiency and Uplift*; and P. Meiskins, 'Scientific management

and class relations', *Theory and Society* 13 (1984), pp. 177–209, p. 178.

52 Quoted in Copley, *Frederick W. Taylor*, vol. 1, p. 388.

53 This is shown in considerable detail by Meiskins, 'Scientific management'.

54 Litterer, 'Systematic management', p. 370; and see Thompson, *Theory and Practice*, p. 211; and Person, *Scientific Management*, pp. 11–12.

55 Taylor, *The Principles*, p. 43.

56 Nelson, *Managers and Workers*, p. 75; and see Littler, *Development*, p. 181.

57 Noble, *America*, p. 75.

58 Taylor, *The Principles*, p. 31.

59 Layton, *The Revolt*, p. 139.

60 Meiskins, 'Scientific management', pp. 192–3.

61 Stark, 'Class struggle', p. 101.

62 See Noble, *America*, part 1.

63 Quoted ibid., p. 21; and see Layton, *The Revolt*.

64 For details, see Noble, *America*, part 2, and Merkle, *Management*, p. 67.

65 Stark, 'Class struggle', p. 118. Also though see Larson, *The Rise of Professionalisation*; and M. Burrage, 'Democracy and the mystery of the crafts', *Daedalus*, Fall (1972), pp. 141–62, on why engineers did not develop a full 'professional' identity.

66 See Touraine, *Post-industrial Society*, p. 29.

67 See Noble, *America*, ch. 8.

68 Merkle, *Management*, p. 75. Generally here see Larson, *The Rise of Professionalism*: M. S. Larson, 'Proletarianisation and Educated Labour', *Theory and Society* 9 (1980), pp. 131–75, pp. 141–2; B. J. Bledstein, *The Culture of Professionalism* (Norton, New York, 1976); and K. H. Jarausch ed., *The Transformation of Higher Education, 1860–1930* (University of Chicago Press, Chicago, 1983).

69 Noble, *America*, p. 168; also see Abercrombie and Urry, *Capital, Labour*, ch. 6; R. Wiebe, *The Search for Order* (Macmillan, London, 1967); and C. Disco, 'Critical theory as ideology of the new class', *Theory and Society* 8 (1979), pp. 159–214.

70 K. Jarausch, 'Higher education and social change: some comparative perspectives', in *idem.*, *The Transformation of Higher Education*, pp. 108–30, p. 111.

71 See C. B. Burke, 'The expansion of American higher education', in ibid., pp. 108–30, p. 111.

72 See R. Debray, *Teachers, Writers, Celebrities* (Verso, London, 1981); and F. Mulhern, '"Teachers, Writers, Celebrities", intelligentsias and their histories', *New Left Review* 126 (1981), pp. 43–59.

73 See J. Berbst, 'Diversification in American higher education', in Jarausch, *The Transformation of Higher Education*, pp. 196–220, p. 205.

74 Bendix, *Work and Authority*, p. 288; and see L. Baritz, *The Servants of Power* (Greenwood Press, Westport, Conn., 1960), ch. 4.

75 See A. Gedicks, 'American social scientists and the emerging corporate economy, 1885–1915', *Insurgent Sociologist* 5 (1975), pp. 25–48, on the development of an 'organizationally-dependent' sociology; and R. L. Church, 'Economists as experts: the rise of an academic profession in the United States, 1870–1920', in *The University in Society*, ed. L. Stone (Oxford University Press, Oxford, 1974), pp. 571–610, on the growth of economists as experts.

76 See Wiebe, *Search for Order*, p. 113.
77 See C. Lasch, 'The siege of the family', *New York Review of Books* 24 (1977), pp. 15–18.
78 See R. E. Brown, *Rockefeller Medicine Men* (University of California Press, Berkeley, 1980), pp. 50–1, 59, 122.
79 Ibid., p. 59; although note the more sceptical comments of P. Starr, *The Social Transformation of American Medicine* (Basic Books, New York, 1982), pp. 229–30.
80 W. Trattner, *From Poor Law to Welfare State* (Free Press, New York, 1979), p. 140.
81 See ibid., pp. 134–84; A. F. Davis, 'The social workers and the Progressive Party, 1912–1916', *American Historical Review* 69 (1964), pp. 671–88; A. F. Davis, *Spearheads for Reform: the Social Settlements and the Progressive Movement, 1890–1914* (Oxford University Press, New York, 1967).
82 See Trattner, *From Poor Law*; A. J. Altmeyer, *The Formative Years of Social Security* (University of Wisconsin Press, Madison, Wisconsin, 1966). On the 'new class', see Bruce-Briggs ed., *The New Class?* (McGraw-Hill, New York, 1979), especially the chs by Bell, Lipset and Podhoretz.
83 Stark, 'Class struggle', p. 119, as well as Bruce-Biggs, *New Class*.
84 See K. Burgess, *The Challenge of Labour* (Croom Helm, London, 1980), ch. 4; and Littler, *Development*, ch. 7.
85 C. Maier, 'Between Taylorism and technocracy: European ideologies and the vision of industrial productivity in the 1920s', *Journal of Contemporary History* 5 (1970), pp. 27–61, p. 37.
86 Quoted in M. J. Wiener, *English Culture and the Decline of the Industrial Sprit, 1850–1980* (Cambridge University Press, Cambridge, 1981); also see L. Urwick and E. F. L. Brech, *Management in British Industry* (Management Publications Trust, London, 1946), ch. 7.
87 L. Urwick, *The Meaning of Rationalisation* (Nisbet, London, 1929), p. 58.
88 Ibid., p. 70.
89 A. Shadwell, 'The welfare of factory workers', *The Edinburgh Review*, October (1916), pp. 375–6; and see *idem, Industrial Efficiency*, 2 vols (Longman, London, 1906).
90 See J. A. Hobson, *Incentives in the New Industrial Order* (Parsons, London, 1922), although note his less critical comments in 'Scientific management', *Sociological Review* 6 (1913), pp. 197–212; S. Webb, *The Works Manager Today* (Longman, London, 1918); E. Cadbury, 'Some principles of industrial organization: the case for and against scientific management', *Sociological Review* 7 (1914), pp. 99–125, and *idem*, 'Reply to C. B. Thompson', *Sociological Review* 7 (1914), pp. 266–9.
91 See A. L. Levine, *Industrial Retardation in Britain, 1880–1914* (Weidenfeld and Nicolson, London, 1967).
92 *The Engineer*, April 25th, 1913, p. 413.
93 E. T. Elbourne, *Factory Administration and Accounts* (Longman, London, 1914), p. 169.
94 Thompson, *Theory and Practice*, p. 39; and see Levine, *Industrial Retardation*, p. 67.
95 Levine, *Industrial Retardation*, pp. 52–4.
96 Burgess, *Challenge of Labour*, p. 166; and see S. Pollard, *The Development of*

the British Economy, 1914–67 (Edward Arnold, London, 1969), pp. 53–6, 81–2.
97 This is convincingly demonstrated in Littler, *Development*, pp. 99–100.
98 C. Bedaux, *The Bedaux Efficiency Course for Industrial Application* (Bedaux Industrial Institute, 1917); P. Livingstone, 'Stop the stopwatch', *New Society*, 10th July, 1969, pp. 49–51; E. Layton, *Revolt*; and especially Littler, *Development*, chs 8 and 9; and *idem*, 'Deskilling and changing structures of control', in *The Degradation of Work*, ed. S. Wood (Hutchinson, London, 1982), pp. 122–45.
99 Littler, *Development*, p. 107.
100 See Layton, *Revolt*, p. 382 and *passim*.
101 Livingstone, 'Stop the stopwatch', p. 50.
102 See G. C. Brown, 'AFL Report on the Bedaux System', *American Federationist* 42 (1935), pp. 936–43; and Littler, *Development*, p. 112.
103 See the discussion in Nadworny, *Scientific Management*, p. 134.
104 Littler, *Development*, pp. 113–14; and *idem*, 'The bureaucratisation of the shop-floor; the development of the modern work-system', London PhD, Appendix A.
105 Littler, *Development*, pp. 118–33.
106 Ibid., ch. 9.
107 As reflected, for example, in the TUC Report, *Bedaux Report* (1933), p. 16.
108 See Littler, *Development*, p. 141.
109 See ibid., p. 103, on the Calico Printers Association founded in 1899 which possessed 128 directors and eight managing directors! Also see Burgess, *Challenge of Labour*, p. 113, on capital export.
110 A. Marshall, *Principles of Economics* (Macmilland, London, 1938), p. 21.
111 Wiener, *English Culture*, p. 128.
112 Ibid., pp. 128–9; and see G. Ingham, *Capitalism Divided* (Macmillan, London, 1984); and S. Wood and J. Kelly, 'Taylorism, responsible autonomy and management strategy', in *Degradation of Work*, ed. Wood, pp. 74–89.
113 See Levine, *Industrial Retardation*, pp. 122–4.
114 See Littler, *Development*, pp. 183–5.
115 E. H. Brown and M. H. Browne, *A Century of Pay* (Macmillan, London, 1967), p. 67.
116 Burgess, *Challenge of Labour*, p. 97; and see Levine, *Industrial Retardation*, pp. 76–8.
117 See Littler, *Development*, p. 95.
118 Hobson, *Incentives*, pp. 62, 81.
119 Quoted in Levine, *Industrial Retardation*, p. 70. The Wedgwoods claimed in 1884 that they did not employ any chemists! See Wiener, *English Culture*, p. 201.
120 Maier, 'Between Taylorism and technocracy', p. 59.
121 Wiener, *English Culture*, pp. 88–90.
122 See ibid., pp. 138–9. On the differences between rugby union and American football, see P. Clark, 'Interpreting responsible autonomy and direct control: unravelling Anglo-American predispositions in work organization', Work Organisation Research Centre, Aston, Sept. 1983.
123 D. C. Coleman, 'Gentlemen and players', *Economic History Review* 26 (1933), pp. 92–116, p. 113.
124 See M. Shanks, 'The comforts of stagnation', in *Suicide of a Nation?*, ed. A. Koestler (Hutchinson, London, 1963), pp. 51–69.

125 P. Sargent Florence, *Investment, location and size of plant* (Cambridge University Press, Cambridge, 1948), p. 143.

126 See Wiener, *English Culture*, p. 15; and Larson, *The Rise of Professionalism*, p. 103.

127 See W. D. Rubinstein, 'Wealth, elites and class structure in Britain', *Past and Present* 76 (1977), pp. 99–126. For further details see H. Perkin, 'Middle class education and employment in the nineteenth century: a critical note', *Economic History Review* 14 (1961/2), pp. 122–30, pp. 128–9. It should also be noted that part of the process of nineteenth-century professionalization was to 'masculinize' especially the medical profession and to drive out, or reduce in status, or prevent from entering, women 'healers' of various sorts. See A. Witz, *Midwifery and Medicine* (Lancaster Regionalism Group Working Paper No. 13, 1985).

128 See T. Nichols, *Ownership, Control and Ideology* (Allen & Unwin, London, 1969), pp. 88–9.

129 R. Whitley, A. Thomas, J. Marceau, *Masters of Business* (Tavistock, London, 1981), p. 1; more generally see chs 1, 2, 3.

130 Ibid., p. 33; and see J. Child, *British Management Thought* (Allen & Unwin, London, 1969).

131 See Whitley, Thomas, Marceau, *Masters*, ch. 3.

132 F. Ringer, *Education and Society in Modern Europe* (Indiana University Press, Bloomington, 1979), pp. 250–1.

133 M. Gowring, *Science, Technology and Education* (The Wilkins Lecture 1976, Royal Society of London, London, 32, 1977). J. S. Mill's pronouncements in 1867 are instructive here:

> There is a tolerable agreement about what a university is not. It is not a place of professional education. Universities are not intended to teach the knowledge required to fit men for some special mode of gaining a livelihood. Their object is not to make skilful lawyers and physicians and engineers, but capable and cultivated human beings (cited Musgrove, 1981, p. 59).

134 See B. Martin, *A Sociology of Contemporary Cultural Change* (Basil Blackwell, Oxford, 1981).

135 Perhaps the most telling summary of the state of education in Britain can be found in Oscar Wilde's *The Importance of Being Earnest*, where Lady Bracknell states that:

> I do not approve of anything that tampers with natural ignorance. Ignorance is like a delicate exotic fruit; touch it and the bloom is gone. The whole theory of modern education is unsound. Fortunately in England, at any rate, education produces no effect whatsoever. If it did, it would prove a serious danger to the upper classes, and probably lead to acts of violence in Grosvenor Square (sic).

136 J. Kocka, 'Entrepreneurs and managers in German industrialisation', in *Cambridge Economic History of Europe*, vol. 7, ed. P. Mathias and M. M. Postan (Cambridge University Press, Cambridge, 1978), pp. 492–589. Also see the useful contemporary account, P. Devinat, *Scientific Management in Europe* (ILO, Geneva, 1927).

137 J. Kocka, *White-Collar Workers in America, 1890–1940* (Sage, London, 1980), pp. 456ff.; and see Levine, *Industrial Retardation*, pp. 46, 75, 147.

138 Bendix, *Work and Authority*, p. 214.
139 See Kocka, 'Entrepreneurs and managers', *idem*, *White-Collar Workers*, p. 464.
140 G. Winter, *Der Taylorismus: Handbuch der wissenschaftlichen Betriebs- und Arbeitsweise für die Arbeitenden alle Klassen, Stände, und Berufe* (Verlag von S. Hirzel, Leipzig, 1920).
141 See J. Kocka, *Unternehmensverwaltung und Angestelltenschaft am Beispiel Siemens 1847–1914* (Klett, Stuttgart, 1969); and R. Torstendahl, 'Engineers in industry, 1850–1910: professional men and new bureaucrats. A comparative approach', in *Science, Technology and Society in the Time of Alfred Nobel*, ed. G. Bernhard, E. Crawford, P. Sorborn (Pergamon, London, 1982), pp. 253–70, pp. 261–4.
142 See Torstendahl, 'Engineers in industry', p. 262. Also see G. Ahlstrom, 'Higher technical education and the engineering profession in France and Germany during the 19th century', *Economy and History* 21 (1978), pp. 51–88.
143 See Ringer, *Education and Society*; McClelland, *State, Society and University in Germany, 1700–1914* (Cambridge University Press, Cambridge, 1980), p. 240 and part 4 *passim*.
144 P. W. Musgrave, 'The labour force: some relevant attitudes', in *Where Did We Go Wrong?*, ed. G. Roderick and M. Stephens (Falmer Press, Lewes, 1981), pp. 46–66, pp. 59–61.
145 D. H. Aldcroft, 'The economy, management and foreign competition', ibid., pp. 13–32, p. 25; Ahlstrom, 'Higher technical education', pp. 61–8; and J. C. Smail, *Trade and Technical Education in Germany and France* (London County Council, London, 1914).
146 C. McClelland, 'Professionalization and higher education in Germany', in Jarausch *The Transformation of Higher Education*, pp. 306–20, p. 307.
147 See ibid., p. 309.
148 Ahlstrom, 'Higher technical education', pp. 74–6.
149 See J. Kocka, 'Capitalism and bureaucracy in German industrialization before 1914', *Economic History Review* 34 (1981), pp. 455–68; and S. Hutton and P. Lawrence, *German Engineers* (Clarendon Press, Oxford, 1981).
150 B. R. Mitchell, *European Labour Statistics* (Cambridge University Press, Cambridge, 1975), p. 775.
151 See Torstendahl, 'Engineers in industry', p. 257; generally see B. Berner, *Teknikens värld* (Kristianstad, Lund, 1981), ch. 7.
152 Torstendahl, 'Engineers in industry', p. 259.
153 See ibid., p. 265.
154 See N. Runeby, 'Americanism, Taylorism and social integration', *Scandinavian Journal of History* 3 (1978), pp. 21–46, p. 22.
155 Ibid., p. 27.
156 Ibid., pp. 30–2.
157 This was particularly the argument of Nils Fredriksson, who went on study trips to the USA and wrote *The American Brick Industry*. Estimates were made that 30–50% of the work-process constituted 'lost time'. See ibid., p. 33.
158 See ibid., fn. 46; and Berner, *Teknikens värld*, ch. 10.
159 See the comments of Erik Forsberg summarized in Runeby, 'Americanism, Taylorism', p. 39. Forsberg stated:

> Work intensity. It is deliberately obstructed. Can be cured through organization. Good salary and cheap work. Compare America.

160 See ibid., pp. 41–2.
161 Ibid., pp. 45–6.
162 Bendix, *Work and Authority*, pp. 214, 218.
163 Mitchell, *European Labour Statistics*, p. 776.
164 R. Eyerman, 'Rationalizing intellectuals', *Theory and Society* 14 (1985), pp. 777–807, p. 802; and for details, see L. Pettersson, *Ingenjörsutbildning och kapitalbildning 1933–1973* (Studentlitteratur, Lund, 1983).
165 See Ahlstrom, 'Higher tehcnical education', p. 55; and Devinat, *Scientific Management*, p. 39.
166 See Ahlstrom, 'Higher technical education', pp. 60, 66.
167 See D. Landes, *Unbound Prometheus* (Cambridge University Press, Cambridge, 1969).
168 See Devinat, *Scientific Management*, pp. 30–2; Maier, 'Beyond Taylorism and technocracy', pp. 37–8; E. Layton, 'The diffusion of scientific management and mass production from the US in the twentieth century', *International Congress in the History of Science* 4 (1974), pp. 377–86.
169 See M. Levy-Leboyer, 'The contribution of French scientists and engineers to the development of modern managerial practices in the early part of the twentieth century', in *Science, Technology and Society*, ed. G. Bernhard et al., pp. 283–97, p. 288.
170 See ibid., p. 289; on Clemenceau see Copley, *Frederick W. Taylor*, vol. 1, p. xxi. Incidentally there was no substantial international exchange of scientific management ideas until after the First World War. The first international congress was held in Prague in 1924 attended by delegates from six European countries and from the USA. Further congresses were held in 1925 and 1927 when 1400 delegates heard over 170 papers. In 1927 the ILO established at Geneva the International Management Institute to collate, classify and disseminate all known schemes of scientific management. See Urwick, *The Meaning of Rationalisation*, pp. 75f.
171 See Levy-Leboyer, 'Contribution of French scientists', pp. 288–94.
172 Ibid., p. 293.
173 See discussion in ibid., pp. 294–5.
174 See Whitley, Thomas and Marceau, *Masters of Business*, ch. 4.
175 See J. Story and M. Parrott, 'An essay on management in France: does it work?', *International Herald Tribune*, 5th May, 1977.
176 Quoted in Whitley, Thomas and Marceau, *Masters of Business*, p. 61.
177 Mitchell, *European Labour Statistics*, p. 774; and see Whitley, Thomas and Marceau, *Masters of Business*, ch. 4, on the changes in French management education in the post-war period.
178 Much of this is applied in Abercrombie and Urry, *Capital, Labour*, part 2.

7 INDUSTRY, FINANCE, POLITICS

1 J. Dunning and R. Pearce, *The World's Largest Industrial Enterprise* (Gower, Farnborough, 1981), p. 64. The ratio is based on the proportion of the total sales of the largest 20 companies accounted for by the three largest companies. See P. Cooke, 'Spatial development processes: organized or disorganized?', *Nordplan Seminar*, Cambridge, Dec. 1985, who maintains that this merely involves a 'reorganization' and not disorganization.

2 See M. Piore and C. Sabel, *The Second Industrial Divide* (Basic Books, New York, 1984), ch. 4.

3 See ibid., p. 185. More generally on the increased competition for American corporations, see S. Bowles, D. Gordon and T. Weisskopf, *Beyond the Wasteland* (Verso, London, 1984), p. 84.

4 *Eurofutures. The Challenges of Innovation*, the FAST Report (Butterworths, Commission of European Communities with Futures, 1984), p. 132.

5 Quoted in B. Badcock, *Unfairly Structured Cities* (Basil Blackwell, Oxford, 1984), p. 154.

6 Ibid., p. 155.

7 L. Hannah and J. A. Kay, *Concentration in Modern Industry* (Macmillan, London, 1977), p. 45.

8 See 'Trade war across the Pacific', *Sunday Times*, 10 March, 1985, p. 67.

9 See A. Giddens, *A Contemporary Critique of Historical Materialism* (Macmillan, London, 1981), on the notion of 'time–space distanciation'.

10 See J. Short, *The Urban Arena* (Macmillan, London, 1984), figure 2.1, which shows that the net rate of return in Britain fell from 17% to 4% between the late 1950s and 1980.

11 Piore and Sabel, *Second Industrial Divide*, p. 134.

12 See ibid.; and L. Hirschhorn, *Beyond Mechanization* (MIT Press, Cambridge, Mass., 1984), pp. 106f.

13 Piore and Sabel, *Second Industrial Divide*, p. 210.

14 Ibid., pp. 211–213.

15 Quoted ibid., p. 212.

16 Ibid., pp. 213–15; and see C. Sabel, *Work and Politics* (Cambridge University Press, Cambridge, 1982) on high technology cottage industry.

17 See Piore and Sabel, *Second Industrial Divide*, pp. 216–20; see ch. 9 for an extensive discussion of the possibilities of the widespread development of 'flexible specialization'. Piore and Sabel perhaps overstate the potentiality of this development when they state: 'in flexible specialization it is hard to see where society (in the form of family and school ties or community celebrations of ethnic and political identity) ends, and where economic organization begins. Among the ironies of the resurgence of craft is that its deployment of modern technology depends on its reinvigoration of affiliations that are associated with the pre-industrial past' (p. 275).

18 Hirschhorn, *Beyond Mechanization*, p. 106. For discussion of some political implications see R. Murray, 'Bennetton Britain', *Marxism Today*, Nov., 1985.

19 See for a most interesting discussion of this, J. Gough, 'Industrial policy and

socialist strategy; restructuring and the unity of the working class', *Capital and Class* (29 (1986), pp. 58–61.

20 Hirschhorn, *Beyond Mechanization*, pp. 106–7.

21 Ibid., p. 109.

22 Our thinking on this topic is much indebted to the work of Gershuny. See especially J. Gershuny and I. Miles, *The New Service Economy* (Frances Pinter, London, 1983). Also see J. Urry, 'Some social and spatial aspects of services', *Society and Space*, (forthcoming).

23 See G. Ingham, *Capitalism Divided* (Macmillan, London, 1984).

24 See Ibid., pp. 40–1.

25 See chapter 2 above.

26 For two important exceptions, see G. Junne, 'Multinational banks, the state, international integration', in *German Political Studies* 1 (1976), pp. 117–37; and E. Brett, *International Money and Capitalist Crisis* (Heinemann, London, 1983).

27 Junne, 'Multinational banks', p. 117.

28 Ibid., pp. 120–5.

29 See ibid., pp. 118–20.

30 See Brett, *International Money*; W. P. Hogan and I. F. Pearce, *The Incredible Eurodollar* (Unwin, London, 1984); A. Lipietz, 'How monetarism choked Third World industrialization', *New Left Review* 145 (1984), pp. 71–87; K. van der Pijl, *The Making of an Atlantic Ruling Class* (Verso, London, 1984); T. Evans, 'Money makes the world go round', *Capital and Class* 24 (1985), pp. 99–124; and F. Block, *The Origins of International Economic Disorder* (University of California Press, Berkeley, 1977), ch. 8.

31 Evans, 'Money', p. 105.

32 Van der Pijl, *The Making of an Atlantic Ruling Class*, ch. 6.

33 Evans, 'Money', p. 106.

34 See Brett, *International Money*, p. 184; van der Pijl, *The Making of an Atlantic Ruling Class*.

35 For details, see Hogan and Pearce, *The Incredible Eurodollar*, ch. 4.

36 Evans, 'Money', pp. 108–9. The Chairman of New York's Citibank explained why London became the centre of the Eurodollar market:

> The Eurodollar market exists in London because people believe that the British government is not about to close it down. That's the basic reason and it took you a thousand years of history (cited Ingham, *Capitalism Divided*, p. 41).

37 Evans, 'Money', p. 109.

38 Brett, *International Money*, p. 210.

39 Hogan and Pearce, *The Incredible Eurodollar*, p. 1.

40 Ibid., p. 3.

41 Ibid., pp. 150–1.

42 Ibid., pp. 158–60.

43 Ibid., p. 169.

44 See E. Mandel, *The Second Slump* (New Left Books, London, 1978), pp. 29–30; and see M. Aglietta, 'World capitalism in the eighties', *New Left Review* (136 (1982), pp. 23–4.

45 See Brett, *International Money*, p. 215.

46 See Block, *Origins of International Economic Disorder*, pp. 203–4.

47 See Evans, 'Money', p. 111.
48 See A. Maddison, *Phases of Capitalist Development* (Oxford University Press, Oxford, 1982), pp. 137–9.
49 Evans, 'Money', p. 113.
50 Ibid., pp. 118–19. And see Brett, *International Money*, ch. 6; and C. Edwards, *The Fragmented World* (Methuen, London, 1985), pp. 167–94, generally on the enormous problems for Third World countries of these various developments. The ratio of debt service payments to total exports for all non-oil exporting developing countries rose from 21% in 1973 to 37% in 1982. Also see E. Brett, *The World Economy Since the War: the Politics of Uneven Development* (Macmillan, London, 1985).
51 Evans, 'Money', p. 119; and see Brett, *International Money*, pp. 87–8.
52 See Brett, *International Money*, p. 223.
53 See Edwards, *Fragmented World*, pp. 189–90.
54 *The Economist*, 16 October, 1982, p. 23.
55 Brett, *International Money*, p. 224; on more recent developments in the USA see N. Gilbert, 'Banking on the rocks', *Sunday Times*, 14 April, 1985, p. 67.
56 See van der Pijl, *The Making of an Atlantic Ruling Class*, pp. 262–5 on the following points.
57 J. Scott and C. Griff, *Directors of Industry* (Polity Press, Cambridge, 1984), chs 5 and 6, and p. 166 in particular.
58 I. Williams, 'The new men from the Pru', *Sunday Times*, Jan. 5, 1985, p. 53. On developments in stock exchanges, see D. T. Ayling, *The Internationalisation of Stockmarkets* (Gower, Aldershot, 1986).
59 Scott and Griff, *Directors*, p. 72.
60 van der Pijl, *The Making of an Atlantic Ruling Class*, pp. 280–2.
61 See Aglietta, 'World capitalism', pp. 27–31.
62 Hogan and Pearce, *The Incredible Eurodollar*, p. 176.
63 See Junne, 'Multinational banks', pp. 126–30 on these various points.
64 Aglietta, 'World capitalism', p. 25.
65 On A. Gorz's, *Farewell to the Working Class* (Pluto, London, 1982), see A. Hirsch, *The French New Left* (South End Press, London, 1981); and D. Byrne, 'Just hang on a minute there: a rejection of Andre Gorz's 'Farewell to the Working Class'', *Capital and Class* 24 (1985), pp. 75–99. On Hobsbawm, see the various papers in M. Jacques and F. Mulhern, *The Forward March of Labour Halted?* (Verso, London, 1981), On Britain also see J. Curran ed., *The Future of the Left* (Polity Press, Cambridge, 1984).
66 Gorz, *Farewell*, p. 28.
67 Ibid., p. 30.
68 Byrne, 'Just hang on a minute there', p. 78.
69 See E. Hobsbawm, 'The Forward March of Labour Halted?', in Jacques and Mulhern, *Forward March*, pp. 1–19; this was originally published in 1978.
70 G. Therborn, 'The prospects of labour and the transformation of advanced capitalism', *New Left Review* 145 (1984), pp. 5–38.
71 See W. Korpi, *The Democratic Class Struggle* (Routledge & Kegan Paul, London, 1983), p. 40.
72 See R. Alford, *Party and Society. The Anglo-American Democracies* (Greenwood, Westport, Conn., 1963), p. 102.

73 Korpi, *The Democratic Class Struggle*, p. 35.
74 For a convenient and recent summary, see I. Crewe, 'The electorate: partisan dealignment ten years on', *West European Politics* 6 (1983), pp. 183–215. More generally on how the British party system is no longer sustained by the class system see M. Franklin, 'How the decline of class voting opened the way to radical change in British politics', *British Journal of Political Science* 14 (1984), pp. 483–508.
75 See P. Dunleavy and C. Husbands, *British Democracy at the Crossroads* (Allen & Unwin, London, 1985), ch. 1; and P. Dunleavy, 'Voting and the electorate', in *Developments in British Politics*, ed. H. Drucker et al. (Macmillan, London, 1984), pp. 30–58.
76 See B. Särlvik and I. Crewe, *Decade of Dealignment* (Cambridge University Press, Cambridge, 1983), p. 88.
77 Dunleavy, 'Voting and the electorate', p. 37. It should also be noted that there was a considerable increase in Social Democratic/Liberal Alliance voting among trade unionists.
78 See Dunleavy and Husbands, *British Democracy at the Crossroads*, p. 138; as well as P. Dunleavy, 'The urban basis of political alignment: social class, domestic property ownership, and state intervention in consumption processes', *British Journal of Political Science* 9 (1979), pp. 409–43; and I. Crewe, 'The disturbing truth behind Labour's rout', *The Guardian*, 13 June, 1983, p. 5. Note also the tremendous increase in home ownership in Britain, from 29% of the housing stock in 1950 to almost 60% currently.
79 Dunleavy, 'The urban basis of political alignment', p. 442.
80 For example, of the Labour voters in 1979 who bought their council home in the next four years, a staggering 59% failed to vote Labour in 1983; see Crewe, 'The disturbing truth', p. 5.
81 See W. L. Miller, 'Social class and party choice in England: a new analysis', *British Journal of Political Science* 8 (1978), pp. 257–84; W. L. Miller, 'Class, region and strata at the British general election of 1979', *Party Affairs* 32 (1979), pp. 376–82; J. Curtice and M. Steed, 'Electoral choice and the production of government: the changing operation of the electoral system in the United Kingdom since 1955', *British Journal of Political Science* 12 (1982), pp. 249–98; and especially A. Warde, 'Space, class and voting in Britain', in *Politics, Geography and Social Stratification*, ed. E. Koffman and K. Haggett (Croom Helm, London, 1986).
82 Miller, 'Class region and strata', p. 378; note that he only here anlysed English constituencies. See Warde, 'Space, class and voting', p. 6.
83 See the extensive discussion of the 'neighbourhood effect' in P. J. Taylor and R. J. Johnson, *Geography of Elections* (Croom Helm, London, 1979), ch. 5.
84 See the discussion of these in Warde, 'Space, class and voting', p. 15. Note incidentally that major differences in male/female voting patterns have now mostly disappeared in Britain. See L. Lovendulski and J. Hills eds, *The Politics of the Second Electorate* (Routledge & Kegan Paul, London, 1981); although Dunleavy and Husbands, *British Democracy at the Crossroads*, pp. 124–9, presents some counter-argument from the 1983 election.
85 See Crewe, 'The electorate', p. 212.
86 Ibid., p. 212.
87 See Dunleavy, 'Voting and the electorate', pp. 40–6, for a brief summary. See Särlvik and Crewe, *Decade of Dealignment*, more generally here.

88 This is most effectively described in J. Ross, *Thatcher and Friends* (Pluto Press, London, 1983), ch. 4. Also see D. W. Urwin, 'Territorial structures and political development in the United Kingdom', in *The Politics of Territorial Identity*, ed. S. Rokkan and D. Urwin (Sage, London, 1982), pp. 19–74, p. 47, on how the 'nationalization' of British politics reached its peak in the 1950s. There were 'two main parties which competed everywhere, and the swing between them...was remarkably uniform'.

89 Ibid., p. 8 and ch. 8.

90 Ibid., p. 74.

91 Ibid., p. 9.

92 Ibid., p. 13; note that the last figure is for the Alliance as a whole.

93 Crewe, 'The disturbing truth', p. 5.

94 See Särlvik and Crewe, *Decade of Dealignment*, p. 61.

95 Dunleavy, 'Voting and the electorate', p. 47.

96 Särlvik and Crewe, *Decade of Dealignment*, p. 68.

97 See Crewe, 'The disturbing truth', p. 5.

98 See D. Salisbury, 'Scandinavian party politics reexamined: Social Democracy in decline?', *West European Politics* 7 (1984), pp. 66–102, p. 80; more generally on Scandinavian politics from 1870 onwards, see N. Elder, A. Thomas and D. Arter, *The Consensual Democracies* (Martin Robertson, Oxford, 1982).

99 S. Berglund and U. Lindstrom, *The Scandinavian Party System(s)* (Student Litteratur, Lund, 1978), p. 108.

100 M. D. Hancock, *Sweden. The Politics of Postindustrial Change* (Dryden, Illinois, 1972), pp. 55–6.

101 See Berglund and Lindstrom, *The Scandinavian Party System(s)*, p. 28.

102 See Salisbury, 'Scandinavian party politics reexamined', pp. 84–8.

103 See Berglund and Lindstrom, *The Scandinavian Party System(s)*, p. 123, on the former point; and Korpi, *The Democratic Class Struggle*, p. 86, on the latter point.

104 See Korpi, *The Democratic Class Struggle*, p. 88; Salisbury, 'Scandinavian party politics reexamined', p. 80; D. Webber, 'Combating or acquiescing in unemployment? Economic crisis management in Sweden and West Germany', *West European Politics* 6 (1983), pp. 23–43, p. 36.

105 See on the last point S. Ersson and J. E. Lane, 'Polarisation and political economy crisis: the 1982 Swedish election', *West European Politics* 6 (1983), pp. 287–96.

106 Korpi, *The Democratic Class Struggle*, p. 133.

107 Ibid., pp. 134–7, on these various points.

108 See Alford, *Party and Society*, p. 103. There is some evidence of a growing alignment of the parties around not occupation but income. See T. Edsall, 'Republican America', *New York Review of Books* 33 (April 24, 1986), pp. 3–6, p. 4.

109 See D. E. Stokes, 'Parties and the nationalization of electoral forces', in *The American Party Systems: Stages of Political Development*, ed. W. W. Chambers and W. D. Burnham (Oxford University Press, New York, 1967), pp. 182–202; W. Claggett, W. Flanigan and N. Zingale, 'Nationalization of the American electorate', *American Political Science Review* 78 (1984), pp. 77–91.

110 T. E. Mann, *Unsafe at any margin* (American Enterprise Institute, Washington DC, 1978).

362 NOTES TO CHAPTER 7

111 Claggett, Flanigan and Zingale, 'Nationalization', p. 90.
112 See G. Rabinowitz, P-H. Curian, S. Macdonald, 'The structure of presidential elections and the process of realignment, 1944 to 1980', *American Journal of Political Science* 18 (1984), pp. 611–35; H. Norpoth and J. Rusk, 'Partisan dealignment in the American electorate: itemizing the deductions since 1964', *American Political Science Review* 76 (1982), pp. 522–37.
113 P. Abramson and J. Aldrich, 'The decline of electoral participation in America', *American Political Science Review* 76 (1982), pp. 502–21, p. 502.
114 See S. Flanagan and R. Dalton, 'Parties under stress: realignment and dealignment in advanced industrial societies', *West European Politics* (1984), pp. 7–23, pp. 10, 17; Therborn, 'The prospects of labour', p. 31. Note incidentally that the religious differences in voting behaviour, once of considerable importance, had more or less disappeared by the 1970s.
115 U. Feist, M. Gullner and K. Liepelt, 'Structural assimilation versus ideological polarization: on changing profiles of political parties in West Germany', in *German Political Studies* 3 (ed. M. Kaase and K. von Beyme) (1978), pp. 171–90, p. 174.
116 Ibid., p. 178.
117 A. Rothacher, 'The Green Party in German politics', *West European Politics* 7 (1984), pp. 109–16.
118 Ibid., p. 113.
119 See G. Therborn, 'Prospects for the European left', *Marxism Today* (November, 1981), pp. 21–5. For general background see R. W. Johnson, *The Long March of the French Left* (Macmillan, London, 1981); and S. Lash, *The Militant Worker* (Heinemann, London, 1984), ch. 9.
120 Therborn, 'Prospects', p. 21.
121 Ibid., p. 22; and see Therborn, 'Prospects of labour and the transformation of advanced capitalism', p. 30.
122 See M. Lewis-Beck, 'France: the stalled electorate', in R. Dalton, S. Flanagan and P. Beck, *Electoral Change in Advanced Industrial Societies* (Princeton University Press, Princeton, NJ, 1984), pp. 425–48.
123 Ibid., p. 22.
124 See Lovendulski and Hills, *The Politics of the Second Electorate*.
125 See P. Bacot, *Les dirigeants du Parti Socialiste* (Presses Universitaires de Lyon, Lyon, 1979), pp. 75–80, 126–30;. J. F. Bizot, *Au Parti des socialistes* (Grasset, Paris, 1975), pp. 57–72.
126 See J. Habermas, 'New social movements', *Telos* 49 (1981), pp. 33–7, p. 33.
127 See R. Inglehart, *The Silent Revolution. Changing Values and Political Styles Among Western Publics* (Princeton University Press, Princeton, NJ, 1977); and K. Hildebrandt and R. Dalton, 'The new politics: political change and sunshine politics', *German Political Studies* 3 (1978), pp. 66–96. On some of the electoral consequences, see Dalton, Flanagan and Beck, *Electoral Change*.
128 Hildebrandt and Dalton, 'The new politics', p. 79.
129 See R. Inglehart, 'The changing structure of political cleavages in western societies', in *Electoral Change*, pp. 25–68, p. 30.
130 See V. Granow and C. Offe, 'Political culture and the politics of the Social Democratic government', *Telos* 53 (1982), pp. 67–80.
131 Ibid., p. 70; and see K. Baker, R. Dalton and K. Hildebrandt, *Germany*

NOTES TO CHAPTER 7

Transformed. Political Culture and the New Politics (Harvard University Press, Cambridge, Mass., 1981), especially p. 275.

132 Ibid., p. 75.

133 Ibid., pp. 75–6.

134 See C. Spretnak and F. Capra, *Green Politics. The Global Promise* (Paladin, London, 1985), pp. 35–9.

135 S. Hall, 'Popular-democratic vs authoritarian populism: two ways of "taking democracy seriously"'', in A. Hunt ed., *Marxism and Democracy* (Lawrence and Wishart, London, 1980), pp. 157–85. And see E. Laclau, *Politics and Ideology in Marxist Theory* (New Left Books, London, 1977).

136 See Granow and Offe, 'Political culture', p. 76.

137 Ibid., p. 80; also here see K. Baker, R. Dalton and K. Hildebrandt, *Germany Transformed* (Harvard University Press, Cambridge, Mass., 1981); and D. Conradt, 'Changing German political culture', *The Civic Culture Revisited*, ed. G. Almond and S. Verba (Little, Brown, Boston, 1980), pp. 212–72.

138 See A. Toffler and H. Toffler, 'An appointment with the future', *Sunday Times*, 7 February, 1985, p. 16; and see M. Davis, 'The AFL-CIO's second century', *New Left Review* 136 (1982), pp. 43–54.

139 D. Vogel, 'The power of business in America: a re-appraisal', *British Journal of Political Science* 13 (1983), pp. 19–43, p. 20.

140 D. Howell, 'The uncharted country', *Sunday Times*, 28 April, 1985, p. 16.

141 Ibid., p. 16.

142 See S. Hall, 'Labour's love still lost', *New Socialist* 15 (February 1980), pp. 7–9, p. 7; and more generally see J. Curran ed., *The Future of the Left* (Polity Press, Cambridge, 1984). See further discussion in chapter 9 below.

143 See M. Boddy and C. Fudge eds, *Local Socialism?* (Macmillan, London, 1984).

144 See S. Rowbotham, L. Segal and H. Wainwright, *Beyond the Fragments* (Merlin, London, 1980) on the inability of the left in Britain to respond to, or connect with, the dominant concerns of the contemporary women's movement.

145 J. Keane, 'Civil Society and the Peace Movement in Britain', *Thesis Eleven*, 8 (1984), pp. 5–22.

146 See C. Rootes, 'Protest, social movement, revolution?', *Social Alternatives* 4 (1984), p. 5.

147 See J. Mattausch, 'The sociology of NCD', BSA Conference, Hull, April 1985, p. 9.

148 Keane, 'Civil Society', p. 6.

149 Ibid., p. 9.

150 See G. Day and D. Robbins, 'Activists for peace: the social basis of a local peace movement', BSA Conference, Hull, April 1985. More generally on the rediscovery of a variety of decentralizing tendencies in modern societies, see L. J. Sharpe ed., *Decentralist Trends in Western Democracies* (Sage, London, 1979).

151 *The Guardian*, 19 Jan., 1985.

152 For a general history of the British and American women's movement, see O. Banks, *Faces of Feminism* (Martin Robertson, Oxford, 1981). It is often said that the women's movement is a 'new' social movement. In its various forms this is manifestly incorrect as Banks' book shows. Indeed, more radical versions of feminism did not disappear in Britain between 1920 and the 1960s – as

D. Spender, *Time and Tide Wait for No Man* (Pandora, London, 1984) demonstrates. However, we would argue that during the period of 'organized capitalism', the main *effect* of such feminist struggles was on existing political struggles, especially on the Democratic Party and the New Deal in the 1930s in the United States, and on the Labour Party and its commitment to 'welfarism' in the 1940s in Britain. The complex issues raised by 'women and politics' are discussed in part in L. Murgatroyd, M. Savage, D. Shapiro, J. Urry, S. Walby and A. Warde, *Localities, Class and Gender* (Pion, London, 1985).

153 See G. Almond and S. Verba, *The Civil Culture: Political Attitudes and Democracy in Five Nations* (Princeton University Press, Princeton, NJ, 1963); S. Beer, *Britain against Itself* (Faber and Faber, London, 1982). ch. 4. On the ecology movement in Britain, see J. Porritt, *Seeing Green. The Politics of Ecology Explained* (Basil Blackwell, Oxford, 1984), and P. Lowe and J. Goyder, *Environmental Groups in Politics* (Allen & Unwin, London, 1983).

154 D. Kavanagh, 'Political culture in Great Britain: the decline of the civic culture', in Almond and Verba eds., *The Civic Culture Revisited*, pp. 124–76, p. 170.

155 Ibid., p. 170.

156 See A. Marsh, *Protest and Political Consciousness* (Sage, Beverly Hills and London, 1977), pp. 176–7.

157 See Beer, *Britain against Itself*, pp. 126–32.

156 Ibid., p. 153.

158 Ibid., p. 153.

159 Ibid., pp. 12f. More generally here see K. Middlemas, *Politics in Industrial Society* (Andre Deutsch, London, 1979), especially pp. 460–2.

160 Ibid., p. 35.

161 Ibid., p. 36.

162 K. Newton, *Second City Politics* (Clarendon Press, Oxford, 1976).

163 See S. Brittan, 'The economic contradictions of democracy', *British Journal of Political Science* 5 (1975), pp. 129–59; and see R. R. Benjamin, *The Limits of Politics* (University of Chicago Press, Chicago, 1980), p. 21.

164 See M. Olson, *The Logic of Collective Action* (Harvard University Press, Cambridge, Mass., 1965), p. 127.

165 See W. Korpi, *The Democratic Class Struggle* (Routledge & Kegan Paul, London, 1983), pp. 144f; and M. D. Hancock, *Sweden. The Politics of Post-industrial Change* (Dryden Press, Hinsdale, Illn., 1972), p. 80f.

166 Korpi, *Democratic Class Struggle*, p. 148.

167 See ibid., p. 154. The figure in the USA was 71%, in the UK 67%, in France 64% and in West Germany 59%.

168 Ibid., p. 156.

169 Ibid., p. 156.

170 Therborn, 'The prospects of labour', pp. 34–5.

171 See P. Cerny ed., *Social Movements and Protest in France* (Frances Pinter, London, 1982); see also A. Touraine, 'La revolution culturelle que nous vivons', *Le Nouvel Observateur* (1 Aug., 1978), who says of the women's movement in France:

> One of its most basic aspects is its opposition to military and financial models of organisation, to the power of money and giant organisations. It represents a will to organise one's own life. . . Of all the social movements, the women's movement

is the one most able to oppose the growing hold exercised over our daily lives... What began as a form of cultural self-defence can become a directly social and political struggle against a world of managers, sub-managers and employees...

172 J. L. Cohen, 'Beyond "reform or revolution"'? The problem of French socialism', *Telos* 55 (1983), pp. 5–12, p. 7.

173 Ibid., p. 9; and see A. Lipietz, 'Which social forces are for change?', *Telos* 55 (1983), pp. 13–35, pp. 21–2.

174 Ibid., p. 35.

175 J. Alt, 'Beyond class', *Telos* 18 (1971), pp. 55–80.

176 See J. Seabrook, *What Went Wrong?* (Victor Gollancz, London, 1978), p. 31.

177 Ibid., p. 131.

178 Alt, 'Beyond class', p. 72. Note both the reduction in hours worked by the typical industrial worker, and the increased proportion of expenditure on consumer durables. See G. Moore and J. Hedges, 'Trends in labor and leisure', *Monthly Labor Review* (February, 1971), pp. 3–11; and J. Gershuny, *After Industrial Society?* (Macmillan, London, 1978).

179 See the very effective critique of such views in J. A. Cronin, 'Politics, class structure, and the enduring weakness of British social democracy', *Journal of Social History* 16 (1983), pp. 123–42.

180 See H. Beynon ed., *Digging Deeper* (Verso, London, 1985), on the extraordinary British miners' strike of 1984–5.

181 See W. Korpi and M. Shalev, 'Strikes, power, and politics in the western nations, 1900–1976', *Political Power and Social Theory* 1 (ed. M. Zeitlin) (1980), pp. 301–34, p. 313.

182 Cronin, 'Politics, class structure', p. 139.

183 See Therborn, 'The prospects for labour', especially p. 27.

184 See P. Flora and A. Heidenheimer, Introduction to *The Development of Welfare States in Europe and America* (Transaction Books, New Brunswick, NJ, 1981), pp. 5–14, p. 11.

185 On the significance of such 'liberal' notions for feminism, see Z. Eisenstein, *The Radical Future of Liberal Feminism* (Longman, London, 1981).

186 See Therborn, 'The prospects for labour', p. 34.

187 Ibid., p. 29, on these various points.

188 See O. Banks, *Faces of Feminism* (Martin Robertson, Oxford, 1981), pp. 175 and 174:

> We can see that, in Britain as in the United States, the alliance between feminism and welfare dominated the feminist movement in the years after women's suffrage had at last been granted... The effect was to turn feminism increasingly away from its roots in the Enlightenment doctrine of equal rights and to give support to the ideal of male and female differentiation [and]... to a large extent we may see the welfare state in Britain as a product of an alliance between welfare feminism and the Labour Party, albeit with the latter as the dominant element.

189 P. Dunleavy, 'The growth of sectoral cleavages and the stabilization of state expenditures', *International Sociological Association Conference on Industrial Restructuring, Social Change and the Locality*, Sussex, April, 1985, p. 8. And see F. G. Castles and R. D. McKinlay, 'Public welfare provision, Scandinavia, and the sheer futility of the sociological approach to politics', *British Journal*

of Political Science 9 (1979), pp. 157–71, who show that the only plausible explanation of high welfare expenditure in Denmark, Norway and Sweden is the 'historic strength and unity of the working class movement (p. 169) which in turn stems from the absence of a unified right wing party likely to oppose such developments.

190 See S. Rosenberry, 'Social insurance, distributive criteria and the welfare backlash: a comparative analysis', *British Journal of Political Science* 12 (1982), pp. 421–47, on some further determinants of a welfare backlash.

191 Therborn, 'The prospects of labour', p. 35, notes that a quarter of the Swedish workforce is now employed in what he calls the 'public reproductive sector'.

192 See T. Skocpol, 'America's incomplete welfare state', in *Stagnation and Renewal in Social Policy*, ed. G. Esping-Andersen, M. Rein and L. Rainwater (M. E. Sharpe, USA, forthcoming).

8 THE CHANGING STRUCTURE OF TRADE-UNIONISM

1 See, for example, most of the writers in *Order and Conflict in Contemporary Capitalism*, ed. J. H. Goldthorpe (Clarendon, Oxford, 1984).

2 This conception differs on a few points from Schmitter's classic, and we think very fruitful, notion. See P. Schmitter, 'Still the century of corporatism?', *Review of Politics* 36 (1974), pp. 85–131.

3 Here we disagree with Charles Maier's argument that synchronization of national union confederation and political party formation was the crucial factor. See C. Maier, 'Preconditions for corporatism', in *Order and Conflict*, ed. Goldthorpe, pp. 39–59.

4 On comparative national union formation and union–party relations, see H. Mitchell, 'Labour and the origins of social democracy in Britain, France and Germany, 1890–1914', in *European Labor Movements: the Working Classes and the Origins of Social Democracy*, ed. *idem.* and P. Stearns (Peacock, Itasca, Ill., 1971); R. Geary, *European Labour Protest 1848–1939* (Methuen, London, 1984); L. Ullman, *The Rise of the National Trade Union* (Harvard University Press, Cambridge, Mass., 1955), ch. 2.

5 See, e.g., A. Lipietz, 'Mondialisation de la crise globale du fordisme: 1967–1984', *Les Temps Modernes* 41 (1984), pp. 696–736.

6 We do not fully accept Lipietz's concept of 'fordism', but do think that what he takes to be fordism is a condition of existence of corporatism. See, e.g., A. Lipietz, 'Which social forces are for change?', *Telos* 55 (1983), pp. 13–36. On consumption and collective identity, see *Resistance through Rituals*, ed. S. Hall and T. Jefferson (Hutchinson, London, 1976).

7 See, e.g., S. Beer, *Britain against Itself* (Faber, London, 1982); E. Laclau and C. Mouffe, *Hegemony and Socialist Strategy: Towards a Radical Democratic Politics* (Verso, London, 1985).

8 *Pluto World View 1983* (Pluto, London, 1983).

9 See R. O. Åberg, 'Market-independent income distribution: efficiency and legitimacy', in *Order and Conflict*, ed. Goldthorpe, pp. 209–32.

10 For a more detailed account of the 1983–4 events, see S. Lash, 'The end of neo-corporatism: the breakdown of centralised bargaining in Sweden', *British Journal of Industrial Relations* 23 (1985), pp. 215–40.

11 See G. Ross and P. Gourevitch, 'Conclusion', in *Unions and Economic Crisis: Britain, West Germany and Sweden*, ed. P. Gourevitch et al. (Allen & Unwin, London, 1984), p. 384.

12 On earlier public-sector growth in Sweden, see A. Heidenheimer, 'Professional unions, public sector growth and the Swedish equality policy', *Comparative Politics* 9 (1976), pp. 49–73.

13 We spoke of the origins of the manual-worker trade union confederation (the LO) in chapter 2 above.

14 On legislative change here, see H. Gospel, 'Trade unions and the legal obligation to bargain: an American, Swedish and British comparison', *British Journal of Industrial Relations* 21 (1983), pp. 343–57.

15 L. Bengtsson, A. Ericsson and P. Sederblad, 'The associative action of Swedish business interests', Research Report No. 10, Statsvetenskapliga institutionen, Stockholms universitet, 1984, pp. 5–6.

16 Martin, ibid., pp. 202–12; B. Rothstein, The success and export of the Swedish labour market policy: the organizational connection to policy' (Lund University, Department of Political Science, 1983); G. Rehn, 'Swedish active labor market policy: retrospect and prospect', *Industrial Relations* 24 (1985), pp. 68–89.

17 W. Korpi, *The Democratic Class Struggle* (Routledge, London, 1983), pp. 46–52, 142–54.

18 Martin, 'Strategic responses', pp. 268f.

19 See A. Kjellberg, 'Radikalisieurung oder Japanisierung? Die Entwicklung des "schwedischen Modells" industrieller Beziehungen in den achtziger Jahren', *Prokla* 54 (1984), pp. 59–76.

20 U. Himmelstrand, et al., *Beyond Welfare Capitalism* (Heinemann, London, 1982), pp. 257f.

21 Korpi, *Class Struggle*, p. 229.

22 Interview with R. Meidner, 18 May, 1984, Stockholm; C. Gill, 'Swedish wage-earner funds: the road to economic democracy?', *Journal of General Management* 9 (1984), pp. 37–59.

23 Gill, ibid., pp. 51–6; Korpi, *Class Struggle*, pp. 232–6; Martin, 'Strategic responses', p. 329.

24 Martin, ibid., p. 328.

25 For an account of the strike, see E. Hoglund, *Storkonflikten i den politiska debatten* ('Tidens Forlag', Stockholm, 1981), pp. 70–106; and Martin, ibid., pp. 314–23.

26 Bengtsson et al., 'Associative action', p. 54.

27 Ibid., pp. 58–9; K. O. Faxen, 'Incomes policy and centralized wage formation' (Swedish Employers Federation (SAF), Stockholm, Feb. 1982).

28 Bengtsson et al., 'Associative Action', p. 65.

29 Interview with confederal representatives of SAF, 16 May, 1984, Stockholm.

30 LO, 'Rattvisa loner, En skrift om LOs solidariska Lönepolitik' (Tiba Tryck, Stockholm, 1983).

31 Interview with Å. Norlander, managing director of the Swedish Engineering Employers Association (CF), Stockholm, 17 May, 1984.

32 Svenska Metallindustriarbetareförbundet, 'Verksamhetsberättelse 1983', Stockholm, 1984, pp. 2–3.

33 Swedish Metalworkers Union, *The Value of Work*, Action Programme adopted by the union Congress in June 1981 (Stockholm, 1981), p. 29.

34 Interview with press officer of Swedish Metalworkers Union, 16 May, 1984, Stockholm.

35 Interview with representative of Swedish Fabrikarbetareförbundet, 15 May, 1984, Stockholm.

36 Interview with I. Ohlsson, chief statistician to LO, 18 May, 1984, Stockholm.

37 Metall, 'Verksamhetsberättelse', pp. 93–4.

38 Interview with chief statistician to LO.

39 See R. Adams, *The Growth of White-collar Unionism in Britain and Sweden* (University of Wisconsin Industrial Relations Research Institute Monograph, Madison, Wisconsin, 1975).

40 Privattjänstemannkartellen, *Behind the headlines: Information about the PTK* (Privattjänstemannkartellen, Stockholm, 1982).

41 Interview with chief cartel negotiator and other PTK officials, Stockholm, 15 May, 1984.

42 KTK, *Verksamhetsberättelse 1983* (Nordisk Bokindustri, Stockholm, 1984); interview with chief negotiator to KTK, 17 May, 1984, Stockholm.

43 Interview with negotiators from Svenska Kommunalarbetareförbundet (SKAF), 14 May, 1984, Stockholm.

44 Svenska kommunalarbetareförbundet, *Kommunal, En Broschyr om Svenska Kommunalarbetareförbundet, medlemmarna, jobben och offentliga sektorn* (Stockholm, 1982). The feminization of the workforce is a more important factor in Sweden than in most countries for a number of reasons. First, a very high proportion of the female population is economically active. Second, an unusually high proportion of women are unionized (there are much greater disparities in union density between Sweden and other countries among females than among males). Third, women are concentrated in the largest national unions. Two of the four largest LO unions are over 70% female in membership. The powerful white-collar cartels (discussed above) cannot be understood apart from this feminization. The PTK is 50–60% female and though the predominantly male better-paid members of its SIF component are now the strongest group in the cartel, the greatest increase in total membership is coming in recent years from commercial employees who are predominantly female and relatively unqualified. The KTK on the other hand organized largely among the lower professional managerial ranks and is 80% female: it has large constituencies among part-time workers in nursing and day-care centre employees with intermediate-level educational qualifications. Fourth, the workforce in unions with predominantly female membership can be more effectively mobilized for industrial action than in most countries. (PTK, interview 1984; KTK, *Verksamhetsberättelse 1983*.)

45 Höglund, *Storkonflikten*, pp. 151–68.

46 In this context it should be noted that representatives from the metalworkers, the engineering employers and the municipal employers interviewed considered that 1984 bargaining was a further step away from centralization, while municipal workers and LO officials spoken to considered that it was a step back towards a central solution.

47 See A. Martin, 'The dynamics of change in a Keynesian political economy: the Swedish case and its implications', in *State and Economy in Contemporary Capitalism*, ed. C. Crouch (Croom Helm, London, 1979), pp. 83–121; M. Kesselman, 'Prospects for democratic socialism in advanced capitalism: class

struggle and compromise in Sweden and France', *Politics and Society* 11 (1982), pp. 397–438.
48 Interview with Anna Hedborg at LO headquarters, 19 May 1984; interview with Ohlsson.
49 See, e.g., Eric Wolf, *Europe and the People without History* (University of California Press, Berkeley, 1982).
50 A. Hedborg and R. Meidner, *Folkhemsmodellen* (Stockholm, 1983).
51 Interview with I. Ohlsson, 18 May, 1984.
52 Interview with Hedborg, 19 May, 1984.
53 A. Kjelberg, 'The 1984/85 collective bargaining round in Sweden', Sociology Department, Lund University, June 1985.
54 J. Hirsch, 'Developments in the political system of West Germany since 1945', in *The State in Western Europe*, ed. R. Scase (Croom Helm, London, 1980), pp. 115–41, pp. 116, 125; H. Popitz et al., *Das Gesellschaftsbild des Arbeiters* (Mohr, Tübingen, 1957), pp. 177f.
55 See J. Bergmann, O. Jacobi and W. Müller-Jentsch, *Gewerkschaften in der Bundesrepublik, Band I, Gewerkschaftliche Lohnpolitik zwischen Mitglieder-interessen und ökonomischen Systemzwängen* (Campus Verlag. Frankfurt, 1979), pp. 153–5; M. Nolan and C. Sabel, 'Class conflict and the Social Democratic reform cycle in Germany', in *Political Power and Social Theory* 3, JAI Press (1982), pp. 158–62; A. Markovits and C. Allen, 'Trade unions and economic crisis: the West German case', in *Unions and Economic Crisis*, P. Gourevitch et al., pp. 120–5; W. Streeck, 'Organizational consequences of neo-corporatist co-operation in West German labour unions', in *Patterns of Corporatist Policy-Making* (Sage, London, 1982), pp. 51–65. For a comparison with Britain, see W. Streeck, P. Seglow and P. Wallace, 'Competition and monopoly in interest representation: a comparative analysis of trade-union structure in the railway industries of Great Britain, and West Germany', *Organization Studies* 2 (1981), pp. 314–18.
56 Markovits and Allen, 'West German case', pp. 112–18; Bergmann et al., *Gewerkschaftliche Lohnpolitik*, pp. 160–72. On the effect of strike trends here see W. Müller-Jentsch, 'Strikes and strike trends in West Germany 1950–1978', *Industrial Relations Journal* 12 (1981), pp. 37–44.
57 See D. Miller, 'Trade union workplace representation in the Federal Republic of Germany: an analysis of the post-war Vertrauensleute policy of the German Metalworkers Union (1952–1977)', *British Journal of Industrial Relations* 16 (1978), pp. 338–42.
58 W. Streeck, 'Qualitative demands and neo-corporatist manageability of industrial relations', *British Journal of Industrial Relations* 19 (1981), pp. 149–69.
59 W. Müller-Jentsch and H. Sperling, 'Economic development, labour conflicts and the industrial relations system in West Germany', in *The Resurgence of Class Conflict in Western Europe since 1968*, vol. 1, *National Studies*, ed. C. Crouch and A. Pizzorno (Macmillan, London, 1978), pp. 257–8; Markovits and Allen, 'The West German case', pp. 104–8.
60 Bergmann et al., *Gewerkschaftliche Lohnpolitik*, pp. 240–5; Markovits and Allen, 'West German case', pp. 111, pp. 125–6.
61 C. Offe, 'The attribution of public status to interest groups: observations on the West German case', in *Organizing Interest in Western Europe*, ed. S. Berger,

(Cambridge University Press, Cambridge, 1981), pp. 133–6; J. Clark, 'Concerted action in the Federal Republic of Germany', *British Journal of Industrial Relations* 17 (1969), pp. 245–8; M. Hudson, '"Concerted action"': wages policy in West Germany, 1967–1977', *Industrial Relations Journal* 11 (1980), pp. 5–16, pp. 6–8, 13.

62 Bergmann et al., *Gewerkschaftliche Lohnpolitik*, pp. 249–56, 404–8; Markovits and Allen, 'West German case, pp. 136–41; Müller-Jentsch and Sperling, 'Economic development', pp. 262–72, 291–2.

63 W. Streeck, 'Co-determination: the fourth decade', Discussion Paper, Labour Market Policy, Internationales Institut für Management und Verwaltung, Berlin, 1983 (all citations from this unpublished paper, later published in *International Yearbook of Organizational Democracy*, vol. II (Wiley, New York State, 1984)).

64 Streeck, ibid., pp. 7–11; W. Tegtmeier, *Wirkungen der Mitbestimmung der Arbeitnehmer* (Vandenhoeck & Ruprecht, Gottingen, 1973).

65 Streeck, 'Neo-corporatist co-operation', pp. 44–7; H. Niedenhoff, *Mitbestimmung in der Bundesrepublik Deutschland* (Deutscher Instituts-Verlag, Koln, 1979).

66 See W. Streeck, *Industrial Relations in Germany* (Heinemann, London, 1984), pp. 56–81, for an example of this in the case of manpower policy at Volkswagen in the mid-1970s. Also see Streeck, 'Co-determination', pp. 13–14, 20–3; and Heinz Hartmann, 'Co-determination today and tomorrow', *British Journal of Industrial Relations* 13 (1975), pp. 54–64.

67 H. Weber, 'Konkurrenz und Solidarität – Zur Arbeitskampfstrategie der metall-industriellen Arbeitgeber in dem Tarifkonflikt 1984', Bielefeld University, May, 1985, pp. 1–6; K. Hinrichs, C. Offe and H. Wiesenthal, 'Crisis of the welfare state and alternative modes of work redistribution', Bielefeld University, Sociology Department, Dec., 1984, pp. 10–17. The causes of the 1984 strike began in 1978–9 with the defeat of a seven-week IGM strike for reduced working time. The settlement, which included an extension of paid vacation to six weeks, was for a continuation of the 40-hour week and provided that work hours could not be rebargained until 1983/4. The other industrial branches then followed to arrive at similar settlements. In the lead-up to 1983/4 negotiations the CDU/Free Democrat coalition government in conjunction with the Federation of German Employers, proposed instead an early-retirement scheme. This proposal seemed more in line with the wishes of employees, a Bielefeld University survey found; only a small minority of respondents here were attracted by the 35-hour week demand of IG Metall and only a small proportion wanted reduced working hours as an end in itself. Further, there was an unexpected range of preferred schemes of reduction of work hours; a plurality, however, favoured early retirement. In the event, employers' associations in most branches offered a substantial pay rise linked to the introduction of an early retirement scheme; unions in food, textile, construction and banking signed, retaining the 40-hour week until 1986. The IGM chose Nordwürttemburg-Nordbaden as a first front for the strike followed by a second front in Hesse. The former area was chosen because of its strike-experienced workforce and leadership; the low level of unemployment in the prosperous region; its compact size which minimized lockouts, since the 1980 legislation which forbade offensive lockouts. Additionally, employers in Nordwürttemburg-Nordbaden were conflict-tested and known to be conciliatory as well as very influential within Gesamtmetall, the metallurgy employers' federation. Finally and

perhaps most important, this region and Hesse are key locations for the automobile and electrotechnical industries. A strike here would quickly have heavily deleterious effects on automobile firms in other regions, whose suppliers were in Nordwürttemburg-Nordbaden. Indeed, the strike was kicked off with only 15,000 to 18,000 strikers, largely concentrated in automobile supply plants. See K. Hinrichs, W. Roche and H. Wiesenthal, 'Working time policy as class-oriented strategy: unions and shorter working hours in Great Britain and West Germany', Universitat Bielefeld/University College Dublin, Oct., 1984, pp. 13–16; Weber, 'Konkurrenz und Solidaritat', pp. 12, 21–2; Arbeitgebersverband der hessischen Metallindustrie, 'Arbeitskampf '84 in Hessen', pp. 36–45. More generally see K. Hinrichs, C. Offe and H. Wiesenthal, 'Die Streit um die Zeit', in Arbeitszeit-politik, ed. idem (Campus, Frankfurt, 1981), pp. 8–15.

68 H. Weber, ibid., pp. 36–7; Hinrichs et al., 'Working time policy', pp. 18, 25.

69 F. Scharpf, 'Economic and institutional constraints of full-employment strategies: Sweden, Austria and West Germany 1973–1982', in Order and Conflict, ed. Goldthorpe, pp. 281–6; Markovits and Allen, 'The West German case', pp. 132–3; M. Gurdon, 'Equity participation by employees: the growing debate in West Germany', Industrial Relations 24 (1985), pp. 113–30, p. 113.

70 W. Streeck, 'Neo-corporatist industrial relations and the economic crisis in West Germany', in Order and Conflict, ed. Goldthorpe, pp. 291–314; Gurdon, 'Equity participation', pp. 120–6; Markovits and Allen, 'The West German case', pp. 164–5; D. Toscano, 'Labour–management co-operation and the West Germany system of co-determination', Industrial Relations Journal 12 (1981), pp. 61–4.

71 R. Kuisel, Capitalism and the State in Modern France (Cambridge University Press, Cambridge, 1981), pp. 178–81.

72 M. Margairaz, 'Autour des accords Blum-Byrnes: Jean Monnet entre le consensus national et le consensus atlantique', Histoire, Economie et Société 1, part 2 (1982), pp. 439–70.

73 A. Shonfield, Modern Capitalism (Oxford University Press, Oxford, 1965), ch. 8; C. Gruson, Origine et éspoirs de la planification en France (Paris, 1968); Y. Ullmo, La Planification en France (Dalloz, Paris, 1975).

74 On political-institutional changes this view is consistent with standard textbook accounts; see, e.g., H. Ehrmann, Politics in France (Little, Brown, Boston, 1976). On political sociology of elections see J. Charlot, Quand la gauche peut gagner...les élections législatives des 4–11 mars 1973 (Moreau, Paris, 1973).

75 See, e.g., J. Bron, Histoire du mouvement ouvrier français: la lutte des classes aujourd'hui, 1950–1972 (Editions Ouvrières, Paris, 1973), pp. 119–51. On the Socialists see P. Bacot, Les dirigeants du Parti socialiste (Presses Universitaires de Lyon, 1979), pp. 126–30, 201–19; and J. Bizot, Au parti des socialistes (Grasset, Paris, 1975).

76 P. Lange, G. Ross and M. Vannicelli, Unions, Change and Crisis: French and Italian Union Strategy and the Political Economy, 1945–1980 (Allen & Unwin, London, 1982), pp. 30–5.

77 J. Keeler, 'Situating France on the pluralism-corporatism continuum', Comparative Politics 17 (1985), pp. 235, 240; Lipietz, 'Social forces', pp. 22–3; Daniele Linhart, L'Appel de la sirène (Sycorne, Paris, 1981).

78 Lange et al., Unions, Change and Crisis, p. 65.

79 See chapter 3 above.

80 Lange et al., *Unions, Change and Crisis*, pp. 56f. On CFDT recentrage see H. Hamon and P. Rotman, *La Deuxième Gauche, Histoire intellectuelle et politique de la CFDT* (Ramsay, Paris, 1982), pp. 293–333; and R. Shyrock, 'The CFDT: beyond really attainable French socialism?', *Telos* 55 (1983), pp. 84–9. More generally on CFDT–CGT relations, see W. R. Smith, 'Dynamics of plural unionism in France: the CGT, CFDT and industrial conflict', *British Journal of Industrial Relations* 22 (1984), pp. 15–33.

81 Lange et al., *Unions, Change and Crisis*, pp. 61–5; René Mouraix, *La CGT* (Éditions du Seuil, Paris, 1982), pp. 119–25; C. Durand and O. Kourchid, 'Débat sur Longwy en lutte', *Sociologie du travail* 1/82 (1982), pp. 85–94.

82 F. Wilson, 'French interest group politics, pluralist or neocorporatist', *American Political Science Review* 77 (1983), p. 903.

83 See *International Labor Organization Yearbook of Labor Statistics 1984* (ILO, Geneva, 1984), pp. 854–5).

84 F. Wilson, 'Interest group politics', p. 898. More generally on the issue of corporatism in France see F. Wilson, 'Alternative models of interest intermediation: the case of France', *British Journal of Political Science* 12 (1982), pp. 173–200; Wilson, 'Les groupes d'interêt sous la Cinquième République', *Revue Française de Science Politique* 33 (1983), pp. 220–54; P. Birnbaum, 'The state versus corporatism', *Politics and Society* 11 (1982), pp. 477–501.

85 D. Mothé, 'What prospects for democracy at the workplace?', *Telos* 55 (1983), pp. 98–103; Shyrock, 'The CFDT', pp. 91–2; F. Eyraud and R. Tchobanian, 'The Auroux reforms and company level industrial relations in France', *British Journal of Industrial Relations* 23 (1985), pp. 241–59; J. Lojkine, *La classe ouvrière en mutations* (Messidor, Éditions sociales, Paris, 1986), pp. 133–62. On the balance of power at plant level during the crisis see O. Kourchid, *Les Ouvriers entre la crise et l'entreprise: contribution à l'étude comparative de la condition salariale dans les regions de Paris et Los Angeles* (CNRS – Groupe de Sociologie de Travail, Paris, 1984).

86 See, e.g., S. Zukin, 'French socialists vs deindustrialization', *Telos* 55 (1983), pp. 139–51; Lipietz, 'Which social forces', pp. 19–20; Keeler, 'Situating France', pp. 243–4.

87 A. Touraine, 'State and social forces in socialist France', *Telos* 55 (1983), pp. 179–85; F. Hincker, *Le Parti communiste au carrefour* (Albin Michel, Paris, 1981). More generally here see Kesselman, 'Prospects for democratic socialism'.

88 K. Middlemas, *Politics in Industrial Society* (Andre Deutsch, London, 1979), pp. 174–243; C. Crouch, 'The intensification of industrial conflict in the United Kingdom', in *Resurgence of Class Conflict*, vol. 1, ed. *idem*, and Pizzorno, pp. 201–2, 225–34; M. Terry, 'Shop steward development and managerial strategies', in *Industrial Relations in Britain*, ed. G. Bain (Basil Blackwell, Oxford, 1983), pp. 67–91, pp. 67–8.

89 C. Crouch, *Class Conflict and the Industrial Relations Crisis* (Heinemann, London, 1977), ch. 11; L. Panitch, *Social Democracy and Industrial Militancy* (Cambridge University Press, Cambridge, 1976), chs 3–6.

90 S. Bornstein and P. Gourevitch, 'Unions in a declining economy: the case of the British TUC', in *Unions and Economic Crisis*, Gourevitch et al., pp. 40–6.

91 D. Coates, *Labour in Power?* (Longman, London, 1980), pp. 56–9.

92 Bornstein and Gourevitch, 'Declining economy', pp. 60–2; Coates, *Labour in Power*, pp. 234–52.

93 R. Hyman, 'Trade unions: structure, policies and politics', in *Industrial Relations*, ed. Bain, pp. 36–7; G. Bain and R. Price, 'Union growth: Dimensions, determinants and density', ibid., p. 14.

94 D. Winchester, 'Industrial relations in the public sector', ibid., pp. 166–8; A. Thompson and P. Beaumont, *Public Sector Bargaining: a Study of Relative Gain* (Saxon House, Farnborough, 1978).

95 Winchester, 'Industrial relations', pp. 171–5.

96 See, specifically on Thatcherism and the unions, C. Leys, 'Thatcherism and British manufacturing: a question of hegemony', *New Left Review* 151 (1985), pp. 5–25, pp. 9–10; and D. Strinati, 'State intervention, the economy and the crisis', in *Contemporary Britain*, ed. A. Stewart (Routledge, London, 1983), pp. 75–6). More generally in this context see G. Thompson, 'Rolling back the state? Economic intervention, 1975–1982', in *State and Society in Contemporary Britain*, ed. G. McLennan et al. (Polity Press, Cambridge, 1984), pp. 289–93; S. Holland, 'Out of the crisis: international economic recovery', in *The Future of the Left*, ed. J. Curran (Polity/New Socialist, London, 1984), pp. 256–60; C. Vogler, *The National State: the Neglected Dimension of Class* (Gower, Aldershot, 1985).

97 K. Sisson and W. Brown, 'Industrial relations in the private sector: Donovan revisited', in *Industrial Relations*, ed. Bain, p. 151; J. Purcell and K. Sisson, 'Strategies and practice in the management of industrial relations', ibid., pp. 100–1.

98 W. Brown, *The Changing Contours of British Industrial Relations* (Basil Blackwell, Oxford, 1981), pp. 32–3, 42–3.

99 Ibid., pp. 43–4, 54–9; Terry, 'Shop steward development', p. 70.

100 Ibid., pp. 111–13; Sisson and Brown, 'Private sector', p. 142.

101 W. Daniel and N. Millward, *Workplace Industrial Relations in Britain, The DE/PSI/SSRC Survey* (Heinemann, London, 1983), pp. 179, 188; Sisson and Brown, 'Private sector', pp. 147–8.

102 Purcell and Sisson, 'Strategies and practice', p. 110; Daniel and Millward, *Workplace Industrial Relations*, p. 192; Hyman, 'Structure, policies and politics', p. 48; C. Offe and H. Wiesenthal, 'Two logics of collective action', *Political Power and Social Theory* 1 (1980), pp. 67–115.

103 Daniel and Millward, *Workplace Industrial Relations*, p. 212; Purcell and Sisson, 'Strategies and practice', pp. 118–19; Terry, 'Shop steward development', p. 90. On the EEPTU and billets, see J. Torode, 'Militancy will still make its ballot mark', *The Guardian*, 31 December, 1985, p. 21.

104 P. Carter, 'Striking the right note', *Marxism Today*, March, 1985, p. 28; H. Francis, 'NUM united: a team in disarray', *Marxism Today*, April, 1985, pp. 29–30; 'The miners' strike: a balance sheet', Roundtable Discussion, *Marxism Today*, April, 1985, p. 21. And see Torode, 'Militancy'.

105 More generally see R. Samuel, 'Breaking up is very hard to do', *The Guardian*, 2 December, 1985, p. 19, especially on what he describes as a very widespread 'waning of corporate loyalties', which are 'no longer thought of as the repository of moral values, as incarnations of collective virtue or as bearers of collective ideals.'

106 Carter, 'Right note', p. 30; Francis, 'NUM united', p. 32; H. Beynon, 'The miners' strike in Easington', *New Left Review* 148 (1984), pp. 104–15; see more generally on these and other points, *Digging Deeper: Issues in the Miners' Strike* (Verso, London, 1985).
107 See, for example, the interview with Neil Kinnock in *New Musical Express*, 27 April, 1985, pp. 12–16.
108 See S. Lash, *The Militant Worker* (Heinemann, London, 1984), ch. 9, *passim*; A. Wolfe, *America's Impasse: the Rise and Fall of the Politics of Growth* (Pantheon, NY, 1981); G. Wilson, *Unions in American Politics* (Macmillan, London, 1979). On profit-sharing schemes in particular and recent changes more generally in American industrial relations, see H. Katz, 'The US automobile collective bargaining system in transition', *British Journal of Industrial Relations* 22 (1984), pp. 205–17; and D. T. Mroczkowski, 'Is the American labour–management relationship changing?', *British Journal of Industrial Relations* 22 (1984), pp. 47–62.

9 POST MODERN CULTURE AND DISORGANIZED CAPITALISM

1 On the eclipse of 'aura' in art see of course Walter Benjamin, 'The work of art in the age of mechanical reproduction', in *Illuminations* (London: Fontana/Collins, 1973), pp. 219–54.
2 Peter Bürger, *Theory of the Avant-Garde* (Manchester University Press, 1984).
3 Some suggestive connections between punk and avant-garde are made in Dick Hebdige, *Subcultures* (Methuen, London, 1979).
4 Jean Baudrillard, *For a Critique of the Political Economy of the Sign* (Telos Press, St Louis, Mo., 1981), pp. 130ff. See John Brenkman, 'Mass media: from collective experience to the culture of privatization', *Social Text* 1 (1979), pp. 94–109, p. 108.
5 Mark Poster, 'Technology and culture in Habermas and Baudrillard', *Contemporary Literature* 22.4 (1981), pp. 456–76, p. 471.
6 Jean Baudrillard, *In the Shadow of Silent Majorities. . .or The End of the Social* (Semiotexte, New York, 1983), p. 36.
7 Mark Poster, *Foucault, Marxism and History: Mode of Production versus Mode of Information* (Polity Press, Cambridge, 1984).
8 Baudrillard, *Silent Majorities*, pp. 98–9.
9 Ibid., p. 102.
10 Ibid., p. 86. This absorption of meaning into the hyperreality of spectacle is one form of 'implosion', a concept for which Baudrillard has become well known. Implosion, which might be defined as a cataclysmic bursting inwards of the previously disparate in the same flat plane, has two other important aspects. The first is the implosion of subjectivity, or of the interiority of the subject. Here Baudrillard is referring both to expressive and unconscious subjectivity. Previously, he considers, we had private selves, were in possession of unconscious and expressive subjectivities, which invested desire into objects. In contemporary hyperreality however we become objects (terminals) like other objects. Gone is the unconscious, the private, gone is passion; instead all is transparent. We have become control screens. The previous interiority of 'expression, investment

of desire, passion and seduction' have imploded into the immediately visible hyperreality of 'ecstasy', 'obscenity', 'fascination' and 'communication' (see Baudrillard, 'The ecstasy of communication', in H. Foster (ed.), *Postmodern Culture* (Pluto, London, 1984), pp. 126–34). Whereas, previously, paradigmatic psychopathologies such as paranoia and hysteria were pathologies of expression, paradigmatic for the society of the spectacle in schizophrenia with its flatness and transparency. When schizophrenics attach double meaning to objects, the second meaning, which for most people is mere connotation, takes on a real and immediate, often frightening reality of its own. Rather similar has been the observation in clinical psychology textbooks of a decrease in neuroses, properly speaking, in which unconscious drives have suffered from an hypertrophy of superego and defence mechanisms, and an increase in personality disorders in which there has been insufficient screening of unconscious drives, which appear so to speak on the surface, especially in psychopaths and sociopaths. The work of Heinz Kohut and the observations of Christopher Lasch on narcissism would tend to provide confirmatory evidence for Baudrillard's speculations about the contemporary flattening or implosion of unconscious subjectivity (See, especially C. Lasch, *The Culture of Narcissism* (Sphere, London, 1980)). Bryan Turner has also noted a shift in dominant psychopathologies from hysteria to narcissism and anorexia. He comments that hysteria is a disease concerning the internal regulation of desire, while anorexia and narcissism are 'diseases of presentation', in which 'anxiety is directed at the surface of the body' (Bryan Turner, *The Body and Society* (Basil Blackwell, Oxford, 1984), pp. 93–4).

The first two types of Baudrillardian implosion, which we think sensitizes contemporary audiences to post-modern culture, were the implosion first of the signified or meaning, and the second of the subject into the hyperreality of spectacle. The third is the implosion of the object, the real or the referent. This is what Baudrillard is speaking of in his famous pronouncements on the 'dissolution of the social'. What Baudrillard seems to designate here are several loosely connected phenomena. First, he speaks of the attempt in consumer capitalism of power to 'dominate' the masses through the attachment of signifieds (meanings) to images as 'socialization', or as an attempt by power to 'explode' the social through its massive networks of information and communication. When the masses refuse to attach any meanings to these images, he speaks of the social as being rolled back or imploded. Second, when the masses as discussed above themselves simulate the media they depart from social reality and enter the hyperreality of the spectacle; in this sense the social also is imploded. Finally the work of Michel Foucault suggests that notions of the social and the popular only came to gain significance in the disciplinary conditions of modernity. Baudrillard's post-modern dissolution of the social is signalled by what he sees as the demise of significance of ideas of the social, the popular and the proletariat as the real referents of history.

11 William Leiss, 'The icons of the marketplace', *Theory, Culture and Society* 1.3 (1983), pp. 10–21, pp. 16–17.

12 Ibid., p. 19; W. Leiss, S. Kline and S. Jhally, *Social Communication in Advertising: Persons, Products and Images of Well-being* (Methuen, New York, 1986).

13 Simon Frith, 'Frankie Said...but what did they mean?' unpublished paper, (Warwick University, Sociology Department, 1985), p. 7.

376 NOTES TO CHAPTER 9

14 S. Frith, 'Art ideology and pop practices', ed. C. Nelson and L. Grossberg (University of Illinois Press, Champaign-Urbana, Ill., 1986), p. 7.
15 These observations on punk are indebted to conversations with Brian Longhurst, and have drawn on his lectures for the Popular Culture course in Lancaster University, Sociology Department. Flaws are of course our own. On the 'first time' being already the 'second time' see Frederic Jameson, 'Reification and utopia in mass culture', *Social Text* 1 (1979), pp. 130–148, p. 136.
16 Frith, 'Frankie said', p. 6.
17 Ibid., p. 6.
18 Frith, 'Pop practice', pp. 11–12. And see T. Henry, 'Punk and avant-garde art', *Journal of Popular Culture'* 18 (1984), pp. 30–6.
19 Frith, 'Frankie said', pp. 10–14.
20 Ibid., p. 15.
21 F. Jameson, 'Postmodernism and consumer society', in H. Foster ed., *Postmodern Culture*, p. 123.
22 See Mike Featherstone, 'Lifestyle and consumer culture', paper presented at Conference on Everyday Life, Leisure and Culture, Catholic University of Tilbury, Holland, Dec., 1985, p. 9. Featherstone is to our knowledge the first to make explicit links between post-modern culture and the new middle classes. He does this, as we do below, via Bourdieu. We have learnt much from Featherstone's work, though we draw rather differently on the veritable goldmine of information and insights in Bourdieu's *Distinction*.
23 Pierre Bourdieu, *Distinction: a Social Critique of the Judgement of Taste* (Routledge & Kegan Paul, London, 1984), pp. 466–72. We would like to thank Mike Featherstone and John Thompson for rather forcefully directing our attention to Bourdieu's work. Any shortcomings in interpretation are ours.
24 Ibid., p. 474.
25 Ibid., p. 476.
26 Ibid., pp. 245–6.
27 Bernice Martin, *A Sociology of Contemporary Cultural Change* (Basil Blackwell, Oxford, 1981), ch. 2.
28 See discussion in A. Ellis and K. Kumar eds, *Dilemmas of Liberal Democracies* (Tavistock, London, 1983) and S. Lash and J. Urry, 'The dissolution of the social?', in *Sociological Theory in Transition*, ed. M. Wardell and S. Turner (Allen & Unwin, London, 1986), pp. 15–112, pp. 98–9.
29 Bourdieu, *Distinction*, pp. 251–4.
30 Ibid., pp. 287–8.
31 Ibid., pp. 218–20.
32 Ibid., pp. 310–315.
33 Jameson, 'On Diva', *Social Text* 6 (Fall, 1982), pp. 114–19.
34 Bourdieu, *Distinction*, pp. 345, 359.
35 Ibid., p. 358; Featherstone, 'Lifestyle', pp. 14–15.
36 Bourdieu, *Distinction*, p. 370.
37 Ibid., pp. 358–9.
38 Ibid., pp. 360–6.
39 Ibid., p. 370.
40 Featherstone, 'Leisure', p. 20.
41 Bourdieu, *Distinction*, p. 365.

42 Ibid., pp. 370–1.
43 Martin, *Cultural Change*, ch. 7, *passim*.
44 Joshua Meyrowitz, *No Sense of Place. The Impact of Electronic Media on Social Behaviour* (Oxford University Press, New York, 1985), p. 131.
45 Ibid., p. 136.
46 For an excellent critical analysis of this, see John Keane, *Public Life and Late Capitalism* (Cambridge University Press, Cambridge, 1984).
47 Meyrowitz, *Sense of Place*, p. 157.
48 Ibid., pp. 165–6.
49 Ibid., p. 211.
50 Ibid., p. 143.
51 J. F. Lyotard, *The Postmodern Condition* (University of Manchester Press, Manchester, 1984).
52 Frederic Jameson, *The Political Unconscious* (Methuen, London, 1981).
53 Jameson, 'Postmodern and consumer society', p. 118.
54 Jameson, 'Reification', p. 142; Jameson, *Political Unconscious*, p. 22.
55 Lasch, *Narcissism*; Bell, *Cultural Contradictions*, p. 90.
56 Featherstone, 'Lifestyle'.
57 See John Keane, *Public Life and Late Capitalism* (Cambridge University Press, Cambridge, 1984), pp. 185–6.
58 Thus the popularity of social-scientific figures such as Dietmar Kamper in contemporary West Germany. See, e.g. D. Kamper (ed.), *Macht und Ohnmacht der Phantasie* (Luchterhand, Darmstadt and Neuweid, 1986).
59 Stuart Hall and M. Jacques (eds), *The Politics of Thatcherism* (Lawrence & Wishart, London, 1983).
60 S. Beer, *Britain Against Itself* (Faber, London, 1982), pp. 151–4.
61 E. Laclau and C. Mouffe, *Hegemony and Socialist Strategy* (Verso, London, 1985).

Index